FINANCIAL MARKET PLACE

Editorial Advisers

FINANCIAL MARKET PLACE

A Directory of Major Corporations, Institutions, Services, and Publications

Compiled and Edited by
Dr. Steven E. Goodman
in association with
Reference Development
Corporation

R. R. BOWKER COMPANY
New York & London, 1972
A Xerox Education Company

XEROX

Published by R. R. Bowker Co. (a Xerox Education Company)
1180 Avenue of the Americas, New York, N.Y. 10036

Printed and bound in the United States of America

Library of Congress Cataloging in Publication Data

Goodman, Steven E
  Financial market place.

  1. Finance—United States—Directories.
2. Financial institutions—United States—Directories.
I. Title.
HG65.G62   332'.025'73   72-1736
ISBN 0-8352-0545-2

9/24/73

CONTENTS

EDUCATIONAL PROGRAMS AND RESOURCES

ASSOCIATIONS AND ORGANIZATIONS

PROFESSIONAL SERVICES
51.	Major Certified Public Accounting Firms	269
52.	Transmitters of Financial and Securities Data	270
	Ticker Information	270
	Bid-Asked Information	270
53.	Financial and Business Mailing Lists	271
54.	Financial News Services	272
55.	Major Financial Printers	273
56.	Financial Writers and Publicists	273
57.	Major Law Firms	276

APPENDIXES
Glossary of Investing Terms ... 279
Selected Financial Statistics ... 304

INDEX ... 349

PREFACE

Financial Market Place has been created to provide a one-volume directory which is useful to laymen, librarians, students, educators, members of the financial community, and others interested in the "financial world" in the broadest sense. A useful, accurate, and comprehensive directory of information and sources of information about the financial world has been a long-awaited need, now fulfilled. It is the hope of the editor that users of this publication will now be able to spend their valuable time in the analysis of financial material, rather than in the tedious process of locating information sources.

This publication is dedicated in some sense to the many librarians whom I have contacted during the past year. A common statement heard by the editor in attempting to locate sources of information on specific topics was, "We don't seem to have any material or information about that topic. . . . Please let us know if your search has been successful!" This book represents the collected fruits of that long search.

The determination of which organizations, institutions, services and publications were to be included in the "largest" or "major" categories was based upon the industry-wide data available from both published and unpublished sources. There was *no* attempt to equate "largest" or "major" with "best." In this light, it must be emphasized that the author and publisher have created this publication with the understanding that neither is engaged in rendering legal, accounting, investment, or business advisory services of any type. It is also noted that editorial choice has been exercised in the completion of the publication. No claim is made that any of the sections are all-inclusive, nor does the author or publisher have legal responsibility for accidental omissions or errors in the data included.

The author wishes to thank many individuals and organizations for their assistance and contributions. Thanks are in order to those librarians who contributed prepublication suggestions concerning areas to be covered; those associations, corporations and individuals who granted permission to include some of their copyrighted material; Mrs. Jane Schrader, Librarian, Fairleigh Dickinson University, for her assistance; and Mrs. Barbara Colucci whose personal and secretarial skills translated my poorly written notes into final manuscript form.

Dr. Steven E. Goodman
July 1972

BANKS

1. Federal Reserve Banks and Branches

BANKS

National Office

Board of Governors of the Federal
  Reserve System
Washington, D.C. 20551

Atlanta

Federal Reserve Bank of Atlanta
  Federal Reserve Sta., Atlanta, Ga.
  30303

Boston

Federal Reserve Bank of Boston
  30 Pearl St., Boston, Mass. 02106

Chicago

Federal Reserve Bank of Chicago
  P.O. Box 834, Chicago, Ill. 60690

Cleveland

Federal Reserve Bank of Cleveland
  P.O. Box 6387, Cleveland, Ohio
  44101

Dallas

Federal Reserve Bank of Dallas
  Sta. K, Dallas, Tex. 75222

Kansas City

Federal Reserve Bank of Kansas City
  Federal Reserve P.O. Sta., Kansas
  City, Mo. 64198

Minneapolis

Federal Reserve Bank of Minneapolis
  Minneapolis, Minn. 55440

New York

Federal Reserve Bank of New York
  Federal Reserve P.O. Sta., New York,
  N.Y. 10045

Philadelphia

Federal Reserve Bank of Philadelphia
  925 Chestnut St., Philadelphia, Pa.
  19101

Richmond

Federal Reserve Bank of Richmond
  P.O. Box 27622, Richmond, Va.
  23261

St. Louis

Federal Reserve Bank of St. Louis
  P.O. Box 442, St. Louis, Mo. 63166

San Francisco

Federal Reserve Bank of San Francisco
San Francisco, Calif. 14120

BRANCHES

Baltimore

Federal Reserve Bank Branch of
Baltimore
Baltimore, Md. 21203

Birmingham

Federal Reserve Bank Branch of
Birmingham
Birmingham, Ala. 35202

Buffalo

Federal Reserve Bank Branch of
Buffalo
Buffalo, N.Y. 14240

Charlotte

Federal Reserve Bank Branch of
Charlotte
Charlotte, N.C. 28201

Cincinnati

Federal Reserve Bank Branch of
Cincinnati
Cincinnati, Ohio 45201

Denver

Federal Reserve Bank Branch of Denver
Denver, Colo. 80217

Detroit

Federal Reserve Bank Branch of
Detroit
Detroit, Mich. 48231

El Paso

Federal Reserve Bank Branch of El
Paso
El Paso, Tex. 79901

Helena

Federal Reserve Bank Branch of Helena
Helena, Mont. 59601

Houston

Federal Reserve Bank Branch of
Houston
Houston, Tex. 77001

Jacksonville

Federal Reserve Bank Branch of
Jacksonville
Jacksonville, Fla. 32203

Little Rock

Federal Reserve Bank Branch of Little
Rock
Little Rock, Ark. 72203

Los Angeles

Federal Reserve Bank Branch of Los
Angeles
Los Angeles, Calif. 90051

Louisville

Federal Reserve Bank Branch of
Louisville
Louisville, Ky. 40201

Memphis

Federal Reserve Bank Branch of
Memphis
Memphis, Tenn. 38101

Miami

Federal Reserve Bank Branch of Miami
Miami, Fla. 33101

Nashville

Federal Reserve Bank Branch of
Nashville
Nashville, Tenn. 37203

New Orleans

Federal Reserve Bank Branch of New
Orleans
New Orleans, La. 70160

Oklahoma City

Federal Reserve Bank Branch of Oklahoma City
Oklahoma City, Okla. 73125

Omaha

Federal Reserve Bank Branch of
Omaha
Omaha, Nebr. 68102

Pittsburgh

Federal Reserve Bank Branch of
Pittsburgh
Pittsburgh, Pa. 15230

Portland

Federal Reserve Bank Branch of
Portland
Portland, Oreg. 97208

Salt Lake City

Federal Reserve Bank Branch of Salt
Lake City
Salt Lake City, Utah 84110

San Antonio

Federal Reserve Bank Branch of San
Antonio
San Antonio, Tex. 78295

Seattle

Federal Reserve Bank Branch of
Seattle
Seattle, Wash. 98124

2. One Hundred Largest Commercial Banks

BancOhio Corp.
  51 North High St., Columbus, Ohio
  43216
  614-221-2211
  Pres.: Philip F. Searle

BankAmerica Corp.
  555 California St., San Francisco,
  Calif. 94120
  415-622-3456
  Pres.: A. W. Clausen

Bank of California National Assn.
  400 California St., San Francisco,
  Calif. 94120
  415-765-0400
  Pres.: John M. Schutt

Bank of the Commonwealth
  719 Griswold, Detroit, Mich. 48231
  313-965-8800
  Pres.: John E. Thompson

Bank of New York
  48 Wall St., New York, N.Y. 10015
  212-530-1784
  Pres.: Elliott Averett

Bankers Trust New York Corp.
  280 Park Ave., New York, N.Y.
  10017
  212-577-2345
  Pres.: William H. Moore

Charter New York Corp.
  1 Wall St., New York, N.Y. 10005
  212-553-1212
  Pres.: George A. Murphy

Chase Manhattan Corp.
  1 Chase Manhattan Plaza, New York,
  N.Y. 10015
  212-552-2222
  Pres.: Herbert P. Patterson

Chemical New York Corp.
  20 Pine St., New York, N.Y. 10015
  212-770-1234
  Pres.: Howard W. McCall, Jr.

Citizens & Southern National Bank
  22 Bull St., Savannah, Ga. 31401
  404-588-2121
  Pres.: Mills B. Lane, Jr.

Cleveland Trust Co.
  Euclid Ave. & East 9th St., Cleveland, Ohio 44115
  216-621-1600
  Pres.: Everett Ware Smith

Continental Illinois National Bank & Trust
  231 South La Salle St., Chicago, Ill. 60690
  312-828-2345
  Pres.: T. Cummings

Crocker National Corp.
  1 Montgomery St., San Francisco, Calif. 94120
  415-983-0456
  Pres.: Joseph F. Hogan

Detroit Bank & Trust Co.
  Fort At Washington, Detroit, Mich. 48231
  313-222-3400
  Pres.: C. Boyd Stockmeyer

Fidelity Corp. of Pennsylvania
  1200 East Lancaster Ave., Bryn Mawr, Pa. 19010
  215-527-3188
  Pres.: Carl K. Dellmuth

First Bank System, Inc.
  120 South 6th St., Minneapolis, Minn. 55402
  612-333-1451
  Pres.: Donald R. Grangaard

First National Bank of Chicago
  38 South Dearborn St., Chicago, Ill. 60603
  312-732-4000
  Exec. Officer: G. A. Freeman

First National Bank in Dallas
  1401 Elm St., Dallas, Tex. 75202
  214-749-4011
  Pres.: W. Dewey Presley

First National Boston Corp.
  1 Federal St., Boston, Mass. 02110
  617-434-2200
  Pres.: Richard D. Hill

First National City Corp.
  399 Park Ave., New York, N.Y. 10022
  212-559-1000
  Pres.: Walter B. Wriston

First Pennsylvania Banking & Trust Co.
  555 City Line Ave., Bala Cynwyd, Pa. 19004
  215-568-1700
  Pres.: John R. Bunting

First Wisconsin Bankshares Corp.
  735 North Water St., Milwaukee, Wisc. 53202
  414-276-6100
  Pres.: George F. Kasten

Franklin National Bank
  189 Montague St., Brooklyn, N.Y. 11201
  212-425-1400
  Pres.: James G. Smith

Girard Co.
  Bala & City Line Ave., Bala Cynwyd, Pa. 19004
  215-667-4156
  Pres.: Stephen S. Gardner

Harris Trust & Savings Bank
  111 West Monroe St., Chicago, Ill. 60690
  312-461-2121
  Pres.: William F. Murray

Lincoln First Banks, Inc.
  183 Main St., East Rochester, N.Y. 14603
  716-262-2000
  Pres.: Wilmont R. Craig

Manufacturers Hanover Corp.
  350 Park Ave., New York, N.Y. 10022
  212-350-3300
  Pres.: Gabriel Hauge

Manufacturers National Bank of Detroit
  151 West Fort St., Detroit, Mich. 48226
  313-222-4000
  Pres.: Dean E. Richardson

Marine Midland Banks, Inc.
241 Main St., Buffalo, N.Y. 14203
716-842-2424
Pres.: George R. Williams

Mellon National Bank & Trust Co.
Mellon Square, Pittsburgh, Pa.
15230
412-232-4100
Pres.: A. Bruce Bowden

J. P. Morgan & Co.
23–25 Wall St., New York, N.Y.
10015
212-425-2323
Pres.: Ellmore C. Paterson

National Bank of Commerce
2nd At Spring, Seattle, Wash. 98101
206-587-2111
Pres.: Maxwell Carlson

National Bank of Detroit
611 Woodward Ave., Detroit, Mich.
48232
313-965-6000
Senior V.P.: Joseph G. Conway

National Bank of North America
60 Hempstead Ave., West Hempstead, N.Y. 11552
516-481-9000
Pres.: John H. Vogel

National City Bank of Cleveland
623 Euclid Ave., Cleveland, Ohio
44101
216-861-4900
Pres.: Claude M. Blair

North Carolina National Bank
200 South Tryon St., Charlotte, N.C.
28201
704-374-5000
Pres.: T. I. Storrs

Northern Trust Co.
50 South LaSalle St., Chicago, Ill.
60690
312-346-5500
Pres.: Douglas R. Fuller

Northwest Bancorp.
1200 Northwest Bank Bldg., Minneapolis, Minn. 55480

612-372-8123
Pres.: Henry T. Rutledge

Philadelphia National Bank
Broad & Chestnut Sts., Philadelphia,
Pa. 19101
215-569-2100
Pres.: G. M. Dorrance, Jr.

Pittsburgh National Corp.
1 Oliver Plaza, Pittsburgh, Pa. 15230
412-355-2000
Pres.: Merle E. Gilliand

Republic National Bank of Dallas
Pacific & Ervay Sts., Dallas, Tex.
75222
214-749-5000
Pres.: James W. Keay

Seattle-First National Bank
P.O. Box 3586, Seattle, Wash. 98124
206-583-3131
Pres.: Robert S. Beaupre

Security Pacific National Bank
561 South Spring St., Los Angeles,
Calif. 90013
213-620-6211
Pres.: Carl E. Hartnack

Shawmut Assn., Inc.
82 Devonshire St., Boston, Mass.
02109
617-742-4900
Pres.: John K. Benson

Union Bank of Los Angeles
5th and Figueroa St., Los Angeles,
Calif. 90054
213-687-6877
Pres.: George A. Thatcher

U.S. National Bank of Oregon
P.O. Box 4412, Portland, Oreg.
97208
503-225-6111
Chmn. of the Bd.: L. B. Stauer

Valley National Bank
141 North Central Ave., Phoenix,
Ariz. 85001
602-261-2900
Pres.: Earl L. Bimson

Wachovia Corp.
  301 North Main St., Winston-Salem,
    N.C. 27101
  919-761-5000
  Pres.: James H. Styers

Wells Fargo Bank
  464 California St., San Francisco,
    Calif. 94120

415-396-2902
Pres.: Richard P. Cooley

Western Bancorporation
  600 South Spring St., Los Angeles,
    Calif. 90054
  213-627-7981
  Pres.: Clifford Tweter

3. Largest Mutual Savings Banks

Anchor Savings Bank
  5323 Fifth Ave., Brooklyn, N.Y.
    11220
  212-439-7300
  Pres.: D. J. Thomas

Boston Five Cents Savings Bank
  30 School St., Boston, Mass. 02108
  617-742-6000
  Pres.: G. C. Francis

Bowery Savings Bank
  110 East 42nd St., New York, N.Y.
    10017
  212-697-1414
  Pres.: J. W. Larsen

Bronx Savings Bank
  Tremont & Park Aves., Bronx, N.Y.
    10457
  212-299-3000
  Pres.: J. M. Nosworthy

Brooklyn Savings Bank
  Fulton & Montague Sts., Brooklyn,
    N.Y. 10001
  212-624-4100
  Pres.: W. G. Hampton

Buffalo Savings Bank
  545 Main St., Buffalo, N.Y. 14203
  716-852-5130
  Pres.: W. H. Harder

Central Savings Bank
  2100 Broadway, New York, N.Y.
    10023
  212-787-4500
  Pres.: J. J. Bloor

Charleston Savings Bank
  55 Summer St., Boston, Mass. 02110
  617-482-2600
  Pres.: J. E. Wilkinson

Community Savings Bank
  Main & Clinton, Rochester, N.Y.
    14604
  716-454-6200
  Pres.: J. P. Schubert

Dime Savings Bank of Brooklyn
  DeKalb Ave. & Fulton, Brooklyn,
    N.Y. 11201
  212-643-4200
  Pres.: C. H. Miller

Dollar Savings Bank
  2530 Grand Concourse, Bronx, N.Y.
    10458
  212-584-6000
  Pres.: H. G. Waltemade

Dollar Savings Bank
  4th Ave. & Smithfield, Pittsburgh,
    Pa. 15230
  412-261-4900
  Pres.: F. B. Nimick, Jr.

Dry Dock Savings Bank
  742 Lexington Ave., New York,
    N.Y. 10022
  212-753-0600
  Pres.: R. J. Horsfield

East New York Savings Bank
  2644 Atlantic Ave., Brooklyn, N.Y.
    11207
  212-270-6000
  Pres.: J. P. McGrath

East River Savings Bank
  26 Cortland St., New York, N.Y.
  10007
  212-267-4200
  Pres.: A. S. Murphy

Emigrant Savings Bank
  5 East 42nd St., New York, N.Y.
  10007
  212-883-5800
  Pres.: R. A. Gray

Empire Savings Bank
  221 West 57th St., New York, N.Y.
  10019
  212-247-6400
  Pres.: J. P. Billhardt

Erie County Savings Bank
  1 Main Place, Buffalo, N.Y. 14202
  716-842-5454
  Pres.: H. J. Swift

Farmers & Mechanics Savings
  90 South 6th St., Minneapolis,
  Minn. 55402
  612-339-2515
  Pres.: H. S. Kingman, Jr.

Franklin Savings Bank
  Eighth Ave. & 42nd St., New York,
  N.Y. 10036
  212-736-3000
  Pres.: H. H. Bock

Greater New York Savings Bank
  Fifth Ave., 9 & 10 Sts., Brooklyn,
  N.Y. 11215
  212-499-7000
  Pres.: A. Casazza

Green Point Savings Bank
  807 Manhattan Ave., Brooklyn,
  N.Y. 11222
  212-383-2600
  Pres.: J. W. Raber

Greenwich Savings Bank
  Broadway & Sixth Ave., New York,
  N.Y. 10003
  212-524-8800
  Pres.: W. S. Brennen

Harlem Savings Bank
  205 East 42nd St., New York, N.Y.
  10017
  212-686-5252
  Pres.: W. R. Brennan, Jr.

Howard Savings Institute
  768 Broad St., Newark, N.J. 07101
  201-643-1000
  Pres.: J. W. Kress

Jamaica Savings Bank
  161–01 Jamaica Ave., Jamaica, N.Y.
  11432
  212-526-1500
  Pres.: P. T. Adikes

Kings Highway Savings Bank
  Kings Highway & East 16 St.,
  Brooklyn, N.Y. 11229
  212-339-4000
  Pres.: E. G. Flowers

Lincoln Savings Bank
  551 Broadway, Brooklyn, N.Y.
  11206
  212-782-6000
  Pres.: E. G. Murphy

Long Island Savings Bank
  Bridge Plaza North, Long Island City,
  N.Y. 11101
  212-392-5000
  Pres.: H. J. Dirkes

Manhattan Savings Bank
  385 Madison Ave., New York, N.Y.
  10017
  212-688-3000
  Pres.: R. G. Smith

New York Bank for Savings
  22nd St. & Park Ave., New York,
  N.Y. 10003
  212-473-5656
  Pres.: A. J. Quinn

Old Stone Savings Bank
  86 South Main St., Providence, R.I.
  02901
  401-274-7800
  Pres.: F. A. Strom

Onondaga Savings Bank
101 South Salina St., Syracuse, N.Y.
13202
315-471-4151
Pres.: W. G. Morton

Peoples Savings Bank
221 Main St., Bridgeport, Conn.
06601
203-366-7811
Pres.: M. R. Waterman

Philadelphia Savings Fund Society
1212 Market St., Philadelphia, Pa.
19107
215-925-5800
Pres.: R. S. Rauch

Provident Institute Savings
36 Temple Pl., Boston, Mass. 02105
617-423-9600
Pres.: J. Howe

Queens County Savings Bank
38–25 Main St., Flushing, N.Y.
11354
212-359-6400
Pres.: G. S. Tarbell, Jr.

Ridgewood Savings Bank
Myrtle & Forest Aves., Ridgewood,
N.Y. 11227
212-821-4600
Pres.: W. J. Hess

Rochester Savings Bank
40 Franklin St., Rochester, N.Y.
14604
716-263-4400
Pres.: F. S. DeVoy

Savings Bank of Baltimore
Charles & Baltimore, Baltimore, Md.
21203
301-539-3360
Pres.: R. W. Thon, Jr.

Seamens Bank for Savings
30 Wall St., New York, N.Y. 10005

212-797-5000
Chmn. of the Bd. Pres.: E. Conway

Society for Savings
31 Pratt St., Hartford, Conn. 06103
203-524-8321
Pres.: B. P. Terry

South Brooklyn Savings Bank
130 Court St., Brooklyn, N.Y.
11202
212-624-6620
Pres.: R. H. MacKinnon

Suffolk Franklin Savings
45 Franklin St., Boston, Mass.
02110
617-482-7530
Pres.: E. Kehoe

Union Dime Savings Bank
1065 Ave. of Americas, New York,
N.Y. 10018
212-695-2300
Pres.: R. T. Hills

United Mutual Savings Bank
20 Union Square, New York, N.Y.
10003
212-777-5300
Pres.: E. J. Maude

Washington Mutual Savings Bank
1101 Second Ave., Seattle, Wash.
98101
206-682-1101
Pres.: A. I. Eyring

Western Saving Fund Society
Broad & Chestnut Sts., Philadelphia,
Pa. 19107
215-545-1010
Pres.: T. E. Munson

Williamsburgh Savings Bank
1 Hanson Pl., Brooklyn, N.Y. 11217
212-857-9100
Pres.: J. A. Kaiser

4. Largest Savings and Loan Associations

American Savings & Loan of California
9535 Wilshire Blvd., Beverly Hills,
Calif. 90212
Exec.: S. Taper

Astoria Federal Savings & Loan
37-16 30th Ave., Long Island City,
N.Y. 11103
Exec.: E. A. Riesbeck

Atlanta Federal Savings & Loan
22 Marietta St., Atlanta, Ga. 30301
Exec.: W. S. Duvall

Baltimore Federal Savings & Loan
Fayette & St. Paul Sts., Baltimore,
Md. 21202
Exec.: H. C. Irr

Bell Federal Savings & Loan Assn.
79 West Monroe St., Chicago, Ill.
60603
Exec.: H. V. Halleen

Broadview Savings & Loan
4221 Pearl Rd., Cleveland, Ohio
44109
Exec.: E. P. Rupert

California Federal Savings & Loan
5670 Wilshire Blvd., Los Angeles,
Calif. 90036
Exec.: A. M. Freston

Capital Federal Savings & Loan
700 Kansas Ave., Topeka, Kans.
66603
Exec.: H. R. Bubb

Carteret Savings & Loan Assn.
866 Broad St., Newark, N.J. 07102
Exec.: M. A. Rice

Citizens Federal Savings & Loan
700 Market St., San Francisco,
Calif. 94102
Exec.: F. R. Donahoe

Coast & Southern Federal Savings &
Loan
855 South Hill St., Los Angeles,
Calif. 90014
Exec.: J. Crail

Community Federal Savings & Loan
8944 St. Charles Rd., Saint Louis,
Mo. 63114
Exec.: J. M. Armbruster

County Federal Savings & Loan
53 North Park Ave., Rockville
Center, N.Y. 11571
Exec.: H. H. Peterson

Dade Federal Savings & Loan
101 East Flagler St., Miami, Fla.
33101
Exec.: J. F. Lipton

Dallas Federal Savings & Loan
1505 Elm, Dallas, Tex. 75201
Exec.: L. Bowles

Equitable Savings & Loan
1300 Southwest Sixth Ave., Portland, Oreg. 97201
Exec.: H. P. Cake

Equitable Savings & Loan Assn.
8150 Sunset Blvd., Los Angeles,
Calif. 90046
Exec.: G. A. Edwards

Farm & Home Savings Assn.
221 West Cherry, Nevada, Mo.
64772
Exec.: C. W. Duncan

Fidelity Federal Savings & Loan
225 East Broadway, Glendale, Calif.
91209
Exec.: N. A. Hayhurst

Fidelity Savings & Loan Assn.
2323 Shattuck Ave., Berkeley, Calif.
94704
Exec.: A. M. Meyer

First Federal Savings & Loan
100 N.E. First Ave., Miami, Fla.
33132
Exec.: R. J. Walker

First Federal Savings & Loan
First Federal Bldg., St. Petersburg,
Fla. 33731
Exec.: D. H. Kreutz

First Federal Savings & Loan
1 South Dearborn St., Chicago, Ill.
60603
Exec.: E. M. Enlund

First Federal Savings & Loan
1001 Woodward Ave., Detroit,
Mich. 48226
Exec.: H. D. Gehrke

First Federal Savings & Loan
320 Main St. East, Rochester, N.Y.
14604
Exec.: W. J. Almekinder

First Federal Savings & Loan of
Broward
301 East Las Olas Blvd., Fort Lauder-
dale, Fla. 33302
Exec.: E. A. Wilburn

Franklin Society Federal Savings &
Loan
217 Broadway, New York, N.Y.
10007
Exec.: C. J. Plumb

Gibraltar Savings Assn.
2302 Fannin St., P.O. Box 2, Houston, Tex. 77002
Exec.: E. H. Lallinger

Gibraltar Savings & Loan Assn.
P. O. Box 878, Beverly Hills, Calif.
90213
Exec.: H. Young, Sr.

Glendale Federal Savings & Loan
401 North Brand Blvd., Glendale,
Calif. 91209
Exec.: R. W. Edwards

Great Western Savings & Loan
4401 Crenshaw Blvd., Los Angeles,
Calif. 90043
Exec.: C. Ford

Home Federal Savings & Loan
1200 4th Ave., San Diego, Calif.
92101
Exec.: F. J. Morton

Home Federal Savings & Loan Assn. of
Chicago
201 South State St., Chicago, Ill.
60604
Exec.: D. T. Preisler

Home Savings & Loan
761 South Broadway, Los Angeles,
Calif. 90014
Exec.: H. K. Ahmanson

Lincoln Savings & Loan
630 West 6th St., Los Angeles, Calif.
90017
Exec.: D. L. McDonald

Loyola Federal Savings & Loan Assn.
1300 North Charles St., Baltimore,
Md. 21201
Exec.: R. C. Israel

Miami Beach Federal Savings & Loan
401 Lincoln Rd., Miami, Fla. 33139
Exec.: J. M. Payne

Midwest Savings & Loan Assn.
Nicollet Mall 8th St., Minneapolis,
Minn. 55402
Exec.: H. V. Greenwood, Jr.

Minnesota Federal Savings & Loan
355 Minnesota St., Saint Paul, Minn.
55107
Exec.: F. O. Bjorlund

Mutual Savings & Loan Assn.
315 East Colorado St., Pasadena,
Calif. 91109
Exec.: L. R. Vincenti

Pacific First Federal Savings & Loan
Assn.
204 South 11th St., Tacoma, Wash.
98402
Exec.: G. A. Ende

Palo Alto Salinas Savings & Loan Assn.
300 Hamilton Ave., Palo Alto,
Calif. 94301
Exec.: F. S. Gryp

Perpetual Building Assn.
11 and East N.W., Washington, D.C.
20004
Exec.: T. P. Owen

Standard Federal Savings & Loan
P.O. Box 859, Detroit, Mich. 48231
Exec.: R. W. Hutton

Talman Federal Savings & Loan
5501 South Kedzie Ave., Chicago,
Ill. 60629
Exec.: B. S. Polek

Twin City Federal Savings & Loan
801 Marquette Ave., Minneapolis,
Minn. 55402
Exec.: R. Johnson

Washington Heights Federal Savings
& Loan
1390 St. Nicholas Ave., New York,
N.Y. 10033
Exec.: G. H. Mooney

West Side Federal Savings & Loan
1790 Broadway, New York, N.Y.
10019
Exec.: M. A. Zarrilli

Western Federal Savings & Loan
700 17th St., Denver, Colo. 80202
Exec.: J. J. Baxter

Worcester Federal Savings & Loan
22 Elm St., Worcester, Mass. 01608
Exec.: R. L. Harold

5. Major World Banks

ARGENTINA

Banco de la Nación Argentina
Bartoleme Nitre 326, Capital Federal,
Buenos Aires

AUSTRIA

Creditanstalt-Bankverein
Schottengasse 6, A-1010 Vienna

AUSTRALIA

Bank of New South Wales
60 Martin Pl., Sydney, New South
Wales

Australia and New Zealand Banking
Group Ltd.
394–396 Collins St., Melbourne

BELGIUM

Societe Generale de Banque
3, Montagne du Parc, b-1000
Brussels

BRAZIL

Banco de Brasil SA
Setor Bancario Seil-Lote 23, Plan o
Piloto P.O. Box 562, Brasilia

BULGARIA

Bulgarian Foreign Trade Bank
2, Sofiiska Konouna St., Sofia

BURMA, Union of

Union Bank of Burma
24–26 Sule Pagoda Rd., P.O. Box
184, Rangoon

CANADA

Royal Bank of Canada
Montreal 1, Quebec

Canadian Imperial Bank of Commerce
25 King St. West 1, Toronto 1

CHILE

Banco del Estado de Chile
Alameda Bernardo O'Higgins 1111,
Correo 24, Santiago

CHINA, People's Republic of

The People's Bank of China
87 Chiao Ming Hsiang, Peking

COLUMBIA

Banco Central Hipotecario
Carrera 6, No. 15 - 32/48, Apartado
Aereo 3637, Bogota

CONGO, Republic of

Banque Commerciale Congolaise
Ave, du 28 Aout 1940, Box 79,
Brazzaville

CONGO, Democratic Republic of

Banque du Congo
8–10 Avenue Paul Hauzeur, P.O.
Box 2798, Kinshasa

CZECHOSLOVAKIA

Ceskoslovenska Obchodni Banka AS
Na Prikope 14, Praha 1, Prague

DENMARK

Copenhagen Handelsbank
Holmens Kanal 2, DK-1091,
Copenhagen

EGYPT

National Bank of Egypt
24 Sherif St., Cairo

FINLAND

Kansalus-Osake-Pankki
Alenksanterinkatu 42, Helsinki 10

FRANCE

Banque Nationale de Paris SA
16 Boulevard des Italiens 75, P.O.
Box 229–C9, Paris 9e

Credit Lyonnais
19 Boulevard des Italiens, P.O. Box
12, Paris 2e

Societe Generale
29, Boulevard Haussman, Paris 9e

GERMANY

Bayerische-Hypotheken-Und Wechsel
Bank
Theatener Strasse 8–17, P.O. Box
200527, 8 Munich 2

Norddeutsche Landesbank Girozentrale
Georgsplatz 1, P.O. Box 290, 3
Hannover

Westdeutsche Landesbank Girozentrale
56 Friedrichstrasse 4, P.O. Box
1128, Dusseldorf

Duetsche Bank Aktiengesellschaft
5–11 Junghofstrasse, P.O. Box
3629, Frankfort

GREECE

National Bank of Greece
86 Eolou St., Athens 21

HONG KONG

Hong Kong and Shanghi Banking Corp.
1 Queens Rd., Central Box 64

INDIA

State Bank of India
P.O. Box 12, Bombay 1

IRAN

Bank Melli Iran
Ferdows Ave., Tehran

IRAQ

Central Bank of Iraq
Rashid St., P.O. Box 64, Baghdad

INDONESIA

Bank Negara Indonesia
1 Djalan Lada, P.O. Box 1412/DAK,
Djakarta

IRELAND

Munster and Leinster Bank Ltd.
66 South Mall, Cork

Bank of Ireland
College Green, P.O. Box 9a, Dublin 2

ISRAEL

Bank Leumi-Le-Israel B.M.
24–32 Yehuda Halevi St., Box 2,
Tel-Aviv

ITALY

Banca Nazionale del Lauoro
119 Via Vittorio Veneto, Rome

Banco di Napoli
Via Roma 177-178, Naples

Banca Commerciale Italiana
Piazza della Scala, 6-20-100 Milan

JAPAN

Sumitomo Bank Ltd.
22 5-Chome Kitahama, Higashi-Ku,
Box 45, Osaka Central, Osaka

Tokai Bank Ltd.
21-24 Nishiki 3-Chome, Naka-Ku,
Box 160, Nagoya

Hokkaido Takushoku Bank Ltd.
7 Nishi 3-Chome, Odori, P.O. Box
27, Sapparo

Fuji Bank Ltd.
5, 1-Chome Otemachi, Chiyoda-Ku,
C.P.O. Box 148, Tokyo

KENYA, Republic of

Commercial Bank of Africa Ltd.
Wabera St., P.O. Box 30437, Nairobi

KOREA

Korea Exchange Bank
10 Kwanchul-Dong, Chongro-Ku,
P.O. Box 1, Seoul

KUWAIT

National Bank of Kuwait SAK
Abdulla Al Salim St., P.O. Box 95,
Kuwait

LAOS

Banque Nationale du Laos
Rue Yonnet, P.O. Box 19, Vietiane

LUXEMBOURG

Banque Internationale A Luxembourg
Societe Anonyme
2 Boulevard Royal, P.O. Box 20

MEXICO

Banco de Comercio, SA
Venustiano Carranza, No. 44, P.O.
Box 9, B15, Mexico City

MOROCCO

Banque Commerciale du Maroc
1 Rue Ldriss Lahrizi, P.O. Box 141,
Casablanca

NETHERLANDS

Algeme Bank Nederland NV
32 Vilzelstraat, P.O. Box 659,
Amsterdam

Coopertieve Centrale Raiffeisen Bank
St. Jacobsstraat 30, P.O. Box 2098,
Amsterdam

NEW ZEALAND

Bank of New Zealand
239-247 Lambton Quay, P.O. Box
2392, Wellington, C.I.

NIGERIA

Barclays Bank of Nigeria Ltd.
40 Marina, Lagos

NORTHERN IRELAND

Northern Bank Ltd.
16 Victoria St., Belfast BT 1-3GQ

NORWAY

Den Norske Creditbank
Kirkegaten 21, Oslo 1

PAKISTAN

Habib Bank Ltd.
Chundrigar Rd., Karachi 21

PERU

Banco De Credito del Peru,
Lima

PHILLIPINES

Phillipines National Bank
257 Escolta St., P.O. Box 1844,
Manila

POLAND

Bank Handlowy W. Warszawie Spolka
Akcyjna
Warszawa Traugutta 7, Warsaw

PORTUGAL

Banco Portugues do Atlantico
Praca D/Joao 1, Palacio Atlantico,
P.O. Box 80, Oporto

Banco Espirito Santo E. Commercial
de Lisboa
Rue do Comercio 95-119, P.O. Box
2105, Lisbon

SCOTLAND

Royal Bank of Scotland
42 St. Andrews Square, P.O. Box
31, Edinburgh EH 2 2YE

SOUTH AFRICA

Trust Bank of South Africa
112 Adderly St., P.O. Box 353,
Capetown

Standard Bank of South Africa Ltd.
78 Fox St., P.O. Box 1155,
Johannesburg

SPAIN

Banco Español de Crédito
Paseo de la Castellana 7, P.O. Box
297, Madrid 1

SWEDEN

Svenska Handelsbanken
27, Ostra Hamngatan, Goteborg

Svenska Handelsbanken
11 Arsenalsgatan, Box 16, 341
S-10326, Stockholm 16

SWITZERLAND

Banque Nationale Swisse
Place Federale 1, 3003 Berne

Swiss Bank Corp.
1 Aeschenvorstadt, Basle

Union Bank of Switzerland
Bahnhofstrasse 45, 8021 Zurich

TAIWAN

Bank of Taiwan
120 Chungking South Rd., Section
1, P.O. Box 305, Taipei

THAILAND

Bangkok Bank Ltd.
3-9 Sucpa Rd., P.O. Box 95,
Bangkok

TURKEY

Turkiye Cumhuriyeti Ziraat Bankasi
Bankalar Caddesi, Ankara

UNITED KINGDOM

National Westminster Bank Ltd.
41, Lothbury, London CC 2P, 2 BP

Barclays Bank Ltd.
54 Lombard St., London EC 3

UNION OF SOVIET SOCIALIST REPUBLICS (USSR)

Bank for Foreign Trade of the USSR
3/5 Kopievski Lane, Moscow

URUGUAY

Banco de la Republica Oriental del
Uruguay
Calles Cerrito Zabala Solis &
Piedros, Montevideo

VENEZUELA

Banco Central de Venezuela
Esquina de Carmelitas Ave. Urdaneta,
P.O. Box 2017, Caracas

VIETNAM

National Bank of Vietnam
17 Quay Chuong Duong, Saigon

YUGOSLAVIA

Banque Nationale de Yougoslavie
Siege Centrale 15, Bulevar Revolucije,
P.O. Box 1010, Belgrade

6. Major Foreign Exchange Establishments

BOSTON

The First National Bank of Boston
100 Federal St., Boston, Mass.
02109
617-434-2080

CHICAGO

Continental Illinois National Bank &
Trust Co. of Chicago
231 South LaSalle St., Chicago, Ill.
60690
312-828-2742

First National Bank of Chicago
1 First National Plaza, Chicago, Ill.
60670
312-735-5811

CLEVELAND

Central National Bank of Cleveland
800 Superior Ave., Cleveland, Ohio
44114
216-861-1378

DETROIT

National Bank of Detroit
611 Woodward Ave., Detroit, Mich.
48232
313-965-2366

LOS ANGELES

Security Pacific National Bank
610 South Broadway, Los Angeles,
Calif. 90014
213-620-6110

United Californian Bank, International Div.
600 South Spring St., Los Angeles,
Calif. 90054
213-627-0143

MILWAUKEE

First Wisconsin National Bank of
Milwaukee
743 North Water St., Milwaukee,
Wisc. 53403
414-276-6100

MINNEAPOLIS

Northwestern National Bank of
Minneapolis
7 Marquette Ave., Minneapolis,
Minn. 55480
612-372-8233

NEWARK

Englehard Minerals & Chemicals Corp.
Englehard Industries Div., 430
Mountain Ave., Murray Hill, N.J.
07974
201-464-7000

NEW ORLEANS

Whitney National Bank of New Orleans
228 St. Charles St., New Orleans,
La. 70160
504-529-7272

NEW YORK CITY

American Express International Banking Corp.
65 Broadway, New York, N.Y. 10006
212-944-2000

Bank of America, International
37 Broad Street, New York, N.Y. 10004
212-269-5900

The Bank of New York, International Div.
20 Broad St., New York, N.Y. 10005
212-530-3652

Bankers Trust Co.
280 Park Ave. New York, N.Y. 10017
212-692-7100

Brown Brothers Harriman & Co.
59 Wall St., New York, N.Y. 10005
212-483-1818

The Chase Manhattan Bank
1 Chase Manhattan Plaza, New York, N.Y. 10015
212-552-5438

Chemical Bank
20 Pine St., New York, N.Y. 10015
212-770-1966

First National City Bank
111 Wall St., New York, N.Y. 10015
212-825-2321

Hambro American Bank & Trust Co.
25 Broad St., New York, N.Y. 10004
212-425-1150

Irving Trust Co.
1 Wall St., New York, N.Y. 10015
212-553-2831

Manufacturers Hanover Trust Co.
4 New York Plaza, New York, N.Y. 10015
212-623-4481

Marine Midland Grace Trust Co. of New York
140 Broadway, New York, N.Y. 10015
212-797-8180

Morgan Guaranty Trust Co. of New York
23 Wall St., New York, N.Y. 10005
212-425-2323

PHILADELPHIA

The Fidelity Bank
Broad & Walnut St., Philadelphia, Pa. 19109
215-985-7251

The First Pennsylvania Banking & Trust Co.
15th & Chestnut St., Philadelphia, . Pa. 19101
215-568-1226

PITTSBURGH

Mellon National Bank & Trust Co.
Mellon Square, Pittsburgh, Pa. 15222
412-232-4100

PROVIDENCE

Industrial National Bank of Rhode Island
P.O. Box 368, Providence, R.I. 02901
401-521-9700

SAN FRANCISCO

The Bank of California, N.A. International Div.
400 California St., San Francisco, Calif. 94120
415-765-2351

Crocker National Bank, International Div.
1 Sansome St., San Francisco, Calif. 94138
415-983-2977

Wells Fargo Bank
   464 California St., San Francisco,
      Calif. 94120
   415-396-2573

SEATTLE

First National Bank
   P.O. Box 3586, Seattle, Wash. 98124
   206-583-3374

INVESTMENT ORGANIZATIONS

7. Two Hundred Largest Investment Banking Firms

Abraham & Co.
170 Broadway, New York, N.Y.
10005
212-732-7200
Partner: Henry L. Froy

Adams & Peck
120 Broadway, New York, N.Y.
10005
212-374-6200
Partner: Braman B. Adams

Advest Co.
6 Central Row, Hartford, Conn.
06103
203-525-1421
Partner (Hartford): Bertrand
McTeague
Partner (New York): Hunter B.
Grant

Allen & Co.
30 Broad St., New York, N.Y.
10004
212-422-2600
Genl. Mgr.: Murray R. Lavin

Almstedt Brothers
425 West Market St., Louisville, Ky.
40202

502-585-3264
Partners: Robert D. Bastin; J. R.
Burkholder, III

American Securities Corp.
25 Broad St., New York, N.Y.
10004
212-422-3200
Pres.: H. T. Freeland

American UBS Corp.
40 Wall St., New York, N.Y.
10005
212-943-5900
V.Ps.: Owen Jaeger; Donald E.
Williams

Anderson & Strudwick
913 East Main St., Richmond, Va.
23212
703-644-3071
Partner: George W. Anderson

Andresen & Co.
140 Broadway, New York, N.Y.
10005
212-363-6300
Genl. Partner: William D. Whitlaw

Arnhold & S. Bleichroeder, Inc.
30 Broad St., New York, N.Y.
10004
212-943-9200
Pres.: Stephen M. Kellen

Asiel & Co.
20 Broad St., New York, N.Y.
10005
212-422-5000
Senior Partner: John Wasserman

Bache & Co. Inc.
100 Gold St., New York, N.Y.
10038
212-797-3600
Senior V.P.: Charles W. Rendigs, Jr.

Bacon, Whipple & Co.
135 South LaSalle St., Chicago, Ill.
60603
312-782-3100
Partners: Gordon Bent; Robert B.
Krell

Robert W. Baird & Co.
731 North Water St., Milwaukee,
Wisc. 53201
414-273-3100
V.P.: Robert A. Stephan

Baker, Watts & Co.
Calvert & Redwood Sts., Baltimore,
Md. 21203
301-685-2600
Partners: John J. Jackson; Edgar M.
Boyd

Baker, Weeks & Co., Inc.
1 Battery Park Plaza, New York,
N.Y. 10004
212-785-3900
V.P.: G. Bruce Leib

Ball, Burge & Kraus
1414 Union Commerce Bldg., Cleveland, Ohio 44115
216-696-6464
Genl. Partners: Donald G. Rundle;
Bruce B. Ranney

Bateman Eichler, Hill Richards, Inc.
460 South Spring St., Los Angeles,
Calif. 90013
213-625-3545

Senior V.P.: William T. Walker, Jr.
Exec. V.P.: Peter J. Eichler

Bear, Stearns & Co.
1 Wall St., New York, N.Y. 10005
212-344-8500
Partner: V. Theodore Low

A. G. Becker & Co., Inc.
First National Plaza, Chicago, Ill.
60670
312-786-5000
V.P.: Stanley S. Wirt

D. H. Blair & Co.
437 Madison Ave., New York, N.Y.
10022
212-935-6400
Senior Partner: J. Morton Davis

William Blair & Co.
135 South LaSalle St., Chicago, Ill.
60603
312-236-1600
Partners: Donald T. Fletcher; Lee H.
Ostrander

Blunt Ellis & Simmons Inc.
111 West Monroe St., Chicago, Ill.
60603
312-346-9000
V.P.: Robert M. Clark

Blyth & Co., Inc.
14 Wall St., New York, N.Y. 10005
212-732-1900
Exec. V.P.: Frank L. Mansell

Boettcher & Co.
828 17th St., Denver, Colo. 80202
303-292-1010
Partner: James M. Powell
Special Partner: Robert F. Bardwell

Bosworth, Sullivan & Co., Inc.
660 17th St., Denver, Colo. 80202
303-534-1177
Pres.: John J. Sullivan

J. C. Bradford & Co.
J. C. Bradford Bldg., Nashville,
Tenn. 37219
615-244-6600
Partners: W. L. Simons, Jr.; J. C.
Bradford, Jr.

Partner (New York City): B. C. Pinkerton

Bregman & Co.
4 Albany St., New York, N.Y. 10006
212-732-0600
Partner: Paul M. Rosenthal

Alex. Brown & Sons
135 East Baltimore St., Baltimore, Md. 21203
301-727-1700
Partners: F. Barton Harvey, Jr.; John Pohlhaus

Burnham & Co.
60 Broad St., New York, N.Y. 10004
212-344-1400
Partners: J. N. Daley; Graham E. Jones; Jon M. Burnham

Butcher & Sherrerd
1500 Walnut St., Philadelphia, Pa. 19102
215-985-5000
Managing Partner: John B. Richter

CBWL–Hayden, Stone Inc.
767 Fifth Ave., New York, N.Y. 10022
212-350-0500
V.Ps.: Thomas L. Piper; Donald Stroben

Cartwright & Co.
141 West Jackson Blvd., Chicago, Ill. 60604
312-922-2535
Pres.: Levering Cartwright

The Chicago Corp.
208 South LaSalle St., Chicago, Ill. 60604
312-782-4100
Pres.: Milton S. Emrich

Clark, Dodge & Co., Inc.
140 Broadway, New York, N.Y. 10005
212-944-5600
V.P.: John E. Eckelberry

Crowell, Weedon & Co.
1 Wilshire Blvd., Los Angeles, Calif. 90017
213-620-1850
Partners: Donald W. Crowell; Warren H. Crowell

Dain, Kalman & Quail, Inc.
100 Dain Tower, Minneapolis, Minn. 55402
612-371-2711
Chief Exec. Officer: Wheelock Whitney

Shelby Cullom Davis & Co.
116 John St., New York, N.Y. 10038
212-233-0626
Partner: Kenneth C. Ebbitt

Dempsey & Co.
135 South LaSalle St., Chicago, Ill. 60603
312-346-2626
Pres.: J. R. Dempsey

Dick & Merle Smith
48 Wall St., New York, N.Y. 10005
212-944-0440
Managing Partner: Fergus Reid, III

Dillon, Read & Co., Inc.
46 William St., New York, N.Y. 10005
212-422-2828
Exec. V.P.: Arthur B. Treman, Jr.

Discount Corp. of New York
58 Pine St., New York, N.Y. 10005
212-943-4400
Pres.: Andrew K. Marckwald

Dishy, Easton & Co.
40 Exchange Pl., New York, N.Y. 10005
212-425-4580
Partner: Bernard Dishy

Dominick & Dominick, Inc.
14 Wall St., New York, N.Y. 10005
212-227-4600
V.Ps.: James Callery; Peter M. Kennedy; Norman A. Cooledge

Donaldson, Lufkin & Jenrette, Inc.
140 Broadway, New York, N.Y. 10005
212-943-0300
Exec. V.P.: Carl H. Tiedermann

Drexel Firestone, Inc.
1500 Walnut St., Philadelphia, Pa.
19101
215-545-4100
V.P. & Dir.: John E. Friday

F. I. duPont, Glore Forgan & Co.
1 Wall St., New York, N.Y. 10005
212-344-2000
Partner: Thomas W. Thompson

Eastman Dillon, Union Securities
& Co.
1 Chase Manhattan Plaza, New York,
N.Y. 10005
212-770-8000
Partner: William B. Harvey

F. Eberstadt & Co., Inc.
61 Broadway, New York, N.Y.
10006
212-944-8787
V.P.: W. A. Lubanko

A. G. Edwards & Sons, Inc.
1 North Jefferson, St. Louis, Mo.
63103
314-289-3039
V.P.: Bill F. Sarni

Edwards & Hanly
1 Whitehall St., New York, N.Y.
10004
212-425-9000
Partner: James M. Kingsbury

Elkins, Morris, Stroud & Co.
Stock Exchange Bldg., 17th & San-
som Sts., Philadelphia, Pa. 19103
215-568-1975
Partner: Theodore E. Eckfeldt

Eppler, Guerin & Turner, Inc.
3900 First National Bank Bldg.,
Dallas, Tex. 75202
214-741-3441
Chmn.: John W. Turner

Equitable Securities, Morton & Co.,
Inc.
65 Broadway, New York, N.Y.
10005
212-483-9800
Pres.: Peter V. N. Philip

Estabrook & Co., Inc.
80 Pine St., New York, N.Y. 10005
212-944-7800
Synd. Mgr.: John M. Perkins

Evans & Co., Inc.
300 Park Ave., New York, N.Y.
10022
212-753-6200
Exec. V.P.: George C. Bradley

Fahnestock & Co.
110 Wall St., New York, N.Y.
10005
212-943-8900
Partner: Thomas Grant

Faulkner, Dawkins & Sullivan
1 New York Plaza, New York, N.Y.
10004
212-623-6100
Partner: Richard B. Dawkins

Faulkner, Dawkins & Sullivan Securities, Inc.
1 New York Plaza, New York, N.Y.
10004
212-623-6100
Pres.: Richard B. Dawkins

Ferris & Co.
1720 Eye St., N.W., Washington,
D.C. 20006
202-298-4500
Senior Partner: George M. Ferris, Sr.

The First Boston Corp.
20 Exchange Pl., New York, N.Y.
10005
212-344-1515
Pres.: Paul L. Miller

First California Co.
555 California St., San Francisco,
Calif. 94120
415-622-7900
Exec. V.P.: R. F. Bjorkquist

First Manhattan Co.
30 Wall St., New York, N.Y. 10005
212-344-2525
Partner: John Wallace

First of Michigan Corp.
1200 Buhl Bldg., Detroit, Mich.
48226
313-962-2055
Pres.: John G. Martin

First Southwest Co.
Mercantile Bank Bldg., 9th Floor,
Dallas, Tex. 75201
214-742-6461
V.P.: John P. Boone

Folger, Nolan, Fleming, Douglas Inc.
725 15th St., N.W., Washington,
D.C. 20005
202-783-5252
Pres.: James Parker Nolan

Freehling & Co.
120 South LaSalle St., Chicago,
III. 60603
312-346-2680
Partners: Willard M. Freehling; Stanley Freehling; Karl Guiney

Albert Fried & Co.
77 Water St., New York, N.Y. 10005
212-344-5656
Managing Partner: Albert Fried, Jr.

Glover & MacGregor, Inc.
586 Union Trust Bldg., Pittsburgh,
Pa. 15219
412-218-2007
Pres.: M. G. Hulme

Goldman, Sachs & Co.
55 Broad St., New York, N.Y.
10004
212-676-8000
V.P., Synd. Dept.: Michael K.
Travers

Gruss & Co.
55 Broad St., New York, N.Y.
10004
212-422-7066
Partner: Albert B. Cohen

Haas Securities Corp.
120 Broadway, New York, N.Y.
10005
212-233-1700
V.P. & Treas.: George Sarner

Halle & Stieglitz, Inc.
52 Wall St., New York, N.Y.
10005
212-797-2550
Senior V.P.: Robert A. W. Brauns

Hallgarten & Co.
44 Wall St., New York, N.Y.
10005
212-269-9000
Partners: Frederick M. Peyser; Alvin Rumi

Halsey, Stuart & Co., Inc.
123 South LaSalle St., Chicago, III.
60690
312-782-3900
V.P.: John T. Riha

Hardy & Co.
25 Broad St., New York, N.Y.
10004
212-344-7800
Partner: Benjamin Wetzler

Harris, Upham & Co., Inc.
120 Broadway, New York, N.Y.
10005
212-374-7000
Pres.: Henry U. Harris, Jr.

H. Hentz & Co.
72 Wall St., New York, N.Y.
10005
212-797-8800
First V.P.: Arthur Parent

Herzfeld & Stern
30 Broad St., New York, N.Y.
10004
212-344-2600
Partner: Paul A. Cohen

Hettleman & Co.
61 Broadway, New York, N.Y.
10006
212-943-5770
Genl. Partner: Phillip Hettleman

Hill & Co.
1717 Provident Tower, Cincinnati,
Ohio 45202
513-241-8600
Partner: Richard G. Meyer

Hoppin, Watson & Co.
55 Broad St., New York, N.Y.
10004
212-344-6111
Partner: James F. Stebbins

Hornblower & Weeks-Hemphill, Noyes
8 Hanover St., New York, N.Y.
10004
212-344-6600
V.P. Synd.: Roy J. Remite

Howard, Weil, Labouisse, Friedrichs
Inc.
211 Carondelet St., New Orleans,
La. 70130
504-581-2711
V.P.: Forres M. Collins, Sr.

E. F. Hutton & Co., Inc.
1 Battery Park Plaza, New York,
N.Y. 10004
212-742-5000
Exec. V.P.: John S. R. Shad

W. E. Hutton & Co.
14 Wall St., New York, N.Y. 10005
212-732-3300
Partners: James J. Lee; J. Logan
Burke, Jr.

Johnson, Lane, Space, Smith & Co.,
Inc.
34 Broad St. N.W., Atlanta, Ga.
30303
404-523-3692
Pres. (Savannah): David T. Johnson

Johnston, Lemon & Co.
900 Southern Bldg., Washington,
D.C. 20005
202-783-3130
Senior Partner: James H. Lemon

Edward D. Jones & Co.
101 North 4th St., St. Louis, Mo.
63102
314-231-7600
Partner: Edward J. Costigan

Josephthal & Co.
120 Broadway, New York, N.Y.
10005
212-964-5000

Partners: Bernard E. Pollak; Louis H.
Serlen; Sydney Parlow

Kalb, Voorhis & Co.
27 William St., New York, N.Y.
10005
212-425-6000
Senior Partner: Arthur Vare

Keefe, Bruyette & Woods, Inc.
140 Broadway, New York, N.Y.
10005
212-425-3232
Pres.: Harry V. Keefe, Jr.

Kidder, Peabody & Co., Inc.
20 Exchange Pl., New York, N.Y.
10005
212-770-7000
Exec. V.P.: Ralph D. DeNunzio

Kohlmeyer & Co.
147 Carondelet St., New Orleans,
La. 70130
504-529-3771
Partners: Herman S. Kohlmeyer, Jr.;
Robert W. Newman

Kuhn, Loeb & Co.
40 Wall St., New York, N.Y. 10005
212-797-2100
Partner: William H. Todd

Ladenburg, Thalmann & Co.
25 Broad St., New York, N.Y.
10004
212-422-8570
Partner: Carl K. Erpf

Laird, Bissell & Meeds, Inc.
DuPont Bldg., Wilmington, Del.
19899
302-658-4241
V.P.: William H. Foulk, Jr.

Laird Inc.
140 Broadway, New York, N.Y.
10005
212-269-4900
Pres.: George T. Weymouth

Cyrus J. Lawrence & Sons
115 Broadway, New York, N.Y.
10006
212-962-2200
Genl. Partner: Gene Apruzzi

Lazard Freres & Co.
44 Wall St., New York, N.Y. 10005
212-422-1200
Partner: Francis J. Madden

Legg, Mason & Co., Inc.
22 Light St., Baltimore, Md. 21203
301-539-3400
Partner: Philip O. Rogers

Lehman Brothers Inc.
1 William St., New York, N.Y.
10004
212-269-3700
Managing Dirs.: Robert F. Shapiro;
Jonathan Smith

Arthur Lipper Corp.
140 Broadway, New York, N.Y.
10005
212-425-8900
Exec. V.P.: Nancy L. Stuart

Loeb, Rhoades & Co.
42 Wall St., New York, N.Y. 10005
212-530-4000
Partners: J. Howard Carlson; Albert
Parker, Jr.

Loewi & Co., Inc.
225 East Mason St., Milwaukee, Wis.
53202
414-272-5100
Pres.: W. L. Liebman

Lynch, Jones & Ryan
20 Exchange Pl., New York, N.Y.
10005
212-344-8400
Partners: John B. Lynch; Harry H.
Jones

Carl Marks & Co. Inc.
77 Water St., New York, N.Y. 10005
212-437-7000
Pres.: Edwin S. Marks

A. E. Masten & Co.
1 Oliver Plaza, Pittsburgh, Pa. 15222
412-261-7300
Partner: L. W. Young, Jr.

McDonald & Co.
2100 Central National Bank Bldg.,
Cleveland, Ohio 44114

216-523-2000
Partner: Joseph H. Thomas

Merrill Lynch, Pierce, Fenner & Smith
Inc.
70 Pine St., New York, N.Y. 10005
212-944-1212
Grp. V.P.: Julius H. Sedlmayr

Mesirow & Co.
135 South LaSalle St., Chicago, Ill.
60603
312-346-1700
Partners: Sheldon Pekin; Norman
Mesirow

The Milwaukee Co.
207 East Michigan St., Milwaukee,
Wisc. 53202
414-276-6075
Pres.: Robert G. Stenger

Mitchell, Hutchins & Co., Inc.
1 Battery Park Plaza, New York,
N.Y. 10004
212-344-0700
V.P. & Treas.: Charles Peterson

Mitchum, Jones & Templeton, Inc.
510 South Spring St., Los Angeles,
Calif. 90013
213-625-3511
Senior V.P.: James W. Lewis

Model, Roland & Co., Inc.
120 Broadway, New York, N.Y.
10005
212-964-5300
V.P.: J. Anthony Lockhart

Moore, Leonard & Lynch, Inc.
Union Trust Bldg., Pittsburgh, Pa.
15219
412-281-0358
V.P.: Richard A. Hay

Morgan Stanley & Co. Inc.
140 Broadway, New York, N.Y.
10005
212-732-2100
Managing Partner: H. Lawrence
Parker

F. S. Moseley & Co.
50 Congress St., Boston, Mass.
02109

617-482-1300
Partner (New York): Frederick C. Braun, Jr.

Neuberger & Berman
120 Broadway, New York, N.Y. 10005
212-267-2600
Partner: Peter Strauss

Newhard, Cook & Co.
400 Olive St., St. Louis, Mo. 63102
314-231-5585
Partner: Harry W. Newhard

New York Hanseatic Corp.
60 Broad St., New York, N.Y. 10004
212-363-2000
V.Ps.: Lawrence B. Illoway; Ernest M. Grunebaum

New York Securities Co. Inc.
1 New York Plaza, New York, N.Y. 10004
212-425-2800
V.P.: Stanford H. Brainerd

John Nuveen & Co., Inc.
61 Broadway, New York, N.Y. 10006
212-344-8300
Pres.: Frank P. Wendt

The Ohio Co.
51 North High St., Columbus, Ohio 43215
614-221-4431
V.P.: George G. Scully

Oppenheimer & Co.
4 New York Plaza, New York, N.Y. 10004
212-344-4460
Managing Partner: Jack Nash

Paine, Webber, Jackson & Curtis Inc.
140 Broadway, New York, N.Y. 10005
212-437-2121
V.Ps.: Albert Pratt; A. T. Wenzell ·

Paribas Corp.
40 Wall St., New York, N.Y. 10005
212-425-5151
Pres.: Christian M. Cardin

Parker/Hunter Inc.
Union Trust Bldg., Pittsburgh, Pa. 15219
412-281-5400
Exec. V.P.: David W. Hunter

Pershing & Co.
120 Broadway, New York, N.Y. 10005
212-964-4300
Partner: Michael A. Dreitlein

Carl H. Pforzheimer & Co.
70 Pine St., New York, N.Y. 10005
212-422-5484
Genl. Partner: C. H. Pforzheimer, III

Piper, Jaffray & Hopwood Inc.
115 South 7th St., Minneapolis, Minn. 55402
612-371-6111
Pres.: George Fox

Wm. E. Pollock & Co., Inc.
160 Water St., New York, N.Y. 10038
212-425-5700
Pres.: George W. Hall

Prescott, Merrill, Turben & Co.
900 National City Bank Bldg., Cleveland, Ohio 44114
216-696-1000
Partners: John A. Kruse; William S. Gray

R. W. Pressprich & Co., Inc.
80 Pine St., New York, N.Y. 10005
212-483-1100
Senior V.P.: Edward M. Rowan

Chas. E. Quincey & Co.
115 Broadway, New York, N.Y. 10006
212-422-4410
Senior Partner: M. A. Gilmartin, Jr.

Rauscher Pierce Securities Corp.
1200 Mercantile Dallas Bldg., Dallas, Tex. 75201
214-748-0111
Senior V.P.: Charles C. Pierce, Jr.

Reinholdt & Gardner
506 Olive St., St. Louis, Mo. 63101
314-231-6640
Partner: John R. Gardner

Reynolds & Co.
120 Broadway, New York, N.Y.
10005
212-558-6000
Genl. Partner: John F. Bryan

Riter, Pyne, Kendall & Hollister
100 Wall St., New York, N.Y. 10005
212-785-7000
Genl. Partner: Allen J. Nix

The Robinson Humphrey Co., Inc.
2 Peachtree St. N.W., Atlanta, Ga.
30303
404-577-3700
Pres.: Alexander Yearley, IV

Rodman & Renshaw, Inc.
209 South LaSalle St., Chicago, Ill.
60604
312-332-0560
V.P.: Joel H. Jastromb

Wm. C. Roney & Co.
Buhl Bldg., Detroit, Mich. 48226
313-963-6700
Partner: Clyde L. Hagerman

L. M. Rosenthal & Co., Inc.
5 Hanover Square, New York, N.Y.
10004
212-425-7800
V.P.: Charles M. Rosenthal

L. F. Rothschild & Co.
99 William St., New York, N.Y.
10038
212-425-3300
Genl. Partners: Chester W. Viale;
   Walter W. Hess, Jr.

Rowles, Winston & Co., Inc.
200 Houston National Gas Bldg.,
   Houston, Tex. 77002
713-225-9221
Exec. V.P.: Roger G. Stotler

Salomon Brothers
1 New York Plaza, New York, N.Y.
10004
212-747-7000
Partner: John Gutfreund

G. A. Saxton & Co., Inc.
100 Wall St., New York, N.Y. 10005

212-483-1600
Pres.: Gerald C. McNamara

M. A. Schapiro & Co., Inc.
1 Chase Manhattan Plaza, New York,
   N.Y. 10005
212-425-6600
Pres.: Morris A. Schapiro

Scherck, Stein & Franc, Inc.
506 Olive St., St. Louis, Mo. 63101
314-421-0225
Pres.: Elliot H. Stein

Schweickart & Co.
2 Broadway, New York, N.Y.
10004
212-363-4300
V.P.: M. L. Rothenberg

Scott & Stringfellow
P.O. Box 1575, Richmond, Va.
23213
703-643-1811
Partner: Joseph J. Muldowney

Second District Securities Co., Inc.
1 Chase Manhattan Plaza, New York,
   N.Y. 10005
212-943-1900
Exec. V.P.: Edward L. Madden, Jr.

Seiden & deCuevas Inc.
110 Wall St., New York, N.Y.
10005
212-943-2465
Pres.: Melvin R. Seiden

Shearson, Hammill & Co., Inc.
14 Wall St., New York, N.Y. 10005
212-558-2323
Pres.: Alger B. Chapman, Jr.

Shields & Co.
44 Wall St., New York, N.Y. 10005
212-785-2400
Genl. Partners: Macrae Sykes;
   Thomas McGlade; Joseph V. Mis-
   sett, III

Shuman, Agnew & Co., Inc.
650 California St., San Francisco,
   Calif. 94108
415-981-0900
Pres.: Iver Lyche

I. M. Simon & Co.
315 North 4th St., St. Louis, Mo.
63102
314-231-3550
Partner: Elvin K. Popper

Singer, Deane & Scribner
1045 Union Trust Bldg., Pittsburgh,
Pa. 15219
412-471-4700
Partner: Richard E. Fisher

Singer & Mackie, Inc.
40 Exchange Pl., New York, N.Y.
10005
212-422-9000
Chmn.: Herbert Singer

Smith, Barney & Co., Inc.
1345 Ave. of the Americas, New
York, N.Y. 10019
212-344-9600
V.P. & Dir.: J. Frederick Van
Vranken, Jr.

Smith, Hague & Co.
539 Penobscot Bldg., Detroit, Mich.
48226
313-963-5535
Partner: Hal H. Smith, III

F. S. Smithers & Co., Inc.
1 Battery Park Plaza, New York,
N.Y. 10004
212-943-3300
V.P.: Ray P. Foote, Jr.

Spear, Leeds & Kellogg
111 Broadway, New York, N.Y.
10006
212-349-1000
Senior Partner: Raymond E.
Grabowski

Steiner, Rouse & Co., Inc.
19 Rector St., New York, N.Y.
10006
212-422-0700
V.P.: Philip M. Waterman, Jr.

Stephens, Inc.
114 East Capitol Ave., Little Rock,
Ark. 72201
501-374-4361
V.P.: Vernon J. Giss

Stern Brothers & Co.
9 West 10th St., Kansas City, Mo.
64199
816-471-6460
Exec. V.P.: J. L. Gumbiner

Stern, Lauer & Co.
120 Broadway, New York, N.Y.
10005
212-349-2800
Managing Partner: Charles A.
Bernheim

Stifel, Nicolaus & Co., Inc.
314 North Broadway, St. Louis,
Mo. 63102
314-421-1980
V.P.: Robert V. Strano

Stone & Webster Securities Corp.
90 Broad St., New York, N.Y.
10004
212-269-4200
V.P.: Winchester F. Hotchkiss

Stone & Youngberg
1 California St., San Francisco,
Calif. 94111
415-981-1314
Partner & Contractor: Edward C.
Kern

J. S. Strauss & Co.
4650 Bank of America Center, San
Francisco, Calif. 94104
415-392-8515
Sec./Treas.: William P. Held

Stuart Brothers
55 Broad St., New York, N.Y.
10004
212-944-2300
Partners: Alan L. Stuart; James M.
Stuart; Howard Kelting, Jr.

Sutro & Co., Inc.
460 Montgomery St., San Francisco,
Calif. 94104
415-392-0900
Senior V.P.: Paul N. Duggan

Swiss American Corp.
100 Wall St., New York, N.Y. 10005
212-943-7424
Pres.: Henry Stravitz

TPO Inc.
61 Broadway, New York, N.Y.
10006
212-425-2288
V.P.: Richard Gamsu

Thomson & McKinnon, Auchincloss,
Inc.
2 Broadway, New York, N.Y.
10004
212-422-5100
V.Ps.: H. Kelly McLaughlin; Harry
Zisson

Spencer Trask & Co., Inc.
60 Broad St., New York, N.Y.
10004
212-422-4300
Senior V.P.: Allan C. Eustis, Jr.

Tucker, Anthony & R. L. Day
120 Broadway, New York, N.Y.
10005
212-732-8300
Partner: Ernest W. Borkland

Tweedy, Browne & Knapp
52 Wall St., New York, N.Y. 10005
212-422-4694
Genl. Partner: Howard S. Browne

Underwood, Neuhaus & Co., Inc.
724 Travis St., Houston, Tex.
77002
713-224-1224
Pres.: Philip R. Neuhaus

C. E. Unterberg, Towbin Co.
61 Broadway, New York, N.Y.
10006
212-425-3090
Partner: A. Robert Towbin

Van Alstyne, Noel & Co.
4 Albany St., New York, N.Y.
10006
212-233-2000
Partners: Lorrin C. Mawdsley; John
P. Sellas

Vance, Sanders & Co., Inc.
111 Devonshire St., Boston, Mass.
02109
617-482-8900
Treas.: Eric Pierce

H. C. Wainwright & Co.
1 Boston Pl., Boston, Mass. 02108
617-723-7300
Partner: Francis V. Ward

G. H. Walker & Co.
45 Wall St., New York, N.Y. 10005
212-422-4000
Genl. Partner: Charles H. Symington,
Jr.

Walston & Co., Inc.
77 Water St., New York, N.Y. 10005
212-437-7440
V.P.: Alexander W. Small

Watling, Lerchen & Co.
Ford Bldg., Detroit, Mich. 48226
313-962-5525
Partner: S. P. Bayekian

Weeden & Co.
25 Broad St., New York, N.Y.
10004
212-344-2300
Pres.: Alan N. Weeden

Weis, Voisin & Co., Inc.
17 Battery Pl. North, New York,
N.Y. 10006
212-964-7300
Pres.: Arthur J. Levine

Wertheim & Co.
1 Chase Manhattan Plaza, New York,
N.Y. 10005
212-558-3300
Partner: William D. Kerr

Wheat & Co., Inc.
801 East Main St., Richmond, Va.
23211
703-649-2311
V.P.: L. Gordon Miller, Jr.

Wheeler, Munger & Co.
618 South Spring St., Los Angeles,
Calif. 90014
213-624-7715
Partner: Charles T. Munger

White, Weld & Co.
20 Broad St., New York, N.Y.
10005
212-944-4900
Genl. Partner: Alexander M. White,
Jr.

Dean Witter & Co., Inc.
  45 Montgomery St., San Francisco,
    Calif. 94106
  415-392-7211
  Pres.: Lawrence B. Morris, Jr.

William D. Witter, Inc.
  1 Battery Park Plaza, New York,
    N.Y. 10004
  212-483-0800
  V.P.: Peter Shipman

Wood, Struthers & Winthrop, Inc.
  20 Exchange Pl., New York, N.Y.
    10005
  212-269-3313
  Exec. V.P.: H. K. L'Hommedieu

Wood, Walker & Co.
  63 Wall St., New York, N.Y. 10005
  212-944-7870
  Partner: Charles L. Hewitt

B. C. Ziegler & Co.
  215 North Main St., West Bend,
    Wisc. 53095
  414-334-5521
  Pres.: Thomas J. Kenny

Zuckerman, Smith & Co.
  30 Broad St., New York, N.Y.
    10004
  212-422-5300
  Partner: James W. Wolff

8. Investment Counselors and Portfolio Managers

Alexander, Van Cleef, Jordan & Wood,
    Inc.
  National City Bank Bldg., Cleveland,
    Ohio 44114
  216-621-2150

Argus Investors' Counsel, Inc.
  140 Broadway, New York, N.Y.
    10005
  212-425-7500

E. W. Axe & Co., Inc.
  400 Benedict Ave., Tarrytown, N.Y.
    10591
  914-631-8131

David L. Babson & Co., Inc.
  1 Boston Pl., Boston, Mass. 02108
  617-723-7540

Beck, Mack & Oliver
  6 East 43rd St., New York, N.Y.
    10017
  212-661-2640

John N. Blewer, Inc.
  685 Fifth Ave., New York, N.Y.
    10022
  212-838-4860

Boyd Watterson & Co.
  1500 Union Commerce Bldg., Cleve-
    land, Ohio 44115
  216-771-3450

Bridges Investment Counsel, Inc.
  256 Swanson Bldg., 8401 West
    Dodge Rd., Omaha, Nebr. 68114
  402-397-4700

Brundage, Story & Rose
  90 Broad St., New York, N.Y.
    10004
  212-BO9-3050

Neil F. Campbell, Inc.
  10889 Wilshire Blvd., Suite 945, Los
    Angeles, Calif. 90024
  213-478-5023

Campbell, Henderson & Co.
  3100 First National Bank Bldg.,
    Dallas, Tex. 75202
  214-742-4117

Chase Investment Counsel Corp.
  415 4th St. N.E., Charlottesville,
    Va. 22901
  703-293-9104

Clifford Associates
639 South Spring St., Los Angeles,
Calif. 90014
213-627-2228

Franklin Cole & Co., Inc.
2 Wall St., New York, N.Y. 10005
212-349-1110

Cooke & Bieler, Inc.
Philadelphia National Bank Bldg.,
Broad & Chestnut Sts., Philadelphia, Pa. 19107
215-LO7-1101

Dahlberg, Kelly and Wisdom, Inc.
803 Hibernia Bank Bldg., New Orleans, La. 70112
504-525-6285

Danforth Associates
384 Washington St., Wellesley Hills,
Mass. 02181
617-235-9100

Davidge & Co.
1747 Pennsylvania Ave. N.W., Washington, D.C. 20006
202-223-6090

Dodge & Cox, Inc.
3500 Crocker Plaza, Post at Montgomery St., San Francisco, Calif.
94104
415-981-1710

Eaton & Howard, Inc.
24 Federal St., Boston, Mass. 02110
617-482-8260

Lionel D. Edie & Co.
530 Fifth Ave., New York, N.Y.
10022
212-697-8900

Gofen & Glossberg
135 South LaSalle St., Chicago,
Ill. 60603
312-782-3512

Everett Harris & Co.
550 South Flower St., Room 719,
Los Angeles, Calif. 90017
213-625-2677

Heber–Fuger–Wendin, Inc.
810 Ford Bldg., Detroit, Mich.
48226
313-961-6205

James Hotchkiss Associates, Inc.
208 South LaSalle St., Chicago, Ill.
60604
312-368-4633

Hunter, Miller & Fleming, Inc.
120 Montgomery St., San Francisco,
Calif. 94104
415-392-8577

Douglas T. Johnson & Co., Inc.
460 Park Ave., New York, N.Y.
10022
212-679-2700

Dale A. Lindsay
21 West Putnam Ave., Greenwich,
Conn. 06830
203-TO9-5155

Loomis, Sayles & Co., Inc.
225 Franklin St., Boston, Mass.
02110
617-482-2450

Mairs & Power, Inc.
West 2062 First National Bank Bldg.,
St. Paul, Minn. 55101
612-222-8478

McCuen & McCuen, Inc.
2020 Union Bank Bldg., San Diego,
Calif. 92101
714-239-3034

Montag & Caldwell, Inc.
2901 First National Bank Tower,
Atlanta, Ga. 30303
404-522-0210

Neville, Rodie & Shaw, Inc.
100 Park Ave., New York, N.Y.
10017
212-725-1440

Paul, Armstrong & Tindall, Inc.
9601 Wilshire Blvd., Beverly Hills,
Calif. 90210
213-272-9157

John G. Pell & Co.
1 Wall St., New York, N.Y. 10005
212-WH3-1182

Post & Astrop
1500 Rhodes-Haverty Bldg., Atlanta, Ga. 30303
214-748-7037

T. Rowe Price & Associates, Inc.
1 Charles Center, Baltimore, Md. 21201
301-539-1992

Professional Economics, Inc.
850 Boylston St., Chestnut Hill, Mass. 02167
617-731-6850

Pulsifier & Hutner, Inc.
14 Wall St., New York, N.Y. 10005
212-349-0200

Frederic Samuels
1747 Van Buren St., Suite 950, Hollywood, Fla. 33020
305-923-8515

Fayez Sarofim & Co.
1405 First City National Bank Bldg., Houston, Tex. 77002
713-224-5301

Scudder, Stevens & Clark
345 Park Ave., New York, N.Y. 10022
212-350-8200

Securities Counsel, Inc.
408 Wildwood Ave., Jackson, Mich. 49201
517-784-7128

Arthur H. Spiegel, Investment Counsel
504 Sunshine Bldg., Albuquerque, N.M. 87101
505-243-2259

Standish, Ayer & Wood, Inc.
50 Congress St., Boston, Mass. 02109
617-CA7-7744

Stein, Roe & Farnham
150 South Wacker Dr., Chicago, Ill. 60606
312-368-7700

Stephenson & Evers
220 Montgomery St., San Francisco, Calif. 94104
415-362-5637

Templeton, Dobrow & Vance, Inc.
177 North Dean St., Englewood, N.J. 07631
201-LO7-2000

Trainer, Wortham & Co., Inc.
345 Park Ave., New York, N.Y. 10022
212-759-7755

Wentworth, Dahl & Belden
2900 Crocker Plaza, San Francisco, Calif. 94104
415-981-6911

Windsor Assn., Inc.
954 1 Main Pl., Dallas, Tex. 75250
214-748-7037

9. Largest Municipal Bond Dealers

Arthurs, Lestrange & Short
2 Gateway Center, Pittsburgh, Pa. 15222
412-391-3131
Partner: S. R. Robb, Jr.

Bache & Co., Inc.
100 Gold St., New York, N.Y. 10038
212-797-3600
Senior V.P.: Charles W. Rendigs, Jr.

Bear, Stearns & Co.
1 Wall St., New York, N.Y. 10005
212-344-8500
Partner: V. Theodore Low

A. G. Becker & Co., Inc.
First National Plaza, Chicago, Ill.
60670
312-786-5000
V.P.: Stanley S. Wirt

Boettcher & Co.
828 17th St., Denver, Colo. 80202
303-292-1010
Partner: James M. Powell

Alex Brown & Sons
135 East Baltimore St., Baltimore,
Md. 21203
301-727-1700
Partner: John Pohlhaus

Butcher & Sherrerd
1500 Walnut St., Philadelphia, Pa.
19102
215-985-5000
Managing Partner: John B. Richter

Clark, Dodge & Co., Inc.
140 Broadway, New York, N.Y.
10005
212-944-5600
V.P.: John E. Eckelberry

Dain, Kalman & Quail, Inc.
100 Dain Tower, Minneapolis, Minn.
55402
612-371-2711
Chief Exec. Officer: Wheelock
Whitney

Dominick & Dominick, Inc.
14 Wall St., New York, N.Y. 10005
212-227-4600
V.P.: James Callery

F. I. duPont, Glore Forgan & Co.
1 Wall St., New York, N.Y. 10005
212-344-2000
Partner: Thomas W. Thompson

Eastman Dillon, Union Securities &
Co.
1 Chase Manhattan Plaza, New York
N.Y. 10005

212-770-8000
Partner: William B. Harvey

First of Michigan Corp.
1200 Buhl Bldg., Detroit, Mich.
48226
313-962-2055
President: John G. Martin

Goldman, Sachs & Co.
55 Broad St., New York, N.Y.
10004
212-676-8000
Partner: Lewis M. Weston

J. J. B. Hilliard, W. L. Lyons & Co.
545 South Third St., Louisville, Ky.
40202
502-583-6651
Partner: Watson B. Dabney

Hornblower & Weeks-Hemphill, Noyes
8 Hanover St., New York, N.Y.
10004
212-344-6600
V.P. Synd.: Roy J. Remite

Kidder, Peabody & Co., Inc.
20 Exchange Place, New York, N.Y.
10005
212-770-7000
Exec. V.P.: Ralph D. DeNunzio

Kuhn, Loeb & Co.
40 Wall St., New York, N.Y. 10005
212-797-2100
Partner: William H. Todd

Lazard Freres & Co.
44 Wall St., New York, N.Y. 10005
212-422-1200
Partner: Francis J. Madden

Lehman Brothers, Inc.
1 William St., New York, N.Y.
10004
212-269-3700
Managing Dir.: Robert F. Shapiro

McDonald & Co.
2100 Central National Bank Bldg.,
Cleveland, Ohio 44114
216-523-2000
Partner: Joseph H. Thomas

Merrill Lynch, Pierce, Fenner & Smith, Inc.
70 Pine St., New York, N.Y. 10005
212-944-1212
V.P.: Thomas L. Chrystie

Moore, Leonard & Lynch, Inc.
Union Trust Bldg., Pittsburgh, Pa. 15219
412-281-0358
V.P.: Richard A. Hay

Piper, Jaffray & Hopwood, Inc.
115 South 7th St., Minneapolis, Minn. 55402
612-371-6111
Pres.: George Fox

Rauscher Pierce Securities Corp.
1200 Mercantile Dallas Bldg., Dallas, Tex. 75201
214-748-0111
Senior V.P.: Charles C. Pierce, Jr.

The Robinson-Humphrey Co., Inc.
2 Peachtree St. N.W., Atlanta, Ga. 30303
404-577-3700
Pres.: Alexander Yearley, IV

L. F. Rothschild & Co.
99 William St., New York, N.Y. 10038
212-425-3300
Genl. Partner: Chester W. Viale

Rowles, Winston & Co., Inc.
200 Houston National Gas Bldg., Houston, Tex. 77002
713-225-9221
Exec. V.P.: Roger G. Stotler

Salomon Brothers
1 New York Plaza, New York, N.Y. 10004
212-747-7000
Partner: John Gutfreund

Shields & Co.
44 Wall St., New York, N.Y. 10005
212-785-2400
Genl. Partner: Macrae Sykes

Singer, Deane & Scribner
1045 Union Trust Bldg., Pittsburgh, Pa. 15219
412-471-4700
Partner: Richard E. Fisher

Smith, Barney & Co., Inc.
1345 Ave. of the Americas, New York, N.Y. 10019
212-344-9600
V.P. & Dir.: J. Frederick Van Vranken, Jr.

F. S. Smithers & Co., Inc.
1 Battery Park Plaza, New York, N.Y. 10004
212-943-3300
V.P.: Ray P. Foote, Jr.

Stifel, Nicolaus & Co., Inc.
314 North Broadway, St. Louis, Mo. 63102
314-421-1980
V.P.: Robert V. Strano

Underwood, Neuhaus & Co., Inc.
724 Travis St., Houston, Tex. 77002
713-224-1224
Pres.: Philip R. Neuhaus

Walston & Co., Inc.
77 Water St., New York, N.Y. 10005
212-437-7440
V.P.: Alexander W. Small

Wertheim & Co.
1 Chase Manhattan Plaza, New York, N.Y. 10005
212-558-3300
Partner: William D. Kerr

White, Weld & Co.
20 Broad St., New York, N.Y. 10005
212-944-4900
Genl. Partner: Alexander M. White, Jr.

10. Largest Put and Call Dealers

M. C. Adams & Co., Inc.
61 Broadway, New York, N.Y.
10006
212-WH3-4488
Exec. Officer: Merritt C. Adams

Henry Blair & Co., Inc.
39 Broadway, New York, N.Y.
10006
212-944-9100
Exec. Officer: Henry Blair

Cohn, Ivers & Co., Inc.
122 East 42nd St., New York, N.Y.
10017
212-YU6-0630
Exec. Officer: Philip Ivers

Daniel Daly
2301 Clipper St., San Mateo, Calif.
94403
415-345-6563
Exec. Officer: Daniel Daly

Joseph Ezra & Co., Inc.
150 Broadway, New York, N.Y.
10038
212-962-1744
Exec. Officer: Joseph Ezra

Alvin V. Filer & Co., Inc.
30 Broad St., New York, N.Y.
10004
212-422-2565
Exec. Officer: William J. Kehoe

Filer, Schmidt & Co., Inc.
26 Broadway, New York, N.Y.
10004
212-425-8383
Exec. Officer: Herbert Filer, Jr.

Godnick & Son, Inc.
30 Broad St., New York, N.Y.
10004
212-HA2-3832
Exec. Officer: Berton W. Godnick

Jerry D. Goldstein
16 Bingham Hill Circle, Rumson,
N.J. 07760

201-842-5311
Exec. Officer: Jerry D. Goldstein

Samuel Gomberg, New York Produce
Exchange
2 Broadway, New York, N.Y. 10004
212-269-3400
Exec. Officer: Samuel Gomberg

Harco Options, Inc.
19 Rector St., New York, N.Y.
10006
212-248-3350
Exec. Officer: Max Gertler

International Option Corp.
120 Broadway, New York, N.Y.
10005
212-233-4554
Exec. Officer: Gregory B. Hillman

Paul Karp
5401 Collins Ave., Miami Beach,
Fla. 33140
305-864-8302
Exec. Officer: Paul Karp

Lawrence Kotkin Associates, Inc.
40 Exchange Pl., New York, N.Y.
10005
212-422-1115
Exec. Officer: Lawrence Kotkin

Krinski, Cassio Co., Inc.
19 Rector St., New York, N.Y.
10006
212-HA2-3986
Exec. Officer: John R. Cassio

Saul Lerner Co., Inc.
61 Broadway, New York, N.Y.
10006
212-344-0155
Exec. Officer: Saul Lerner

Lombard Street, Inc.
170 Broadway, New York, N.Y.
10038
212-349-7760
Exec. Officer: James A. Sawyer

Marsh, Block, Leibler & Co., Inc.
132 Nassau St., New York, N.Y.
10038
212-349-7330
Exec. Officer: Max Leibler

Ragnar Option Corp.
39 Broadway, New York, N.Y.
10006
212-248-2460
Exec. Officer: Everett H. Moffat

Joseph Z. Simons
Zuckerman, Smith & Co., 30 Broad
St., New York, N.Y. 10004
212-422-5300
Exec. Officer: Joseph Z. Simons

Spiegel Securities, Inc.
708 Ashbourne Rd., Elkins Park,
Pa. 19117
215-CA4-8100
Exec. Officer: Dr. Henry Spiegel

Thomas, Haab & Botts
50 Broadway, New York, N.Y.
10004
212-269-8100
Exec. Officer: Lawrence G. Botts

U. S. Option Corp.
77 Water St., New York, N.Y.
10005
212-944-7111
Exec. Officer: Martin Askowitz

Vogel-Lorber, Inc.
29 Broadway, New York, N.Y.
10006
212-344-2500
Exec. Officer: Henry G. Vogel

Wilkins-Rose, Inc.
111 Broadway, New York, N.Y.
10006
212-964-2274
Exec. Officer: Nathan Rosenblatt

CAPITAL FIRMS

11. Small Business Investment Companies

ALASKA

Alaska-Pacific Capital Corp.
425 G St., Suite 710, Anchorage
99501
905-272-3508
Attorney: Chancy Croft
A*12

ARIZONA

CSC Capital Corp. (branch)
3550 North Central Ave., United
Bank Bldg., Suite 1600, Phoenix
85012
602-277-5479
Chmn. of Exec. Committee: Mel
Decker
D§12 (See Texas; see also
California)

First Midwest Capital Corp. (branch)
3003 North Central Ave., Suite
1200, Phoenix 85012
602-274-3625
C*5, 8, 12 (See Minnesota)

First Southwest Small Business Investment Co.
1611 East Camelback, Phoenix
85016
602-274-3623
Pres.: William Howard O'Brien
A§1, 5, 7, 11

CALIFORNIA

ABCO Equity Funds, Inc.
9220 Sunset Blvd., Suite 222, Los
Angeles 90069
213-273-2562
Pres.: M. D. Sharpe
A*5, 9, 12

Arcata Investment Co.
2750 Sand Hill Rd., Menlo Park
94025
415-854-0461
Mgr.: Ronald N. Hope
A*MESBIC

Bryan Capital, Inc.
235 Montgomery St., San Francisco
94104
415-421-9990
Pres.: John M. Bryan
B§1, 5, 6, 8

CSC Capital Corp. (branch)
61 South Lake St., Suite 305,
Pasadena 91101
213-681-5141 or 681-5142
V.P.: W. W. Hass
D§12 (see Texas; see also Arizona)

C. S. & W. Investment Co.
385 Grand Ave., Oakland 94610
415-421-2484
Pres.: Harry Stevenson
A§12

Capital City Equity Co.
P.O. Box 689, Santa Ana 94702
714-540-0450
Pres.: Robert F. Palmer
B§1, 5, 9, 12

City Capital Corp.
9255 Sunset Blvd., Suite 1011, Los
Angeles 90069
213-878-2080 or 273-4080
Pres.: Morton A. Heller
B§1, 5, 8

City of Commerce Investment Co.
1117-B south Goodrich Blvd., Los
Angeles 90022
213-724-6141
Genl. Mgr.: Manuel Aregon, Jr.
A*MESBIC

Continental Capital Corp.
Bank of America Center, San
Francisco 94104
415-989-2020
Pres.: Frank G. Chambers
C§1, 5, 6, 7, 8

Creative Capital Corp. (branch)
Russ Bldg., San Francisco 94104
415-932-3900
Regional Mgr.: David B. Wood
D§1, 2, 5, 8, 10, 12 (See New York)

Crocker Capital Corp.
405 Florence St., Palo Alto 94301

415-322-6236
Pres.: John J. Holwerda
C§5, 8, 12

Developers Equity Capital Corp.
9348 Santa Monica Blvd., Beverly
Hills 90210
213-878-2533 or 278-3611
Pres.: Larry Sade
A*2, 6, 11

Diversified Equities Corp.
625 Market St., San Francisco
94104
415-781-0605
Genl. Mgr.: R. Alan McClung
A§4, 5, 12

First Small Business Investment Co.
of California
215 West 6th St., Los Angeles 90014
213-620-8241
Pres.: Timothy Hay
C§5, 12

Krasne Fund for Small Business, Inc.
9350 Wilshire Blvd., Suite 416,
Beverly Hills 90212
213-274-7007
Pres.: Clyde A. Krasne
A*2

Midland Capital Corp. (branch)
626 Wilshire Blvd., Los Angeles
90017
213-627-6757
V.P. & Resident Mgr.: Harry E.
Christiansen
D§12 (See New York)

Pioneer Enterprises Inc.
11255 West Olympic Blvd., Los
Angeles 90064
213-479-4374
Pres.: Miles Rubin
A*MESBIC

Roe Financial Corp.
9885 Charleville Blvd., Beverly Hills
90212
213-278-5717 or 272-5717
Pres.: Martin J. Roe
A§12

San Joacquin Small Business Investment Co.
P.O. Box 5266, Santa Monica
90405
213-823-4737
Pres.: Morris E. Harrison
A§12

Unionamerica Capital Corp.
445 South Figueroa St., Los
Angeles 90017
213-687-5587
Pres.: Dennis A. Repp
C*5, 8, 12

Wells Fargo Investment Co.
475 Sansome St., San Francisco
94111
415-396-3293
V.P.: R. G. Perring
C§12

Westamco Investment Co.
7805 Sunset Blvd., Los Angeles
90046
213-876-2120
Pres.: Leonard G. Muskin
A*2, 6, 12

Western Business Funds
235 Montgomery St., San Francisco
94104
415-982-3637
Pres.: Harold L. Moose, Jr.
B§2, 12

Westland Capital Corp.
11661 San Vicente Blvd., Suite 707,
Los Angeles 90049
213-826-6581
V.P.: B. K. Hagopian
C§12

COLORADO

Central Investment Corp. of Denver
811 Central Bank Bldg., Denver
80202
303-825-3351
Pres.: Blaine E. D'Arcey
B§1, 3, 5, 12

Colorado Small Business Investment
Co.
P.O. Box 5168, Terminal Annex,
Denver 80217
303-222-0465
Exec. V.P.: H. W. DeGooyer
A§12

CONNECTICUT

Connecticut Capital Corp.
488 Whalley Ave., New Haven
06511
203-387-5218
V.P.: Myron Blumenthal
A*5, 8, 9

Conresco Corp.
10 River St., Stamford 06901
203-324-4157
Pres.: Lawrence C. Widdoes
B§1, 6, 8

Dewey Investment Corp.
18 Asylum St., Room 911, Hartford
06103
203-522-3765
Pres.: Samuel N. Rosenstein
A*12

The First Connecticut Small Business
Investment Co.
177 State St., Bridgeport 06603
203-366-4726
Pres.: David Engelson
D*2, 6, 12 (See also New York)

First Miami Small Business Investment
Co. (branch)
P.O. Box P, Orange 06647
203-799-2056
A*7, 10, 12 (See Florida)

Hartford Community Capital Corp.
777 Main St., Hartford 06115
203-547-2841
Pres.: William M. Keresey, Jr.
A*MESBIC

Investors Capital Corp.
955 Main St., Bridgeport 06603
203-334-0109
Pres.: Edward Helfer
A*12

Manufacturers Small Business Investment Co., Inc.
1488 Chapel St., New Haven 06511
203-777-3042
Exec. Dir. & Secy.: Louis W.
Mingione
A§12

Marwit Capital Corp.
19 West Elm St., Greenwich 06830
203-661-8594
Pres.: Martin W. Witte
D*12 (See also New York)

Northern Business Capital Corp.
P.O. Box 711, South Norwalk
06856
203-866-1000 or 866-1954
Pres.: Joseph Kavanewsky
A§1, 5, 7

Nutmeg Capital Corp.
125 Market St., New Haven 06510
203-776-0643
Exec. V.P.: Leigh B. Raymond
A*2, 4, 10

The Small Business Investment Co.
of Connecticut
855 Main St., Bridgeport 06601
203-367-3282
Sigmund L. Miller
A†12

DISTRICT OF COLUMBIA

Allied Capital Corp.
1625 Eye St. N.W., Suite 603,
Washington 20006
202-393-4276
Pres.: George C. Williams
B§1, 5, 12

Capital Investment Co. of Washington
1001 Connecticut Ave. N.W., Suite
901, Washington 20036
202-659-4660
Dir. of Investments: Solomon
Berenson
B*1, 2, 4, 6, 12

Distribution Services Investment Corp.
1725 K St. N.W., Washington 20006
202-659-2338

Pres.: Paul L. Courtney
B†9

Greater Washington Industrial Investments, Inc.
1015 18th St. N.W., Washington
20036
202-466-2210
Pres.: Don A. Christensen
C§5, 8, 12

FLORIDA

First Miami Small Business Investment Co.
420 Lincoln Rd., Miami Beach
33139
305-531-0891
Pres.: Irve L. Libby
A*2, 7, 12 (See also Connecticut)

Gold Coast Capital Corp.
1451 North Bayshore Dr., Miami
33132
305-371-5456
Pres.: William I. Gold
B§12

Market Capital Corp.
P.O. Box 1048, Tampa 33601
813-247-1357
Pres.: Ernest E. Eads
A*1, 2, 5, 9

Small Business Assistance Corp.
P.O. Box 12038, Panama City
32401
904-234-3359
Chmn.: J. R. Arnold
B*4, 12

GEORGIA

CSRA Capital Corp.
P.O. Box 854, 914 Georgia Railroad
Bank Bldg., Augusta 30903
404-724-3579
Pres.: Allen F. Caldwell, Jr.
B§2, 4, 6

The Citizens & Southern Capital Corp.
P.O. Box 4899, Atlanta 30303
404-588-3372

Pres.: S. D. Clark
C§5, 12

Dixie Capital Corp.
2400 First National Bank Bldg.,
Atlanta 30303
404-524-4168
Pres.: DeJongh Franklin
A§1, 4, 12

First American Investment Corp.
300 Interstate North, Suite 305,
Atlanta 30339
404-432-3211
V.P. & Mgr.: Jerry J. Pezzella, Jr.
C§2, 12

Southeastern Capital Corp.
3204 First National Bank Bldg.,
Atlanta 30303
404-521-3926
Pres.: J. Ray Efird
C§12

HAWAII

Small Business Investment Co. of
Hawaii, Inc.
1575 South Beretania St., Honolulu
96814
818-949-3677
Chmn. of the Board: James W. Y.
Wong
A§2, 4, 9

IDAHO

Industrial Investment Corp.
413 West Idaho St., Boise 83702
208-543-5114
Pres.: J. Robert Tullis
A§12

ILLINOIS

Business Capital Corp.
120 South LaSalle St., Suite 656,
Chicago 60603
312-782-8862
Pres.: Edgar S. Meredith
D§12

Central Capital Corp.
4 Madison St., Oak Park 60302
Pres.: David M. Tomaso
A*4, 5, 12

Chicago Equity Corp.
188 West Randolph St., Chicago
60601
312-ST2-1758
Pres.: Morris Weiser
A§2, 5, 12

Conill Venture Corp.
231 South LaSalle St., Chicago
60604
312-828-8023
Pres.: John L. Hines
C*12

First Capital Corp. of Chicago
1 First National Plaza, Chicago
60670
312-723-8060
Pres.: Stanley C. Golder
D§1, 5, 12

LaSalle Street Capital Corp.
10 South LaSalle St., Chicago
60603
312-236-1597
Pres.: Daniel J. Donahue
C§5, 12

North Central Capital Corp.
P.O. Box 998, 201 North Main St.,
Rockford 61101
815-963-8261
Pres.: Willard C. Mills
B*12

INDIANA

Great Lakes Small Business Investment
Corp.
P.O. Box 285, Tipton 46072
317-675-6420
Pres.: Max H. Suite
B§5, 7, 9, 11

Incentive Capital Corp.
569 Broadway, Gary 46402
219-885-4188
Pres.: J. C. Nagle
A§1, 5

Indiana Capital Corp.
927 South Harrison, Fort Wayne
46802
219-742-7364
Pres.: Samuel A. Rea
B§5, 7, 8

Indiana Capital Corp. (branch)
Chamber of Commerce Building,
Indianapolis 46204
317-632-7518
Pres.: Samuel A. Rea
B§5, 7, 8

IOWA

Iowa Growth Investment Co.
200 American Bldg., Cedar Rapids
52401
319-363-0261
Pres.: Peter F. Bezanson
B*5, 6, 10, 12

LOUISIANA

Commercial Capital, Inc.
P.O. Box 939, Covington 70433
504-892-1334
Pres.: Alfred R. Blossman, Jr.
A*12

Delta Capital Corp.
P.O. Box 708, Slidell 70458
504-643-7666
Exec. V.P. & Secy.: John L. C.
Leslie
B§2, 5, 12 (See also North Carolina)

First Small Business Investment Co.
of Louisiana, Inc.
736 Poydras St., New Orleans
70130
504-529-5272
Pres.: Mrs. Alma O. Galle
A*12

Royal Street Investment Corp.
520 Royal St., New Orleans 70130
504-524-4376
Exec. V.P.: William D. Humphries
C§1, 4, 5, 6, 8, 10

Southern Small Business Investment
Co., Inc.
8137 Oleander St., New Orleans
70118
504-486-7861
Secy.: Gerald H. Schreiber
A*2, 4, 12

MAINE

Maine Small Business Investment Co.
284 Water St., Augusta 04330
Chmn.: Francis T. Finnegan
A*12

MASSACHUSETTS

Atlas Capital Corp.
200 City Bank Bldg., 55 Court St.,
Boston 02108
617-482-1218
Pres.: Herbert Carver
B†12

Eastern Seaboard Investment Corp.
73 State St., Room 212, Springfield
01103
413-732-8531
Pres.: Herbert M. Goldstein
A*5, 9, 12

Federal Street Capital Corp.
75 Federal St., Room 914, Boston
02110
617-542-1380
Pres.: John H. Lamothe
C§1, 5, 8

Financial Investors of Boston, Inc.
185 Devonshire St., Boston 02110
617-482-4077
Pres.: James V. Slidell
B*12

First Capital Corp. of Boston
1 Federal St., Boston 02110
617-434-2456
V.P.: Richard A. Farrell
B§12

Massachusetts Capital Corp.
225 Franklin St., Boston 02110

617-423-6044
Pres.: Arthur P. Contas
A§2, 6, 12

Pilgrim Capital Corp.
10 Pleasant St., Boston 02146
617-566-5212
Pres.: Bernard G. Berkman
B§2, 4, 6, 7, 9, 12

Worcester Capital Corp.
446 Main St., Worcester 01608
617-853-7460
Mgr.: Christopher W. Bramley
A§12

MICHIGAN

Michigan Capital and Service, Inc.
P.O. Box 28, Ann Arbor 48108
313-663-0702
Treas. & Mgr.: Kenneth Heininger
A§5, 8, 12

Motor Enterprises, Inc.
7-166 General Motors Bldg., 3044
West Grand Blvd., Detroit 48202
Herbert F. Lorenz
A*MESBIC

MINNESOTA

First Midwest Capital Corp.
703 Northstar Center, 110 South 7
St., Minneapolis 55402
Pres.: Alan K. Ruvelson
C*5, 8, 12 (See also Arizona)

Minnesota Small Business Investment
Co.
2338 Central Ave. Northeast,
Minneapolis 55418
612-789-2471, Ext. 82
V.P.: Walter L. Tiffin
B§5, 10, 12

Northland Capital Corp.
402 West 1st St., Duluth 55802
218-722-0545
Pres.: George G. Barnum, Jr.
B§12

Northwest Growth Fund, Inc.
  960 Northwestern Bank Bldg.,
    Minneapolis 55402
  612-333-2275
  Pres.: Thomas M. Crosby
  C§5, 8, 12

MISSISSIPPI

Sunflower Investment Corp.
  P.O. Box 670, Indianola 38751
  601-887-3211
  Pres.: Morris Lewis, Jr.
  A†9

Vicksburg Small Business Investment
  Co.
  302 First National Bank Bldg.,
    Vicksburg 39180
  601-636-4762
  Secy.: George W. Rogers, Jr.
  A*12

MISSOURI

Atlas Small Business Investment Corp.
  1808 Main St., Kansas City 64108
  816-842-8700
  V.P.: Herbert D. Sharpe
  A*2, 10, 12

MONTANA

Capital Investors Corp.
  Front & Ryman Sts., Capital Bldg.,
    Missoula 59801
  406-543-7888
  Pres.: Alan Bradley
  B*12 (See also Washington)

Small Business Improvement Co.
  P.O. Box 1175, Billings 59103
  406-252-3805
  Pres.: T. N. Reynolds
  A*9

NEVADA

J & M Investment Corp.
  P.O. Box 1328, Reno 89503
  702-323-1051
  Pres.: Jacques J. Morvay
  A§12

NEW JERSEY

Capital Small Business Investment Co.
  143 East State St., Trenton 08608
  609-394-3161 or 394-5221
  Pres.: Isadore Cohen
  A§12

Engle Investment Co.
  241 Main St., Hackensack 07601
  201-489-3583
  Pres.: Murray Hendel
  A*2, 5, 8, 12

Main Capital Investment Corp.
  818 Main St., Hackensack 07601
  201-489-2080
  Pres.: S. Sam Klotz
  A§3, 5, 12

Monmouth Capital Corp.
  P.O. Box 480, Toms River 08753
  201-341-9000
  Pres.: Eugene W. Landy
  B*12

Monmouth Capital Corp. (branch)
  P.O. Box 335, Eatontown 07724
  201-542-4555
  B*12

NEW MEXICO

New Mexico Capital Corp.
  1420 Carlisle N.E., Suite 203,
    Albuquerque 87110
  505-265-6421
  Pres.: Ed Leslie
  A§12

NEW YORK

Avionics Investing Corp.
  375 Park Ave., New York 10022
  212-355-5400
  V.P.: Alan Franklin
  B§5, 6, 12

Basic Capital Corp.
  40 West 37th St., New York 10018
  212-868-9645
  Pres.: Paul W. Kates
  B*4, 5, 7

Bonan Equity Corp.
60 East 42nd St., Suite 2530,
New York 10017
212-687-8010
Pres.: S. B. Bonan
B§2

Broad Arrow Investment Corp.
Route 5S, Fort Hunter Rd.,
Amsterdam 12010
518-843-3900
Pres.: Charles N. Belim
A*MESBIC

CMNY Capital Co., Inc.
20 Broad St., New York 10005
212-425-4060
V.P.: Robert Davidoff
B§5, 8, 12

Capital For Future, Inc.
635 Madison Ave., New York 10022
212-759-8060
Pres.: Jay Marc Schwamm
C§2, 7

Capital for Technology Corp.
75 East 55th St., New York 10022
212-758-1846
Exec. V.P.: L. L. Monnett, Jr.
C§5, 6, 7, 8

The Central New York Small Business
Investment Co., Inc.
738 Erie Blvd. East, Syracuse 13210
315-475-1631
Pres.: Robert E. Romig
A*5, 7, 8

Chase Manhattan Capital Corp.
1 Chase Manhattan Plaza, New York
10005
212-522-6811
Pres.: Louis L. Allen
C§5, 8

Creative Capital Corp.
56 Beaver St., New York 10004
212-422-3442
Pres.: Milton D. Stewart
D§1, 2, 5, 8, 10, 12 (See also
California)

Equitable Small Business Investment
Corp.
350 Fifth Ave., Suite 5805,
New York 10001
212-564-5420
Pres.: David Goldberg
A*2, 6, 12

Equi-Tronics Capital Corp.
1441 Broadway, New York 10018
212-565-6150
Pres.: Ned Tanenbaum
C*1, 4, 12

Excelsior Capital Corp.
115 Broadway, New York 10006
212-964-2220
Pres.: Solomon Scharf
A§12

FNCB Capital Corp.
399 Park Ave., New York 10022
212-559-0405
Pres.: Philip B. Smith
D§5, 8, 12

15 Broad Street Resources Corp.
15 Broad St., New York 10005
212-425-2323, Ext. 2079
Pres.: Alfred S. Foote
C§5, 8, 12

The First Connecticut Small Business
Investment Co. (branch)
60 Wall St., New York 10005
212-HA5-1222
D*2, 6, 12 (See Connecticut)

First Realty Capital Funds Corp.
770 Lexington Ave., New York
10021
212-TE8-2010
Pres.: Alfred R. Bachrach
B*2, 8, 12

The Franklin Corp.
118 Pearl St., Mt. Vernon 10550
914-664-0123
Pres.: H. E. Goodman
C§1, 2, 5, 7, 10, 12

The Franklin Corp. (branch)
1410 Broadway, New York 10018
212-565-6200
C§1, 2, 5, 7, 10, 12

Great Eastern Small Business Investment Corp.
230 Park Ave., New York 10017
212-686-8030
Mgr.: Howard A. Jaffe
A§4, 10, 12

The Hamilton Capital Fund, Inc.
660 Madison Ave., New York 10021
212-838-8382
Pres.: Joel I. Berson
B§2, 5, 6, 12

The Hanover Capital Corp.
485 Madison Ave., New York 10022
212-687-7300
Pres.: Arnold S. Askin
B§12

Hemisphere Capital Corp.
100 Merrick Rd., Rockville
Centre 11571
516-764-2800
Pres.: Carl Monte
A§12

Intercoastal Capital Corp.
18 East 48th St., New York 10017
212-PL8-0209
Pres.: Herbert Krasnow
B†2, 4

Inverness Capital Corp.
345 Park Ave., New York 10022
212-486-1800
Pres.: G. Stanton Geary
B§12

Lake Success Capital Corp.
5000 Brush Hollow Rd., Westbury
11590
516-333-7600
Pres.: H. H. Schneider
B§2

M & T Capital Corp.
1 M & T Plaza, Buffalo 14203
716-842-4200
Pres.: Andrew B. Craig, III
B§5, 8, 12

Marwit Capital Corp. (branch)
6 East 43rd St., New York 10017
212-585-5128
D*12 (See Connecticut)

Midland Capital Corp.
110 William St., New York 10038
212-732-6580
Chmn. & Pres.: C. Edgar Schabacker, Jr.
D§12 (See also California)

New York Business Assistance Corp.
51 East 42nd St., New York 10017
212-687-1646
Pres.: Lawrence A. Blatte
A*2, 5, 10

New York Enterprise Capital Corp.
500 Old Country Rd., Garden City
11530
516-741-1300
Pres.: George Feldman
B*2, 5

Pioneer Capital Corp.
1440 Broadway, Suite 1967,
New York 10018
212-594-4860
Pres.: L. W. Bergesch
A*MESBIC

R & R Financial Corp.
1451 Broadway, New York 10036
212-564-4500
V.P.: Sylvan Schoenberg
A§2, 5, 12

Real Estate Capital Corp.
111 West 40th St., New York 10018
212-279-0900
Pres.: Samuel M. Fox
B†2

Royal Business Funds Corp.
250 Park Ave., New York 10017
212-986-8463
Pres.: Stephen M. Pollan
D*12

Securus Corp. of America
32 East 57th St., New York 10022
212-355-3621
Pres.: Sigmund A. Siegel
A*2, 4, 6, 12

Small Business Electronics Investment
Corp.
1350 Broadway, New York 10018
212-594-6960

Pres.: Leonard Randell
A*12

Small Business Investment Co. of
New York, Inc.
64 Wall St., New York 10005
212-943-9580
Chmn. of the Bd.: Edward J.
Bermingham, Jr.
D§1, 3, 5, 8

Southern Tier Capital Corp.
219 Broadway, Monticello 12701
914-794-2030
Pres.: Irving Brizel
A*4, 6, 12

Struthers Capital Corp.
630 Fifth Ave., New York 10020
212-757-3927
Pres.: Victor Harz
C§12

Talco Capital Corp.
405 Lexington Ave., Room 3306,
New York 10017
212-661-2290
V.P.: Ike Cohen
A*12

Tappan Zee Small Business Investment
Corp.
120 North Main St., New City,
10956
914-634-8822 or 212-562-9333
Treas. & Chmn. of the Bd.: Irving A.
Garson
A§1, 5, 12

Union Small Business Investment Co.,
Inc.
572 Madison Ave., New York 10022
212-736-3240
Pres.: Robert A. Rosen
A§12

NORTH CAROLINA

Cameron–Brown Capital Corp.
900 Wade Ave., Raleigh 27605
919-828-2581
V.P.: Harold E. Russell, Jr.
B§2, 4, 5

Delta Capital, Inc. (branch)
1200 North Carolina National Bank
Bldg., Charlotte 28202
704-333-9641
Pres.: Herman B. McManaway, Jr.
B§2, 5, 12 (See Louisiana)

Eastern Capital Corp.
P.O. Box 398, Spruce Pine 28777
704-765-4286
Pres.: Bradley E. Ragan
A*9

Forsyth County Investment Corp.
Suite 305, Pepper Bldg., 4th &
Liberty Sts., Winston-Salem
27101
919-724-3676
Exec. Dir.: James P. Hansley
A*MESBIC

OHIO

Gries Investment Co.
922 National City Bank Bldg.,
Cleveland 44114
216-861-1146
Pres.: Robert D. Gries
C§12

Karr Investment Corp.
1134 Corrugated Way, Columbus
43201
614-253-7750
Pres.: William V. Karr
B§12

Ohio Valley Capital Corp.
18 East 4th St., Cincinnati 45202
513-621-2513
V.P.: Dr. John E. McDavid
B§5, 8, 9

OKLAHOMA

Alliance Business Investment Co.
500 McFarlin Bldg., Tulsa 74103
918-584-3581
Chmn. of the Bd.: Elliott Davis
C§3, 5, 12 (See also Texas)

Capital, Inc.
  2106 Liberty Bank Bldg., Oklahoma
    City 73102
  405-236-3729
  Pres.: I. Jack Stephens
  B§3, 5, 9

Founders Capital Corp.
  1900 United Founders Life Tower,
    Oklahoma City 73112
  405-843-9351
  V.P.: Jack T. Massey
  A*5, 6, 10

Investment Capital, Inc.
  P.O. Box 687, Duncan 73533
  405-255-3140
  Pres.: Lloyd O. Pace
  A*2, 5, 6, 10

OREGON

Preferred Growth Capital, Inc.
  217 Oregon Bldg., Portland 97204
  503-225-4281
  Pres.: A. F. Coats
  B§2, 5, 12

The San Francisco-Pacific Fund, Inc.
  812 Southwest Washington St.,
    Portland 97205
  503-226-6377
  Pres.: C. M. Armstrong
  B§12

PENNSYLVANIA

Capital Corp. of America
  121 South Broad St., Philadelphia
    19107
  215-546-7820
  Pres.: Barton M. Banks
  A*12

Delaware Valley Small Business Invest-
    ment Co.
  Wolf Bldg., Market Square, Chester
    19103
  215-876-2669
  Pres.: William J. Wolf
  C*12

Delaware Valley Small Business Invest-
    ment Co. (branch)
  1604 Walnut St., 5th Floor,
    Philadelphia 19103
  215-546-0135
  V.P.: George Banet
  C*12

Fidelity America Small Business
    Investment Co.
  113 South 21st St., Philadelphia
    19103
  215-568-4820
  Pres.: Howard I. Green
  B*4, 9, 12

Great Eastern Capital Corp.
  43 East Main St., Norristown 19401
  215-275-8800
  Pres.: Leonard L. Zeidman
  A*12

Greater Pittsburgh Capital Corp.
  419 Wood St., Pittsburgh 15222
  412-261-5553
  Pres.: J. R. McCartan
  A*5, 10, 12

Osher Capital Corp.
  535 Pennsylvania Ave., Ft.
    Washington 19034
  215-643-4224
  Pres.: L. Cantor
  A§5, 8, 12

Pennsylvania Capital Growth Corp.
  2000 Girard Trust Bldg.,
    Philadelphia 19102
  215-564-1950
  Exec. V.P.: Stanley F. Frankel
  A§12

Sharon Small Business Investment Co.
  385 Shenango Ave., Sharon 16146
  412-981-1500
  Pres.: H. D. Rosenblum
  A*9

PUERTO RICO

Popular Investment Co., Inc.
  G.P.O. Box 2708, San Juan 00936
  809-765-9800 Ext. 5790, and
    765-6441

Pres.: Jose Luis Carrion
B*5, 9, 10, 12

RHODE ISLAND

Industrial Capital Corp.
P.O. Box 368, Providence 02903
401-521-9700
V.P.: Kenneth B. Bourdrie
B§1, 5, 8, 12

Narragansett Capital Corp.
10 Dorrance St., Providence 02903
401-421-6727
Treas.: Robert L. Cummings
E*5, 8, 12

SOUTH CAROLINA

Charleston Capital Corp.
19 Broad St., Charleston 29401
803-723-6464
Pres.: Henry Yaschik
B*4, 5, 12

Falcon Capital Corp.
89 Broad St., Charleston 29401
803-723-8624 or 723-8625
Pres.: Mrs. Mona G. Sokol
A*12

Lowcountry Investment Corp.
Box 10447, Charleston 29411
803-744-7486
Pres.: J. T. Newton, Jr.
B§9

SOUTH DAKOTA

Berkshire Capital, Inc.
405 8th Ave. N.W., Aberdeen 57401
605-225-5166
Pres.: Dr. Robert E. Bormes
A*6, 12

TENNESSEE

Financial Resources, Inc.
1909 Sterick Bldg., Memphis 38103
901-527-9411
Chmn.: Milton Picard
A§5, 8, 12

TEXAS

Admiral Investment Co., Inc.
1302 Rusk, Houston 77002
713-224-5061
V.P.: Charles Ward
A*2

Alliance Business Investment Co.
(branch)
2212 Tennessee Bldg., 1010 Milam
St., Houston 77002
713-228-5143
Pres.: Leon Davis
C§3, 5, 12 (See Oklahoma)

CSC Capital Corp.
750 Hartford Bldg., Dallas 75201
214-747-5117
Pres. & Chmn. of the Bd.: M. E.
Singleton, Jr.
D§12 (See also California and
Arizona)

Capital Marketing Corp.
9001 Ambassador Row, Dallas
75247
214-638-1913
Genl. Mgr.: Harry Cook
B†2, 9

Enterprise Capital Corp.
210 Central National Bank Bldg.,
Houston 77002
713-224-9905
Pres.: Paul Z. Brochstein
B§1, 2, 5, 9, 10

First Dallas Capital Corp.
1401 Elm St., Dallas 75202
214-749-4457
Pres.: Q. Allen Sanders
C§1, 5, 11

First Texas Investment Co.
P.O. Box 495, South Houston
77587
713-644-6193
Pres.: George Leavesley
A§5, 10, 12

The Small Business Investment Co. of
Houston
640 West Bldg., Houston 77002
713-223-5337

Pres.: William E. Ladin
B§2, 5, 12

Tarrant Capital Corp.
Box 2050, Fort Worth 76101
817-334-8115
Pres.: O. Roy Stevenson
A§5, 9, 12

Texas Capital Corp.
2424 Houston Natural Gas Bldg.,
Houston 77002
713-222-8861
Pres.: Lamar E. Ozley, Jr.
C§1, 5, 12

Texas Equity Corp.
215 Cotton Exchange Bldg., Dallas
75201
214-747-2541
Pres.: William D. Felder, Jr.
A§12

Trammell Crow Investment Co.
201 Stemmons Tower South, Dallas
75207
214-631-4114
Pres.: Trammell Crow
B§1, 8, 12

United Business Capital, Inc.
P.O. Box 1396, LaPorte 77571
713-471-1155
Pres.: Ben Fleming
A*12

West Central Capital Corp.
P.O. Box 412, Dumas 79029
806-935-3902
Pres.: Howard W. Jacob
A§2, 5, 12

Western Capital Corp.
2123 First National Bank Bldg.,
Dallas 75202
214-748-3321
Pres.: W. C. Miller
A*2, 9, 12

UTAH

Intermountain Capital Corp. of Utah
79 South State, Salt Lake City
84111

801-328-0317
Pres.: John M. Whiteley
A*2, 6, 9

VIRGINIA

Virginia Capital Corp.
808-West United Virginia Bank
Bldg., Richmond 23219
703-644-5496
Pres.: Robert H. Pratt
B§12

WASHINGTON

Capital Investors Corp. (branch)
Suite 1005, O.N.B. Bldg., Spokane
99210
V.P.: Neal Fosseen
B*12 (See Montana)

Northwest Business Investment Corp.
929 West Sprague Ave., Spokane
99204
509-838-3111
Pres.: C. Paul Sandifur
A*1, 7, 8

Washington Capital Corp.
P.O. Box 1517, Walla Walla 99362
509-525-3500
V.P.: Frederic R. Swauger
B*4, 6, 9

WISCONSIN

Commerce Capital Corp.
6001 North 91st St., Milwaukee
53225
414-353-8200
Pres.: Edward L. Machulak
D§2, 7

Commerce Capital Corp. (branch)
9 South Main St., Fond du Lac
54935
Mgr.: Hubert R. Murphy
D§2, 7

Commerce Capital Corp. (branch)
126 Grand Ave., Wausau 54401
Mgr.: G. Robert Viele
D§2, 7

Commerce Capital Corp. (branch)
106 West 2nd St., Ashland 54806
Mgr.: Richard F. Wartman
D§2, 7

First Wisconsin Investment Corp.
735 North Water St., Milwaukee
53202
414-276-6100

Exec. V.P.: Kenneth Bradbury
A§5, 8, 10

Growth Small Business Investment Co.
811 East Wisconsin Ave., Suite 940,
Milwaukee 53202
414-276-3239
Pres.: C. Paul Johnson
B*12

12. Venture Capital Firms

AVCO
1275 King St., Greenwich, Conn.
06830
203-552-1800

AVTEK Corp.
234 Industrial Bank Bldg.,
Providence, R.I. 02903
401-421-3835

Allen & Co.
30 Broadway, New York, N.Y.
10004
212-HA 2-2600

Allied Capital Corp.
1625 Eye Street N.W., Washington,
D.C. 20006
202-393-4276

Allstate Insurance Co.
Allstate Plaza, Northbrook, Ill.
60062
312-291-5000

Amadon Corp.
31 Milk St., Boston, Mass.
02109
617-482-6775

American Express Investment Management Co.
550 Laurel St., San Francisco, Calif.
94119
415-563-7900

American Research & Development
Corp.
200 Berkeley St., Boston, Mass.
02116
617-426-7060

American Science Associates
1345 Ave. of the Americas, New
York, N.Y. 10019
212-765-4771

Andresen & Co.
140 Broadway, New York, N.Y.
10005
212-363-6300

Aurora Ventures
Tower East Bldg., Shaker Heights,
Ohio 44120
216-283-2110

Bay Securities Corp.
100 California St., San Francisco,
Calif. 94111
415-421-2700

Bessemer Securities Corp.
245 Park Ave., New York, N.Y.
10017
212-986-6900

William Blair & Co.,
135 South LaSalle St., Chicago, Ill.
60603
312-236-1600

Boothe Computer Investment Corp.
1 Maritime Plaza, San Francisco,
Calif. 94111
415-989-6580

Boston Capital Corp.
535 Boyleston St., Boston, Mass.
02116
617-536-4900

William A. M. Burden & Co.
630 Fifth Ave., New York, N.Y.
10020
212-489-1200

C. G. Securities Corp.
900 Cottage Grove Rd., Bloomfield,
Conn. 06002
203-243-8811

Case Pomeroy & Co.
6 East 43rd St. New York, N.Y.
10017
212-867-2211

Central Securities
375 Park Ave., New York, N.Y.
10022
212-688-3011

Chase Manhattan Capital Corp.
1 Chase Manhattan Plaza, New York,
N.Y. 10005
212-552-6812

Clark Dodge & Co.
70 Federal St., Boston, Mass.
02110
617-423-5970

Cogan, Berlind, Weill & Levitt, Inc.
55 Broad St., New York, N.Y.
10004
212-350-0500

Collins Securities Corp.
26 Beaver St., New York, N.Y.
10004
212-425-4087

Continental Capital Corp.
555 California St., San Francisco,
Calif. 94104
415-989-2020

Creative Capital Corp.
56 Beaver St., New York, N.Y.
10004
212-986-5595

Creative Strategies, Inc.
885 North San Antonio Rd., Los
Altos, Calif. 94022
415-964-8900

Data Science Ventures, Inc.
221 Nassau St., Princeton, N.J.
08540
609-924-6420

Diebold Venture Technology Corp.
430 Park Ave., New York, N.Y.
10022
212-755-9510

Diversified Technology, Inc.
30 Rockefeller Plaza, New York,
N.Y. 10020
212-246-6414

Donaldson, Lufkin & Jeurette, Inc.
140 Broadway, New York, N.Y.
10005
212-943-0300

Dyson–Kissner Corp.
230 Park Ave., New York, N.Y.
10017
212-MU 6-9270

Eastman Dillon Union Securities Corp.
1 Chase Manhattan Plaza, New York,
N.Y. 10005
212-770-8000

Equity Research Associates
55 Broadway, New York, N.Y.
10006
212-797-4500

FNCB Capital Corp.
399 Park Ave., New York, N.Y.
10022
212-559-1000

Faulkner, Dawkins & Sullivan
60 Broad St., New York, N.Y.
10004
212-623-6100

Federal Street Capital Corp.
75 Federal St., Boston, Mass.
02110
617-542-1380

Federated Capital Corp.
565 Fifth Ave., New York, N.Y.
10017
212-OX 7-8989

15 Broad Street Resources Corp.
15 Broad St., New York, N.Y.
10004
212-944-5117

First Midwest Capital Corp.
703 Northstar Center, Minneapolis,
Minn. 55402
612-339-9391

Philip A. Fisher Investments
220 Bush St., San Francisco, Calif.
94104
415-362-4631

The Foothill Group
1900 Ave. of the Stars, Los Angeles,
Calif. 90067
213-655-5620

The Ford Foundation
320 East 43rd St., New York, N.Y.
10017
212-573-5000

Geiger & Fialkov
1 Rockefeller Plaza, New York,
N.Y. 10020
212-581-3980

Goldwater, Valente, Fitzpatrick &
Schall
5 Hanover Square, New York, N.Y.
10005
212-483-1350

Goodman & Mautner
5250 Century Rd., Los Angeles,
Calif. 90045
213-776-4011

Greater Washington Investors, Inc.
1725 K St. N.W., Washington, D.C.
20006
202-466-2210

Greylock Management Co.
225 Franklin St., Boston, Mass.
02110
617-423-5525

Hambrecht & Quist
235 Montgomery St., San Francisco,
Calif. 94104
415-433-1720

Hayden Stone, Inc.
28 Broad St., New York, N.Y.
10004
212-363-3100

Heizer Corp.
20 North Wacker Dr., Chicago, Ill.
60606
312-641-2200

Hohenberg & Associates, Inc.
8732 Sunset Blvd., Los Angeles,
Calif. 90069
213-274-8393

Inverness Capital Corp.
345 Park Ave., New York, N.Y.
10022
212-486-1800

The Island Co.
630 Fifth Ave., New York, N.Y.
10020
212-757-2277

Jersey Enterprises
30 Rockefeller Plaza, New York,
N.Y. 10020
212-974-3000

Alexander L. Keyes
100 East 42nd St., New York, N.Y.
10017
212-YU 6-4191

Kidder, Peabody & Co.
20 Exchange Pl., New York, N.Y.
10020
212-770-7000

Robert R. Kley Associates, Inc.
2920 Aurora, Ann Arbor, Mich.
48105
313-761-3655

Laird, Inc.
140 Broadway, New York, N.Y.
10005
212-269-4900

Laird Systems, Inc.
1901 Ave. of the Stars, Los Angeles,
Calif. 90067
213-680-9811

LaSalle Street Capital Corp.
10 South LaSalle St., Chicago, Ill.
60606
312-236-1597

Loeb, Rhoades & Co.
42 Wall St., New York, N.Y.
10005
212-530-4000

Madison Consultants
424 Madison Ave., New York, N.Y.
10017
212-759-9050

Marine Midland Bank
110 Williams St., New York, N.Y.
10038
212-797-4000

Massachusetts Mutual Life Insurance
Co.
1295 State St., Springfield, Mass.
01101
413-788-8411

Mayo Foundation
701 4th St. Southwest, Rochester,
Minn. 55901
507-289-3379

Midland Capital Corp.
110 Williams St., New York, N.Y.
10038
212-RE 2-6580

Narragansett Capital
10 Dorrance St., Providence, R.I.
02903
401-421-6727

Ness Industries, Inc.
422 Waverly St., Palo Alto, Calif.
94301
415-328-7036

New Business Resources
6116 North Central Expressway,
Dallas, Tex. 75206
214-239-1378

New Court Securities Corp.
70 Pine St., New York, N.Y.
10005
212-425-9210

Patents International Affiliates
680 Fifth Ave., New York, N.Y.
10019
212-581-7654

Payson & Trask
748 Madison Ave., New York, N.Y.
10021
212-TR 9-0300

R. W. Pressprich & Co., Inc.
80 Pine St., New York, N.Y.
10005
212-483-1100

Robertson, Coleman & Sebol
235 Montgomery St., San Francisco,
Calif. 94104
415-989-2050

Arthur Rock & Co.
1635 Russ Bldg., San Francisco,
Calif. 94104
415-981-3921

S.M.C. Investment Corp.
606 South Olive St., Los Angeles,
Calif. 90014
213-277-1700

Sassower, Jacobs & Schneider, Inc.
4 New York Plaza, New York, N.Y.
10004
212-344-8666

Shelter Rock Corp. (Wm. S. Paley)
51 West 42nd St., New York, N.Y.
10036
212-765-3333

Smith, Barney & Co., Inc.
20 Broad St., New York, N.Y.
10004
212-344-9600

S. F. Smithers
45 Wall St., New York, N.Y.
10005
212-943-3300

The Sperry & Hutchinson Co.
330 Madison Ave., New York, N.Y.
10017
212-983-2000

Starwood Corp.
  100 Park Ave., New York, N.Y.
  10017
  212-679-3620

State Mutual Life Assurance Co. of
  America
  440 Lincoln St., Worchester, Mass.
  01605
  617-852-1000

Ralph I. Straus
  375 Park Ave., New York, N.Y.
  10022
  212-421-6847

Sutro & Co., Inc.
  460 Montgomery St., San Francisco,
  Calif. 94104
  415-392-0900

Sutter Hill Capital Co.
  2600 El Camino Real, Palo Alto,
  Calif. 44306
  415-326-9830

Talcott National Corp.
  1290 Ave. of the Americas, New
  York, N.Y. 10019
  212-956-3000

Tucker, Anthony & R. L. Day
  120 Broadway, New York, N.Y.
  10005
  212-732-8300

Unionamerica Capital Corp.
  Figueroa at Fifth St., Los Angeles,
  Calif. 90017
  213-687-6300·

C. E. Unterberg, Towbin Co.
  61 Broadway, New York, N.Y.
  10006
  212-425-3090

Value Line Development Capital
  Corp.
  5 East 44th St., New York, N.Y.
  10017
  212-687-3965

Venture Research & Development
  Corp.
  145 Witherspoon St., Princeton,
  N.J. 08540
  609-921-9434

L. G. Victors, Gold & Co.
  1501 North Miracle Mile, Tucson,
  Ariz. 85705
  602-624-6606

Wachtel & Co., Inc.
  1000 Vermont Ave. N.W.,
  Washington, D.C. 20005
  202-347-9588

E. M. Warburg & Co., Inc.
  60 Broadway, New York, N.Y.
  10004
  212-425-3838

Weiss, Peck & Greer
  120 Broadway, New York, N.Y.
  10005
  212-349-6660

Wells Fargo Investment Co., Inc.
  464 California St., San Francisco,
  Calif. 94120
  415-396-2902

White, Weld & Co.
  20 Broad St., New York, N.Y.
  10004
  212-944-4900

J. H. Whitney & Co.
  630 Fifth Ave., New York, N.Y.
  10020
  212-PL7-0500

Wisconsin Alumni Research
  Foundation
  506 North Walnut St., Madison,
  Wis. 53705
  608-257-4851

William D. Witter & Co.
  14 Wall St., New York, N.Y.
  10005
  212-483-0800

CREDIT AND COLLECTION SERVICES

13. Commercial Collection Agencies

Allied Credit Bureau, Inc.
P.O. Box 149, Las Vegas, Nev.
89101
Pres.: Frederic S. Weichman

Amalgamated Credit Bureau, Inc.
Box 986, Raritan Center, Edison,
N.J. 08817
Pres.: Leonard Ritterman

American Bureau of Collections, Inc.
Brisbane Bldg., Buffalo, N.Y.
14203
Pres.: Harvey L. Herer

American Bureau of Collections of
New York, Inc.
1 East 42nd St., New York, N.Y.
10017
Pres.: Ralph D. Hochman

Baron & Chestney, Inc.
1109 North Vermont, Los Angeles,
Calif. 90029
Pres.: Mark D. Chestney, Jr.

Biehl & Biehl
608 South Dearborn St., Chicago,
Ill. 60605
Pres.: William E. Biehl

Bruhnke & Wilver
1140 North Silver Lake Rd., Cary,
Ill. 60013
Pres.: Augustus C. Bruhnke

CST Co.
811 South 2nd St., Louisville, Ky.
40203
Pres.: C. Addison Brown

Caine & Weiner Co., Inc.
520 South Virgil Ave., Los Angeles,
Calif. 90020
Pres.: Sidney C. Caine

The Chicago-Midwest Credit Service
Corp.
165 North Canal St., Chicago, Ill.
60606
Pres.: B. C. Chaitman

Commercial Claims, Inc.
P.O. Box 1344, Kansas City, Kan.
66117
Pres.: Bill Mullarky

Commercial Collection Corp. of New
York
2690 Sheridan Dr., Tonawanda, N.Y.
14151
Pres.: Bernard M. Engel

Continental Credit Control Div.
Credit Clearing House, Inc.
531 Central Ave., Scarsdale, N.Y.
10583
Pres.: Stanley Greenfield

Continental Credit Corp.
701 North 1st St., Phoenix, Ariz.
85004
Pres.: William L. Hayes

Cosmopolitan Service Corp.
505 Talcott Rd., Park Ridge, Ill.
60068
Pres.: J. Thomas Akouris

Credit & Adjustment Corp.
175 Fifth Ave., New York, N.Y.
10010
Pres.: Sol Rosen

Credit Managers Service, Inc.
360 Robert St., St. Paul, Minn.
55101
Pres.: S. B. Slocum

Creditors' House
1725 Beverly Blvd., Los Angeles,
Calif. 90026
Pres.: Murry Wagner

Dun & Bradstreet, Inc.
P.O. Box 803, Church St. Sta., New
York, N.Y. 10008
V.P./Commercial Collections: Bill
Harris

Eastern States Adjustment Co.
100 Quimby St., Westfield, N.J.
07090
Pres.: R. J. Langford

Equitable Adjustment Service, Inc.
P.O. Box 588, Clifton, N.J.
07012
Pres.: John K. Gordana

Federated Financial Service, Inc.
407 South Dearborn St., Chicago,
Ill. 60605
Pres.: James F. Walzer

Field Adjustment Bureau
401 Broadway, New York, N.Y.
10013
Pres.: H. Field

The Finn Co., Inc.
30 Vesey St., New York, N.Y.
10007
Pres.: Thomas Zoda

S. J. Foil, Ltd.
19 West 44th St., New York, N.Y.
10036
Pres.: Samuel J. Foil

Fresno Credit Bureau
P.O. Box 942, Fresno, Calif.
93714
Pres.: Robert C. Kempen

Fulton Adjustment Bureau, Inc.
156 William St., New York, N.Y.
10038
Pres.: Morris M. Goldstein

Furst & Furst
Box 375, Chicago, Ill. 60645
Pres.: Louis H. Lewis

General American Credits, Inc.,
Subsidiary of Payco American
Corp.
P.O. Box 15248, Columbus, Ohio
43215
Pres.: Richard E. Cooley

Gro-Tel Adjustments, Ltd.
960 Ave. of the Americas, New York
York, N.Y. 10001
Pres.: Gerald Grossman

William Hudson Co.
412 West 6th St., Los Angeles,
Calif. 90014
Pres.: William I. Hudson

The Kaighn Co.
786 Broad St., Newark, N.J. 07102
Pres.: John Q. Robinson

Kemble & Mills of Pittsburgh, Inc.
P.O. Box 7909, Pittsburgh, Pa.
15216
Pres.: Richard C. Mills

Keystone Collection Bureau
258 Broadway, New York, N.Y.
10007
Pres.: Milton Schiele

Lumbermen's Credit Assn., Inc.
600 South Michigan Ave., Chicago,
Ill. 60605
Pres.: William C. Clancy

Mid-Continent Adjustment Co.
2043 West Howard St., Chicago,
Ill. 60645
Pres.: Benjamin P. Waldman

Morton Mercantile Co.
3525 West Peterson, Chicago, Ill.
60645
Pres.: Alan J. Gabor

National Clearing House Adjustment
Corp.
905 Public Square Bldg., Cleveland,
Ohio 44113
Pres.: William A. Sindelar

National Mercantile Agency
930 G St., Sacramento, Calif. 95806
Pres.: E. D. Bullock

National Mercantile Agency, Inc.
Drawer K, Woodbridge, Conn. 06525
Pres.: Alton L. McLain

National Mercantile Agency, Inc.
486 Totten Pond Rd., Waltham,
Mass. 02154
Pres.: N. Arthur

National Mercantile Agency, Inc.
715 Park Ave., East Orange, N.J.
07017
Pres.: Edward G. Henneberg

Joseph J. Ostro
150 Fifth Ave., New York, N.Y.
10011

R. & W. Otte, Inc.
142 Lexington Ave., New York, N.Y.
10016
Pres.: William Otte

Reed & Reed
1133 Braodway, New York, N.Y.
10010
Pres.: Edward Reiss

Rogers & Rogers, Inc.
3000 Lake Success Quadrangle, Lake
Success, N.Y. 11040
Pres.: Robert D. Rogers

Rosman Adjustment Corp.
5941 North Lincoln Ave., Chicago,
Ill. 60645
Pres.: Sanford N. Bernay

SKO, Inc.
1615 Northern Blvd., Manhasset,
N.Y. 11030
Pres.: Edward F. O'Rourke

S. S. Sampliner & Co., Inc.
48 West 48th St., New York, N.Y.
10036
Pres.: Samuel S. Sampliner

Bernard Sands Collection Agency, Inc.
505 Eighth Ave., New York, N.Y.
10018
Pres.: Bernard Sands

Allyn M. Schiffer, Inc.
461 Eighth Ave., New York, N.Y.
10001
Pres.: Allyn M. Schiffer

R. J. Sheridan
P.O. Box 174, Canton, Mass. 02021

Slattery & Lieberman, Inc.
50 Court St., Brooklyn, N.Y.
11201
Pres.: Gary Slattery

Samuel B. Smith & Associates
115 North 6th St., Springfield, Ill.
62701
Pres.: Samuel B. Smith

Stanley Tulchin Associates
350 Fifth Ave., New York, N.Y.
10001
Pres.: Stanley Tulchin

United Mercantile Agencies, Inc.
600 South 7th St., Louisville, Ky.
40201

Wilshire Credit Co.
4032 Wilshire Blvd., Los Angeles,
Calif. 90005
Pres.: Nat Karish

World Wide Adjustment Bureau
38 West 32nd St., New York, N.Y.
10001
Pres.: Allen Golden

14. Largest Personal Credit Institutions

Allied Finance Co.
2808 Fairmount St., Dallas, Tex.
75201
214-748-9261
V.P.: Bruce M. Steere

American Credit
201 South Tryon St., Charlotte, N.C.
28201
704-333-7791
Pres.: J. G. Burnside, Jr.

American Finance Systems, Inc.
1100 Wilmington Trust, Wilmington,
Del. 19801
302-656-8279
Pres.: L. B. Holroyd

American Financial Corp.
3955 Montgomery Rd., Cincinnati,
Ohio 45212
513-579-2121
Chmn. of the Bd & Pres.: C. R.
Lindner

American Investment Co.
8251 Maryland Ave., St. Louis, Mo.
63105
314-725-7575
Chmn. of the Bd.: D. L. Barnes, Jr.

Associate Investment Co.
1700 Mishawaka Ave., South Bend,
Ind. 46616
219-288-9141
Chief Exec. Officer: J. S. Barnette

Associates Capital Corp.
601 Broadway, Nashville, Tenn.
37203
615-254-1731
Pres.: J. V. Beall

Avco Delta
750 Third Ave., New York, N.Y.
10017
212-867-8620
Chief Exec. Officer: H. H. Taterno

Avco Financial Services
818 W. 7th St., Los Angeles,
Calif. 90017

213-629-5551
Pres.: H. W. Merryman

B-W Acceptance Corp.
4001 West Devon, Chicago, Ill.
60646
312-282-6200
Pres.: R. E. Laroche

Beneficial Finance Co.
1300 Market St., Wilmington, Del.
19899
302-658-5171
Pres.: C. E. Benadom

Budget Finance Plan
6434 Wilshire Blvd., Los Angeles,
Calif. 90048
213-653-9550
Chmn. of the Bd. & Pres.: C. S.
Offer

Capital Finance Corp.
100 East Broad St., Columbus, Ohio
43215
614-235-3406
Chief Exec. Officer: H. L. Fuller

Carte Blanche
3460 Wilshire Blvd., Los Angeles,
Calif. 90005
213-381-7111
Pres.: J. E. Hawthorne

Chrysler Financial Corp.
16250 Northland Dr., Southfield,
Mich. 48075
313-353-0900
Pres.: G. S. Areen

Commonwealth Loan Co.
1010 East 86th St., Indianapolis,
Ind. 46240
317-846-6138
Pres.: C. E. Benadom

Credit Thrift Financial Corp.
601 Northwest 2nd St., Evansville,
Ind. 47708
812-424-8031
Pres.: R. H. Tyring

Dial Finance Co.
 207 9th St., Des Moines, Iowa
  50307
 515-243-2131
 Pres.: E. D. Glazer

Economy Finance Corp.
 108 East Washington St.,
  Indianapolis, Ind. 46204
 317-638-1331
 Chmn. of the Bd. & Pres.: W. L.
  Schloss

Family Finance Corp.
 919 Market St., Wilmington, Del.
  19899
 302-654-9951
 Pres.: J. H. Louis

Federal Discount Corp.
 14th & Central Ave., Dubuque,
  Iowa 52001
 319-582-5494
 Pres.: E. K. Jansen

Fidelity Acceptance Corp.
 910 Plymouth Bldg., Minneapolis,
  Minn. 55402
 612-336-8971
 Pres. Treas.: E. E. Fiterman

Ford Motor Credit Co.
 American Rd., Dearborn, Mich.
  48121
 313-322-3000
 Pres.: J. C. Dean

Gelco Corp.
 P.O. Box 8055, Minneapolis, Minn.
  55416
 612-935-7746
 Pres.: Bud Grossman

General Acceptance Corp.
 1105 Hamilton St., Allentown, Pa.
  18101
 215-437-8000
 Pres. & Exec. V.P.: J. C. Trombley

General Finance Corp.
 1301 Central St., Evanston, Ill.
  60201
 312-273-4160
 Pres.: R. J. Trenkmann

General Motors Acceptance
 767 Fifth Ave. at 58th, New York,
  N.Y. 10022
 212-486-5000
 Pres.: J. O. Zemmerman

Government Employees Finance
 41 East Colfax Ave., Denver, Colo.
  80202
 303-292-2970
 Pres.: R. F. Rodgers

Great Western Financial Corp.
 9601 Wilshire Blvd., Beverly Hills,
  Calif. 90210
 213-878-5670
 Pres.: C. W. Ford

Hawthorne Financial Corp.
 13005 South Hawthorne Blvd.,
  Hawthorne, Calif. 90250
 213-679-4346
 Pres.: V. J. Herbst

Household Finance Corp.
 Prudential Plaza, Chicago, Ill. 60601
 312-944-7174
 Pres.: W. W. Rasmussen, Jr.

ITT Aetna Finance Co.
 212 South Central Ave., St. Louis,
  Mo. 63105
 314-863-8010
 Pres.: D. Corwin

Industrial Finance & Thrift
 546 Carondelet St., New Orleans,
  La. 70130
 504-524-0833
 Pres.: M. M. Ainsworth

Kentucky Finance Co.
 200 East Main St., Lexington,
  Ky. 40507
 606-255-3641
 Chmn. of the Bd. & Pres.: G. Kincaid

Laurentide Finance California
 405 Montgomery St., San Francisco,
  Calif. 94106
 415-HU 6-9440
 Chief Exec. Officer: M. E. Goeglein

Liberty Loan Corp.
7438 Forsyth Blvd., St. Louis, Mo.
63105
314-726-5800
Pres.: D. L. Lichtenstein

Local Finance Corp.
179 Wayland Ave., Providence, R.I.
02906
401-331-7885
Chmn. of the Bd.: R. M. Patterson

Local Loan Co.
105 West Madison St., Chicago, Ill.
60602
312-332-7300
Pres.: T. J. Dillon

Montgomery Ward Credit
4 Denny Rd., Wilmington, Del.
19809
302-762-5252
Chief Exec. Officer: H. A. Sortor

Morlan Pacific Corp.
715 Market St., San Francisco, Calif.
94103
415-397-4522
Chief Exec. Officer: R. H. Larson

Murphy Finance Co.
174 East 6th St., Saint Paul, Minn.
55101
612-227-7381
Chief Exec. Officer: C. A. Claude

Nationwide Consumer Services Co.
246 North High St., Columbus, Ohio
43216
614-228-4711
Pres.: E. F. Wagner

Oxford Finance Cos.
6701 North Broad St., Philadelphia,
Pa. 19126

215-947-4000
Chmn. of the Bd. & Pres.: A. A. Gold

Ritter Financial Corp.
Church Rd. & Greenwood, Wyncote,
Pa. 19095
215-887-3200
Pres. & Treas.: K. Wenk, Jr.

Southwestern Investment
205 East 10th Ave., Amarillo, Tex.
79101
806-374-0361
Chmn. of the Bd. & Pres.: R. E.
O'Keefe

Stephenson Finance Co.
518 South Irby St., Florence, S.C.
29501
803-662-9341
Pres.: Leonard L. Hutchison

Sun Finance & Loan Co.
1015 Euclid Ave., Cleveland, Ohio
44115
216-696-7500
Pres.: J. E. Lampl, Jr.

Texas Consumer Finance Corp.
304 West 77th St., Fort Worth, Tex.
76102
817-336-2081
Chmn. of the Bd. & Pres.-Treas.:
Wallace C. Jay

Thorp Finance Corp.
East Stanley St., Thorp, Wisc. 54771
715-669-5551
Pres.: H. V. Mason

Transamerica Financial Corp.
1150 South Olive St., Los Angeles,
Calif. 90015
213-746-1234
Pres.: D. E. Speer

15. Major Credit Card Issuers

PERSONAL CREDIT CARDS

American Express Company, Credit
Card Department
P.O. Box 38, Church St. Sta., New
York, N.Y. 10008
212-677-5500

Bank of America NT and SA
1453 Mission St., San Francisco,
Calif. 94103
415-622-3456

Bankamericard
Bankers Trust Co., 1775 Broadway,
New York, N.Y. 10019
212-765-3250

Carte Blanche Division
First National City Bank of New
York, 399 Park Ave., New York,
N.Y. 10017
212-559-1000

Central Charge Service, Inc.
1215 E Street N.W., Washington,
D.C. 20004
202-783-7800

Community Charge Plan
395 Main St., Hackensack, N.J.
07601
201-343-3080

Diners Club
10 Columbus Circle, New York,
N.Y. 10019
212-245-1500

Inter Bank Credit Card Assn.
"Mastercharge"
7th Floor, Hills Bldg., Syracuse,
N.Y. 13202

Uni-Card
2000 Marcus Ave., New Hyde Park,
N.Y. 11040
516-328-2700

OIL COMPANY CREDIT CARDS

Amerada–Hess Co.
1 Hess Plaza, Woodbridge, N.J.
07095

American Oil Co.
910 South Michigan Ave., Chicago,
III. 60680

Ashland Oil & Refining Co.
1409 Winchester Ave., Box 391,
Ashland, Ky. 41101

Atlantic Richfield Co.
717 Fifth Ave., New York, N.Y.
10022

BP Oil Corp.
245 Park Ave., New York, N.Y.
10017

Cities Service Oil Co.
1436 South Boulder, Box 300,
Tulsa, Okla. 74102

Continental Oil Co.,
1300 Main St., Box 2197, Houston,
Tex. 77001

Crown Central Petroleum Corp.
1 North Charles St., Baltimore,
Md. 21203

Getty Oil Co.
660 Madison Ave., New York, N.Y.
10021

Gulf Oil Co.
U.S. Box 1519, Houston, Tex.
77001

Humble Oil and Refining Co.
Box 2180, Houston, Tex. 77001

Kerr–McGee Corp.
Kerr–McGee Bldg., 306 North
Robinson, Oklahoma City, Okla.
73102

Lion Oil Co.
Lion Oil Bldg., El Dorado, Ark.
71730

Marathon Oil Co.
539 South Main St., Findlay,
Ohio 45840

Mobil Oil Corp.
150 East 42nd St., New York, N.Y.
10017

Murphy Oil Corp.
200 Jefferson Ave., El Dorado, Ark.
71730

Phillips Petroleum Co.
348 Adams Bldg., Bartlesville, Okla.
74003

The Signal Companies, Inc.
1010 Wilshire Blvd., Los Angeles,
Calif. 90017

Skelly Oil Co.
606 West 47th St., Box 436, Kansas
City, Mo. 64141

Standard Oil Co.
Box 1446, Starks Bldg., Louisville,
Ky. 40201

Standard Oil Co.
Midland Bldg., Cleveland, Ohio
44115

Standard Oil of California
225 Bush St., Box 3495, San
Francisco, Calif. 94120

Shell Oil Co.
50 West 50th St., New York, N.Y.
10020

Sun Oil Co.
1608 Walnut St., Philadelphia, Pa.
19103

Sun Oil Co., DX Division
Box 2039, Tulsa, Oklahoma
74102

Tenneco Oil Co.
Box 2511, Tennessee Bldg., Houston,
Tex. 77001

Texaco, Inc.
135 East 42nd St., New York, N.Y.
10017

Union Oil Co.
P.O. Box 7600, Los Angeles, Calif.
90054

AIRLINE CREDIT CARDS

Air Canada
600 Madison Ave., New York, N.Y.
10022

Air West
1740 Broadway, New York, N.Y.
10019

American Airlines
633 Third Ave., New York, N.Y.
10017

Braniff International
135 East 42nd St., New York, N.Y.
10017

British Overseas Airways Corp.
245 Park Ave., New York, N.Y.
10017

Eastern Airlines
10 Rockefeller Plaza, New York,
N.Y. 10020

National Airlines
219 East 42nd St., New York, N.Y.
10017

Northeast Airlines
299 Park Ave., New York, N.Y.
10017

Northwest Airlines
537 Fifth Ave., New York, N.Y.
10017

Pan American Airways
Pan American Bldg., New York,
N.Y. 10017

Southern Airlines
80 East 42nd St., New York, N.Y.
10017

Swissair
608 Fifth Ave., New York, N.Y.
10020

Trans World Airlines, Inc.
605 Third Ave., New York, N.Y.
10016

United Airlines
277 Park Ave., New York, N.Y.
10017

Western Airlines International
609 Fifth Ave., New York, N.Y.
10017

16. Business Credit Institutions

Advance Mortgage Corp.
First National Bldg., Detroit, Mich.
48226
313-424-2200
Pres.: Irving Rose

Allis Chalmers Credit Corp.
1126 South 70th St., Milwaukee,
Wisc. 53214
414-475-3225
Pres.: P. A. Dunham

A. J. Armstrong Co.
850 Third Ave., New York, N.Y.
10022
212-752-5300
Pres.: D. H. Seiler

Associates Corp. of North America
1 Gulf & Western Pl., New York,
N.Y. 10023
212-333-4744
Pres.: J. D. Barnette

Associates Investment
Associates Bldg., South Bend, Ind.
46624
219-288-9141
Pres.: J. G. Barnette

Century Industries Co., Inc.
444 Fifth Ave., New York, N.Y.
10018
212-565-6300
Pres.: Daniel Niederman

Citizens Financial
33 Public Square, Cleveland, Ohio
44113
216-692-1800
Chmn. of the Bd.: J. Cozzens

Clark Equipment Credit Corp.
128 East Front St., Bushanan, Mich.
49107

616-697-8000
Pres.: John R. Wood, Jr.

Coburn Corp. of America
100 Merrick Rd,. Rockville Center,
N.Y. 11570
516-764-2800
Pres.: Irving L. Bernstein

Commercial Credit Co.
300 St. Paul Pl., Baltimore, Md.
21202
301-685-1400
Pres.: Donald S. Jones

Commercial Securities Co., Inc.
1755 Florida St., Baton Rouge,
La. 70821
504-348-0001
Pres.: J. Noland Singletary

Theodore H. Davies & Co., Ltd.
Financial Plaza, Honolulu, Hawaii
96802
808-531-8531
Pres.: M. H. Pickup

John Deere Credit Co.
John Deere Rd., Moline, Ill.
61265
309-792-8000
Pres.: William A. Hewitt

Fruehauf Finance Co.
10900 Harper Ave., Detroit, Mich.
48232
313-921-2410
Pres.: Russell G. Howell

General Electric Credit Corp.
570 Lexington Ave., New York,
N.Y. 10022
212-750-2000
Pres.: Charles G. Klock

Walter E. Heller & Co.
105 West Adams St., Chicago, III.
60603
312-346-2300
Pres.: Franklin A. Cole

International Harvester Credit
401 North Michigan Ave., Chicago,
III. 60611
312-527-0200
Pres.: Robert E. LaVelle

Mack Financial Corp.
2100 Mack Blvd., Allentown, Pa.
18105
215-439-3687
Pres.: Zenon C. R. Hansen

Rosenthal & Rosenthal, Inc.
1451 Broadway, New York, N.Y.
10036
212-564-4500
Pres.: Andor Rosenthal

Shapiro Brothers Factors
1441 Broadway, New York, N.Y.
10018

212-244-5500
Pres.: E. O. Lewis

Standard Financial Corp.
277 Park Ave., New York, N.Y.
10017
212-922-4000
Pres.: Ezra Denerstein

Talcott National Corp.
1290 Ave. of the Americas, New
York, N.Y. 10019
212-956-3000
Pres.: Kenneth B. Wackman

Union Investment Co.
First National Bldg., Detroit, Mich.
48231
313-963-7474
Pres.: J. Richard Cooper

Westinghouse Credit Corp.
933 Penn Ave., Pittsburgh, Pa.
15222
412-255-4100
Pres.: J. R. McClester

STOCK AND COMMODITY EXCHANGES

17. Commodity Exchanges

Board of Trade of the City of Chicago
141 West Jackson Blvd., Chicago, Ill.
60604
312-WA 2-2800
Pres.: Henry H. Wilson, Jr.

Board of Trade of Kansas City,
Missouri
4800 Main St., Kansas City, Mo.
64112
816-PL 3-7363
Pres.: J. H. Rockwell

Chicago Mercantile Exchange
110 North Franklin St., Chicago, Ill.
60606
312-RA 6-6490
Pres.: Everette B. Harris

Chicago Open Board of Trade
343 South Dearborn St., Chicago, Ill.
60604
312-939-0606
Pres.: J. R. Collins

Commodity Exchange, Inc.
81 Broad St., New York, N.Y.
10004
212-943-5282
Pres.: Matthew S. Fox

International Commercial Exchange
2 Broadway, New York, N.Y. 10004
212-269-3400
Pres.: Murray Borowitz

Kansas City Board of Trade
4800 Main St.,
Kansas City, Mo. 64112
816-753-7363

Minneapolis Grain Exchange
150 Grain Exchange Bldg.,
Minneapolis, Minn. 55415
612-336-6361
Pres.: A. C. Owens

New York Cocoa Exchange
82 Beaver St., New York, N.Y.
10005
212-422-5985
Pres.: John E. Hoch

New York Coffee & Sugar Exchange,
Inc.
79 Pine St., New York, N.Y. 10005
212-269-8637
Pres.: Charles W. Chapin

New York Cotton Exchange
37 Wall St., New York, N.Y. 10005
212-269-7880
Pres.: F. Marion Rhodes

Citrus Associates of the New York
Cotton Exchange, Inc.
37 Wall St., New York, N.Y. 10005
212-269-7880
Pres.: John H. Fitzgerald

Wool Associates of the New York
Cotton Exchange, Inc.
37 Wall St., New York, N.Y. 10005
212-269-7880
Pres.: Malcolm A. Fellman

New York Mercantile Exchange
6 Harrison St., New York, N.Y.
10013

212-966-2600
Pres.: Richard B. Levine

New York Produce Exchange
2 Broadway, New York, N.Y. 10004
212-269-3400
Pres.: Norman L. Sirota

West Coast Commodity Exchange, Inc.
643 South Olive St., Los Angeles,
Calif. 90014
213-485-7171
Pres.: David Callahan

18. U.S. and Canadian Stock Exchanges

U.S. STOCK EXCHANGES

American Stock Exchange
86 Trinity Pl., New York,
N.Y. 10006

Boston Stock Exchange
53 State St., Boston, Mass.
02109

Chicago Board of Trade
141 West Jackson Blvd., Chicago,
Ill. 60603

Cincinnati Stock Exchange
209 Dixie Terminal Bldg.,
Cincinnati, Ohio 45202

Colorado Springs Stock Exchange
418 Mining Exchange Bldg.,
Colorado Springs, Colo. 80902

Detroit Stock Exchange
2314 Penobscot Bldg., Detroit,
Mich. 48226

Honolulu Stock Exchange
843 Fort St., Honolulu, Hawaii
96813

Midwest Stock Exchange
120 South LaSalle St., Chicago, Ill.
60603

National Stock Exchange, Inc.
91 Hudson St., New York, N.Y.
10013

New York Stock Exchange
11 Wall St., New York, N.Y. 10005

Pacific Coast Stock Exchange
301 Pine St., San Francisco, Calif.
94104
618 South Spring St., Los Angeles,
Calif. 90014

Philadelphia–Baltimore–Washington
Stock Exchange
17th St. & Stock Exchange Pl.
Philadelphia, Pa. 19002

Pittsburgh Stock Exchange
333 4th Ave., Pittsburgh Branch,
Pittsburgh, Pa. 15222

Richmond Stock Exchange
P. O. Box 77, Richmond, Va. 23201

Salt Lake Stock Exchange
39 Exchange Pl., Salt Lake City,
Utah 84101

Spokane Stock Exchange
206 Radio Central Bldg., Spokane,
Wash. 99004

Wheeling Stock Exchange
1219 Chapline St., Wheeling, W. Va.
26003

CANADIAN STOCK EXCHANGES

Calgary Stock Exchange
Anglo Avenue Bldg., 330-9 Ave.
SW, Calgary, Alberta

Canadian Stock Exchange
P. O. Box 1626, Place d' Armes,
Montreal, Quebec

Montreal Stock Exchange
P. O. Box 1626, Place d' Armes,
Montreal, Quebec

Toronto Stock Exchange
234 Bay St., Toronto, Ontario

Vancouver Stock Exchange
536 Howe St., Vancouver, B.C.

Winnipeg Stock Exchange
704-213 Notre Dame Ave.,
Winnipeg 2, Manitoba

19. Foreign Stock Exchanges

Austria Stock Exchange
Wiener Börse Wipplingerstade 34,
Vienna 1, Austria

Denmark Stock Exchange
Kø Benhauns Føndbørs, Børsen
Copenhagen, Denmark

Finland Stock Exchange
Helsingin Arvopaperiporssi,
Fabianinkatu 14, Helsinki, Finland

France Stock Exchange
Bourse de Paris, 4 Place de la Bourse,
Paris 2e, France

Germany Stock Exchange
Berliner Wertpapierbörse,
Hardenbergstrasse 16-18, Berlin
12, Germany

Greece Stock Exchange
Chrimatisterion Athenon,
Sophocles 10, Athens, Greece

Ireland Stock Exchange
Dublin Stock Exchange, 24-28
Anglesea St., Dublin 2, Ireland

Cork Stock Exchange, 12 Marl-
borough St., Cork, Ireland

Italy Stock Exchange
Borsa Valori di Roma, via del Burro
147, Rome, Italy

Luxembourg Stock Exchange
Bourse de Luxembourg, 11 rue de la
Porte Neuve, Luxembourg

Netherlands Stock Exchange
Bond voor die Geld, en
Effectenhandel, Koninginnegracht
15 's-Gravenhage, The Hague,
Netherlands

Norway Stock Exchange
Oslo Bors, Tøllbugaten 2, Oslo,
Norway

Scotland Stock Exchange
75 St. George's Pl., Glasgow C2,
Scotland

Spain Stock Exchange
Bolsa Oficial de Comercio de Madrid,
Plaza de la Lealtad, Madrid, Spain

Sweden Stock Exchange
Stocklhoms Fondbörs, Borshuset,
Stockholm C, Sweden

Switzerland Stock Exchange
Berner Börse, Aarbergergasse 30,
Bern, Switzerland

United Kingdom Stock Exchange
The Stock Exchange, London EC2,
England

INVESTMENT GROUPS

20. Major Hedge Funds

Atalanta Partners
  767 Fifth Ave., New York, N.Y.
  10022

Berger-Kent Associates
  280 Park Ave., New York, N.Y.
  10017

Berman, Kalmbach & Co.
  345 Park Ave., New York, N.Y.
  10022

Boston Equity Associates
  50 Federal St., Boston, Mass. 02110

Boxwood Associates
  41 West Putnam Ave., Greenwich,
  Conn. 06830

Broadstreet Partners
  c/o Allen & Co., 30 Broadway,
  New York, N.Y. 10004

Century Partners
  605 Third Ave., New York, N.Y.
  10016

Cerberus Associates
  14-35 150th St., Whitestone,
  N.Y. 11357

City Associates
  20 Exchange Pl., New York, N.Y.
  10005

FBE Partners
  330 Madison Ave., New York,
  N.Y. 10017

Fairfield Partners
  170 Mason St., Greenwich, Conn.
  06830

First Security Co.
  245 Park Ave., New York, N.Y.
  10017

Goodnow, Gray & Co.
  1 Greenwich Plaza, Greenwich,
  Conn. 06830

Harborside Associates
  c/o Allen & Co., 30 Broadway,
  New York, N.Y. 10004

Hartwell & Associates
  345 Park Ave., New York, N.Y.
  10022

A.W. Jones Associates
  9 Bishopsgate, London EC2,
  England

Lincoln Partners
  208 South LaSalle St., Chicago,
  Ill. 60604

Merridohn Associates
   345 Park Ave., New York, N.Y.
   10022

New Court Partners
   70 Pine St., New York, N.Y. 10005

S.S.T. Partners
   20 Vessey St., New York, N.Y.
   10007

Steinhardt, Fine, & Berkowitz
   90 Park Ave., New York, N.Y.
   10016

Strand & Co.
   c/o Samuel M. Stayman, 1000 Park
   Ave., New York, N.Y. 10028

21. Largest Mutual Funds

STOCK FUNDS (LOAD)

Aberdeen Fund
   919 18th St., N.W., Washington,
   D. C. 20006
   Assets in millions: 40

Admiralty Funds
   9601 Wilshire Blvd., Beverly Hills,
   Calif. 90210
   Assets in millions: 53

Advisers Fund
   300 East Fall Creek Blvd.,
   Indianapolis, Ind. 46205
   Assets in millions: 3

Affiliated Fund
   63 Wall St., New York, N.Y. 10005
   Assets in millions: 1,714

All American Fund
   9465 Wilshire Blvd., Beverly Hills,
   Calif. 90212
   Assets in millions: 3

American Diversified Investors Fund
   303 East Washington St.,
   Bloomington, Ill. 61701
   Assets in millions: 3

American Express Capital Fund
   P. O. Box 7650, San Francisco,
   Calif. 94119
   Assets in millions: 223

American Express Stock Fund
   P. O. Box 7650, San Francisco,
   Calif. 94119
   Assets in millions: 84

American Growth Fund
   650 17th St., Denver, Colo. 80202
   Assets in millions: 17

American Mutual Fund
   611 West 6th St., Los Angeles,
   Calif. 90017
   Assets in millions: 405

American National Growth Fund
   Moody Ave. & Market St.,
   Galveston, Tex. 77550
   Assets in millions: 11

Anchor Growth Fund
   Westminster at Parker, Elizabeth,
   N.J. 07207
   Assets in millions: 558

Axe–Houghton Stock Fund
   400 Benedict Ave., Tarrytown,
   N.Y. 10591
   Assets in millions: 86

Axe Science Corp.
   400 Benedict Ave., Tarrytown,
   N.Y. 10591
   Assets in millions: 53

Bayrock Growth Fund (formerly
   Florida Growth Fund)
   516 Gulf Life Tower, Jacksonville,
   Fla. 32203
   Assets in millions: 9

Bondstock Corp.
   1200 Washington Bldg., Tacoma,
   Wash. 98402
   Assets in millions: 34

Broad Street Investing Corp.
65 Broadway, New York, N.Y.
10006
Assets in millions: 412

Brown Fund of Hawaii
915 Fort St., Honolulu, Hawaii
96813
Assets in millions: 6

Bullock Fund
1 Wall St., New York, N.Y. 10005
Assets in millions: 180

Businessman's Fund
111 Broadway, New York, N.Y.
10006
Assets in millions: 18

Capamerica Fund
2727 Alien Parkway, Houston,
Tex. 77001
Assets in millions: 2

Capital Investors Growth Fund
2727 Alien Parkway, Houston,
Tex. 77001
Assets in millions: 3

Capital Shares
2727 Alien Parkway, Houston,
Tex. 77001
Assets in millions: 52

Century Shares Trust
111 Devonshire St., Boston,
Mass. 02109
Assets in millions: 112

Channing Funds
280 Park Ave., New York,
N.Y. 10017
Assets in millions: 442

The Chase Fund of Boston
535 Boylston St., Boston,
Mass. 02116
Assets in millions: 115

Chemical Fund
61 Broadway, New York,
N.Y. 10006
Assets in millions: 620

The Colonial Fund
75 Federal St., Boston, Mass. 02110
Assets in millions: 231

Colonial Growth Shares
75 Federal St., Boston, Mass. 02110
Assets in millions: 77

Commerce Fund
711 Polk St., Houston, Tex. 77002
Assets in millions: 95

Common Stock Fund of State Bond &
Mortgage Co.
28 North Minnesota St., New Ulm,
Minn. 56073
Assets in millions: 33

Commonwealth Fund Indenture of
Trust Plans A & B
155 Berkeley St., Boston, Mass.
02116
Assets in millions: 34

Commonwealth Fund Indenture of
Trust Plan C
155 Berkeley St., Boston, Mass.
02116
Assets in millions: 56

Composite Fund
402 Spokane & Eastern Bldg.,
Spokane, Wash. 99201
Assets in millions: 49

Corporate Leaders Trust Fund
Certificates, Series "B"
177 North Dean St., Englewood,
N.J. 07631
Assets in millions: 66

Crown Western Investments
P. O. Box 1372, Houston, Tex.
77001
Assets in millions: 30

Decatur Income Fund
7 Penn Center Plaza, Philadelphia,
Pa. 19103
Assets in millions: 154

Delaware Fund
7 Penn Center Plaza, Philadelphia,
Pa. 19103
Assets in millions: 519

Diversified Fund of State Bond &
Mortgage Co.
28 North Minnesota St., New Ulm,
Minn. 56073
Assets in millions: 3

Dividend Shares
1 Wall St., New York, N.Y. 10005
Assets in millions: 376

Dreyfus Fund
767 Fifth Ave., New York,
N.Y. 10022
Assets in millions: 2,489

Eaton & Howard Stock Fund
24 Federal St., Boston, Mass.
02110
Assets in millions: 237

Egret Growth Fund
110 Milk St., Boston, Mass. 02109
Assets in millions: 37

Enterprise Fund
1888 Century Park East,
Los Angeles, Calif. 90067
Assets in millions: 511

Equity Fund
520 United Pacific Bldg.,
Seattle, Wash. 98104
Assets in millions: 45

Equity Progress Fund
1900 Ave. of the Stars,
Los Angeles, Calif. 90067
Assets in millions: 24

F-D Capital Fund
67 Broad St., New York, N.Y.
10004
Assets in millions: 1

Fairfield Fund
250 Park Ave., New York,
N.Y. 10017
Assets in millions: 55

Fidelity Capital Fund
35 Congress St., Boston, Mass.
02109
Assets in millions: 658

Fidelity Fund
35 Congress St., Boston, Mass.
02109
Assets in millions: 872

Fidelity Trend Fund
35 Congress St., Boston, Mass.
02109
Assets in millions: 1,113

Financial Industrial Fund
P. O. Box 2040, Denver, Colo.
80201
Assets in millions: 318

First Investors Fund
120 Wall St., New York, N.Y.
10005
Assets in millions: 34

First National Fund
155 Sansome St., San Francisco,
Calif. 94104
Assets in millions: 9

First Sierra Fund
Crocker Plaza, San Francisco,
Calif. 94104
Assets in millions: 37

Founders Growth Fund
2400 First National Bank Bldg.,
Denver, Colo. 80202
Assets in millions: 67

Founders Mutual Fund
2400 First National Bank Bldg.,
Denver, Colo. 80202
Assets in millions: 203

Foursquare Fund
27 State St., Boston, Mass. 02109
Assets in millions: 12

Franklin Custodian Funds (Growth
Series)
99 Wall St., New York, N.Y. 10006
Assets in millions: 15

Fund of America
1900 Ave. of the Stars, Los Angeles,
Calif. 90067
Assets in millions: 83

Fundamental Investors
Westminster at Parker, Elizabeth,
N.J. 07207
Assets in millions: 1,135

Group Securities
1 Exchange Plaza, Jersey City,
N.J. 07302
Assets in millions: 352

Hamilton Funds Series H-DA
777 Grant St., Denver, Colo. 80203
Assets in millions: 680

Harbor Fund
1888 Century Park East,
Los Angeles, Calif. 90067
Assets in millions: 160

Hedberg & Gordon Fund
1 Station Square, Paoli, Pa. 19301
Assets in millions: 16

The Heritage Fund
130 William St., New York, N.Y.
10038
Assets in millions: 2

The ICM Financial Fund
500 Denver Club Bldg., Denver,
Colo. 80202
Assets in millions: 3

ISI Trust Fund
100 California St., San Francisco,
Calif. 94120
Assets in millions: 556

Imperial Capital Fund
P. O. Box 1386, Minneapolis,
Minn. 55440
Assets in millions: 39

Imperial Growth Fund
P. O. Box 1386, Minneapolis,
Minn. 55440
Assets in millions: 20

Independence Fund
70 Federal St., Boston, Mass.
02110
Assets in millions: 28

Industries Trend Fund
711 Polk St., Houston, Tex. 77002
Assets in millions: 104

Integon Growth Fund
420 North Spruce St., Winston
Salem, N.C. 27102
Assets in millions: 10

The Investment Co. of America
611 West 6th St., Los Angeles,
Calif. 90017
Assets in millions: 1,328

Investment Trust of Boston
140 Federal St., Boston, Mass.
02110
Assets in millions: 84

Investors Research Fund
924 Laguna St., Santa Barbara,
Calif. 93101
Assets in millions: 6

Investors Stock Fund
1000 Roanoke Bldg., Minneapolis,
Minn. 55402
Assets in millions: 2,459

Investors Variable Payment Fund
1000 Roanoke Bldg., Minneapolis,
Minn. 55402
Assets in millions: 1,008

Istel Fund
345 Park Ave., New York, N.Y.
10022
Assets in millions: 133

Ivest Fund
28 State St., Boston, Mass. 02109
Assets in millions: 333

Keystone Custodian Funds
50 Congress St., Boston, Mass.
02109
Assets in millions: 1,406

The Knickerbocker Fund
20 Exchange Pl., New York, N.Y.
10005
Assets in millions: 13

Knickerbocker Growth Fund
20 Exchange Pl., New York, N.Y.
10005
Assets in millions: 12

Lexington Research Fund
177 North Dean St., Englewood,
N.J. 07631
Assets in millions: 135

Liberty Fund
245 Park Ave., New York, N.Y.
10017
Assets in millions: 16

Life & Growth Stock Fund
2100 Republic Bank Tower, Dallas,
Tex. 75201
Assets in millions: 11

Life Insurance Investors
170 Fourth Ave. North, Nashville,
Tenn. 37219
Assets in millions: 86

Magna Income Trust
185 Cross St., Fort Lee, N.J. 07024
Assets in millions: 6

Manhattan Fund
245 Park Ave., New York, N.Y.
10017
Assets in millions: 179

Horace Mann Fund
216 East Monroe St., Springfield,
Ill. 62701
Assets in millions: 18

Massachusetts Investors Growth Stock
Fund
200 Berkeley St., Boston, Mass.
02116
Assets in millions: 1,391

Massachusetts Investors Trust
200 Berkeley St., Boston, Mass.
02116
Assets in millions: 2,159

Mid America Mutual Fund
375 Collins Rd. N.E., Cedar Rapids,
Iowa 52406
Assets in millions: 22

Mutual Investing Foundation
246 North High St., Columbus,
Ohio 43216
Assets in millions: 226

Mutual Securities Fund of Boston
4 Liberty Square, Boston, Mass.
02109
Assets in millions: 3

NEA Mutual Fund
1156 15th St. N.W., Washington,
D. C. 20005
Assets in millions: 26

National Investors Corp.
65 Broadway, New York, N.Y.
10006
Assets in millions: 888

National Securities
120 Broadway, New York, N.Y.
10005
Assets in millions: 644

New World Fund
4680 Wilshire Blvd., Los Angeles,
Calif. 90054
Assets in millions: 9

Newton Fund
330 East Mason St., Milwaukee,
Wisc. 53202
Assets in millions: 20

Old Dominion Investors' Trust
110 Bank St., Suffolk, Va. 23434
Assets in millions: 4

Oppenheimer Fund
1 New York Plaza, New York, N.Y.
10004
Assets in millions: 498

Over-The-Counter Securities Fund
Plymouth & Walnut Aves., Oreland,
Pa. 19075
Assets in millions: 6

Pacific Standard Fund
421 Seventh Ave., Pittsburgh, Pa.
15219
Assets in millions: 10

Paramount Mutual Fund
225 North Barranca Ave., West
Covina, Calif. 91790
Assets in millions: 8

Philadelphia Fund
110 Wall St., New York, N.Y.
10005
Assets in millions: 99

Pilgrim Fund
185 Cross St., Fort Lee, N.J. 07024
Assets in millions: 16

Pioneer Enterprise Fund
28 State St., Boston, Mass. 02109
Assets in millions: 6

Pioneer Fund
28 State St., Boston, Mass. 02109
Assets in millions: 214

Planned Investment Fund
4 Liberty Square, Boston, Mass.
02109
Assets in millions: 3

Pligrowth Fund
111 North Broad St., Philadelphia,
Pa. 19107
Assets in millions: 19

Puritan Fund
35 Congress St., Boston, Mass.
02109
Assets in millions: 859

Putnam Growth Fund
265 Franklin St., Boston, Mass.
02110
Assets in millions: 796

Putnam Investors Fund
265 Franklin St., Boston, Mass.
02110
Assets in millions: 354

Revere Fund
123 South Broad St., Philadelphia,
Pa. 19109
Assets in millions: 20

Salem Fund
35 Congress St., Boston, Mass.
02109
Assets in millions: 120

Security Equity Fund
700 Harrison St., Topeka,
Kans. 66603
Assets in millions: 133

Security Investment Fund
700 Harrison St., Topeka, Kans.
66603
Assets in millions: 24

Selected American Shares
135 South LaSalle St., Chicago,
Ill. 60603
Assets in millions: 214

Shareholders' Trust of Boston
535 Boylston St., Boston, Mass.
02116
Assets in millions: 126

Sigma Investment Shares
3801 Kennett Pike, Wilmington,
Del. 19807
Assets in millions: 56

Southwestern Investors
P. O. Box 2994, Dallas, Tex. 75221
Assets in millions: 28

Sovereign Investors
Philadelphia National Bank Bldg.,
Philadelphia, Pa. 19107
Assets in millions: 8

State Street Investment Corp.
225 Franklin St., Boston, Mass.
02110
Assets in millions: 424

Steadman American Industry Fund
919 18th St. N.W., Washington, D. C.
20006
Assets in millions: 54

Steadman Associated Fund
919 18th St. N.W., Washington, D. C.
20006
Assets in millions: 69

Steadman Fiduciary Investment Fund
919 18th St. N.W., Washington,
D. C. 20006
Assets in millions: 12

Technology Fund
120 South LaSalle St., Chicago, Ill.
60603
Assets in millions: 692

Twentieth Century Investors
605 West 47th St., Kansas City,
Mo. 64112
Assets in millions: 12

United Funds
20 West 9th St., Kansas City,
Mo. 64105
Assets in millions: 2,521

United Mutual Shares
207 Guaranty Bldg., Indianapolis,
Ind. 46204
Assets in millions: 14

The Value Line Fund
5 East 44th St., New York, N.Y.
10017
Assets in millions: 64

The Value Line Income Fund
5 East 44th St., New York,
N.Y. 10017
Assets in millions: 88

The Value Line Special Situations
Fund
5 East 44th St., New York, N.Y.
10017
Assets in millions: 204

Vanderbilt Mutual Fund
530 B St., San Diego, Calif.
92101
Assets in millions: 17

Varied Industry Plan
P. O. Box 929, Fort Wayne, Ind.
46801
Assets in millions: 13

Venture Securities Fund
6 Bryn Mawr Ave., Bryn Mawr,
Pa. 19010
Assets in millions: 2

Viking Growth Fund
1712 Commerce St., Dallas, Tex.
75201
Assets in millions: 3

Wall Street Growth Fund
1 Wall St., New York, N.Y. 10005
Assets in millions: 15

Washington Mutual Investors Fund
Southern Bldg., Washington, D. C.
20005
Assets in millions: 329

Western Industrial Shares
780 East South Temple St.,
Salt Lake City, Utah 84110
Assets in millions: 8

Windsor Fund
3001 Philadelphia Pike, Claymont,
Del. 19703
Assets in millions: 526

Winfield Growth Fund
155 Bovet Rd., San Mateo, Calif.
94402
Assets in millions: 138

Wisconsin Fund
225 East Michigan St., Milwaukee,
Wisc. 53202
Assets in millions: 33

STOCK FUNDS (NO-LOAD)

Leon B. Allen Fund
120 Broadway, New York, N.Y.
10005
Assets in millions: 3

American Investment Counseling Fund
615 South Flower St., Los Angeles,
Calif. 90017
Assets in millions: 3

American Investors Fund
88 Field Point Rd., Greenwich,
Conn. 06830
Assets in millions: 241

David L. Babson Investment Fund
301 West 11th St., Kansas City,
Mo. 64105
Assets in millions: 55

Concord Fund
366 Madison Ave., New York, N.Y.
10017
Assets in millions: 2

Consultant's Mutual Investments
211 South Broad St., Philadelphia,
Pa. 19107
Assets in millions: 16

De Vegh Mutual Fund
20 Exchange Pl., New York, N.Y.
10005
Assets in millions: 97

Dodge & Cox Stock Fund
3500 Crocker Plaza, San Francisco,
Calif. 94104
Assets in millions: 10

Drexel Equity Fund
1500 Walnut St., Philadelphia, Pa.
19101
Assets in millions: 50

Energy Fund
120 Broadway, New York, N.Y.
10005
Assets in millions: 161

Farm Bureau Mutual Fund
1000 Merchandise Mart, Chicago,
III. 60654
Assets in millions: 12

General Securities
133 South 7th St., Minneapolis,
Minn. 55402
Assets in millions: 9

Growth Industry Shares
135 South LaSalle St., Chicago, III.
60603
Assets in millions: 46

Guardian Mutual Fund
120 Broadway, New York, N.Y.
10005
Assets in millions: 59

Ivy Fund
155 Berkeley St., Boston, Mass.
02116
Assets in millions: 68

The Johnston Mutual Fund
460 Park Ave., New York, N.Y.
10022
Assets in millions: 198

Loomis–Sayles Capital Development
Fund
225 Franklin St., Boston, Mass.
02110
Assets in millions: 71

Mairs & Power Growth Fund
2062 West First National Bank Bldg.,
St. Paul, Minn. 55101
Assets in millions: 9

Market Growth Fund
431 Fifth Ave., New York, N.Y.
10016
Assets in millions: 3

Mathers Fund
1 First National Plaza, Chicago, III.
60670
Assets in millions: 81

Moody's Capital Fund
28 Park Pl., New York, N.Y. 10007
Assets in millions: 33

Mutual Shares Corp.
200 East 42nd St., New York, N.Y.
10017
Assets in millions: 10

Mutual Trust
4901 Main St., Kansas City, Mo.
64112
Assets in millions: 10

Nassau Fund
P. O. Box 629, Princeton, N.J.
08540
Assets in millions: 8

National Industries Fund
1880 Century Park East,
Los Angeles, Calif. 90067
Assets in millions: 9

Nelson Fund
345 Park Ave., New York, N.Y.
10022
Assets in millions: 5

The One William Street Fund
1 William St., New York, N.Y.
10004
Assets in millions: 286

Penn Square Mutual Fund
451 Penn Square, Reading, Pa.
19603
Assets in millions: 173

Pine Street Fund
20 Exchange Pl., New York, N.Y.
10005
Assets in millions: 53

T. Rose Price Growth Stock Fund
1 Charles Center, Baltimore, Md.
21201
Assets in millions: 865

Rowe Price New Horizons Fund
1 Charles Center, Baltimore, Md.
21201
Assets in millions: 268

Scudder Special Fund
10 Post Office Square, Boston, Mass.
02109
Assets in millions: 210

Scudder Stevens & Clark Balanced
Fund
10 Post Office Square, Boston, Mass.
02109
Assets in millions: 91

Scudder Stevens & Clark Common
Stock Fund
10 Post Office Square, Boston, Mass.
02109
Assets in millions: 159

Stein Roe & Farnham Stock Fund
150 South Wacker Dr., Chicago, Ill.
60606
Assets in millions: 149

Variable Stock Fund
9th & Main Sts., Richmond, Va.
23218
Assets in millions: 3

CLOSED-END INVESTMENT COMPANIES

Abacus Fund
76 Beaver St., New York, N.Y.
10005
Assets in millions: 58

Adams Express
48 Wall St., New York, N.Y.
10005
Assets in millions: 186

Carriers & General Corp.
1 Wall St., New York, N.Y. 10005
Assets in millions: 22

Central Securities
375 Park Ave., New York, N.Y.
10022
Assets in millions: 50

Consolidated Investment Trust
35 Congress St., Boston, Mass.
02109
Assets in millions: 75

Dominick Fund
30 Broad St., New York, N.Y.
10004
Assets in millions: 61

General American Investors
60 Broad St., New York, N.Y.
10004
Assets in millions: 118

International Holdings
1 State St., New York, N.Y. 10004
Assets in millions: 97

Japan Fund
25 Broad St., New York, N.Y.
10004
Assets in millions: 77

The Lehman Corp.
1 South William St., New York, N.Y.
10004
Assets in millions: 522

Madison Fund
919 Market St., Suite 501
Wilmington, Del. 19801
Assets in millions: 331

National Aviation
630 Fifth Ave., New York, N.Y.
10020
Assets in millions: 110

Niagara Share Corp.
70 Niagara St., Buffalo, N.Y.
14202
Assets in millions: 106

Petroleum Corp. of America
48 Wall St., New York, N.Y. 10005
Assets in millions: 81

Standard Shares
40 Wall St., New York, N.Y. 10005
Assets in millions: 84

Surveyor Fund
90 Broad St., New York, N.Y.
10004
Assets in millions: 150

Tri-Continental Corp.
65 Broadway, New York, N.Y.
10006
Assets in millions: 680

The United Corp.
250 Park Ave., New York, N.Y.
10017
Assets in millions: 138

U. S. & Foreign Securities
767 Fifth Ave., New York, N.Y.
10022
Assets in millions: 160

FUNDS FOR INVESTING ABROAD

Boston Common Stock Fund
111 Devonshire St., Boston, Mass.
02109
Assets in millions: 48

Canadian Fund
1 Wall St., New York, N.Y. 10005
Assets in millions: 28

International Investors
420 Lexington Ave., New York,
N.Y. 10017
Assets in millions: 4

Loomis–Sayles Canadian &
International Fund
225 Franklin St., Boston, Mass.
02110
Assets in millions: 17

Scudder International Investments
44 King St. West, Toronto,
Ontario, Canada
Assets in millions: 15

Stein Roe & Farnham Capital
Opportunities Fund
150 South Wacker Dr., Chicago, Ill.
60606
Assets in millions: 18

Templeton Growth Fund
330 Bay St., Toronto, Ontario,
Canada
Assets in millions: 7

Transatlantic Fund
20 Exchange Pl., New York, N.Y.
10005
Assets in millions: 13

United Funds Canada-International
20 West 9th St., Kansas City, Mo.
64105
Assets in millions: 9

BALANCED FUNDS (LOAD)

American Business Shares
63 Wall St., New York, N.Y. 10005
Assets in millions: 27

American Express Income Fund
P. O. Box 7650, San Francisco,
Calif. 94119
Assets in millions: 147

American Express Investment Co.
P. O. Box 7650, San Francisco,
Calif. 94119
Assets in millions: 172

Anchor Income Fund
Westminster at Parker, Elizabeth,
N.J. 07207
Assets in millions: 140

Axe–Houghton Fund A
400 Benedict Ave., Tarrytown,
N.Y. 10591
Assets in millions: 67

Axe–Houghton Fund B
400 Benedict Ave., Tarrytown,
N.Y. 10591
Assets in millions: 260

Balanced Income Fund
120 South LaSalle St., Chicago, Ill.
60603
Assets in millions: 14

Boston Foundation Fund
421 Seventh Ave., Pittsburgh, Pa.
15219
Assets in millions: 46

Boston Fund
111 Devonshire St., Boston, Mass.
02109
Assets in millions: 241

Channing Funds
280 Park Ave., New York, N.Y.
10017
Assets in millions: 180

Composite Bond & Stock Fund
402 Spokane & Eastern Bldg.,
Spokane, Wash. 99201
Assets in millions: 14

Eaton & Howard Balanced Fund
24 Federal St., Boston, Mass. 02110
Assets in millions: 159

Eaton & Howard Income Fund
24 Federal St., Boston, Mass. 02110
Assets in millions: 21

Financial Industrial Income Fund
P. O. Box 2040, Denver, Colo.
80201
Assets in millions: 113

Franklin Custodian Funds—Income
Series Shares
99 Wall St., New York, N.Y. 10005
Assets in millions: 7

Group Securities—Balanced Fund
1 Exchange Plaza, Jersey City,
N.J. 07302
Assets in millions: 17

Income Fund of Boston
9601 Wilshire Blvd., Beverly Hills,
Calif. 90210
Assets in millions: 40

Investors Mutual
1000 Roanoke Bldg., Minneapolis,
Minn. 55402
Assets in millions: 2,825

Keystone Custodian Funds
50 Congress St., Boston, Mass.
02109
Assets in millions: 106

Massachusetts Fund
70 Federal St., Boston, Mass.
02110
Assets in millions: 218

National Securities
120 Broadway, New York, N.Y.
10005
Assets in millions: 193

Nation-Wide Securities Co.
1 Wall St., New York, N.Y. 10005
Assets in millions: 83

Provident Fund for Income
3 Penn Center Plaza, Philadelphia,
Pa. 19102
Assets in millions: 111

The George Putnam Fund of Boston
265 Franklin St., Boston, Mass.
02110
Assets in millions: 438

Putnam Income Fund
265 Franklin St., Boston, Mass.
02110
Assets in millions: 142

Sigma Trust
3801 Kennett Pike, Wilmington,
Del. 19807
Assets in millions: 18

Wellington Fund
3001 Philadelphia Pike, Claymont,
Del. 19703
Assets in millions: 1,376

Whitehall Fund
65 Broadway, New York, N.Y.
10006
Assets in millions: 18

BALANCED FUNDS (NO-LOAD)

Dodge & Cox Balanced Fund
3500 Crocker Plaza, San Francisco,
Calif. 94104
Assets in millions: 16

Loomis–Sayles Mutual Fund
225 Franklin St., Boston, Mass.
02110
Assets in millions: 169

Northeast Investors Trust
50 Congress St., Boston, Mass.
02109
Assets in millions: 45

Prudential Fund of Boston
50 Congress St., Boston, Mass.
02109
Assets in millions: 3

Stein Roe & Farnham Balanced Fund
150 South Wacker Dr., Chicago, Ill.
60606
Assets in millions: 172

22. Major Offshore and Overseas Funds

Alexander Fund
Bank of New York
48 Wall St., New York, N.Y. 10005

American Express International
American Express Investment
Management Co.
P. O. Box 7650, San Francisco,
Calif. 94119

Anchor B Unit Trust
Management International
Bank of Bermuda Bldg., Hamilton,
Bermuda

Atlantic Exempt
M & G (Cayman) Ltd.
P. O. Box 706, Cardinal Ave., Grand
Cayman, British West Indies

Buttress International
Butterfield Management Co., Ltd.
P. O. Box 195, Hamilton, Bermuda

Capital Growth Fund
Capital Growth Services, Ltd.
1 Mount St., London W1
4PL, England

Caribico Growth Fund
Caribico-Carribean Oil and Gas
Investment Co.
Postfach 129, 9490 Vaduz,
Liechtenstein, Germany

Channel Island Enterprise Fund
Hambros (Guernsey) Ltd.
Hirzel Court, P. O. Box 86, St. Peter
Port, Guernsey, Channel Islands

Chase Selection Fund
Securities Management Co., Inc.
700 Harrison St., Topeka, Kans.
66603

Convertible Bond Fund N.V.
S. G. Warburg
30 Gresham St., London EC2,
England

Delta Dollar Fund
Delta International Management Co.,
Ltd.
P. O. Box N 3229, Nassau, Bahamas

Delta Unit Trust
Delta International Management Co.,
Ltd.
P. O. Box N 3229, Nassau, Bahamas

Dreyfus Offshore Trust
Dreyfus Management International,
Ltd.
P. O. Box 1660, 284 Bay St.,
Nassau, Bahamas

Ebor Channel Capital Trust, Ltd.
Ebor Management
P. O. Box 73, 37 Broad St.,
St. Helier, Jersey, Channel Islands

Enterprise Fund
Share Service GmbH, Briennerstrasse
1, 8 Munich 2, Western Germany

Fidelity International Fund
Fidelity Management and Research
Co.
35 Congress St., Boston, Mass.
02109

First Investors American
First Investors American Trust
37 Rue Notre Dame, Luxembourg
Ville, Luxembourg

Fleming Fund
N. V. Fides
24 Handelskade Willemstad, Curacao,
Netherlands, Antilles

Fleming Japan Fund, S. A.
Fleming Japan Fund
37 Rue Notre Dame, Luxembourg
Ville, Luxembourg

Fonditalia
Investors Overseas Service
119 Rue de Lausanne, 1211 Geneve,
Switzerland

Frontier Growth Fund, Ltd.
Frontier Management, Ltd.
Boyle St., Nassau, Bahamas

Guardian Growth International
Guardian Management International,
Ltd.
P. O. Box 529, Hamilton, Bermuda

Hambros Overseas Fund
Hambros, Ltd.
Hirzel Court, P. O. Box 86, St. Peter
Port, Guernsey, Channel Islands

Hedged Investors Fund
A. W. Jones
9 Bishopsgate, London EC2, England

Hill, Samuel, Guernsey Trust Fund
Hill, Samuel and Co., Ltd.
8 Lefebure St., St. Peter Port,
Guernsey, Channel Islands

Hope Street Fund
Murray Johnstone & Co.
163 Hope St., Glasgow C2,
Scotland

International Pacific Securities
Jardine, Matheson and Co.
Jardine House, 22 Peddar St.,
Victoria, Hong Kong

Japan Growth Fund
Stoope, Vigne and Co.
3 London Wall Bldgs., London EC2,
England

Japan Selection Fund
Formula Selection, Inc.
Postfach 3243, CH 8023, Zurich,
Switzerland

Kleinwort Benson International Fund
Kleinwort Benson (Guernsey) Ltd.
P. O. Box 44, The Grange, St. Peter
Port, Guernsey, Channel Islands

Netherlands Antilles Fund
First National City Bank
55 Wall St., New York, N.Y. 10005

Nippon Fund
Vicker, Da Costa and Co.
Ed. Sassoon Bldg., P. O. Box 4715,
Nassau, Bahamas

North American Bank Stock Fund
Noram Administrative Services
3 Rue du Marche, 1204 Geneva,
Switzerland

North American Investment Fund
Noram Administrative Services
3 Rue du Marche, 1204 Geneva,
Switzerland

Pacific Searboard Fund
Rothschild (N.M.) & Sons
Curacao, Netherlands Antilles

Save & Prosper Dollar Fund
Save and Prosper International, Ltd.
P. O. Box 1434, Hamilton, Ontario,
Canada

Second Bahamas Investment Trust
Fund
Capital Growth Services, Ltd.
Mount St., London W1 4PL, England

Security and Prosperity Fund S.A.
Security and Prosperity Fund
Distributors
Postfach 515, Utoquai 43, 8027
Zurich, Switzerland

Shareholders Excalibur Investment
Corp. Fund
Excalibur Advisory Co., Ltd.
37 Rue Notre Dame, Luxembourg
Ville, Luxembourg

Signet Fund
Bank of Bermuda
Front St., Hamilton, Bermuda

Stanhope Transatlantic Fund
Lepercq, DeNeuflize & Co.
63 Wall St., New York, N.Y. 10005

Stellar Growth Unit Trust Fund
Stellar Unit Managers, Ltd.
P. O. Box 32, 28 Victoria St.,
Douglas, Isle of Man

Target Offshore Fund
Target Trust Managers
P. O. Box 710, Grand Cayman,
Cayman Island, British West Indies

Tokyo Trust Fund
Tokyo Trust S. A., P. O. Box 1447,
330 Bay St., Nassau, Bahamas

Tokyo Valor Fund
Banque De. L'Union, Parisienne
CFCB, 6 & 8 Boulevard
Hausmann, Paris 9e, France

Trafalgar Fund
Trafalgar Fund, Ltd.
Bank of Bermuda Bldg., Hamilton,
Bermuda

U. S. Trust Investment Fund, S.A.
U. S. Trust International Advisory
Co.
7 Ave. Krieg, 1208 Geneva,
Switzerland

Worldwide Special Fund
Burham & Co.
60 Broad St., New York, N.Y.
10004

23. Major Over-the-Counter Stocks

American Express Co.
65 Broadway, New York, N.Y.
10006
212-944-2000
Pres.: William H. Morton

American Greetings Corp.
10500 American Rd., Cleveland,
Ohio 44144
216-252-7300
Pres.: Irving I. Stone

American International Group
102 Maiden Lane, New York, N.Y.
10005
212-344-9200
Pres.: M. R. Greenberg

American National Insurance Co.
Moody Ave. & Market St., Galveston,
Tex. 77550
713-763-4661
Pres.: Glendon E. Johnson

American Re-Insurance Co.
99 John St., New York, N.Y. 10038
212-974-1500
Pres.: Donald R. MacKay

Anheuser–Busch, Inc.
721 Pestalozzi St., St. Louis, Mo.
63118
314-577-0577
Pres.: R. A. Meyer

Bandag, Inc.
1056 Hershey Ave., Muscatine,
Iowa 52761
319-263-3721
Pres.: Stephen Keller

Bankamerica Corp.
555 California St., San Francisco,
Calif. 94120
415-622-3456
Pres.: A. W. Clausen

Bassett Furniture Industries
Highway 57, Bassett, Va. 24055
703-629-2531
Pres.: Robert H. Spilman

Betz Laboratories, Inc.
4636 Somerton Rd., Langhorne, Pa.
19047
215-355-3300
Pres.: John J. Maguire

Block Drug Co., Inc.
257 Cornelison Ave., Jersey City,
N.J. 07302
201-434-3000
Pres.: Leonard Block

Brink's, Inc.
234 East 24th St., Chicago, Ill.
60616
312-326-5300
Pres.: Edgar A. Jones

Cannon Mills Co.
Main St., Kannapolis, N.C. 28081
704-933-1221
Chmn. of the Bd. & Pres.: Don S.
Holt

Chemed Corp.
Dubois Tower, Cincinnati, Ohio
45202
513-762-6000
Pres.: Edward L. Hutton

Chicago Bridge & Iron Co.
901 West 22nd St., Hinsdale, Ill.
60521
312-654-1700
Pres.: Marvin G. Mitchell

Christiana Securities Co.
1007 Market St., Wilmington, Del.
19801
302-774-4357
Pres.: Irenee du Pont, Jr.

Chubb Corp.
90 John St., New York, N.Y. 10038
212-964-1200
Chmn. of the Bd. & Pres.: William
W. Rees

Citizens & Southern National Bank
22 Bull St., Savannah, Ga. 31401
912-234-5101
Pres.: Mills B. Lane, Jr.

Cleveland Trust Co.
900 Euclid Ave., Cleveland, Ohio
44101
216-687-5000
Pres.: Everett Ware Smith

Combined Insurance Co. of America
5050 North Broadway, Chicago, Ill.
60640
312-275-8000
Pres.: Matthew T. Walsh

Commerce Clearing House, Inc.
4025 West Peterson Ave., Chicago,
Ill. 60646
312-267-9010
Pres.: Robert C. Bartlett

Connecticut General Insurance Corp.
900 Cottage Grove Rd., Hartford,
Conn. 06115
203-243-8811
Pres.: Henry R. Roberts

Crum & Forster
110 William St., New York, N.Y.
10038
212-233-1100
Pres.: Bobby P. Russell

DeKalb Agresearch, Inc.
Sycamore Rd., DeKalb, Ill. 60115
815-758-3461

Chmn. of the Bd. & Pres.: T. H.
Roberts, Jr.

Deluxe Check Printers, Inc.
2199 North Pascal, St. Paul, Minn.
55113
612-631-1010
Pres.: J. L. Rose

Dow Jones & Co., Inc.
30 Broad St., New York, N.Y.
10004
212-422-3115
Pres.: William F. Kerby

ERC Corp.
21 West 10th St., Kansas City,
Mo. 64105
816-842-9160
Pres.: Stanford Miller

Economics Laboratory, Inc.
370 Wabasha St., St. Paul, Minn.
55102
612-224-4678
Pres.: Edward B. Osborn

Farmers Group, Inc.
4680 Wilshire Blvd., Los Angeles,
Calif. 90005
213-931-1961
Pres.: C. D. Beshears

Farmers New World Life Insurance
9611 Sunset Highway, Mercer
Island, Wash. 98040
206-232-8400
Pres.: R. T. Vonrosenberg

Fidelity Union Life Insurance Co.
1511 Bryan St., Dallas, Tex. 75221
214-741-1921
Chmn. of the Bd. & Pres.: Carr P.
Collins

First Bank System, Inc.
1400 First National Bank,
Minneapolis, Minn. 55402
612-370-5100
Pres.: Donald R. Grangaard

First Connecticut Bancorp, Inc.
101 Pearl St., Hartford, Conn.
06103
203-249-0871
Pres.: James J. Preble

First National Bank in Dallas
1401 Elm St., Dallas, Tex. 75202
214-749-4011
Pres.: W. Dewey Presley

First Pennsylvania Corp.
Packard Bldg. & 15th, Philadelphia,
Pa. 19102
215-786-5000
Pres.: J. R. Bunting, Jr.

Fort Howard Paper Co.
1919 South Broadway, Green Bay,
Wisc. 54305
414-435-8821
Pres.: John P. Cofrin

Franklin Life Insurance Co.
Franklin Square, Springfield, Ill.
62705
217-528-2011
Chmn. of the Bd. & Pres.: George E.
Hatmaker

General Crude Oil Co.
910 Travis St., Houston, Tex. 77001
713-224-9261
Pres.: K. E. Montaque

General Reinsurance Corp.
400 Park Ave., New York, N.Y.
10022
212-751-5800
Pres.: Harold H. Hudson, Jr.

Government Employees Insurance
1705 L St. N.W., Washington, D. C.
20036
202-656-1000
Pres.: Norman L. Gidden

Hoover Co.
101 East Maple St., Canton, Ohio
44720
216-499-9200
Chmn. of the Bd. & Pres.: Felix N.
Mansager

Illinois Bell Telephone Co.
225 West Randolph St., Chicago, Ill.
60606
312-727-9411
Pres.: Charles L. Brown

Interprovincial Pipe Line Co.
7 King St. East, Toronto 1,
Canada
416-362-1343
Pres.: D. G. Waldon

Kemper Construction Co.
3701 Overland Ave., Los Angeles,
Calif. 90034
213-870-4838
Pres.: M. F. Kemper

Liberty National Life Insurance Co.
3rd Ave. South & 20 St.,
Birmingham, Ala. 35202
205-328-0171
Pres.: Frank P. Samford, Jr.

Lowe's Companies, Inc.
Highway 268 East, North Wilkesboro,
N.C. 28659
919-838-2102
Chmn. of the Bd.: Edwin
Duncan, Sr.

Mallinckrodt Chemical Works
3600 North 2nd St., St. Louis,
Mo. 63160
314-231-8980
Chmn. of the Bd. & Pres.: Harold E.
Thayer

Maryland National Corp.
Baltimore & Light, Baltimore, Md.
21202
301-685-3900
Pres.: Tilton H. Dobbin

Medtronic, Inc.
3055 Old Highway 8, Minneapolis,
Minn. 55418
612-781-6061
Pres.: Earl E. Bakken

Mellon National Bank & Trust Co.
Mellon Square, Pittsburgh, Pa.
15230
412-232-4100
Pres.: A. Bruce Bowden

Monarch Capitol Corp.
1250 State St., Springfield, Mass.
01109
413-785-5811
Pres.: Benjamin F. Jones

Monumental Corp.
Northeast Corner Charles, Baltimore,
Md. 21202
301-727-8080
Pres.: Donald H. Wilson, Jr.

NCNB Corp.
200 South Tryon St., Charlotte,
N.C. 28201
704-374-5000
Pres.: Thomas I. Storrs

NLT Corp.
Nashville, Tenn. 37219
615-747-9443
Pres.: Sam F. Fleming

National Bank of Detroit
Woodward at Fort St., Detroit,
Mich. 48232
313-965-6000
Pres.: Robert M. Surdam

National Bank of North America
44 Wall St., New York, N.Y. 11552
212-623-4000
Pres.: John H. Vogel

National City Bank of Cleveland
623 Euclid Ave., Cleveland, Ohio
44114
216-861-4900
Pres.: Claude M. Blair

National Liberty Corp.
20 Moores Rd., Malvern, Pa. 19355
215-647-5000
Pres.: Arthur DeMoss

National Patent Development
375 Park Ave., New York, N.Y.
10022
212-759-4343
Pres.: Jerome I. Feldman

A. C. Nielsen Co.
2101 Howard St., Chicago, Ill.
60645
312-465-4400
Pres.: A. C. Nielsen, Jr.

Northern Trust Co.
50 South LaSalle St., Chicago, Ill.
60690
312-346-5500
Pres.: Douglas R. Fuller

Noxell Corp.
11050 York Rd., Cockeysville, Md.
21030
301-666-2662
Pres.: Norbert A. Witt

Ocean Drilling & Exploration Co.
1600 Canal St., New Orleans, La.
70160
504-529-2811
Pres.: Alden J. Laborde

Ohio Casualty Corp.
136 North 3rd St., Hamilton, Ohio
45011
513-867-3000
Pres.: J. G. Sloneker

PNB Corp.
Northeast Corner Broad &
Chestnut Sts., Philadelphia, Pa.
19101
215-569-2100
Chmn. of the Bd. & Pres.: G. Morris
Dorrance, Jr.

Pabst Brewing Co.
917 West Juneau Ave., Milwaukee,
Wis. 53201
414-271-0230
Pres.: James C. Windham

Pacific Car & Foundry Co.
777 106th Ave. N.E., Bellevue,
Wash. 98009
206-455-0520
Pres.: Charles M. Pigott

Pennsylvania Life Co.
3130 Wilshire Blvd., Santa Monica,
Calif. 90406
213-828-6411
Pres.: Stanley Beyer

Pennzoil Offshore Gas Operator
Southwest Tower, Houston, Tex.
77002
713-228-8741
Pres.: Wm. A. Hover

Peterson Howell & Heather, Inc.
2701 North Charles St., Baltimore,
Md. 21218
301-338-1000
Pres.: John S. Lalley

Pinkerton's, Inc.
100 Church St., New York, N.Y.
10007
212-233-3144
Pres.: Edward J. Bednarz

Pittsburgh National Corp.
1 Oliver Plaza, Pittsburgh, Pa. 15230
412-355-2000
Pres.: Merle E. Gilliand

Provident Life & Accident Insurance
Co.
Fountain Square, Chattanooga,
Tenn. 37402
615-755-1011
Pres.: Henry C. Unruh

Republic National Bank
P. O. Box 5961, Dallas, Tex. 75222
214-749-5000
Pres.: James W. Keay

Richmond Corp.
914 Capitol St., Richmond, Va.
23219
703-644-8561
Pres.: Warren M. Pace

Rich's, Inc.
45 Broad St. S.W., Atlanta, Ga.
30303
404-522-4636
Pres.: Harold Brockey

Roadway Express, Inc.
1077 Gorge Blvd., Akron, Ohio
44309
216-434-1641
Pres.: J. Robert Wilson

Rouse Co.
2 Wincopin Circle, Ellicott City,
Md. 21043
301-730-7700
Pres.: James W. Rouse

Safeco Corp.
4347 Brooklyn Ave. N.E., Seattle,
Wash. 98105
206-633-0622
Pres.: Gordon H. Sweany

St. Paul Companies, Inc.
385 Washington St., St. Paul, Minn.
55102
612-221-7911
Pres.: R. M. Hubbs

R. P. Scherer Corp.
9425 Grinnell Ave., Detroit, Mich.
48213
313-921-3240
Pres.: Robert P. Scherer, Jr.

Seattle-First National Bank
1001 4th Ave., Seattle, Wash. 98124
206-583-3131
Pres.: Robert S. Beaupre

Security Pacific National Bank
561 South Spring St., Los Angeles,
Calif. 90051
213-620-6211
Pres.: Carl E. Hartnack

Seven-Up Co.
121 South Meramec, St. Louis, Mo.
63105
314-VO 3-7777
Pres.: Ben H. Wells

Snap-On-Tools Corp.
8028-28th Ave., Kenosha, Wisc.
53140
414-654-8681
Pres.: R. L. Grover

Southeast Banking Corp.
100 S. Biscayne Blvd., Miami, Fla.
33131
305-377-3411
Pres.: Charles J. Zwick

Southern New England Telephone
227 Church St., New Haven, Conn.
06506
203-771-5200
Pres.: Alfred W. Van Sinderen

Southland Corp.
2828 North Haskell Ave., Dallas,
Tex. 75221
214-824-8121
Pres.: Herbert Hartfelder

Southwestern Life Insurance Co.
Ross & Akard, Dallas, Tex. 75221
214-742-9101
Pres.: William H. Seay

Stirling Homex Corp.
1150 East River Rd., Avon, N.Y.
14414
716-926-2481
Pres.: William Stirling

Tampax, Inc.
5 Dakota Dr., New Hyde Park, N.Y.
11040
516-437-8800
Chmn. of the Bd. & Pres.: Thomas F.
Casey

Tecumseh Products Co.
East Patterson, Tecumseh, Mich.
49236
313-423-7411
Pres.: William E. Macbeth

Transcontinental Gas Pipe Line Corp.
3100 Travis St., Houston, Tex.
77001
713-524-6351
Pres.: James B. Henderson

Transocean Oil, Inc.
Houston National Gas, 17th Floor,
Houston, Tex. 77002

713-225- 0231
Pres.: R. E. Bennett

Valley National Bank of Arizona
141 North Central Ave., Phoenix,
Ariz. 85004
602-261-2900
Pres.: Earl L. Bimson

Washington National Corp.
1630 Chicago Ave., Evanston, Ill.
60201
312-866-7900
Pres.: Stanley P. Hutchinson

Willamette Industries, Inc.
811 Southwest 6th, Portland,
Ore. 97204
503-227-5585
Pres.: Gene D. Knudson

Yellow Freight System, Inc.
92nd and State Line, Kansas City,
Mo. 64114
816-363-3344
Pres.: Don McMorris

24. Major Real Estate Investment Trusts

Information for this section was provided by Mr. Noel Wallis of Steiner, Rouse,
& Co. of New York City.

American Realty Trust
2000 Jefferson Davis Highway,
Arlington, Va. 22207

Atico Mortgage Investors
150 Southeast Third Ave., Miami,
Fla. 33131

Bradley Real Estate Trust
250 Boylston St., Boston, Mass.
02116

C.I. Mortgage Group
1 Boston Plaza, Boston, Mass. 02108

Cameron–Brown Investment Trust
225 Peachtree St. N.E., Atlanta, Ga.
30303

Chase Manhattan Mortgage & Realty
Trust
60 State St., Boston, Mass. 02109

Citizens Mortgage Investment Trust
24700 Northwestern Highway,
Southfield, Mich. 48075

City Investing Mortgage Trust
980 Madison Ave., New York, N.Y.
10021

Clevetrust Realty Investors
1525 Investment Plaza, Cleveland,
Ohio 44144

Colwell Mortgage Trust
3223 W. 6th St., Los Angeles, Calif.
90005

Cousins Mortgage & Equity Investments
300 Interstate North, Atlanta, Ga.
30339

Denver Real Estate Investment Assn.
650 17th St., Denver, Colo. 80202

First Fidelity Investment Trust
25 East 12th St., Kansas City, Mo.
64106

First General Resources Co.
505 Park Ave., New York, N.Y.
10022

First Union Real Estate Equity &
Mortgage Investments
55 Public Square, Suite 1650, Cleveland, Ohio 44113

Greenfield Real Estate Investment
Trust
2118 Two Girard Plaza, Philadelphia,
Pa. 19102

Guardian Mortgage Investors
47 West Forsyth St., Jacksonville,
Fla. 32202

Gulf Mortgage & Realty Investments
225 Franklin St., Boston, Mass.
02110

Heitman Mortgage Investors
225 Franklin St., Boston, Mass.
02110

Kavanau Real Estate Trust
30 East 42nd St., New York, N.Y.
10017

Larwin Mortgage Investors
9100 Wilshire Blvd., Beverly Hills,
Calif. 90212

Lomas & Mettleton Mortgage Investors
1111 Hartford Bldg., Dallas, Tex.
75201

Midland Mortgage Investors Trust
1421 North Broadway, Santa Ana,
Calif. 92706

Mony Mortgage Investors
10 Post Office Square, Boston, Mass.
02109

B.C. Morton Realty Trust
22 East 40th St., New York, N.Y.
10016

North American Mortgage Investors
249 Washington St., Boston, Mass.
02108

Pennsylvania Real Estate Investment
Trust
Cedarbrook Hill 111, Wyncote, Pa.
19095

Prudent Resources Trust
245 Great Neck Rd., Great Neck,
N.Y. 11021

Real Estate Investment Trust of
America
294 Washington St., Boston, Mass.
02108

Riviere Realty Trust
1832 M St. N.W., Washington, D.C.
20036

B.F. Saul Real Estate Investment Trust
925 15th St. N.W., Washington, D.C.
20005

Security Mortgage Investors
1720 Peachtree Rd. N.W., Atlanta,
Ga. 30309

State Mutual Investors
440 Lincoln St., Worcester, Mass.
01650

Sutro Mortgage Investment Trust
4900 Wilshire Blvd., Los Angeles,
Calif. 90005

Washington Real Estate Investment
Trust
919 18th St. N.W., Washington, D.C.
20006

Wells Fargo Mortgage Investors
P.O. Box 30015, Terminal Annex,
Los Angeles, Calif. 90030

MAJOR CORPORATIONS

25. Major Equipment Leasing Companies

American Pacesetter
650 S. Spring St., Los Angeles, Calif.
90014
213-625-5784

Banister Continental Corp.
9001 Bloomington Freeway,
Minneapolis, Minn. 55420
612-884-9286

Barrington Industries, Inc.
666 Fifth Ave., New York, N.Y.
10019
212-581-8080

Boothe Computer Corp.
555 California St., San Francisco,
Calif. 94104
415-989-6580

CIC Leasing
Statler Hilton Bldg., Buffalo, N.Y.
14202
716-854-2480

CIT Financial Corp.
650 Madison Ave., New York, N.Y.
10022
212-572-6500

Coburn Corp. of America
100 Merrick Rd., Rockville Centre,
N.Y. 11570
516-764-2800

Computer Complex, Inc.
5051 Westheimer Rd., Houston, Tex.
77027
713-681-4891

Computer Investors Group, Inc.
200 Myrtle Ave., Larchmont, N.Y.
10538
914-834-7700

Consolidated Leasing Corp. of America
69 West Washington St., Chicago,
Ill. 60603
312-346-9142

Drew National Leasing Corp.
555 Fifth Ave., New York, N.Y.
10017
212-986-0600

Equity Enterprises
40 West 15th St., New York, N.Y.
10011
212-243-1316

Faness Industries, Inc.
27 Weyman Ave. New Rochelle,
N.Y. 10805
914-632-6501

Feld Leasing Co.
2210 South 7th St., St. Louis,
Mo. 63104
816-842-4383

Gilbert-Flexi-Van Corp.
330 Madison Ave., New York, N.Y.
10017
212-682-4160

Greyhound Computer Corp.
Greyhound Tower, Phoenix, Ariz.
85007
602-248-2900

Greyhound Leasing & Financial Corp.
10 South Riverside Plaza, Chicago,
III. 60606
312-372-9800

Hudson Leasing Corp.
1 Linden Pl., Great Neck, N.Y.
11021
516-487-8610

Industrial Leasing Corp.
2300 Southwest Sixth Ave.,
Portland, Oreg. 97201
503-228-2111

Liberty Leasing Co.
221 N. LaSalle St., Chicago, III.
60601
312-726-6061

MAI Equipment Corp.
300 East 44th St., New York,
N.Y. 10017
212-557-3500

McCullagh Leasing, Inc.
30803 Little Mack, Roseville,
Mich. 48066
313-294-7800

NCC Industries, Inc.
299 Park Ave., New York, N.Y.
10017
212-758-9060

Nationwide Industries, Inc.
1603 Orrington Ave., Evanston, III.
60201
312-866-6050

Nicholas Land & Leasing Co.
2940 North Hollywood Way,
Burbank, Calif. 91503
213-842-5171

Pepsico, Inc.
Purchase, N.Y. 10577
914-253-2000

Pullman, Inc.
200 S. Michigan Ave., Chicago, III.
60604
312-939-4262

Russeks, Inc.
6550 East Washington Blvd., Los
Angeles, Calif. 90022
213-723-6321

Saunders Leasing System, Inc.
201 Office Park Dr., Birmingham,
Ala. 35223
205-879-2131

Scientific Resources Corp.
7320 Old York Rd., Philadelphia, Pa.
19126
215-635-5100

Sea Containers, Inc.
345 Park Ave., New York, N.Y.
10022
212-486-1824

Sherwood Diversified Services
277 Park Ave., New York, N.Y.
10017
212-759-7400

James Talcott, Inc.
1290 Ave. of the Americas, New
York, N.Y. 10019
212-956-3000

U.S. Leasing International
633 Battery St., San Francisco,
Calif. 94111
415-397-6464

26. Major Public Franchise Companies

Barbizon Corp.
475 Fifth Ave., New York, N.Y.
10017
212-684-5720
Pres.: Gerald Ritter
Franchise: Modeling and self-improvement schools

H&R Block, Inc.
4410 Main St., Kansas City,
Mo. 64111
816-531-6400
Pres.: Henry W. Bloch
Franchise: Tax service

Chock Full O Nuts Corp.
425 Lexington Ave., New York, N.Y.
10017
Chmn. of the Bd.: William Black
Franchise: Restaurants

Coast to Coast Stores Central
Organization
7500 Excelsior Blvd., Minneapolis,
Minn. 55426
213-235-4161
Pres.: Eric Emergon
Franchise: Hard goods retail stores

Consolidated Foods Corp.
135 South LaSalle St., Chicago, Ill.
60603
312-726-6414
Pres.: William Teets
Franchise: Chicken Delight take-out
foods

Culligan International Co.
1 Culligan Parkway, Northbrook, Ill.
60062
312-498-2000
Pres.: Thomas J. Culligan, Jr.
Franchise: Water conditioning and
supplies

Denny's Restaurants, Inc.
14256 Firestone Blvd., La Mirada,
Calif. 90638
213-625-2126
Pres.: Robert W. Eberle

Downtowner Motor Inns, Inc.
150-202 Union Ave., Memphis,
Tenn. 38101
901-527-6311
Chmn. of the Bd.: Robert L.
Kirkpatrick

Dunkin Donuts, Inc.
Pacella Industrial Park, Box 317,
Randolph, Mass. 02368
617-961-4000
Pres.: Robert M. Rosenberg

Firestone Tire & Rubber Co.,
1200 Firestone Parkway, Akron,
Ohio 44317
216-379-7000
Pres.: Robert D. Thomas
Franchise: Auto supplies and service

Gamble–Skogmo, Inc.
5100 Gamble Dr., Minneapolis,
Minn. 55440
612-374-6123
Pres.: James A. Watson
Franchise: "House of Fabrics"
retail sales of fabrics

B.F. Goodrich Co.
500 South Main St., Akron, Ohio
44318
216-379-2000
Pres.: H.B. Warner
Franchise: Rayco, Inc. auto
accessories and supplies

Goodway Copy Centers, Inc.
11401 Roosevelt Blvd., Philadelphia,
Pa. 19154
Pres.: Donald L. Wolk
Franchise: Quick-copy centers

Goodyear Tire & Rubber Co.
1144 East Market St., Akron, Ohio
44316
216-794-2121
Pres.: Victor Holt, Jr.
Franchise: Tire sales and service

Hardees Food Systems, Inc.
1233 North Church St., Rocky
Mount, N.C. 27801
919-446-5141
Pres.: J. Leonard Rawis, Jr.
Franchise: Restaurants—short menus

Harvest Food Markets, Inc.
2050 Elmwood Ave., Buffalo, N.Y.
14207
716-874-4410
Pres.: Jacob Ablove

Henry's Drive-In, Inc.
1 East Wacker Dr., Chicago, Ill.
60601
312-321-1900
Pres.: Anthony S. DeRosa
Franchise: Drive-in fast food

Holiday Inns of America, Inc.
3742 Lamar Ave., Memphis, Tenn.
38118
901-362-4001
Pres.: William S. Walton

Household Finance Corp.
Prudential Plaza, Chicago, Ill.
60601
312-944-7174
Pres.: A. W. Rasmussen

Howard Johnson's Corp.
1 Howard Johnson Plaza, Boston,
Mass. 02125
617-848-2350
Pres.: Howard B. Johnson

Jewel Companies, Inc.
5725 East River Rd., Chicago, Ill.
60631
312-693-6000
Pres.: Weston R. Christopherson
Franchise: White-Hen Pantry Stores—
convenience food stores

Kelly Services, Inc.
16130 Northland Dr., Southfield,
Mich. 48075
313-352-4000
Pres.: T. E. Adderley
Franchise: Temporary employment
services

Kentucky Fried Chicken Corp.
1441 Gardiner Lane, Louisville, Ky.
40213
502-459-8600
Chmn. of the Bd.: John Y. Brown

Lawn-A-Mat Chemical & Equipment
Corp.
153 Jefferson Ave., Mineola, N.Y.
11501
516-CH 8-7887
Pres.: Daniel Dorfman
Franchise: Lawn care services

Lum's, Inc.
5050 Biscayne Blvd., Miami, Fla.
33137
305-759-8701
Pres.: Melvin Chasen
Franchise: Fast food restaurants

McDonald's Corp.
McDonald's Plaza, Oak Brook, Ill.
60521
312-986-1600
Pres.: Fred L. Turner
Franchise: McDonald's Restaurants—
hamburgers and fast food

McGraw–Edison Co.
333 West River Rd., Elgin, Ill.
60120
312-741-8900
Pres.: Raymond H. Giesecke
Franchise: Self-laundry and dry-
cleaning stores

Manpower, Inc.
820 North Plankinton Ave., Milwaukee, Wisc. 53203
414-272-8510
Pres.: Elmer L. Winter
Franchise: Temporary employment
services

Mansfield Tire & Rubber Co.
515 Newman St., Mansfield, Ohio
44901
419-522-4111
Pres.: James H. Hoffman
Franchise: Auto tire sales

Midas International, Inc.
33 North Dearborn St., Chicago, Ill.
60602
312-782-4433
Pres.: Nathan H. Sherman
Franchise: Auto muffler service

Mr. Sandwich, U.S.A.
2 West 45th St., New York, N.Y.
10036
212-867-5750
Pres.: Thomas Michaels
Franchise: Fast food

Mr. Swiss of America, Inc.
1111 East Commerce, Oklahoma
City, Okla. 73129
405-677-8731
Pres.: Wendell R. Thompson
Franchise: Soft ice cream, sandwich
shops, restaurants, and art galleries

Mutual Enterprises, Inc.
120 Wells Ave., Newton, Mass.
02159
617-969-0400
Pres.: David B. Slater
Franchise: Sandwich restaurants

O. K. Tire & Rubber Co.
1400 Winchester Ave., Ashland, Ky.
41101
606-324-1111
Pres.: Walter A. Ketron
Franchise: Auto tire sales and service

Olin-Matheson Chemical Corp.
275 Winchester Ave., New Haven,
Conn. 06511
Pres.: Gordon Grand
Franchise: Skeet and trap shooting
ranges

Ply Gem Industries, Inc.
182-20 Liberty Ave., Jamaica, N.Y.
11412
212-454-5400
Pres.: Albert Hersch
Franchise: Paneling centers

Robo Wash, Inc.
2 East Gregory, Kansas City, Mo.
64114

816-333-8885
Pres.: Ralph C. Hedges
Franchise: Automatic car washes

Earl Schieb, Inc.
8737 Wilshire Blvd., Beverly Hills,
Calif. 90211
213-652-4880
Chmn. of the Bd.: Earl Schieb
Franchise: Auto painting centers

Snap-On Tools Corp.
8028 28th Ave., Kenosha, Wisc.
53140
414-654-8681
Pres.: R. L. Grover
Franchise: Mechanics' hand tools and
equipment

Stuckey's, Inc.
U.S. Highway 23 South, Eastman, Ga.
31023
912-374-4381
Pres.: James W. Spradley
Franchise: Fast food restaurants

Taco-Si, Inc.
1160 Cranston St., Providence, R.I.
02920
401-942-8000
Pres.: John Hazen White
Franchise: Mexican food

Travelodge Motel Corp.
250 South Cuyamaca, El Cajon,
Calif. 92022
714-442-0311
Pres.: Kenneth E. Cocks

David Wade Industries
11111 North Central Expressway,
Dallas, Tex. 75231
214-363-2578
Pres.: Kevin B. Halter
Franchise: Restaurant endorsement
program

Walter Kidde & Co., Inc.
9 Brighton Rd., Clifton, N.J.
07012
201-777-6500
Chmn. of the Bd.: Fred R. Sullivan
Franchise: FSE security systems

Western Auto Supply Co.
2107 Grand Ave., Kansas City, Mo.
64108
816-421-6700
Pres.: L. A. Fults

White Stores, Inc.
3910 Call Field Rd., Wichita Falls,
Tex. 76308
817-692-3410

Pres.: W. Dean Stewart
Franchise: Auto supplies, appliances,
and hardware stores

Witt Tax Service
107-29 71st Ave., Forest Hills, N.Y.
11375
212-261-1313
Pres.: Mr. Witt

27. Largest Conglomerate Companies

AMF, Inc.
261 Madison Ave., New York, N.Y.
10016
212-687-3100
Pres.: John L. Tullis
V.P. Comptroller: W. Thomas York
Gross sales in millions: 636

AMFAC, Inc.
700 Bishop St., Honolulu, Hawaii
96801
808-546-8111
Pres.: H. A. Walker, Jr.
Senior V.P Finance: E. Laurence Gay
Gross sales in millions: 408

A-T-O, Inc.
4420 Sherwin Rd., Willoughby, Ohio
44094
216-946-9000
Pres.: John J. Tanis
V.P. Treas. Finance: Richard
Patterson
Gross sales in millions: 356

AVCO Corp.
1275 King St., Greenwich, Conn.
06830
203-552-1800
Pres.: James R. Kerr
V.P.: Comptroller: Alan S. Berk
Gross sales in millions: 758

Alco Standard Corp.
Rt. 363 East/South Schuylkill,
Valley Forge, Pa. 19481
215-666-0760

Pres.: Myron S. Gelbach, Jr.
Treas.: O. Gordon Brewer, Jr.
Gross sales in millions: 456

Glen Alden Corp.
888 7th Ave., New York, N.Y.
10019
212-957-8700
Pres.: Paul A. Johnston
V.P. Treas. Finance: D. Irving Obrow
Gross sales in millions: 100

Allied Products Corp.
208 South LaSalle St., Chicago, Ill.
60604
312-236-8278
Pres.: Saul S. Sherman
Senior V.P. Finance Admin.: Richard
F. Doyle
Gross sales in millions: 197

American Standard, Inc.
40 West 40th St., New York, N.Y.
10018
212-484-5100
Pres.: William A. Marquard, Jr.
Comptroller: James P. Sears
Gross sales in millions: 1418

Bangor Punta Corp.
1 Greenwich Plaza, Greenwich,
Conn. 06830
203-661-3900
Pres.: David W. Wallace
V.P. Treas. Admin.: Thomas D.
Stephenson
Gross sales in millions: 294

Brunswick Corp.
  69 West Washington St., Chicago, Ill.
    60602
  312-341-7000
  Chmn. of the Bd. & Pres.: John L.
    Hanigan
  V.P. Finance: Arthur R. Cahill
  Gross sales in millions: 450

Chromalloy-American Corp.
  120 Broadway, New York, N.Y.
    10005
  212-227-3775
  Pres.: Richard P. Seelig
  V. Chmn. of the Bd. Finance: Frank
    P. Nykiel
  Gross sales in millions: 371

City Investing Co.
  767 Fifth Ave., New York, N.Y.
    10022
  212-759-5300
  Pres.: George T. Scharffenberger
  V.P. Finance: Daniel E. Lyons
  Gross sales in millions: 581

Colt Industries, Inc.
  430 Park Ave., New York, N.Y.
    10022
  212-980-3500
  Pres.: David I. Margolis
  V.P. Treas. Finance: Kenneth A.
    Wulff
  Gross sales in millions.: 665

Dart Industries, Inc.
  8480 Beverly Blvd., Los Angeles,
    Calif. 90048
  213-658-2000
  Chmn. of the Bd. & Pres.: Justin W.
    Dart
  Comptroller: William R. Palmer
  Gross sales in millions: 703

Dayco Corp.
  333 West 1st St., Dayton, Ohio
    45401
  513-461-3700
  Chmn. of the Bd. & Pres.: Richard J.
    Jacob
  V.P. Finance Admin.: A. E. Grill
  Gross sales in millions: 321

FMC Corp.
  1105 Coleman Ave., San Jose, Calif.
    95110
  408-289-0111
  Pres.: Jack M. Pope
  V.P. Comptroller: W. Douglas
    Wallace
  Gross sales in millions: 1330

Fuqua Industries, Inc.
  2 Peachtree St. N.W., Atlanta, Ga.
    30303
  404-521-0204
  Pres.: Carl L. Patrick
  V.P. Finance: James A. Goese
  Gross sales in millions: 324

GAF Corp.
  140 West 51st St., New York, N.Y.
    10020
  212-582-7600
  Chmn. of the Bd. & Pres.: Dr. Jesse
    Werner
  Comptroller: W. Richard Margerm
  Gross sales in millions: 599

W. R. Grace & Co.
  3 Hanover Square, New York, N.Y.
    10004
  212-344-1200
  Pres.: Felix E. Larkin
  V.P. Comptroller: A. E. Bollengier
  Gross sales in millions: 1918

Gulf & Western Industries, Inc.
  1 Gulf & Western Plaza, New York,
    N.Y. 10023
  212-333-7000
  Pres.: David N. Judelson
  V.P. Treas.: Norman R. Forson
  Gross sales in millions: 1620

Illinois Central Industries
  135 East 11th Pl., Chicago, Ill.
    60605
  312-939-5313
  Chmn. of the Bd. & Pres.: William B.
    Johnson
  V.P. Finance: George K. Weigel
  Gross sales in millions: 754

Indian Head, Inc.
111 West 40th St., New York, N.Y.
10018
212-695-1260
Pres.: Robert W. Lear
V.P. Treas.: William J. Rust
Gross sales in millions: 414

International Telephone & Telegraph
320 Park Ave., New York, N.Y.
10022
212-752-6000
Chmn. of the Bd. & Pres.: Harold S.
Geneen
Exec. V.P. Finance: Hart Perry
Gross sales in millions: 6364

International Utilities
1500 Walnut St., Philadelphia, Pa.
19102
215-985-6600
Pres.: John M. Seabrook
V.P. Comptroller: James J. Burke
Gross sales in millions: 25

Walter Kidde & Co., Inc.
9 Brighton Rd., Clifton, N.J.
07012
201-777-6500
Chmn. of the Bd. & Pres.: Fred R.
Sullivan
Senior V.P. Finance: James J. Brown
Gross sales in millions: 818

Kinney National Services
10 Rockefeller Plaza, New York,
N.Y. 10020
212-586-0800
Pres.: Steven J. Ross
V.P. Comptroller: Bert W.
Wasserman
Gross sales in millions: 514

Lear Siegler, Inc.
3171 South Bundy Dr., Santa
Monica, Calif. 90406
213-391-0666
Pres.: Robert T. Campion
Comptroller: David Louks
Gross sales in millions: 566

Ling-Temco-Vought, Inc.
1600 Elm St., Dallas, Tex. 75222
214-742-9555

Chmn. of the Bd. & Pres.: Paul
Thayer
V.P. Comptroller: H. M. Eitel
Gross sales in millions: 3709

Litton Industries, Inc.
360 North Crescent Dr., Beverly
Hills, Calif. 90210
213-273-7860
Pres.: Roy L. Ash
Senior V.P. Finance Affairs: Joseph
T. Casey
Gross sales in millions: 2400

Martin Marietta Corp.
277 Park Ave., New York, N.Y.
10017
212-826-5050
Pres.: George M. Bunker
Treas. Comptroller: Robert J.
Norris
Gross sales in millions: 941

Midland–Ross Corp.
55 Public Square, Cleveland, Ohio
44113
216-771-4800
Pres.: Harry J. Bolwell
V.P. Finance: E. C. Gendron
Gross sales in millions: 254

National Industries, Inc.
510 West Broadway, Louisville, Ky.
40202
502-583-7602
Chmn. of the Bd. & Pres.: Stanley R.
Yarmuth
V.P. Finance: Donald G. McClinton
Gross sales in millions: 375

National Service Industries
1180 Peachtree N.E., Atlanta, Ga.
30309
404-892-2400
Pres.: Erwin Zaban
V.P. Treas.: Eugene F. McManus
Gross sales in millions: 319

Northwest Industries, Inc.
400 West Madison St., Chicago, Ill.
60606
312-263-4200
Pres.: Ben W. Heineman
V.P. Finance: Paul J. Weir
Gross sales in millions: 480

Ogden Corp.
161 East 42nd St., New York, N.Y.
10017
212-972-2200
Pres.: M. Lee Rice
Comptroller: Robert DiGia
Gross sales in millions: 1136

SCM Corp.
299 Park Ave., New York, N.Y.
10017
212-752-2700
Chmn. of the Bd. & Pres.: Emerson E.
Mead
V.P. Comptroller: Herbert H. Egli
Gross sales in millions: 854

Signal Companies, Inc.
1010 Wilshire Blvd., Los Angeles,
Calif. 90017
213-482-0722
Pres.: Forrest N. Shumway
Comptroller: Robert J. Runser
Gross sales in millions: 1487

Singer Co.
30 Rockefeller Plaza, New York,
N.Y. 10020
212-581-4800
Chmn. of the Bd. & Pres.: Donald P.
Kircher
Senior V.P. Finance: Donald G.
Robbins, Jr.
Gross sales in millions: 2100

Studebaker–Worthington, Inc.
530 Fifth Ave., New York, N.Y.
10036
212-697-2345
Pres.: Leslie T. Welsh
Comptroller: Bernard P. Lauber
Gross sales in millions: 858

Sybron Corp.
1100 Midtown Tower, Rochester,
N.Y. 14604
716-546-4040
Pres.: William G. vonBerg
V.P. Treas. Finance: Stephen R.
Hardis
Gross sales in millions: 333

TRW, Inc.
23555 Euclid Ave., Cleveland, Ohio,
44117

216-383-2121
Pres.: Dr. R. F. Mettler
V.P. Finance: Charles R. Allen
Gross sales in millions: 1580

Teledyne, Inc.
1901 Ave. of Stars, Los Angeles,
Calif. 90067
213-277-3311
Pres.: George A. Roberts
Treas.: Jerrold V. Jerome
Gross sales in millions: 1216

Tenneco, Inc.
1010 Milan, Houston, Tex. 77001
713-229-2131
Pres.: N. V. Freeman
Exec. V.P. Finance: R. E. McGee
Gross sales in millions: 2525

Textron, Inc.
10 Dorrance St., Providence, R.I.
02903
401-521-3500
Pres.: George William Miller
Exec. V.P. Finance Admin.: Joseph
B. Collinson
Gross sales in millions: 1612

Transamerica Corp.
701 Montgomery St., San Francisco,
Calif. 94111
415-982-2330
Chmn. of the Bd. & Pres.: John R.
Beckett
V.P. Comptroller: Gary L. Depolo
Gross sales in millions: 1400

Universal Oil Products Co.
30 Algonquin Rd., Des Plaines, Ill.
60016
312-824-1155
Pres.: John O. Logan
V.P. Treas. Finance: Frank Wyatt
Gross sales in millions: 494

U.S. Industries, Inc.
250 Park Ave., New York, N.Y.
10017
212-697-4141
Pres.: Charles E. Selecman
Comptroller Accounting: Frank J.
Tanzola
Gross sales in millions: 1232

White Consolidated Industries, Inc.
11770 Berea Rd., Cleveland, Ohio
44111
216-252-3700
Pres.: William H. Johnson
Comptroller: Robert Drainville
Gross sales in millions: 709

Whittaker Corp.
10880 Wilshire Blvd., Los Angeles,
Calif. 90024
213-475-9411
Pres.: Joseph F. Alibrandi
Senior V.P. Finance: Harry S. Derby-
shire
Gross sales in millions: 793

28. Fifty Largest Insurance Companies

Acacia Mutual Life Insurance Co.
51 Louisiana Ave. N.W., Washington,
D.C. 20001
202-628-4506
Chmn. of the Bd. & Pres.: Daniel L.
Hurson

Aetna Life Insurance Co.
151 Farmington Ave., Hartford,
Conn. 06115
203-273-0123
Pres.: Donald M. Johnson

American National Insurance Co.
Moody Ave. at Market, Galveston,
Tex. 77550
713-763-4661
Chmn. of the Bd. Pres.: Phil B. Noah

Bankers Life Co.
711 High St., Des Moines, Iowa
50307
515-284-5111
Pres.: H. G. Allen

Connecticut General Life Insurance
Co.
Hartford, Conn. 06115
203-242-4422
Pres.: Henry R. Roberts

Connecticut Mutual Life Insurance
140 Garden St., Hartford, Conn.
06115
203-249-0631
Pres.: Edward B. Bates

Continental Assurance Co.
310 South Michigan Ave., Chicago,
Ill. 60604

312-822-5000
Pres.: Jacque W. Sammet

Equitable Life Assurance Society U.S.
1285 Ave. of Americas, New York,
N.Y. 10019
212-554-1234
Pres.: J. Henry Smith

Equitable Life Insurance Co. of Iowa
604 Locust St., Des Moines, Iowa
50306
515-284-6911
Pres.: K. R. Austin

Fidelity Mutual Life Insurance Co.
Parkway at Fairmount, Philadelphia,
Pa. 19101
215-765-6500
Pres.: Elmer L. Nicholson

Franklin Life Insurance Co.
Franklin Square, Springfield, Ill.
62705
217-582-2011
Chmn. of the Bd. & Pres.: George E.
Hatmaker

General American Life Insurance Co.
1501 Locust St., St. Louis, Mo.
63166
314-231-1700
Pres.: Armand C. Stainaker

Guardian Life Insurance Co. of
America
Park Ave. South at 17th, New York,
N.Y. 10003
212-473-3000
Pres.: George T. Conklin, Jr.

Home Life Insurance Co.
253 Broadway, New York, N.Y.
10007
212-233-6400
Pres.: Gerald K. Rugger

Jefferson Standard Life Insurance Co.
P.O. Box 21008, Greensboro, N.C.
27420
919-378-2011
Pres.: W. Roger Soles

John Hancock Mutual Life Insurance
Co.
200 Berkeley St., Boston, Mass.
02117
617-421-6000
Pres.: Frank B. Maher

Kansas City Life Insurance Co.
3520 Broadway, Kansas City, Mo.
64111
816-753-7000
Pres.: J. R. Bixby

Liberty National Life Insurance
3rd Ave. South & 20th, Birmingham,
Ala. 35233
205-328-0171
Pres.: Frank P. Samford, Jr.

Life & Casualty Insurance of Tennessee
Life & Casualty Tower, Nashville,
Tenn. 37219
615-254-1511
Senior V.P.: Kenneth Ward-Smith

Life Insurance Co. of Virginia
914 Capitol St., Richmond, Va.
23209
703-644-8561
Pres.: Warren M. Pace

Lincoln National Life Insurance Co.
1301 South Harrison, Fort Wayne,
Ind. 46801
219-742-5421
Pres.: Thomas A. Watson

Massachusetts Mutual Life Insurance
1295 State St., Springfield, Mass.
01101
413-788-8411
Pres.: James R. Martin

Metropolitan Life Insurance Co.
1 Madison Ave., New York, N.Y.
10010
212-578-2211
Pres.: Richard R. Shinn

Minnesota Mutual Life Insurance Co.
345 Cedar St., St. Paul, Minn. 55101
612-224-5544
Exec. V.P.: Coleman Bloomfield

Mutual Benefit Life Insurance Co.
520 Broad St., Newark, N.J. 07101
201-624-6600
Pres.: John J. Magovern, Jr.

Mutual Life Insurance Co. of New
York
1740 Broadway, New York, N.Y.
10019
212-586-4000
Pres.: J. McCall Hughes

National Life & Accident Insurance
National Life Center, Nashville,
Tenn. 37203
615-747-9000
Pres.: William C. Weaver, Jr.

National Life Insurance Co.
Washington County, Montpelier, Vt.
05602
802-223-3431
Pres.: John T. Fey

Nationwide Life Insurance Co.
246 North High St., Columbus, Ohio
43216
614-228-4711
Pres.: Dean W. Jeffers

New England Mutual Life Insurance
551 Boylston St., Boston, Mass.
02117
617-266-3700
Pres.: Abram T. Collier

New York Life Insurance Co.
51 Madison Ave., New York, N.Y.
10010
212-576-7000
Pres.: R. Manning Brown, Jr.

Northwestern Mutual Life Insurance
Co.
720 East Wisconsin Ave., Milwaukee,
Wisc. 53202
414-276-3320
Pres.: Francis E. Ferguson

Northwestern National Life Insurance
Co.
20 Washington Ave., Minneapolis,
Minn. 55440
612-372-5432
Pres.: Harry E. Atwood

Occidental Life Insurance Co. of
California
Box 2101 Terminal Annex, Los
Angeles, Calif. 90054
213-748-8111
Pres.: Earl Clark CLU

Pacific Mutual Life Insurance
Pacific Mutual Bldg., Los Angeles,
Calif. 90054
213-625-1211
Pres.: Stanton G. Hale

Penn Mutual Life Insurance Co.
Independence Square, Philadelphia,
Pa. 19105
215-925-7300
Pres.: Charles R. Tyson

Phoenix Mutual Life Insurance Co.
1 American Row, Hartford, Conn.
06115
203-278-1212
Pres.: Lyndes B. Stone

Provident Life & Accident Insurance
Fountain Square, Chattanooga, Tenn.
37402
615-265-2525
Pres.: Henry C. Unruh

Provident Mutual Life Insurance
Philadelphia
Northwest Corner 46th & Market,
Philadelphia, Pa. 19101
215-474-7000
Pres.: Edward L. Stanley

Prudential Insurance Co. of America
Prudential Plaza, Newark, N.J.
07101
201-336-1234
Pres.: Kenneth C. Foster

Southland Life Insurance Co.
Southland Center, Dallas, Tex.
75201
214-741-1321
Pres.: James B. Goodson

Southwestern Life Insurance Co.
1807 Ross Ave., Dallas, Tex.
75221
214-742-9101
Pres.: William H. Seay

State Farm Life Insurance Co.
State Farm Insurance Bldg.,
Bloomington, Ill. 61701
309-967-6123
Pres.: Edward B. Rust

State Mutual Life Assurance of
America
Worcester, Mass. 01605
617-798-8111
Pres.: W. Douglas Bell

Teachers Insurance Annuity Assn.
of America
730 Third Ave., New York, N.Y.
10017
212-697-7600
Pres.: Thomas C. Edwards, Jr.

Travelers Insurance Co.
Hartford, Conn. 06115
203-277-0111
Pres.: Roger C. Wilkins

Union Central Life Insurance Co.
P.O. Box 179, Cincinnati, Ohio
45201
513-825-1880
Chmn. of the Bd. & Pres.: John A.
Lloyd

United Benefit Life Insurance Co.
33rd & Farnam, Omaha, Nebr.
68131
402-342-7450
Pres.: Gale E. Davis

Washington National Insurance Co.
1630 Chicago Ave., Evanston, Ill.
60201
312-475-7900
Pres.: R. W. Friedner

Western & Southern Life Insurance
400 Broadway, Cincinnati, Ohio
45202
513-421-1800
Pres.: William C. Safford

29. Five Hundred Largest Corporations

ACF Industries, Inc.
750 Third Ave., New York, N.Y.
10017
212-986-8600
Pres.: Henry A. Correa

AMF, Inc.
261 Madison Ave., New York,
N.Y. 10016
212-687-3100
Pres.: John L. Tullis

AMP, Inc.
Eisenhower Blvd., Harrisburg, Pa.
17105
717-564-0101
Pres.: Samuel S. Auchincloss

A-T-O, Inc.
4420 Sherwin Rd., Willoughby, Ohio
44094
216-946-9000
Pres.: James H. Goss

Abbott Laboratories
1400 Sheridan Rd., North Chicago,
Ill. 60064
312-338-1600
Pres.: Henry J. Atwood

Addressograph-Multigraph Corp.
1200 Babbitt Rd., Cleveland, Ohio
44117
216-731-8000
Pres.: William H. Wilson

Admiral Corp.
3800 Cortland St., Chicago, Ill.
60647
312-292-2600
Pres.: Ross D. Siragusa, Jr.

Agway, Inc.
333 Butternut Dr., Dewitt, N.Y.
13214
315-477-7061
Pres.: Jonathan F. Davis

Air Products & Chemicals, Inc.
Trexlertown, Pa. 18087
215-395-4911
Pres.: Edward J. Donley

Air Reduction Co.
AIRCO, 150 East 42nd St., New
York, N.Y. 10017
212-682-6700
Pres.: George S. Dillon

Akzona, Inc.
Asheville, N.C. 28802
704-253-6851
Pres.: Claude Ramsey

Alberto-Culver Co.
2525 Armitage Ave., Melrose Park,
Ill. 60160
312-345-6300
Pres.: Leonard H. Lavin

Alco Standard Corp.
Rt. 363 at E/S Schuykill, Valley
Forge, Pa. 19481
215-666-0300
Pres.: Myron S. Gelbach, Jr.

Allegheny Ludlum Industries
537 Smithfield St., Pittsburgh, Pa.
15222
412-261-5300
Pres.: Roger S. Ahibrandt

Allied Chemical
1411 Broadway, New York, N.Y.
10018
212-422-7300
Pres.: Frederick L. Bissinger

Allied Mills, Inc.
110 North Wacker Dr., Chicago, Ill.
60606
312-346-5060
Pres.: Roy E. Folck, Jr.

Allied Products Corp.
208 South LaSalle St., Chicago, Ill.
60650
312-236-8278
Pres.: Saul S. Sherman

Allis-Chalmers Manufacturing Co.
1205 South 70th St., Milwaukee,
Wisc. 53201
414-475-2000
Chmn. of the Bd. & Pres.: David C.
Scott

Aluminum Co. of America
1501 Alcoa Bldg., Pittsburgh, Pa.
15219
412-553-4545
Pres.: W. H. Krome George

Amerada Hess Corp.
51 West 51st St., New York, N.Y.
10019
212-581-2910
Pres.: A. T. Jacobson

American Bakeries Co.
10 South Riverside Pl., Chicago, Ill.
60606
312-645-7400
Chmn. of the Bd. & Pres.: L. Arthur
Cushman, Jr.

American Beef Packers, Inc.
7000 West Center Rd., Omaha,
Nebr. 68106
402-391-4700
Exec. V.P.: Darrell R. Golden

American Brands, Inc.
245 Park Ave., New York, N.Y.
10017
212-557-7000
Pres.: Robert K. Heimann

American Can Co.
American Lane, Greenwich, Conn.
06830
203-552-2000
Chmn. of the Bd. & Pres.: William
F. May

American Chain & Cable Co.
929 Conn. Ave., Bridgeport, Conn.
06602
202-335-2511
Exec. V.P.: Edward C. Mabbs

American Cyanamid Co.
Berdan Ave., Wayne, N.J. 07470
201-831-1234
Pres.: Clifford D. Siverd

American Hoist & Derrick Co.
63 South Robert St., St. Paul,
Minn. 55107
612-224-4646
Pres.: John E. Carroll

American Home Products Corp.
685 Third Ave., New York, N.Y.
10017
212-986-1000
Exec. V.P.: Herbert W. Blades

American Metal Climax, Inc.
1270 Ave. of Americas, New York,
N.Y. 10020
212-757-9700
Pres.: Donald J. Donahue

American Motors Corp.
14250 Plymouth Rd., Detroit, Mich.
48232
313-493-2000
Pres.: William V. Luneburg

American Petrofina, Inc.
50 Rockefeller Plaza, New York,
N.Y. 10020
212-586-8510
Pres.: Richard I. Galland

American Smelting & Refining Co.
120 Broadway, New York, N.Y.
10005
212-732-9500
Pres.: C. F. Barber

American Standard, Inc.
40 West 40th St., New York, N.Y.
10018
212-695-5600
Pres.: W. D. Eberle

Ampex Corp.
401 Broadway, Redwood City,
Calif. 94063
415-367-2011
Pres.: William E. Roberts

Amstar Corp.
120 Wall St., New York, N.Y. 10005
212-944-7500
Pres.: William F. Oliver

Amsted Industries, Inc.
3700 Prudential Plaza, Chicago, Ill.
60601
312-645-1700
Pres.: Goff Smith

Anaconda Co.
25 Broadway, New York, N.Y.
10004
212-422-6300
Pres.: John G. Hall

Anchor Hocking Corp.
109 North Broad St., Lancaster,
Ohio 43130
614-653-3131
Pres.: John L. Gushman

Anderson Clayton & Co.
1010 Milam St., Houston, Tex.
77002
713-224-6641
Pres.: T. J. Barlow

Anheuser-Busch, Inc.
721 Pestalozzi St., St. Louis, Mo.
63118
314-577-0577
Exec. V.P.: R. A. Meyer

Arcata National Corp.
2750 Sand Hill Rd., Menlo Park,
Calif. 94025
415-854-5222
Pres.: Robert O. Dehlendorf, II

Archer-Daniels Midland Co.
4666 Faries Parkway, Decatur, Ill.
62525
217-423-2571
Pres.: Lowell W. Andreas

Armco Steel Corp.
703 Curtis St., Middletown, Ohio
45042
513-425-6541
Pres.: Calvin William Verity

Armour-Dial, Inc.
111 East Wacker Dr., Chicago, Ill.
60601
312-751-5000
Pres.: David L. Duensing

Armstrong Cork Co.
Liberty & Charlotte Sts., Lancaster,
Pa. 17604
717-397-0611
Pres.: J. H. Binns

Armstrong Rubber Co.
500 Sargent Dr., New Haven, Conn.
06507
203-777-7401
Pres.: Frank L. Dwyer

Arvin Industries, Inc.
East 13th St. & Big 4 R.R.,
Columbus, Ind. 47201
812-372-7271
Pres.: Eugene I. Anderson

Ashland Oil, Inc.
1409 Winchester Ave., Ashland,
Ky. 41101
606-324-1111
Chmn. Exec. Comm. & Pres.: Orin E.
Atkins

Athlone Industries, Inc.
767 Fifth Ave., New York, N.Y.
10022
212-425-6550
Chmn. of the Bd. & Pres.: Harold J.
Miller

Atlantic Richfield Co.
717 Fifth Ave., New York, N.Y.
10022
212-758-2345
Pres.: T. F. Bradshaw

Automation Industries, Inc.
1901 Bldg., Century City, Los
Angeles, Calif. 90067
213-879-2222
Chmn. of the Bd. & Pres.: Corwin D.
Denney

Avco Corp.
1275 King St., Greenwich, Conn.
06830
203-552-1800
Pres.: James R. Kerr

Avnet, Inc.
Time & Life Bldg., New York, N.Y.
10022
212-246-5033
Pres.: Simon Sheib

Avon Products, Inc.
30 Rockefeller Plaza, New York,
N.Y. 10020
212-757-3780
Pres.: Fred G. Fusee

Babcock & Wilcox Co.
161 East 42nd St., New York,
N.Y. 10017
212-687-6700
Pres.: George G. Zipf

Bangor Punta Corp.
1 Greenwich Plaza, Greenwich,
Conn. 06830
203-861-3900
Pres.: David W. Wallace

E. T. Barwick Industries, Inc.
5025 New Peachtree, Chamblee,
Ga. 30341
404-451-4761
Pres.: B. A. Talley

Bath Industries, Inc.
2100 North Mayfair Rd., Milwaukee,
Wisc. 53226
414-778-2100
Pres.: William P. Kyle, Jr.

Baxter Laboratories, Inc.
6301 Lincoln Ave., Morton Grove,
Ill. 60053
312-267-6900
Pres.: William B. Graham

Beatrice Foods Co.
120 South LaSalle St., Chicago,
Ill. 60603
312-782-3820
Pres.: William G. Karnes

Becton Dickinson & Co.
Rutherford, N.J. 07070
201-939-9000
Senior V.P.: William S. Little

Beech Aircraft Corp.
9709 East Central, Wichita,
Kans. 67201
316-685-6211
Pres.: Frank E. Hedrick

Bell & Howell Co.
7100 McCormick Rd., Chicago,
Ill. 60645
312-262-1600
Chmn. of the Bd. & Pres.: Peter G.
Peterson

Bemis Co.
800 Northstar Center, Minneapolis,
Minn. 55402
612-332-7151
Pres.: Judson Bemis

Bendix Corp.
Bendix Center, Southfield, Mich.
48075
313-352-6300
Chmn. of the Bd. & Pres.: A. P.
Fontaine

Bethlehem Steel Corp.
701 East Third St., Bethlehem,
Pa. 18016
215-694-2424
Pres.: Stewart S. Cort

Black & Decker Manufacturing Co.
Joppa Rd., Baltimore, Md. 21204
301-828-3900
Chmn. of the Bd. & Pres.: Alonzo G.
Decker, Jr.

Blue Bell, Inc.
335 Church St., Greensboro, N.C.
27401
919-275-9392
Pres.: Rodger S. LeMatty

Boeing Co.
7735 East Marginal Way South,
  Seattle, Wash. 98124
206-656-2121
Pres.: T. A. Wilson

Boise Cascade Corp.
114 South 10th St., Boise,
  Idaho 83701
208-385-9000
Chmn. of the Bd. & Pres.: Robert V.
  Hansberger

Borden, Inc.
350 Madison Ave., New York,
  N.Y. 10017
212-573-4000
Chmn. of the Bd. & Pres.: Augustine
  R. Marusi

Borg-Warner Corp.
200 South Michigan Ave., Chicago,
  Ill. 60604
312-663-2111
Pres.: James F. Bere

Briggs & Stratton Corp.
3300 North 124th St., Milwaukee,
  Wisc. 53222
414-461-1212
Pres.: C. L. Coughlin

Bristol-Myers Co.
345 Park Ave., New York, N.Y.
  10020
212-644-2100
Pres.: Richard L. Gelb

Brockway Glass Co.
McCullough Ave., Brockway, Pa.
  15824
814-268-3015
Pres.: P. Stuart Holmquest

Brown Shoe Co.
8300 Maryland Ave., St. Louis, Mo.
  63105
314-863-2000
Pres.: W. L. H. Griffin

Brunswick Corp.
69 West Washington St., Chicago,
  Ill. 60602
312-341-7000
Pres.: John L. Hanigan

Budd Co.
2450 Hunting Park Ave.,
  Philadelphia, Pa. 19132
215-225-9100
Pres.: Philip W. Scott

Bunker-Ramo Corp.
1200 Harger Rd., Oakbrook North,
  Hinsdale, Ill. 60521
312-654-3100
Pres.: George S. Trimble

Burlington Industries, Inc.
301 North Eugene St., Greensboro,
  N.C. 27401
919-379-2000
Pres.: Ely R. Callaway, Jr.

Burroughs Corp.
Second Ave., Burroughs, Detroit,
  Mich. 48232
313-972-7000
Pres.: Ray W. Macdonald

CPC International, Inc.
International Plaza, Englewood, N.J.
  07632
201-894-4000
Pres.: James W. McKee, Jr.

Cabot Corp.
125 High St., Boston, Mass. 02110
617-423-6000
Pres.: Robert A. Charpie

Campbell Soup Co.
375 Memorial Ave., Camden, N.J.
  08101
609-964-4000
Pres.: William B. Murphy

Campbell Taggart Associated Bakeries
6211 Lemmon Ave., Dallas, Tex.
  75221
214-352-4861
Pres.–Treas.: C. B. Lane

Cannon Mills Co.
P.O. Box 107, Kannapolis, N.C.
  28081
704-933-1221
Pres.: Don S. Holt

Capitol Industries
1750 North Vine St., Los Angeles,
Calif. 90028
213-462-6251
Pres.: Stanley M. Gortikov

Carborundum Co.
Buffalo at Portage, Niagara Falls,
N.Y. 14303
716-278-2000
Pres.: William H. Wendell

Carnation Co.
5045 Wilshire Blvd., Los Angeles,
Calif. 90036
213-931-1911
Pres.: H. Everett Olson

Carpenter Technology Corp.
101 West Bern St., Reading, Pa.
19601
215-372-4511
Pres.: John Moxon

Carrier Corp.
Carrier Parkway, Syracuse, N.Y.
13201
315-463-8411
Pres.: Charles V. Henn

Castle & Cooke, Inc.
130 Merchant St., Honolulu,
Hawaii 96802
808-548-6611
Pres.: Malcolm MacNaughton

Caterpillar Tractor Co.
100 Northeast Adams St., Peoria,
Ill. 61602
309-675-1000
Pres.: W. H. Franklin

Ceco Corp.
5601 West 26th St., Chicago, Ill.
60650
312-242-2000
Pres.: George R. Wernisch

Celanese Corp.
522 Fifth Ave., New York, N.Y.
10036
212-867-2000
Pres.: John W. Brooks

Central Soya Co.
1300 Fort Wayne National Bank
Bldg., Fort Wayne, Ind. 46802
219-422-8541
Pres.: Dale W. McMillen, Jr.

Cerro Corp.
300 Park Ave., New York, N.Y.
10022
212-688-8822
Pres.: C. Gordon Murphy

Certain-Teed Products Corp.
Valley Forge, Pa. 19481
215-687-5000
Chmn. of the Bd. & Pres.: Malcolm
Meyer

Cessna Aircraft Co.
5800 East Pawnee, Wichita, Kans.
67201
316-685-9111
Pres.: Delbert L. Roskam

Champion Spark Plug Co.
900 Upton Ave., Toledo, Ohio
43601
419-536-3711
Chmn. of the Bd. & Pres.: Robert A.
Stranahan, Jr.

Chemetron Corp.
840 North Michigan Ave., Chicago,
Ill. 60611
312-944-3100
Chmn. of the Bd. & Pres.: John P.
Gallagher

Chesebrough-Pond's, Inc.
485 Lexington Ave., New York,
N.Y. 10017
212-697-4900
Pres.: Ralph E. Ward

Chicago Bridge & Iron Co.
901 West 22nd St., Hinsdale, Ill.
60521
312-654-1700
Pres.: Marvin G. Mitchell

Chromalloy-American Corp.
120 Broadway, New York, N.Y.
10005
212-227-3775
Pres.: Richard P. Seelig

Chrysler Corp.
341 Massachusetts Ave., Detroit,
Mich. 48231
313-956-5252
Pres.: John J. Riccardo

Cincinnati Millacron, Inc.
4701 Marburg Ave., Cincinnati, Ohio
45209
513-475-8100
Pres.: James A. D. Geier

Cities Service Co.
60 Wall St., New York, N.Y. 10005
212-422-1600
Pres.: J. Edgar Heston

City Investing Co.
767 Fifth Ave., New York, N.Y.
10022
212-759-5300
Pres.: George T. Scharffenberger

Clark Equipment Co.
324 East Dewey, Buchanan, Mich.
49107
616-697-8000
Pres.: Bert E. Phillips

Clark Oil & Refining Corp.
8530 West National Ave.,
Milwaukee, Wisc. 53227
414-321-5100
Pres.: Emory T. Clark

Cluett Peabody & Co.
510 Fifth Ave., New York, N.Y.
10036
212-697-6100
Pres.: Henry H. Henley, Jr.

Coastal States Gas Producing
200 Petroleum Tower, Corpus
Christi, Tex. 78403
512-883-5211
Chmn. of the Bd. & Pres.: Oscar S.
Wyatt, Jr.

Coca-Cola Co.
515 Madison Ave., New York, N.Y.
10022
212-355-5475
Chmn. of the Bd. & Pres.: J. Paul
Austin

Colgate-Palmolive
300 Park Ave., New York, N.Y.
10022
212-751-1200
Pres.: David R. Foster

Collins & Aikman Corp.
210 Madison Ave., New York, N.Y.
10016
212-689-3900
Pres.: Albert Laughey

Collins Radio Co.
1200 North Alma Rd., Richardson,
Tex. 75080
214-235-9511
Chmn. of the Bd. & Pres.: Arthur A.
Collins

Colt Industries, Inc.
430 Park Ave., New York, N.Y.
10022
212-980-3500
Pres.: David I. Margolis

Combustion Engineering, Inc.
277 Park Ave., New York, N.Y.
10017
212-826-7100
Pres.: A. J. Santry, Jr.

Commercial Metals Co.
3000 Diamond Park Dr., Dallas,
Tex. 75247
214-631-4120
Pres.-Treas.: Charles W. Merritt

Commonwealth Oil Refining Co., Inc.
200 Park Ave., New York, N.Y.
10017
212-986-6191
Pres.: S. B. Casey

Cone Mills Corp.
Fourth & Maple Sts., Greensboro,
N.C. 27405
919-379-6220
Pres.: Lewis S. Morris

Consolidated Foods Corp.
135 South LaSalle St., Chicago, Ill.
60603
312-726-6414
Chmn. of the Bd. & Pres.: William A.
Buzick, Jr.

Continental Can Co.
633 Third Ave., New York, N.Y.
10017
212-551-7700
Chmn. of the Bd. & Pres.: Ellison L.
Hazard

Continental Oil Co.
30 Rockefeller Plaza, New York,
N.Y. 10020
212-586-2510
Pres.: John G. McLean

Control Data Corp.
8100 34th Ave. South, Minneapolis,
Minn. 55420
612-888-5555
Chmn. of the Bd. & Pres.: William C.
Norris

Cooper Industries, Inc.
2410 First City National Bank Bldg.,
Houston, Tex. 77002
713-224-9181
Chmn. of the Bd. & Pres.: E. L.
Miller

Corning Glass Works
Corning, N.Y. 14830
607-962-4444
Pres.: R. Lee Waterman

Crane Co.
300 Park Ave., New York, N.Y.
10022
212-752-3600
Pres.: Dante C. Fabiani

Crowell Collier & Macmillan
866 Third Ave., New York, N.Y.
10022
212-935-2000
Chmn. of the Bd. & Pres.: Raymond
C. Hagel

Crown Central Petroleum Corp.
1 North Charles St., Baltimore,
Md. 21203
301-539-7400
Pres.: Henry A. Rosenberg, Jr.

Crown Cork & Seal Co.
9300 Ashton Rd., Philadelphia,
Pa. 19136
215-673-5100

Chmn. of the Bd. & Pres.: John F.
Connelly

Crown Zellerbach Corp.
1 Bush St., San Francisco, Calif.
94119
415-981-1700
Pres.: C. R. Dahl

Cudahy Co.
100 West Clarendon Ave., Phoenix,
Ariz. 85013
602-264-7272
Pres.: Elias Paul

Cummins Engine Co.
1000 5th St., Columbus, Ind. 47201
812-372-7211
Pres.: H. B. Schacht

Curtiss-Wright Corp.
1 Passaic St., Wood-Ridge, N.J.
07075
201-777-2900
Chmn. of the Bd. & Pres.: T. Roland
Berner

Cutler-Hammer, Inc.
4201 North 27th St., Milwaukee,
Wisc. 53216
414-442-7800
Pres.: Donald M. Miller

Cyclops Corp.
650 Washington Rd., Pittsburgh,
Pa. 15228
412-343-4000
Pres.: William G. Stewart

Dairylea Cooperative, Inc.
1250 Broadway, New York, N.Y.
10001
212-594-4200
Pres.: Lester W. Martin

Dan River, Inc.
Box 6126 Sta. B, Greenville, S.C.
29606
803-242-5950
Pres.: Robert S. Small

Dana Corp.
4100 Bennett Rd., Toledo, Ohio
43601
419-479-8241
Pres.: Rene C. McPherson

Dart Industries, Inc.
  8480 Beverly Blvd., Los Angeles,
  Calif. 90048
  213-658-2000
  Chmn. of the Bd. & Pres.: Justin W.
  Dart

Dayco Corp.
  333 West 1st St., Dayton, Ohio
  45401
  513-461-3700
  Pres.: Richard J. Jacob

De Soto, Inc.
  1700 South Mt. Prospect Rd., Des
  Plaines, Ill. 60018
  312-296-6611
  Chmn. of the Bd. & Pres.: Bernard
  A. Malm

Deere & Co.
  John Deere Rd., Moline, Ill. 61265
  309-792-8000
  Pres.: Ellwood F. Curtis

Del Monte Corp.
  215 Fremont St., San Francisco,
  Calif. 94119
  415-781-7760
  Chmn. of the Bd. & Pres.: Alfred W.
  Earnes, Jr.

Diamond International, Inc.
  733 Third Ave., New York, N.Y.
  10017
  201-697-1700 .
  Pres.: Richard J. Walters

Diamond Shamrock Corp.
  300 Union Commerce, Cleveland,
  Ohio 44115
  216-621-6100
  Pres.: James A. Hughes

Di Giorgio Corp.
  1 Maritime Plaza, San Francisco,
  Calif. 94101
  415-362-8972
  Pres.: Robert DiGiorgio

Diversified Industries, Inc.
  7701 Forsyth, St. Louis, Mo. 63105
  314-862-8200
  Chmn. of the Bd.: Ben Fixman

R. R. Donnelley & Sons Co.
  2223 M. Luther King Dr., Chicago,
  Ill. 60616
  312-431-8000
  Pres.: Charles W. Lake, Jr.

Dow Chemical Co.
  Midland, Mich. 48640
  517-636-1000
  Chmn. Exec. Comm. & Pres.:
  Herbert D. Doan

Dresser Industries, Inc.
  3000 Republic National Bank Bldg.,
  Dallas, Tex. 75221
  214-748-6411
  Pres.: John V. James

E. I. DuPont DeNemours & Co.
  1007 Market St., Wilmington,
  Del. 19898
  302-774-2421
  Chmn. of the Bd.: Lammot Dupont
  Copeland

ESB Inc.
  5 Penn Center Plaza, Philadelphia,
  Pa. 19103
  215-564-4030
  Pres.: Edward J. Dwyer

Eagle-Picher Industries, Inc.
  American Bldg., Cincinnati, Ohio
  45202
  513-721-7010
  Pres.: William D. Atteberry

Easco Corp.
  201 North Charles St., Baltimore,
  Md. 21201
  301-837-9550
  Pres.: Richard P. Sullivan

Eastern Gas & Fuel Associates
  2900 Prudential, Boston, Mass.
  02199
  617-262-3500
  Pres.: Eli Goldston

Eastman Kodak Co.
  343 State St., Rochester, N.Y.
  14650
  716-325-2000
  Chmn. of the Bd.: Louis K. Eilers

Eaton Yale & Towne, Inc.
100 Erieview Plaza, Cleveland, Ohio
44114
216-523-5000
Pres.: William A. Mattie

Peter Eckrich & Sons, Inc.
1025 Osage St., Fort Wayne, Ind.
46801
219-742-8159
Pres.-Treas.: Donald Eckrich

Eltra Corp.
2 Pennsylvania Pl., New York, N.Y.
10001
212-695-1600
Pres.: J. A. Keller

Emerson Electric Co.
8100 Florissant Ave., St. Louis, Mo.
63136
314-261-1800
Pres.: Edward L. O'Neill

Emhart Corp.
31 Tobey Rd., Bloomfield, Conn.
06002
203-242-8551
Pres.: T. Mitchell Ford

Essex International, Inc.
1601 Wall St., Fort Wayne, Ind.
46804
219-743-0311
Pres.: Paul W. O'Malley

Ethyl Corp.
330 South 4th St., Richmond,
Va. 23219
703-644-6081
Pres.: Bruce C. Gottwald

Evans Products Co.
1121 Southwest Salmon St.,
Portland, Oreg. 97208
503-222-5592
Chmn. of the Bd. & Pres.: Monford
A. Orloff

Ex-Cell-O Corp.
P.O. Box 386, Detroit, Mich. 48232
313-868-3900
Pres.: E. J. Giblin

FMC Corp.
1105 Coleman Ave., San Jose, Calif.
95110
408-289-0111
Pres.: Jack M. Pope

Fairchild Camera & Instrument Corp.
464 Ellis St., Mountain View, Calif.
94040
415-962-5011
Pres.: C. Lester Hogan

Fairchild Hiller Corp.
Fairchild Dr., Germantown, Md.
20767
301-948-9600
Pres.: Edward G. Uhl

Fairmont Foods Co.
3201 Farnam St., Omaha, Nebr.
68131
402-345-9500
Pres.: Gordon Ellis

Farmers Union Central Exchange, Inc.
1185 North Concord South, St.
Paul, Minn. 55075
612-455-8571
Pres.: Norval Ellefson

Farmland Industries, Inc.
3315 North Oak Trafficway, Kansas
City, Mo. 64116
816-453-1400
Pres.: Ernest T. Lindsey

Fedders Corp.
Edison, N.J. 08817
201-549-7200
Chmn. of the Bd.: Salvatore
Giordano

Federal Co.
2900 Sterick Bldg., Memphis, Tenn.
38101
901-525-7382
Chmn. of the Bd. & Pres.: William L.
Taylor

Federal- Mogul Corp.
26555 Northwestern Highway,
Southfield, Mich. 48075
313-353-6700
Chmn. of the Bd. & Pres.: Samuel E.
MacArthur

Fibreboard Corp.
   55 Francisco St., San Francisco,
   Calif. 94133
   415-362-6900
   Pres.: George W. Burgess

Fieldcrest Mills, Inc.
   Eden, N.C. 27288
   919-623-2123
   Chmn. of the Bd. & Pres.: G. William
   Moore

Firestone Tiré & Rubber Co.
   1200 Firestone Parkway, Akron,
   Ohio 44317
   216-379-7000
   Pres.: Robert D. Thomas

Flintkote Co.
   400 Westchester Ave., White Plains,
   N.Y. 10604
   914-761-7400
   Pres.: George J. Pecaro

Ford Motor Co.
   American Rd., Dearborn, Mich.
   48121
   313-322-3000
   Chmn. of the Bd.: Henry Ford II

Foster Wheeler Corp.
   110 South Orange Ave., Livingston,
   N.J. 07039
   201-533-1100
   Pres.: E. F. Wentworth, Jr.

Fruehauf Corp.
   10900 Harper Ave., Detroit, Mich.
   48232
   313-921-2410
   Pres.: William E. Grace

Fuqua Industries, Inc.
   2 Peachtree St. N.W., Atlanta, Ga.
   30303
   404-521-0204
   Pres.: Carl L. Patrick

GAF Corp.
   140 West 51st St., New York, N.Y.
   10020
   212-582-7600
   Chmn. of the Bd. & Pres.: Dr. Jesse
   Werner

Gardner-Denver Co.
   Gardner Expressway, Quincy, Ill.
   62301
   217-222-5400
   Chmn. of the Bd. & Pres.: Cedric H.
   Rieman

General American Transportation
   Corp.
   120 South Riverside Plaza, Chicago,
   Ill. 60680
   312-621-6200
   Pres.: J. R. Scanlin

General Cable Corp.
   730 Third Ave., New York, N.Y.
   10017
   212-986-3800
   Pres.: Donald N. Frey

General Dynamics Corp.
   1 Rockefeller Plaza, New York,
   N.Y. 10020
   212-245-5000
   Chmn. of the Bd. & Pres.: Roger
   Lewis

General Electric Co.
   570 Lexington Ave., New York,
   N.Y. 10022
   212-750-2000
   Chmn. of the Bd.: Fred J. Botch

General Foods Corp.
   250 North St., White Plains, N.Y.
   10602
   914-694-2500
   Pres.: Arthur E. Larkin, Jr.

General Host Corp.
   245 Park Ave., New York, N.Y.
   10017
   212-661-5300
   Pres.: Edward H. Hoornstra

General Instrument Corp.
   65 Gouveneur St., Newark, N.J.
   07104
   201-485-2100
   Chmn. of the Bd.: Moses Shapiro

General Mills, Inc.
   9200 Wayzata Blvd., Minneapolis,
   Minn. 55440
   612-540-2311
   Pres.: James Summer

General Motors Corp.
3044 West Grand Blvd., Detroit,
Mich. 48202
313-556-5000
Pres.: Edward N. Cole

General Refractories Co.
1520 Locust St., Philadelphia, Pa.
19102
215-735-2000
Pres.: Joseph E. Moran

General Signal Corp.
280 Park Ave., New York, N.Y.
10017
212-752-1000
Pres.: Harold A. Strickland, Jr.

General Telephone & Electronics
Corp.
730 Third Ave., New York, N.Y.
10017
212-551-1000
Pres.: Leslie H. Warner

General Tire & Rubber Co.
1 General St., Akron, Ohio 44309
216-798-3000
Pres.: M. G. O'Neill

Genesco, Inc.
111 7th Ave. North, Nashville,
Tenn. 37202
615-747-7000
Pres.: J. Owen Howell

Georgia-Pacific Corp.
900 Southwest Fifth Ave., Portland,
Ore. 97204
503-222-5561
Pres.: William H. Hunt

Gerber Products Co.
445 State St., Fremont, Mich.
49412
606-928-2000
Pres.: John C. Suerth

Getty Oil Co.
3810 Wilshire Blvd., Los Angeles,
Calif. 90054
213-381-7151
Pres.: J. Paul Getty

Gillette Co.
Prudential Tower Bldg., Boston,
Mass. 02199
617-261-8500
Chmn. of the Bd. & Pres.: Vincent
C. Ziegler

Gold Kist, Inc.
3348 Peachtree Rd. North, Atlanta,
Ga. 30301
404-237-2251
Pres.: Warren P. Sewell

B. F. Goodrich Co.
500 South Main St., Akron, Ohio
44318
216-379-2000
Pres.: H. B. Warner

Goodyear Tire & Rubber Co.
1144 East Market St., Akron, Ohio
44316
216-794-2121
Pres.: Victor Holt, Jr.

Gould, Inc.
P.O. Box 3140, St. Paul, Minn.
55101
612-452-1500
Pres.: William T. Ylvisaker

W. R. Grace & Co.
7 Hanover Square, New York, N.Y.
10005
201-344-1200
Pres.: J. Peter Grace

Granite City Steel Co.
20th & State St., Granite City, Ill.
62040
618-452-1100
Pres.: Lyle F. Gulley

Great Northern Nekoosa Corp.
522 Fifth Ave., New York, N.Y.
10036
212-682-5984
Chmn. of the Bd. & Pres.: Peter S.
Paine

Great Western United Corp.
730 17th St. Equitable Bldg.,
Denver, Colo. 80202
303-893-4300

Chmn. of the Bd. & Pres.: William
M. White

Green Giant Co.
1200 Commerce St., Le Sueur,
Minn. 56058
612-665-3515
Pres.: C. J. Tempas

Greyhound Corp.
10 South Riverside Plaza, Chicago,
Ill. 60606
312-346-7560
Pres.: Raymond F. Shaffer

Grolier, Inc.
575 Lexington Ave., New York,
N.Y. 10022
212-741-3600
Pres.: W. J. Murphy

Grumman Corp.
South Oyster Bay Rd., Bethpage,
N.Y. 11714
516-575-0574
Pres.: L. J. Evans

Gulf Oil Corp.
439 7th Ave., Pittsburgh, Pa. 15219
412-391-2400
Pres.: B. R. Dorsey

Gulf & Western Industries, Inc.
1 Gulf & Western Plaza, New York,
N.Y. 10023
212-333-7000
Pres.: David N. Judelson

Hammermill Paper Co.
East Lake Rd., Erie, Pa. 16512
814-456-8811
Pres.: Albert F. Duval

Hanes Corp.
7000 Hanes Mill Rd., Winston-
Salem, N.C. 27102
919-767-3200
Chmn. of the Bd. & Pres.: Gordon
Hanes

Hanna Mining Co.
100 Erieview Plaza, Cleveland, Ohio
44114
216-523-3111
Pres.: Walter A. Marting

Harris-Intertype Corp.
55 Public Square, Cleveland, Ohio
44113
216-861-7900
Pres.: Richard B. Tullis

Harsco Corp.
350 Poplar Church Rd., Camp Hill,
Pa. 17011
717-233-8771
Pres.: Julius G. Underwood

Hart Schaffner & Marx
36 South Franklin St., Chicago, Ill.
60606
312-372-6300
Pres.: Jerome S. Gore

H. J. Heinz Co.
1062 Progress St., Pittsburgh, Pa.
15230
412-231-5700
Pres.: R. Burt Gookin

Hercules, Inc.
910 Market St., Wilmington, Del.
19899
302-656-9811
Pres.: Werner C. Brown

Hershey Foods Corp.
19 East Chocolate Ave., Hershey,
Pa. 17033
717-533-2121
Pres.: H. S. Mohler

Heublein, Inc.
330 New Park Ave., Hartford, Conn.
06101
203-233-4461
Pres.: Stuart D. Watson

Hewlett-Packard Co.
1501 Page Mill Rd., Palo Alto, Calif.
94304
415-326-7000
Pres.: William R. Hewlett

Hobart Manufacturing Co.
World Headquarters Ave., Troy,
Ohio 45373
513-335-7171
Pres.: David B. Meeker

Hoerner Waldorf Corp.
2250 Wabash Ave., St. Paul, Minn.
55114
612-645-0131
Pres.: J. H. Myers

Honeywell, Inc.
2701 4th Ave. South, Minneapolis,
Minn. 55408
612-332-5200
Pres.: Stephen F. Keating

Hoover Ball & Bearing Co.
135 East Bennett St., Saline, Mich.
48176
313-429-2552
Pres.: John F. Daly

Hoover Co.
101 East Maple St., North Canton,
Ohio 44720
216-499-9200
Chmn. of the Bd. & Pres.: Felix N.
Mansager

George A. Hormel & Co.
501 16th Ave. N.E., Austin, Minn.
55912
507-437-5611
Pres.: I. J. Holton

Houdaille Industries, Inc.
1 M & T Plaza, Buffalo, N.Y. 14203
716-854-3456
Chmn. of the Bd. & Pres.: Gerald C.
Saltarelli

Howmet Corp.
475 Steamboat Rd., Greenwich,
Conn. 06830
203-661-4600
Pres.: Andre Jacomet

Hygrade Food Products Corp.
11801 Mack Ave., Detroit, Mich.
48214
313-821-4100
Pres.: Richard T. Berg

Hyster Co.
2902 Northeast Clackamas St.,
Portland, Ore. 97208
503-288-5011
Pres.: Philip S. Hill

I-T-E Imperial Corp.
1900 Hamilton St., Philadelphia,
Pa. 19130
215-561-1500
Pres.: William C. Musham

Illinois Central Industries, Inc.
135 East 11th Pl., Chicago, Ill.
60605
312-922-4811
Chmn. of the Bd. & Pres.: William B.
Johnson

Indian Head, Inc.
111 West 40th St., New York, N.Y.
10018
212-695-1260
Pres.: Robert W. Lear

Ingersoll-Rand Co.
11 Broadway, New York, N.Y. 10004
212-797-2700
Pres.: D. Wayne Hallstein

Inland Container Corp.
120 East Market St., Indianapolis,
Ind. 46206
317-639-2411
Pres.: Henry C. Goodrich

Inland Steel Co.
30 West Monroe St., Chicago, Ill.
60603
312-346-0300
Pres.: Frederick G. Jaicks

Inmont Corp.
1133 Ave. of the Americas, New
York, N.Y. 10036
212-765-1100
Pres.: William R. Barrett, Sr.

Insilco Corp.
1000 Research Parkway, Meriden,
Conn. 06450
203-238-2381
Pres.: Durand B. Blatz

Instrument Systems Corp.
410 Jericho Turnpike, Jericho,
N.Y. 11753
516-822-4200
Chmn. of the Bd. & Pres.: Edward J.
Garrett

Interco, Inc.
1509 Washington Ave., St. Louis,
Mo. 63166
314-241-5045
Pres.: John K. Riedy

Interlake, Inc.
310 South Michigan Ave., Chicago,
Ill. 60604
312-663-1700
Pres.: R. C. MacDonald

International Business Machines Corp.
Armonk, N.Y. 10504
914-765-1900
Pres.: T. Vincent Learson

International Harvester Co.
401 North Michigan Ave., Chicago,
Ill. 60611
312-527-0200
Pres.: Brooks McCormick

International Minerals & Chemical
5401 Old Orchard Rd., Skokie, Ill.
60076
312-966-3000
Pres.: Richard A. Lenon

International Multifoods Corp.
1200 Investors Bldg., Minneapolis,
Minn. 55402
612-339-8444
Pres.: William G. Phillips

International Paper Co.
220 East 42nd St., New York, N.Y.
10017
212-682-7500
Pres.: Edward B. Hinman

International Telephone & Telegraph
320 Park Ave., New York, N.Y.
10022
212-752-6000
Chmn. of the Bd. & Pres.: Harold S.
Geneen

International Utilities of U.S.
1500 Walnut St., Philadelphia, Pa.
19102
215-985-6600
Chmn. of the Bd. & Pres.: John M.
Seabrook

Interpace Corp.
260 Cherry Hill Rd., Parsippany,
N.J. 07054
201-335-1111
Pres.: Hugh F. Kennison

Interstate Brands Corp.
12 East Armour Blvd., Kansas City,
Mo. 64111
816-561-6600
Pres.: E. B. Hueter

Iowa Beef Processors, Inc.
P. O. Box 248, Dakota City, Neb.
68731
402-494-2061
Pres.: Roy Lee, Jr.

Johns-Manville Corp.
22 East 40th St., New York,
N.Y. 10016
212-532-7600
Pres.: Clinton B. Burnett

Johnson & Johnson
501 George St., New Brunswick,
N.J. 08903
201-524-0400
Pres.: R. B. Sellars

Johnson Service Co.
507 East Michigan St., Milwaukee,
Wisc. 53202
414-276-9200
Pres.: Frederick L. Brengel

Jonathan Logan, Inc.
3901 Liberty Ave., North Bergen,
N.J. 07047
212-695-4440
Pres.: Stephen Ross

Joy Manufacturing Co.
535 Smithfield St., Pittsburgh, Pa.
15222
412-471-2140
Pres.: James W. Wilcock

Kaiser Aluminum & Chemical Corp.
300 Lakeside Dr., Oakland, Calif.
94604
415-271-2211
Pres.: Thomas J. Ready

Kaiser Steel Corp.
300 Lakeside Dr., Oakland, Calif.
94612
415-271-2211
Pres.: Jack J. Carlson

Kane-Miller Corp.
355 Lexington Ave., New York,
N.Y. 10017
212-687-3920
Pres.: Daniel Kane

Kayser-Roth Corp.
640 Fifth Ave., New York, N.Y.
10019
212-757-9600
Pres.: Alfred P. Slaner

Keebler Co.
677 Larch Ave., Elmhurst, Ill.
60126
312-379-1525
Pres.: George M. Keller, Jr.

Kellogg Co.
235 Porter St., Battle Creek, Mich.
49016
616-962-5151
Pres.: Joseph E. Lonning

Kellwood Co.
9909 Clayton Rd., St. Louis, Mo.
63124
314-994-9200
Chmn. of the Bd. & Pres.: Fred W.
Wenzel

Kelsey-Hayes Co.
38481 Huron River Dr., Romulus,
Mich. 48174
313-941-2000
Pres.: Wilfred D. Mac Donnell

Kendall Co.
225 Franklin St., Boston, Mass.
02110
617-482-3030
Chmn. of the Bd. & Pres.: Harold T.
Marshall

Kennecott Copper Corp.
161 East 42nd St., New York,
N.Y. 10017
212-687-5800
Pres.: Frank R. Milliken

Kerr-McGee Corp.
Kerr-McGee Bldg., Oklahoma
City, Okla. 73102
405-236-1313
Pres.: Frank C. Love

Keystone Consolidated Industries, Inc.
411 Hamilton Blvd., Peoria, Ill.
61602
309-676-8000
Chmn. of the Bd. & Pres.: Walton B.
Sommer

Walter Kidde & Co.
9 Brighton Rd., Clifton, N.J. 07012
201-759-5000
Pres.: Maurice M. Rosen

Kimberly-Clark Corp.
North Lake St., Neenah, Wisc.
54956
414-722-3311
Pres.: Darwin E. Smith

Knight Newspapers, Inc.
44 East Exchange St., Akron,
Ohio 44308
216-253-4515
Pres.: Lee Hills

Koehring Co.
780 North Water, Milwaukee,
Wisc. 53202
414-273-2300
Pres.: Orville R. Mertz

Koppers Co.
430 Seventh Ave., Pittsburgh, Pa.
15219
412-391-3300
Pres.: Douglas Grymes

Kraftco Corp.
260 Madison Ave., New York, N.Y.
10016
212-686-6100
Pres.: William O. Beers

Land O'Lakes, Inc.
2215 Kennedy St. N.E., Minneapolis,
Minn. 55413
612-331-6330
Pres.: Dan Holtz

Lear Siegler, Inc.
3171 South Bundy Dr., Santa
Monica, Calif. 90406
213-391-0666
Chmn. of the Bd. & Pres.: John G.
Brooks

Lever Brothers Co.
390 Park Ave., New York, N.Y.
10022
212-688-6000
Pres.: Thomas S. Carroll

Levi Strauss & Co.
98 Battery St., San Francisco,
Calif. 94106
415-391-4200
Pres.: Walter A. Haas, Jr.

Libbey–Owens Ford Glass Co.
811 Madison Ave., Toledo, Ohio
43624
419-242-5781
Pres.: R. G. Wingerter

Libby, McNeill & Libby
200 South Michigan Ave., Chicago,
Ill. 60604
312-922-4250
Pres.: David E. Guerrant

Liggett & Myers, Inc.
630 Fifth Ave., New York, N.Y.
10020
212-246-0500
Pres.: Milton E. Harrington

Eli Lilly & Co.
307 East McCarty St., Indianapolis,
Ind. 46206
317-636-2211
Pres.: B. E. Beck

Ling–Temco–Vought, Inc.
1525 Elm St., Dallas, Tex. 75222
214-742-9555
Pres.: James J. Ling

Thomas J. Lipton, Inc.
800 Sylvan Ave., Englewood, N.J.
07632
201-567-8000
Pres.: W. Gardner Barker

Litton Industries, Inc.
360 North Crescent Dr., Beverly
Hills, Calif. 90213
213-273-7860
Pres.: Roy L. Ash

Lockheed Aircraft Corp.
2555 North Hollywood Way,
Burbank, Calif. 91503
213-847-6121
Pres.: A. Carl Kotchian

Loew's Corp.
666 Fifth Ave., New York, N.Y.
10019
212-586-4400
Chmn. of the Bd.: Laurence A.
Tisch

Lone Star Cement Corp.
1 Greenwich Plaza, Greenwich,
Conn. 06830
203-661-3100
Chmn. of the Bd. & Pres.: John R.
Kringel

M. Lowenstein & Sons, Inc.
1430 Broadway, New York, N.Y.
10018
212-560-5000
Pres.: Robert A. Bendheim

Lubrizol Corp.
29400 Lakeland Blvd., Wickliffe,
Ohio 44092
216-943-4200
Pres.: M. Roger Clapp

Lykes–Youngstown Corp.
821 Gravier St., New Orleans, La.
70112
504-522-6661
Pres.: Frank A. Nemec

McDonnell Douglas Corp.
P. O. Box 516, St. Louis, Mo.
63166
314-232-0232
Pres.: David S. Lewis

McGraw–Edison Co.
333 West River Rd., Elgin, Ill.
60120
312-741-8900
Pres.: Raymond H. Giesecke

McGraw-Hill, Inc.
330 West 42nd St., New York, N.Y.
10036
212-971-3333
Pres.: Shelton Fisher

McLouth Steel Corp.
300 South Livernois Ave., Detroit,
Mich. 48217
313-843-3000
Pres.: H. B. Warner

Magnavox Co.
270 Park Ave., New York, N.Y.
10017
212-986-0055
Pres.: Robert H. Platt

Marathon Oil Co.
539 South Main St., Findlay,
Ohio 45840
419-422-2121
Pres.: J. C. Donnell, II

Maremont Corp.
168 North Michigan Ave., Chicago,
Ill. 60601
312-263-7676
Pres.: Richard D. Abelson

Martin Marietta Corp.
277 Park Ave., New York, N.Y.
10017
212-826-5050
Pres.: George M. Bunker

Masonite Corp.
29 North Wacker Dr., Chicago, Ill.
60606
312-372-5642
Pres.: Samuel S. Greeley

Mattel, Inc.
5150 Rosecrans Ave., Hawthorne,
Calif. 90250
213-679-4611
Pres.: Ruth Handler

Max Factor & Co.
1655 North McCadden Pl., Los
Angeles, Calif. 90028
213-462-6131
Pres.: Alfred Firestein

Maytag Co.
403 West 4th Ave., Newton, Iowa
50208
515-792-7000
Pres./Treas.: E. G. Higdon

Mead Corp.
118 West 1st St., Dayton, Ohio
45402
513-222-9561
Pres.: J. W. McSwiney

Merck & Co.
Lincoln Ave., Rahway, N.J.
07065
201-381-5000
Pres.: Henry W. Gadsden

Midland–Ross Corp.
55 Public Square, Cleveland, Ohio
44113
216-771-4800
Pres.: Harry J. Bolwell

Miles Laboratories, Inc.
1127 Myrtle St., Elkhart, Ind.
46514
219-264-8111
Pres.: Walter A. Compton, MD

Minnesota Mining & Manufacturing
Co.
3M Center, St. Paul, Minn. 55101
612-733-1110
Pres.: Harry Heltzer

Missouri Beef Packers, Inc.
P. O. Box 129, Rock Port, Mo.
64482
816-744-5356
Pres.: J. C. Walker

Mobil Oil Corp.
150 East 42nd St., New York,
N.Y. 10017
212-883-4242
Pres.: William P. Tavoulareas

Mohasco Industries, Inc.
57 Lyon St., Amsterdam, N.Y.
12010
518-843-2000
Pres.: Herbert L. Shuttleworth, II

Monsanto Co.
800 North Lindbergh Blvd., St.
Louis, Mo. 63166
314-694-1000
Pres.: Edward J. Bock

Morton–Norwich Products, Inc.
100 North Wacker Dr., Chicago,
Ill. 60606
312-346-1200
Pres.: Lewis F. Bonham

Motorola, Inc.
9401 Grand Ave., Franklin Park,
Ill. 60131
312-451-1000
Pres.: Elmer H. Wavering

NVF Co.
P. O. Box 311, Wilmington,
Del. 19899
302-239-5281
Pres.: Eugene R. Perry

Nalco Chemical Co.
180 North Michigan Ave., Chicago,
Ill. 60601
312-782-2035
Pres.: L. L. Bott

National Biscuit Co.
425 Park Ave., New York, N.Y.
10022
212-751-5000
Pres.: Robert M. Schaeberle

National Can Corp.
5959 South Cicero Ave., Chicago, Ill.
60638
312-735-2400
Pres.: Frank W. Considine

National Cash Register Co.
Main & K Sts., Dayton, Ohio 45409
513-449-2000
Pres.: R. Stanley Laing

National Distillers & Chemical
99 Park Ave., New York, N.Y.
10016
212-697-0700
Pres.: Drummond C. Bell

National Gypsum Co.
325 Delaware Ave., Buffalo,
N.Y. 14202
716-852-5880
Chmn. of the Bd. & Pres.: Colon
Brown

National Homes Corp.
Earl Ave. & Wallace St., Lafayette,
Ind. 47902
317-447-3131
Pres.: George E. Price

National Industries, Inc.
510 West Broadway, Louisville,
Ky. 40202
502-583-7602
Chmn. of the Bd. & Pres.: Stanley R.
Yarmuth

National Lead Co.
111 Broadway, New York, N.Y.
10006
212-732-9400
Pres.: John B. Henrich

National Service Industries
1180 Peachtree N.E., Atlanta, Ga.
30309
404-892-2400
Pres.: Erwin Zaban

National Steel Corp.
2800 Grant Bldg., Pittsburgh, Pa.
15219
412-471-5600
Pres.: G. A. Stinson

Nebraska Consolidated Mills Co.
500 Kiewit Plaza, Omaha, Nebr.
68131
402-346-8004
Pres.: J. A. Mactier

Needham Packing Co., Inc.
220 Badgerow Bldg., Sioux City,
Iowa 51101
712-252-4457
Pres.: Jerry P. Kozney

New York Times Co.
229 West 43d St., New York, N.Y.
10036
212-556-1234

Pres. Publisher: Arthur Ochs
Sulzberger

Newmont Mining Corp.
300 Park Ave., New York, N.Y.
10022
212-753-4800
Chmn. of the Bd. & Pres.: Plato
Malozemoff

Norris Industries, Inc.
5215 South Boyle Ave., Los Angeles,
Calif. 90058
213-588-7111
Pres.: Kenneth T. Norris, Jr.

North American Philips Corp.
100 East 42nd St., New York, N.Y.
10017
212-697-3600
Pres.: Pieter C. Vink

North American Rockwell Corp.
1700 East Imperial Highway,
El Segundo, Calif. 90245
213-647-5000
Pres.: R. Anderson

Northrop Corp.
1800 Century Park East, Los
Angeles, Calif. 90067
213-553-6262
Chmn. of the Bd. & Pres.: Thomas V.
Jones

Northwest Industries, Inc.
400 West Madison St., Chicago, Ill.
60606
312-263-4200
Pres.: Ben W. Heineman

Norton Co.
1 New Bond St., Worcester, Mass.
01606
617-853-1000
Pres.: Robert Cushman

Norton Simon, Inc.
277 Park Ave., New York, N.Y.
10017
212-832-1000
Chmn. of the Bd. & Pres.: David J.
Mahoney

Occidental Petroleum
10889 Wilshire Blvd., Los Angeles,
Calif. 90024
213-477-0066
Pres.: William Bellano

Ogden Corp.
161 East 42nd St., New York, N.Y.
10017
212-972-2200
Pres.: M. Lee Rice

Olin Corp.
120 Long Ridge Rd., Stamford,
Conn. 06904
203-356-2000
Pres.: Gordon Grand

Oscar Mayer & Co., Inc.
910 Mayer Ave., Madison, Wisc.
53701
608-244-1311
Pres.: P. Goff Beach

Otis Elevator Co.
250-260 11th Ave., New York, N.Y.
10001
212-244-8000
Pres.: R. A. Weller

Outboard Marine Corp.
100 Pershing Rd., Waukegan, Ill.
60085
312-689-6200
Pres.: William C. Scott

Owens–Corning Fiberglas Corp.
1 Levis Square, Toledo, Ohio
43659
419-259-3000
Pres.: John J. Thomas

Owens–Illinois, Inc.
405 Madison Ave., Toledo, Ohio
43601
419-242-6543
Pres.: Edwin D. Dodd

PPB Industries, Inc.
1 Gateway Center, Pittsburgh, Pa.
15222
412-434-3131
Pres.: Joseph A. Neubauer

Pabst Brewing Co.
917 West Juneau Ave., Milwaukee, Wisc. 53201
414-271-0230
Pres.: James C. Windham

Pacific Car & Foundry Co.
777 106th Ave. N.E., Bellevue, Wash. 98009
206-455-0520
Pres.: Charles M. Pigott

Parker–Hannifin Corp.
17325 Euclid Ave., Cleveland, Ohio 44112
216-531-3000
Pres.: Patrick S. Parker

Penn–Dixie Cement Corp.
1345 Ave. of Americas, New York, N.Y. 10019
212-687-5000
Chmn. of the Bd. & Pres.: Jerome Castle

Pennwalt Corp.
3 Parkway, Philadelphia, Pa. 19102
215-587-7000
Pres.: Charles H. Rybolt

PepsiCo., Inc.
Anderson Hill Rd., Purchase, N.Y. 10577
914-253-2000
Pres.: Andrall E. Pearson

Perkin–Elmer Corp.
Main Ave., Norwalk, Conn. 06852
203-762-1000
Chmn. of the Bd. & Pres.: Chester W. Nimitz, Jr.

Pet, Inc.
400 South Fourth St., St. Louis, Mo. 63166
314-621-5400
Pres.: Boyd F. Schenk

Pfizer, Inc.
235 East 42nd St., New York, N.Y. 10017
212-573-2323
Chmn. of the Bd. & Pres.: John J. Powers, Jr.

Phelps Dodge Corp.
300 Park Ave., New York, N.Y. 10022
212-751-3200
Pres.: George B. Munroe

Philip Morris, Inc.
100 Park Ave., New York, N.Y. 10017
212-679-1800
Pres.: George Weissman

Phillips Petroleum Co.
Bartlesville, Oklahoma 74003
918-336-6600
Pres.: John M. Houchin

Phillips-Van Heusen Corp.
417 Fifth Ave., New York, N.Y. 10016
212-689-3700
Pres.: Lawrence S. Phillips

Pillsbury Co.
608 Second Ave. South, Minneapolis, Minn. 55402
612-330-4966
Pres.: Terrance Hanold

Pitney-Bowes, Inc.
69 Walnut St., Stamford, Conn. 06902
203-327-3000
Pres.: Fred T. Allen

Pneumo Dynamics Corp.
3781 East 77th St., Cleveland, Ohio 44105
216-341-1700
Pres.: James A. Wood

Polaroid Corp.
730 Main St., Cambridge, Mass. 02139
617-864-6000
Chmn. of the Bd. & Pres.: Dr. Edwin H. Land

H. K. Porter, Inc.
601 Grant St., Pittsburgh, Pa. 15219
412-391-1800
Pres.: J. Stuart Morrow

Potlatch Forests, Inc.
1 Maritime Plaza, San Francisco,
Calif. 94119
415-981-5980
Pres.: Richard B. Madden

Proctor & Gamble Co.
301 East 6th St., Cincinnati,
Ohio 45201
513-421-3100
Pres.: Howard J. Morgens

Pullman, Inc.
200 South Michigan Ave., Chicago,
Ill. 60604
312-939-4262
Pres.: Samuel B. Casey, Jr.

Purex Corp. Ltd.
5101 Clark Ave., Lakewood, Calif.
90712
213-636-0431
Chmn. of the Bd. & Pres.: William R.
Tincher

Quaker Oats Co.
Merchandise Mart Plaza, Chicago,
Ill. 60654
312-222-7111
Pres.: Robert D. Stuart, Jr.

Questor Corp.
1801 Spielbusch Ave., Toledo, Ohio
43601
419-244-7424
Pres.: Pierson M. Grieve

RCA Corp.
30 Rockefeller Plaza, New York,
N.Y. 10020
212-265-5900
Pres.: Anthony L. Conrad

Ralston Purina Co.
835 South 8th St., St. Louis, Mo.
63199
314-982-0111
Chmn. of the Bd.: R. Hal Dean

Rapid-American Corp.
711 Fifth Ave., New York, N.Y.
10022
212-752-0100
Chmn. of the Bd. & Pres.: Mashulum
Rikis

Rath Packing Co.
Sycamore & Elm St., Waterloo,
Iowa 50704
319-235-8900
Pres.: Harry G. Slife

Ratheon Co.
141 Spring St., Lexington, Mass.
02173
617-862-6600
Pres.: Thomas Phillips

Reichhold Chemicals, Inc.
525 North Broadway, White Plains,
N.Y. 10602
914-948-6200
Chmn. of the Bd.: Henry H.
Reichhold

Reliance Electric Co.
24701 Euclid Ave., Cleveland, Ohio
44117
216-266-7000
Pres.: Hugh D. Luke

Republic Corp.
1900 Ave. of Stars, Los Angeles,
Calif. 90067
213-553-3900
Chmn. of the Bd. & Pres.: Sanford
C. Sigoloff

Republic Steel Corp.
25 West Prospect Ave., Cleveland,
Ohio 44101
216-574-7100
Pres.: W. B. Boyer

Revere Copper & Brass, Inc.
605 Third Ave., New York, N.Y.
10016
212-687-4111
Pres.: Fritz C. Hyde, Jr.

Revlon, Inc.
767 Fifth Ave., New York, N.Y.
10022
212-758-5000
Chmn. of the Bd.: Charles Revson

Rex Chainbelt, Inc.
2701 West Greenfield, Milwaukee,
Wisc. 53201
414-384-3000
Pres.: Robert V. Kirkonian

R. J. Reynolds Industries, Inc.
405 North Main St., Winston-
Salem, N.C. 27102
919-761-4000
Pres.: David S. Peoples

Reynolds Metals Co.
6601 Broad St. Rd., Richmond, Va.
23261
703-282-2311
Chmn. of the Bd. & Pres.: Richard
S. Reynolds, Jr.

Rheingold Corp.
41 East 42nd St., New York, N.Y.
10017
212-687-0790
Chmn. of the Bd.: John E. Haigney

Richardson-Merrell, Inc.
122 East 42nd St., New York, N.Y.
10017
212-697-3800
Pres.: H. Robert Marschalk

Riegel Paper Corp.
260 Madison Ave., New York,
N.Y. 10016
212-679-4100
Pres.: William J. Scharffenberger

H. H. Robertson Co.
2 Gateway Center, Pittsburgh, Pa.
15222
412-281-3200
Pres.: Douglas A. Jones

Rockwell Manufacturing Co.
400 North Lexington Ave.,
Pittsburgh, Pa. 15208
412-241-8400
Pres.: A. Clark Daugherty

Rohm & Haas Co.
Independence Mall West,
Philadelphia, Pa. 19105
215-592-3000
Pres.: Vincent L. Gregory

Rohr Corp.
Foot of H St., Chula Vista, Calif.
92010
714-426-7111
Pres.: F. E. McCreery

Roper Corp.
1905 West Court St., Kankakee, Ill.
60901
815-939-3641
Chmn. of the Bd. & Pres.: Charles M.
Hoover

SCM Corp.
299 Park Ave., New York, N.Y.
10017
212-752-2700
Chmn. of the Bd. & Pres.: Emerson
E. Mead

St. Regis Paper Co.
150 East 42nd St., New York, N.Y.
10017
212-697-4400
Pres.: William E. Caldwell, Jr.

Sanders Associates, Inc.
95 Canal St., Nashua, N.H. 03060
603-885-4321
Pres.: Royden C. Sanders, Jr.

F & M Schaeffer Corp.
430 Kent Ave., Brooklyn, N.Y.
11211
212-387-7000
Pres.: Rudolph J. Schaefer

Schering-Plough Corp.
60 Orange St., Bloomfield, N.J.
07003
201-743-6000
Pres.: W. H. Conzen

Jos. Schlitz Brewing Co.
235 West Galena St., Milwaukee,
Wisc. 53201
414-224-5000
Chmn. of the Bd. & Pres.: Robert A.
Uihlein, Jr.

Scott Paper Co.
Scott Plaza, Philadelphia, Pa.
19113
215-724-2000
Pres.: Charles D. Dickey, Jr.

Scovill Manufacturing Co.
99 Mill St., Waterbury, Conn.
60720
203-757-6061
Pres.: John C. Helies

Joseph E. Seagram & Sons, Inc.
375 Park Ave., New York, N.Y.
10022
212-572-7000
Pres.: Edgar M. Bronfman

G. C. Searle & Co.
Searle Parkway, Skokie, Ill. 60076
312-463-2111
Pres.: Daniel C. Searle

Shell Oil Co.
1 Shell Plaza, Houston, Tex. 77002
713-220-6161
Pres.: H. Bridges

Sheller-Globe Corp.
1505 Jefferson Ave., Toledo, Ohio
43624
419-255-8840
Pres.: Chester Devenow

Sherwin-Williams Co.
101 Prospect Ave. N.W., Cleveland,
Ohio 44115
216-566-2000
Pres.: W. O. Spencer

Signal Companies, Inc.
1010 Wilshire Blvd., Los Angeles,
Calif. 90017
213-482-0722
Pres.: Forrest N. Shumway

Signode Corp.
2600-20 North Western, Chicago, Ill.
60647
312-276-8500
Pres.: J. Milton Moon

Simmons Co.
280 Park Ave., New York, N.Y.
10017
212-697-2300
Pres.: Joseph V. Quarles

Singer Co.
30 Rockefeller Plaza, New York,
N.Y. 10020
212-581-4800
Chmn. of the Bd. & Pres.: Donald P.
Kircher

Skyline Corp.
2520 By-Pass Rd., Elkhart, Ind.
46514

219-523-2380
Chmn. of the Bd. & Pres.: Arthur J.
Decio

A. O. Smith Corp.
3533 North 27th St., Milwaukee,
Wisc. 53201
414-873-3000
Pres.: Urban T. Kuechle

Smith Kline & French Laboratories
1500 Spring Garden St.,
Philadelphia, Pa. 19101
215-564-2400
Chmn. of the Bd. & Pres.: Thomas
M. Rauch

Spencer Foods, Inc.
Highway 71 North, Box 1228,
Spencer, Iowa 51301
712-262-4250
Pres.: Gerald L. Pearson

Sperry Rand Corp.
1290 Ave. of Americas, New York,
N.Y. 10019
212-956-2121
Chmn. of the Bd. & Pres.: J. Frank
Forster

Springs Mills, Inc.
205 White St., Fort Mill, S.C.
29715
803-547-2901
Pres.: Peter G. Scotese

Square D Co.
Executive Plaza, Park Ridge, Ill.
60068
312-774-9200
Pres.: Mitchell P. Kartalia

Squibb Beech-Nut, Inc.
480 Park Ave., New York, N.Y.
10022
212-759-8700
Pres.: Richard M. Furlaud

A. E. Staley Manufacturing Co.
2200 East Eldorado St., Decatur,
Ill. 62525
217-423-4411
Pres.: D. E. Nordlund

Standard Brands, Inc.
625 Madison Ave., New York, N.Y.
10022

212-759-4400
Pres.: Henry Weigl

Standard Oil Co. of California
255 Bush St., San Francisco, Calif.
94119
415-894-7700
Pres.: H. J. Haynes

Standard Oil Co. (Ind.)
910 South Michigan Ave., Chicago,
Ill. 60680
312-856-6111
Pres.: Robert C. Gunness

Standard Oil Co. (N.J.)
30 Rockefeller Plaza, New York,
N.Y. 10020
212-974-3000
Pres.: Milo M. Brisco

Standard Oil Co. (Ohio)
101 Prospect Ave. N.W., Cleveland,
Ohio 44115
216-574-4141
Pres.: A. W. Whitehouse, Jr.

Stanley Works
195 Lake St., New Britain, Conn.
06050
203-225-5111
Pres.: Donald W. Davis

Stauffer Chemical Co.
299 Park Ave., New York, N.Y.
10017
212-421-5000
Pres.: Roger W. Gunder

Sterling Drug, Inc.
90 Park Ave., New York, N.Y.
10016
212-972-4141
Pres.: David J. Fitzgibbons

J. P. Stevens & Co., Inc.
1185 Ave. of Americas, New York,
N.Y. 10036
212-575-2000
Pres.: Whitney Stevens

Stokely-Van Camp, Inc.
941 North Meridian St., Indianapolis,
Ind. 46206
317-631-2551
Pres.: Alfred J. Stokely

Studebaker-Worthington, Inc.
530 5th Ave., New York, N.Y.
10036
212-697-2345
Pres.: Leslie T. Welsh

Sun Oil Co.
1608 Walnut St., Philadelphia, Pa.
19103
215-985-1600
Pres.: H. Robert Sharbaugh

Sunbeam Corp.
5400 West Roosevelt Rd., Chicago,
Ill. 60650
312-854-3500
Pres.: W. J. Pfeif

Sundstrand Corp.
4751 Harrison Ave., Rockford, Ill.
61101
815-226-6200
Pres.: Carl L. Sadler, Jr.

Swift & Co.
115 West Jackson Blvd., Chicago,
Ill. 60604
312-431-2000
Pres.: Robert W. Reneker

Sybron Corp.
1100 Midtown Tower, Rochester,
N.Y. 14604
716-546-4040
Pres.: William G. vonBerg

TRW, Inc.
23555 Euclid Ave., Cleveland,
Ohio 44117
216-383-2121
Pres.: Dr. R. F. Mettler

Talley Industries, Inc.
4551 East McKellips, Mesa, Arizona
85201
602-969-7411
Pres.: Franz G. Talley

Tecumseh Products Co.
East Patterson, Tecumseh, Mich.
49286
313-423-7411
Pres.: William E. Macbeth

Teledyne, Inc.
1901 Ave. of Stars, Los Angeles,
Calif. 90067
213-277-3311
Pres.: George A. Roberts

Tenneco, Inc.
1010 Milan, Houston, Tex.
77001
713-229-2131
Pres.: N. V. Freeman

Texaco, Inc.
135 East 42nd St., New York, N.Y.
10017
212-953-6000
Pres.: John K. McKinley

Texas Gulf Sulphur Co.
200 Park Ave., New York, N.Y.
10017
212-972-5000
Pres.: Charles F. Fogarty

Texas Instruments, Inc.
13500 North Central Expressway,
Dallas, Tex. 75222
214-238-2011
Pres.: Mark Shepherd, Jr.

Textron, Inc.
10 Dorrance St., Providence, R.I.
02903
401-521-3500
Pres.: George William Miller

Thiokol Chemical Corp.
Newportville Rd., Bristol, Pa.
19007
215-946-9150
Pres.: R. E. Davis

Time, Inc.
Rockefeller Center, New York, N.Y.
10020
212-586-1212
Pres.: James R. Shepley

Times Mirror Co.
202 West 1st St., Los Angeles,
Calif. 90053
213-625-2345
Pres.: Albert V. Casey

Timken Co.
1835 Dueber Ave. S.W., Canton,
Ohio 44706
216-453-4511
Pres.: H. E. Markley

Todd Shipyards Corp.
1 State St. Plaza, New York, N.Y.
10004
212-344-6900
Pres.: John T. Gilbride

Trane Co.
3600 Pammel Creek, La Crosse,
Wisc. 54601
608-782-8000
Pres.: Thomas Hancock

Trans Union Corp.
111 West Jackson Blvd., Chicago, Ill.
60604
312-431-3111
Pres.: J. W. VanGorkom

Triangle Industries, Inc.
550 Broad St., Newark, N.J.
07102
201-621-6500
Pres.: Edward J. Simmons

USM Corp.
140 Federal St., Boston, Mass.
02110
617-542-9100
Pres.: Herbert W. Jarvis

Union Camp Corp.
1600 Valley Rd., Wayne, N.J.
07470
201-628-9000
Pres.: Alexander Calder, Jr.

Union Carbide Corp.
270 Park Ave., New York, N.Y.
10017
212-551-2345
Pres.: William S. Sneath

Union Oil Co. of California
461 South Boylston St., Los
Angeles, Calif. 90054
213-482-7600
Pres.: Fred L. Hartley

Uniroyal, Inc.
1230 Ave. of the Americas, New York, N.Y. 10020
212-247-5000
Chmn. of the Bd. & Pres.: George R. Vila

United Aircraft Corp.
400 Main St., East Hartford, Conn. 06108
203-565-4321
Pres.: Arthur E. Smith

United Brands Co.
245 Park Ave., New York, N.Y. 10017
212-697-7560
Pres.: John M. Fox

United Merchants & Manufacturers, Inc.
1407 Broadway, New York, N.Y. 10018
212-564-6000
Pres./Treas.: Martin J. Schwab

United States Gypsum Co.
101 South Wacker Dr., Chicago, Ill. 60606
312-321-4000
Pres.: E. W. Duffy

U.S. Industries, Inc.
250 Park Ave., New York, N.Y. 10017
212-697-4141
Pres.: Charles E. Selecman

U.S. Plywood-Champion Papers
777 Third Ave., New York, N.Y. 10017
212-935-3500
Chmn. of the Bd. & Pres.: Karl R. Bendelsen

United States Shoe Corp.
1658 Herald Ave., Cincinnati, Ohio 45207
513-731-5010
Pres.: Philip G. Barach

United States Steel Corp.
71 Broadway, New York, N.Y. 10006
212-558-4444
Pres.: Edgar B. Speer

Universal Oil Products Co.
30 Algonquin Rd., Des Plaines, Ill. 60016
312-824-1155
Pres.: John O. Logan

Upjohn Co.
7000 Portage St., Kalamazoo, Mich. 49001
616-382-4000
Pres.: R. M. Boudeman

VF Corp.
1047 North Park Rd., Reading, Pa. 19610
215-376-7201
Chmn. of the Bd. & Pres.: Manford O. Lee

Varian Associates
611 Hansen Way, Palo Alto, Calif. 94303
415-326-4000
Pres.: Norman F. Parker

Vulcan Materials Co.
1 Off Park, Birmingham, Ala. 35223
205-879-0421
Pres.: John M. Lambert

Wallace-Murray Corp.
299 Park Ave., New York, N.Y. 10017
212-758-4000
Pres.: Fred R. Raach

Jim Walter Corp.
1500 North Dale Mabry, Tampa, Fla. 33607
813-876-4181
Pres.: F. J. Pizzitola

Ward Foods, Inc.
2 Pennsylvania Plaza, New York, N.Y. 10001
212-594-5400
Pres.: Charles W. Call, Jr.

Warnaco, Inc.
350 Lafayette St., Bridgeport, Conn. 06602
203-333-1151
Pres.: John W. Field

Warner-Lambert Co.
201 Tabor Rd., Morris Plains, N.J.
07950
201-285-0234
Pres.: E. Burke Giblin

Wean United, Inc.
3 Gateway Center, Pittsburgh, Pa.
15222
412-261-4534
Pres.: R. J. Wean, Jr.

West Point-Pepperell, Inc.
Corner 4th Ave., West Point, Ga.
31833
404-645-1111
Chmn. Exec. Comm. & Pres.: John
P. Howland

Western Electric Co., Inc.
195 Broadway, New York, N.Y.
10007
212-571-2345
Pres.: Harvey G. Mehlhouse

Western Publishing Co., Inc.
1220 Mound Ave., Racine, Wisc.
53404
414-633-2431
Pres.: G. L. Slade

Westinghouse Electric Corp.
Gateway Center, Pittsburgh, Pa.
15222
412-255-3800
Chmn. of the Bd.: Donald C.
Burnham

Westvaco Corp.
299 Park Ave., New York, N.Y.
10017
212-688-5000
Pres.: David L. Luke, III

Weyerhaeuser Co.
2525 South 336th St., Federal Way,
Wash. 98002
206-924-2345
Pres.: George H. Weyerhaeuser

Wheeling-Pittsburgh Steel Corp.
4 Gateway Center, Pittsburgh, Pa.
15222
412-471-3600
Pres.: Robert E. Lauterbach

Whirlpool Corp.
U.S. 33 North Administration
Center, Benton Harbor, Mich.
49022
616-925-0651
Pres.: John H. Platts

White Consolidated Industries, Inc.
11770 Berea Rd., Cleveland, Ohio
44111
216-252-3700
Pres.: William H. Johnson

White Motor Corp.
100 Erieview Plaza, Cleveland,
Ohio 44101
216-523-5800
Pres.: H. J. Nave

Whittaker Corp.
10880 Wilshire Blvd., Los Angeles,
Calif. 90024
213-475-9411
Pres.: Joseph F. Alibrandi

Willamette Industries, Inc.
811 Southwest 6th, Portland, Oreg.
97204
503-227-5585
Pres.: Gene D. Knudson

Witco Chemical Corp.
277 Park Ave., New York, N.Y.
10017
212-826-1000
Pres.: William Wishnick

Wm. Wrigley, Jr. Co.
410 North Michigan Ave., Chicago,
Ill. 60611
312-644-2121
Pres.: William Wrigley

Xerox Corp.
1200 High Ridge Rd., Stamford,
Conn. 06905
203-329-8711
Chmn. of the Bd.: Joseph C. Wilson

Zenith Radio Corp.
1900 North Austin Ave., Chicago,
Ill. 60639
312-745-2000
Chmn. of the Bd. & Pres.: Joseph S.
Wright

30. Fifty Largest Public Utilities

Allegheny Power System, Inc.
320 Park Ave., New York, N.Y.
10022
212-752-2121
Pres.: D. M. Kammert

American Electric Power Co.
2 Broadway, New York, N.Y.
10004
212-422-4800
Pres.: Donald C. Cook

American Natural Gas Co.
30 Rockefeller Plaza, New York,
N.Y. 10020
212-247-4630
Pres.: Wiber H. Mack

American Telephone & Telegraph Co.
195 Broadway, New York, N.Y.
10007
212-393-9800
Chmn. of the Bd. & Pres.: H. I.
Romnes

Baltimore Gas & Electric Co.
Gas & Electric Bldg., Baltimore, Md.
21203
301-234-5000
Chmn. of the Bd. & Pres.: C. Edward
Utermohle, Jr.

Carolina Power & Light Co.
336 Fayettville St., Raleigh, N.C.
27602
919-828-8211
Chmn. of the Bd. & Pres.: Shearon
Harris

Central & South West Corp.
P.O. Box 1631, Wilmington, Del.
19899
302-655-1526
Pres.: S. B. Philips, Jr.

Cleveland Electric Illuminating Co.
P.O. Box 5000, Cleveland, Ohio
44101
216-623-1350
Pres.: Karl H. Rudolph

Columbia Gas System, Inc.
120 East 41st St., New York, N.Y.
10017
212-679-4500
Pres.: John W. Partridge

Commonwealth Edison Co.
1 First National Plaza, Chicago, Ill.
60690
312-294-4321
Pres.: Thomas G. Ayers

Consolidated Edison New York
4 Irving Pl., New York, N.Y.
10003
212-460-4600
Pres.: Louis H. Roddis, Jr.

Consolidated Natural Gas Co.
30 Rockefeller Plaza, New York,
N.Y. 10020
212-245-5100
Pres.: Robert E. Seymour

Consumers Power Co.
212 West Michigan Ave., Jackson,
Mich. 49201
517-788-0550
Pres.: James H. Campbell

Continental Telephone Corp.
222 South Central, St. Louis, Mo.
63105
314-862-3500
Pres.: Phillip J. Lucier

Detroit Edison Co.
2000 Second Ave., Detroit, Mich.
48226
313-962-2100
Pres.: William G. Meese

Duke Power Co.
422 South Church St., Charlotte,
N.C. 28202
704-332-8521
Pres.: W. B. McGuire

El Paso Natural Gas Co.
P.O. Box 1492, El Paso, Tex.
79999
915-543-2600
Pres.: Hugh F. Steen

Florida Power & Light Co.
4200 Flagler St., Miami, Fla.
33101
305-445-6211
Pres.: Richard C. Fullerton

General Public Utilities Corp.
80 Pine St., New York, N.Y.
10005
212-943-5600
Pres.: William G. Kuhns

Gulf States Utilities Co.
285 Liberty Ave., Beaumont, Tex.
78701
713-838-6631
Pres.: Floyd R. Smith

Houston Lighting & Power Co.
611 Walker St., Houston, Tex.
77001
713-228-9211
Pres.: C. B. Sherman

Illinois Power Co.
500 South 27th St., Decatur, Ill.
62525
217-428-7711
Pres.: Wendell J. Kelley

Long Island Lighting Co.
250 Old Country Rd., Mineola, N.Y.
11501
516-747-1000
Pres.: Edward C. Duffy

Middle South Utilities, Inc.
280 Park Ave., New York, N.Y.
10017
212-687-7181
Pres.: Floyd W. Lewis

New England Electric System
20 Turnpike Rd., Westboro, Mass.
01581
617-366-8811
Pres.: Robert F. Krause

Niagara Mohawk Power Corp.
300 Erie Blvd. West, Syracuse, N.Y.
13202
315-474-1511
Pres.: James A. O'Neill

Northeast Utilities
176 Cumberland Ave., Hartford,
Conn. 06109
203-529-7471
Chmn. of the Bd. & Pres.: Lelan F.
Sillin, Jr.

Northern Natural Gas Co.
2223 Dodge St., Omaha, Nebr.
68102
402-348-4000
Chmn. of the Bd. & Pres.: Willis A.
Strauss

Northern States Power Co.
414 Nicollet Mall, Minneapolis,
Minn. 55401
612-330-5500
Pres.: Robert H. Engels

Ohio Edison Co.
47 North Main St., Akron, Ohio
44308
216-762-9661
Pres.: D. Bruce Mansfield

Pacific Gas & Electric Co.
245 Market St., San Francisco, Calif.
94106
415-781-4211
Pres.: S. L. Sibley

Pacific Lighting Corp.
810 South Flower St., Los Angeles,
Calif. 90017
213-620-0360
Pres.: Paul A. Miller

Pacific Power & Light Co.
920 Southwest Sixth Ave., Portland,
Oreg. 97204
503-226-7411
Pres.: Don C. Frisbee

Panhandle Eastern Pipe Line Co.
3000 Bissonnet, Houston, Tex.
77005
713-664-3401
Pres.: R. L. O'Shields

Pennsylvania Power & Light Co.
901 Hamilton St., Allentown, Pa.
18101
215-434-5151
Pres.: Jack K. Busby

Pennzoil United Co.
900 Southwest Tower, Houston, Tex.
77002
713-228-8741
Pres.: William C. Liedtke

Peoples Gas Co.
122 South Michigan Ave., Chicago,
Ill. 60603
312-431-4000
Pres.: Robert M. Drevs

Philadelphia Electric Co.
1000 Chestnut St., Philadelphia, Pa.
19105
215-922-4700
Pres.: Robert F. Gilkeson

Potomac Electric Power Co.
929 East St. N.W., Washington, D.C.
20004
202-628-8800
Pres.: Stephen R. Woodzell

Public Service Electric & Gas Co.
80 Park Pl., Newark, N.J. 07101
201-622-7000
Pres.: Edward R. Eberle

Southern California Edison Co.
601 West 5th St., Los Angeles, Calif.
90017
213-624-7111
Pres.: T. M. McDaniel, Jr.

Southern Co.
3390 Peachtree N.E., Atlanta, Ga.
30326
404-261-2470
Pres.: Alvin W. Vogtle, Jr.

Texas Eastern Transmission Corp.
P.O. Box 2521, Houston, Tex.
77001

713-224-7961
Pres.: Baxter D. Goodrich

Texas Utilities Co.
1506 Commerce St., Dallas, Tex.
75201
214-742-4742
Pres.: Clarence A. Tatum, Jr.

Transcontinental Gas Pipe Line
3100 Travis St., Houston, Tex.
77001
713-524-6351
Pres.: James B. Henderson

Union Electric Co.
1901 Gratiot St., St. Louis, Mo.
63166
314-621-3222
Pres.: Charles J. Dougherty

United Utilities, Inc.
P.O. Box 11315 Plaza Sta., Kansas
City, Mo. 64112
913-236-9900
Senior V.P.: W. E. Baker

Virginia Electric & Power Co.
700 East Franklin St., Richmond,
Va. 23209
703-771-3000
Pres.: T. Justin Moore, Jr.

Western Union Telegraph Co.
60 Hudson St., New York, N.Y.
10013
212-962-7730
Chmn. of the Bd. & Pres.: Russell W.
McFall

Wisconsin Electric Power Co.
231 West Michigan St., Milwaukee,
Wisc. 53201
414-273-1234
Pres.: John G. Quale

31. Retailing Companies

ARA Services, Inc.
Independence Square West,
Philadelphia, Pa. 19106
215-923-7700
Pres.: William S. Fishman
Chief financial officer: Herman G.
Minter
Nature of business: Vending
machines
Number of outlets: 133,000
vending machines in U.S.
Approximate net sales in millions:
650,000

Acme Markets, Inc.
124 North 15th St., Philadelphia, Pa.
19101
215-568-3000
Pres.: John R. Park
Chief financial officer: Thomas T.
Oyler
Nature of business: Supermarket
Number of outlets: 885
Approx. net sales in millions:
1,650,000

Albertson's, Inc.
1623 Washington, Boise, Idaho
83707
208-344-7441
Pres.: J. L. Scott
Chief financial officer: Robert
Bolinder
Nature of business: Food
Number of outlets: 225
Approx. net sales in millions:
450,000

Allied Stores Corp.
401 Fifth Ave., New York, N.Y.
10016
212-679-0800
Pres.: Thomas M. Macioce
Chief financial officer: Howard E.
Hassler
Nature of business: Department
Number of outlets: 135
Approx. net sales in millions:
1,230,000

Allied Supermarkets, Inc.
8711 Meadowdale Ave., Detroit,
Mich. 48228
313-584-0300
Chmn. of the Bd. & Pres.: Thomas
McMaster
Chief financial officer: Walter Boyle
Nature of business: Supermarket
Number of outlets: 400
Approx. net sales in millions:
960,000

Arden-Mayfair, Inc.
2500 South Garfield Ave., Los
Angeles, Calif. 90054
213-685-5220
Pres.: Albert J. Grosson
Chief financial officer: Bernard
Briskin
Nature of business: Food
Number of outlets: 225
Approx. net sales in millions:
630,000

Associated Dry Goods Corp.
417 Fifth Ave., New York, N.Y.
10016
212-679-8700
Pres.: Arthur J. O'Brien
Chief financial officer: Robert J.
McKim
Nature of business: Department
Number of outlets: 75
Approx. net sales in millions:
800,000

Borman's, Inc.
18718 Borman Ave., Detroit, Mich.
48228
313-931-6600
Pres.: Paul Borman
Chief financial officer: Morris
Tulupman
Nature of business: Food
Number of outlets: 175
Approx. net sales in millions:
445,000

Broadway-Hale Stores, Inc.
600 South Spring St., Los Angeles,
Calif. 90014
213-620-0150
Pres.: Edward M. Carter
Chief financial officer: Howard N.
West
Nature of business: Department
Number of outlets: 50
Approx. net sales in millions:
665,000

City Products Corp.
1700 Wolf Rd., Des Plaines, Ill.
60018
312-299-2261
Pres.: James M. Tait
Chief financial officer: J. B.
Gunderson
Nature of business: Variety
Number of outlets: 2,000
franchised; 800 owned
Approx. net sales in millions:
1,210,000

Colonial Stores, Inc.
2251 North Sylvan Rd., East Point,
Ga. 30344
404-767-7411
Pres.: Ernest F. Boyce
Chief financial officer: J. P. Fowler
Nature of business: Supermarket
Number of outlets: 450
Approx. net sales in millions:
665,000

Cook United, Inc.
16501 Rockside Rd., Cleveland,
Ohio 44137
216-475-1000
President: Roy B. Miner
Chief financial officer: James
Williamson, Jr.
Nature of business & No. of outlets:
Supermarket-75; Department-90;
Drug-25
Approx. net sales in millions: 627,000

Dayton-Hudson Corp.
700 Nicollet Mall, Minneapolis,
Minn. 55402
612-332-1241
Pres.: Kenneth N. Dayton

Chief financial officer: John C.
Curran, Jr.
Nature of business: Department
Number of outlets: 400
Approx. net sales in millions:
970,000

Federated Department Stores, Inc.
222 West 7th St., Cincinnati, Ohio
45202
513-721-7600
Pres.: J. Paul Sticht
Chief financial officer: Albert B.
Glaser
Nature of business: Department
Number of outlets: 100
Approx. net sales in millions:
2,100,000

First National Stores, Inc.
5 Middlesex Ave., Somerville, Mass.
02145
617-623-2400
Pres.: Hilliard J. Coan
Chief financial officer: William A.
Ferrara
Nature of business: Food
Number of outlets: 425
Approx. net sales in millions:
770,000

Fisher Foods, Inc.
5300 Richmond Rd., Cleveland,
Ohio 44146
216-292-7000
Pres.: John Fazio
Chief financial officer: Richard
Schenk
Nature of business: Supermarket
Number of outlets: 100
Approx. net sales in millions:
402,000

Food Fair Stores, Inc.
3175 J.F.K. Blvd., Philadelphia, Pa.
19101
215-382-9500
Pres.: Jack M. Frieland
Chief financial officer: B. F. Lieber
Nature of business: Food
Number of outlets: 600
Approx. net sales in millions:
1,765,000

Gamble-Skogmo, Inc.
5100 Gamble Dr., Minneapolis,
Minn. 55416
612-374-6123
Pres.: James A. Watson
Chief financial officer: Walter H.
Davis
Nature of business: Department
Number of outlets: 800
Approx. net sales in millions:
1,300,000

Giant Food, Inc.
6900 Sheriff Rd., Landover, Md.
20785
301-341-4100
Pres.: Joseph B. Danzansky
Chief financial officer: Emanuel
Cohen
Nature of business: Supermarket
Number of outlets: 90
Approx. net sales in millions:
436,000

Gimbel Brothers, Inc.
1275-87 Broadway, New York, N.Y.
10001
212-564-3300
Pres.: Bruce A. Gimbel
Chief financial officer: Samuel Nass
Nature of business: Department
Number of outlets: 60
Approx. net sales in millions:
720,000

Grand Union Co.
100 Broadway, East Paterson, N.J.
07407
201-796-4800
Pres.: Charles G. Rodman
Chief financial officer: Charles H.
Haight
Nature of business: Supermarket—
550 outlets; Department—30
outlets
Aprox. net sales in millions:
1,200,000

W. T. Grant Co.
1441 Broadway, New York, N.Y.
10018
212-564-1000
Pres.: Richard W. Mayer

Chief financial officer: John G.
Curtin
Nature of business: Variety
Number of outlets: 1,1000
Approx. net sales in millions:
1,260,000

Great Atlantic & Pacific Tea Co.
420 Lexington Ave., New York,
N.Y. 10017
212-689-4000
Pres.: Robert F. Longacre
Chief financial officer: Harry C.
Gillespie
Nature of business: Food
Number of outlets: 4,600
Approx. net sales in millions:
5,650,000

Interstate Stores, Inc.
111 Eighth Ave., New York, N.Y.
10011
212-620-4100
Pres.: Robert Reisner
Chief financial officer: Edward C.
Schenkel
Nature of business: Discount store
Number of outlets: 100
Approx. net sales in millions:
685,000

Jewel Cos., Inc.
5725 East River Rd., Chicago, Ill.
60630
312-693-6000
Pres.: Weston R. Christopherson
Chief financial officer: Howard O.
Wagner
Nature of business & No. of outlets:
Supermarket—400; home service
routes distributors—1800
Approx. net sales in millions:
1,630,000

S. S. Kresge Co.
2727 Second Ave., Detroit, Mich.
48232
313-965-7300
Pres.: R. E. Dewar
Chief financial officer: R. H. Black
Nature of business: Discount store
Number of outlets: 1,000

Approx. net sales in millions:
4,000,000

Kroger Co.
1014 Vine St., Cincinnati, Ohio
45202
513-381-8000
Pres.: James P. Herring
Chief financial officer: James E.
Baker
Nature of business: Food and/or Drug
Number of outlets: 1,800
Approx. net sales in millions:
3,735,000

Lucky Stores, Inc.
1701 Marina Blvd., San Leandro,
Calif. 94577
415-357-2000
Pres.: W. H. Fisher
Chief financial officer: Ivan Owen
Nature of business: Food & Discount
Number of outlets: 400
Approx. net sales in millions:
1,490,000

R. H. Macy & Co.
151 West 34th St., New York, N.Y.
10001
212-695-4400
Pres.: Ernest L. Molloy
Chief financial officer: Jack Hanson
Nature of business: Department store
Number of outlets: 60
Approx. net sales in millions:
910,000

Marcor, Inc.
619 West Chicago Ave., Chicago, Ill.
60607
312-467-8800
Pres.: Leo H. Schoenhofen
Chief financial officer: Gordon R.
Worley
Nature of business/No. of outlets:
Retail—4175; Catalog—925
Approx. net sales in millions:
2,805,000

Marshall Field & Co.
111 North State St., Chicago, Ill.
60690
312-781-1000

Pres.: Gerald A. Sivage
Chief financial officer: George G.
Rinder
Nature of business: Department
Number of outlets: 15
Approx. net sales in millions:
402,000

May Department Stores Co.
6th & Olive Sts., St. Louis, Mo.
63101
314-436-3300
Pres.: Stanley J. Goodman
Chief financial officer: David May,
II
Nature of business: Department
Number of outlets: 90
Approx. net sales in millions:
1,170,000

Melville Shoe Corp.
25 West 43rd St., New York, N.Y.
10036
212-565-6500
Pres.: Francis C. Rooney, Jr.
Chief financial officer: Kenneth K.
Berland
Nature of business: Shoe store
Number of outlets: 1,700
Approx. net sales in millions:
440,000

G. C. Murphy Co.
531 Fifth Ave., Mekeesport, Pa.
15132
412-664-4441
Chmn. of the Bd. & Pres.: Edgar L.
Paxton
Chief financial officer: S. W.
Robinson
Nature of business: Variety
Number of outlets: 525
Approx. net sales in millions:
402,000

National Tea Co.
8303 West Higgins Rd., Chicago, Ill.
60631
312-693-2300
Pres.: F. Bruce Krysiak
Chief financial officer: Paul
Karukstis
Nature of business: Food & drug

No. of outlets: Food—900; drug—
100
Approx. net sales in millions:
1,513,000

J. J. Newberry Co.
245 Fifth Ave., New York, N.Y.
10016
212-689-4240
Pres.: Daryl D. Milius
Chief financial officer: James A.
Heely
Nature of business: Department &
variety
No. of outlets: 750
Approx. net sales in millions:
415,000

J. C. Penney Co.
1301 Ave. of the Americas, New
York, N.Y. 10019
212-957-4321
Pres.: Cecil L. Wright
Chief financial officer: Kenneth S.
Axelson
Nature of business: Department &
variety
No. of outlets: Stores—1,646;
catalog—950
Approx. net sales in millions:
4,150,000

Pueblo International
375 Park Ave., New York, N.Y.
10022
212-935-1710
Pres.: George Tappel
Chief financial officer: Sheldon
Douglass
Nature of business: Supermarket
Number of outlets: 100
Approx. net sales in millions:
460,000

Safeway Stores, Inc.
201 4th St., Oakland, Calif.
94604
415-444-4711
Pres.: William S. Mitchell
Chief financial officer: Neils V.
Lawson
Nature of business: Food

Number of outlets: 2,265
Approx. net sales in millions:
4,870,000

Sears Roebuck & Co.
925 South Homan Ave., Chicago, Ill.
60607
312-265-2500
Pres.: Arthur M. Wood
Chief financial officer: Emory
Williams
Nature of business: Catalog & general
Number of outlets: 900
Approx. net sales in millions:
9,300,000

Southland Corp.
2828 North Haskell, Dallas, Tex.
75204
214-824-8121
Pres.: Herbert Hartfelder
Chief finanial officer: W. K.
Ruppenkamp
Nature of business: Food
Number of outlets: 3,000
Approx. net sales in millions:
951,000

Stop & Shop Cos., Inc.
393 D St., Boston, Mass. 02110
617-463-7000
Pres.: Donald A. Gannon
Chief financial officer: Albert S.
Frager
Nature of business/No. of outlets:
Supermarket—1400; Department—
50; Tobacco Shop—25
Approx. net sales in millions:
790,000

Supermarkets General Corp.
301 Blair Rd., Woodbridge, N.J.
07095
201-636-2400
Pres.: Milton Perlmutter
Chief financial officer: William R.
H. Martin
Nature of business: Supermarket
Number of outlets: 90
Approx. net sales in millions:
810,000

Vornado, Inc.
174 Passaic St., Garfield, N.J.
07026
201-773-4000
Pres.: Murray J. Siegel
Chief financial officer: Norman
Potash
Nature of business: Discount/Department
Number of outlets: 145
Approx. net sales in millions:
840,000

Walgreen Co.
4300 Peterson Ave., Chicago, Ill.
60646
312-777-8400
Pres.: C. R. Walgreen, III
Chief financial officer: C. R.
Campbell
Nature of business: Drug
Number of outlets: 600
Approx. net sales in millions:
745,000

Wickes Corp.
515 North Washington, Saginaw,
Mich. 48607
517-754-0411
Pres.: E. L. McNeely
Chief financial officer: Homer R.
Sessions
Nature of business: Lumber &
building supplies
Number of outlets: 225
Approx. net sales in millions:
515,000

Winn-Dixie Stores, Inc.
5050 Edgewood Court, Jacksonville,
Fla. 32203
904-384-5511
Pres.: Bert L. Thomas
Chief financial officer: F. H. Gibbes,
Jr.
Nature of business: Food
Number of outlets: 800
Approx. net sales in millions:
1,420,000

F. W. Woolworth Co.
229–233 Broadway, New York,
N.Y. 10007
212-227-1000
Pres.: John S. Roberts
Chief financial officer: James R.
Webb
Nature of business: Variety
Number of outlets: 3,700
Approx. net sales in millions:
2,530,000

Zayre Corp.
Framingham, Mass. 01701
617-630-5000
Pres.: Stanley Feidberg
Chief financial officer: Paul
Kwasnick
Nature of business/Number of
outlets: Discount—155; Gas
station—40
Approx. net sales in millions:
685,000

FOREIGN ORGANIZATIONS

32. Foreign Trade
Bureaus in the United States

ARGENTINA

Embassy of the Argentine Republic
1600 New Hampshire Ave. N.W.,
Washington, D.C. 20009
202-332-7100

AUSTRALIA

Australian Embassy, Commercial
Minister
1601 Massachusetts Ave. N.W.,
Washington, D.C. 20036
202-797-3000

Australian Senior Trade Commissioner,
Australian Consulate General
636 Fifth Ave., New York, N.Y.
10020
212-245-4000

Australian Trade Commissioner,
Australian Consulate General
3550 Wilshire Blvd., 17th Floor,
Los Angeles, Calif. 90005
213-380-4611

Australian Trade Commissioner,
Australian Consulate General
1 Post St., Crocker Plaza, 8th Floor,
San Francisco, Calif. 94104
415-362-6160

New South Wales Government Center
680 Fifth Ave., New York, N.Y.
10019
212-582-0336

Sydney Morrell & Co. (for Victoria)
152 East 78th St., New York, N.Y.
10021
212-249-7255

AUSTRIA

Embassy of Austria, Commercial
Attache
2343 Massachusetts Ave. N.W.,
Washington, D.C. 20008
202-483-4474

Austrian Trade Delegate
845 Third Ave., New York, N.Y.
10022
212-421-5250

Austrian Trade Delegate
332 South Michigan Ave., Chicago,
Ill. 60611
312-427-9629

Austrian Trade Delegate
3440 Wilshire Blvd., Los Angeles,
Calif. 90005
213-380-7990

BARBADOS

The Barbados Industrial Development
Corp.
801 Second Ave., 2nd Floor, New
York, N.Y. 10017
212-686-5943

BELGIUM

Belgian Consulate General, Industrial
Section
50 Rockefeller Plaza, New York,
N.Y. 10020
212-JU 6-5110

BRAZIL

Embassy of Brazil, Commercial
Attache
3007 Whitehaven St. N.W., Washington, D.C. 20008
202-265-9880

Brazilian Government Trade Bureau
551 Fifth Ave., New York, N.Y.
10017
212-682-1055

Brazilian Consulate General
630 Fifth Ave., New York, N.Y.
· 10020
212-757-3080

Brazilian Consulate General
20 North Wacker Dr., Chicago, Ill.
60606
312-372-2176

Brazilian Consulate General
1306 International Trade Mart, New
Orleans, La. 70130
504-525-9874

Brazilian Consulate General
5900 Wilshire Blvd., Los Angeles,
Calif. 90036
213-937-5166

Brazilian Consulate
3400 Montrose Blvd., Houston, Tex.
77006
713-526-3941

Brazilian Consulate
100 North Biscayne Blvd., Miami,
Fla. 33132
305-377-1734

CANADA

Canadian Embassy, Commercial
Counsellor
1746 Massachusetts Ave. N.W.,
Washington, D.C. 20036
202-332-1011

Canadian Consulate General, Deputy
Consul General (Commercial)
680 Fifth Ave., New York, N.Y.
10019
212-586-2400

Canadian Consulate General, Consul &
Senior Trade Commissioner
500 Boylston St., Boston, Mass.
02116
617-262-3760

Canadian Consulate, Consul & Trade
Commissioner
1400 Main Pl., 396 Main St.,
Buffalo, N.Y. 14201
716-852-1247

Canadian Consulate General, Consul &
Senior Trade Commissioner
310 South Michigan Ave., Suite
2000, Chicago, Ill. 60604
312-427-1031

Canadian Consulate General, Consul &
Senior Trade Commissioner
Illuminating Bldg., 55 Public Square,
Cleveland, Ohio 44113
216-861-1660

Canadian Consulate, Consul & Trade
Commissioner
2100 Adolphus Tower, 1412 Main
St., Callas, Tex. 75202
214-742-8031

Canadian Consulate, Consul & Trade
Commissioner
1920 First Federal Bldg., 1001
Woodward Ave., Detroit, Mich.
48226
313-965-2811

Canadian Consulate General, Consul &
Trade Commissioner
510 West 6th St., Los Angeles, Calif.
90014
213-627-9511

Canadian Consulate, Consul & Trade
Commissioner
15 South Fifth St., Minneapolis,
Minn. 55402
612-336-4641

Canadian Consulate General, Consul &
Trade Commissioner
2110 International Trade Mart, New
Orleans, La. 70130
504-JA 5-2136

Canadian Consulate, Consul & Trade
Commissioner
3 Parkway Bldg., Suite 1310,
Philadelphia, Pa. 19102
215-561-1750

Canadian Consulate General, Consul &
Trade Commissioner
Commercial Division, 1 Maritime
Plaza, Golden Gateway Center,
San Francisco, Calif. 94111
415-981-2670

Canadian Consulate General, Consul
General & Trade Commissioner
412 Plaza 600, Sixth & Stewart,
Seattle, Wash. 98101
206-MU 2-3515

Quebec Government House, Office of
the Agent General
17 West 50th St., New York, N.Y.
10020
212-581-0770

Quebec Government House
111 Jackson Blvd. West, Chicago,
III. 60604
312-427-7194

Quebec Government House
Park Square Bldg., Suite 409, 31
St. James Ave., Boston, Mass.
02116
617-426-2660

Quebec Government House
1714 Adolphus Tower Bldg., 1412
Main St., Dallas. Tex 75202
214-742-6095

Quebec Government House
510 West 6th St., Suite 1202, Los
Angeles, Calif. 90014
213-680-9156

Government of Ontario, Senior Trade
& Industry Counsellor
11 East Adams St., Suite 705,
Chicago, III. 60603
312-922-2170

Government of Ontario, Senior Trade
& Industry Counsellor
680 Fifth Ave., Suite 1302, New
York, N.Y. 10019
212-247-2744

Government of Ontario, Senior Trade
& Industry Counsellor
606 South Olive St., Suite 1001,
Los Angeles, Calif. 90014
213-627-3531

Government of Ontario, Senior Trade
& Industry Counsellor
607 Boylston St., Suite 412, Boston,
Mass. 02116
617-261-8859

Government of Ontario, Senior Trade
& Industry Counsellor
230 Peachtree St. N.W., Suite 1800,
Atlanta, Ga. 30303
404-577-1883

Government of Ontario, Trade &
Industry Counsellor
Fidelity Bldg., Room 923, 1940 East
6th St., Cleveland, Ohio 44114
216-861-7690

Government of Ontario, Senior Trade
& Industry Counsellor
Chamber of Commerce Bldg., Room
1256, 15 South 5th St., Minneapolis, Minn. 55402
612-339-1800

Government of the Province of Alberta
Suite 703, 510 West 6th St., Los
Angeles, Calif. 90014
213-624-6371

British Columbia House
559 Market St., San Francisco,
Calif. 94105·
415-981-4780

CEYLON

Embassy of Ceylon
2148 Wyoming Ave. N.W.,
Washington, D.C. 20008
202-HU 3-4025

CHILE

Corporacion de Fomento de la
Produccion (CORFO)
80 Pine St., New York, N.Y.
10005
212-344-9800

CHINA (TAIWAN)

Chinese Investment & Trade Office
515 Madison Ave., New York, N.Y.
10022
212-752-2340

COLOMBIA

Colombian Center
140 East 57th St., New York, N.Y.
10022
212-421-8270

CONGO (KINSHASA)

Embassy of the Democratic Republic
of the Congo (Kinshasa)
1800 New Hampshire Ave. N.W.,
Washington, D.C. 20009
202-234-7690

COSTA RICA

Office of Economic Development,
Embassy of Costa Rica
2112 South St. N.W., Washington,
D.C. 20008
202-234-2945

DOMINICAN REPUBLIC

Dominican Republic Consulate
General
30 Rockefeller Plaza, New York,
N.Y. 10022
212-CO 5-0630

ECUADOR

Embassy of Ecuador
2535 15th St. N.W., Washington,
D.C. 20009
202-234-7200

EL SALVADOR

Embassy of El Salvador, Minister for
Economic, Financial and Commercial Affairs
2308 California St. N.W.,
Washington, D.C. 20008
202-265-3480

FINLAND

Embassy of Finland, Commercial/
Economic Section
1900 24th St. N.W., Washington,
D.C. 20008
202-462-0556

Consulate General of Finland, Finland
House
540 Madison Ave., New York, N.Y.
10022
212-832-6550

Consulate General of Finland
120 Montgomery St., San Francisco,
Calif. 94104
415-981-4656

Consulate & Commercial Office of
Finland
3600 Wilshire Blvd., Suite 1610, Los
Angeles, Calif. 90005
213-385-1779

Vice Consulate & Commercial Office of Finland
Box 1484 (111 Church St.),
Evanstown, Ill. 60204
312-491-0551

FRANCE

French Industrial Development Agency
Rockefeller Center, 610 Fifth Ave.,
New York, N.Y. 10020
212-PL 7-9340

GERMANY

Manager, Market Development,
German-American Chamber of Commerce
666 Fifth Ave., New York, N.Y. 10019
212-582-7788

GHANA

Consulate General of Ghana, Ghana Trade & Investment Office
150 East 58th St., New York, N.Y. 10022
212-832-1300

GREECE

Hellenic Industrial Development Bank
1290 Ave. of the Americas, New York, N.Y. 10019
212-757-3523

GUATEMALA

Embassy of Guatemala
2220 R St. N.W., Washington, D.C. 20008
202-332-2865

HAITI

Embassy of Haiti, Commercial Attache
4400 17th St. N.W., Washington, D.C. 20011
202-723-7001

HONG KONG

Hong Kong Trade Development Council
548 Fifth Ave., New York, N.Y. 10036
212-582-6610

Hong Kong Trade Development Council
606 South Hill St., Suite 401/402, Los Angeles, Calif. 90014
213-622-3194

Hong Kong Trade Development Council
333 North Michigan Ave., Suite 1511, Chicago, Ill. 60601
312-726-4515

ICELAND

Embassy of Iceland
2022 Connecticut Ave. N.W., Washington, D.C. 20008
202-265-6653

INDIA

Indian Investment Centre
708 Third Ave., New York, N.Y. 10017
212-TN 7-3390

INDONESIA

Indonesian Consulate General
5 East 68th St., New York, N.Y. 10021
212-879-0600

Embassy of the Republic of Indonesia, Economic Section
2020 Massachusetts Ave. N.W., Washington, D.C. 20036
202-293-1745

IRAN

Iranian Economic Mission
5530 Wisconsin Ave., Washington, D.C. 20015
301-654-7930

IRELAND

Industrial Development Authority
Ireland
410 Park Ave., New York, N.Y.
10022
212-371-8850

Industrial Development Authority
Ireland
1 East Wacker Dr., Chicago, Ill.
60601
312-644-7474

Industrial Development Authority
Ireland
44 Montgomery St., San Francisco,
Calif. 94104
415-434-4758

ISRAEL

Government of Israel Investment &
Export Authority
850 Third Ave., Suite 604, New
York, N.Y. 10022
212-PL 2-5600, ext. 263

Government of Israel Investment &
Export Authority
659 South Highland Ave., Los
Angeles, Calif. 90036
213-938-3691

Government of Israel Investment &
Export Authority
111 East Wacker Dr., Suite 1308,
Chicago, Ill. 60601
312-644-4140

Government of Israel Investment &
Export Authority
805 Peachtree St. N.E., Atlanta, Ga.
30308
404-875-7561

ITALY

Embassy of Italy, Commercial Office
2600 Virginia Ave. N.W., Suite 200,
Washington, D.C. 20037
202-337-3700

Italian Consulate General, Commercial
Office
600 Madison Ave., New York, N.Y.
10022
212-421-4895

Italian Consulate General, Commercial
Office
785 Market St., Suite 604, San Francisco, Calif. 94102
415-YU 2-3551

Italian Trade Commissioner
627 Statler Office Bldg., Boston,
Mass. 02116
617-426-3214

Italian Trade Commissioner
625 North Michigan Ave., Suite 411,
Chicago, Ill. 60611
312-787-3772

Italian Trade Commissioner
212 World Trade Bldg., Houston,
Tex. 77002
713-CA 2-2229

Italian Trade Commissioner
500 Griswold St., Suite 2961,
Detroit, Mich. 48226
313-964-3970

Italian Trade Commissioner
1900 Ave. of the Stars, Gateway
West Bldg., Suite 1870,
Century City, Los Angeles, Calif.
90067
213-879-0950

Italian Trade Commissioner
International Trade Mart, Suite
2414, New Orleans, La. 70112
504-JA 5-9366

Italian Trade Commissioner
2 Penn Center Plaza, Suite 1401,
Philadelphia, Pa. 19102
215-LO 3-0641

IVORY COAST

Embassy of the Republic of Ivory
Coast
2424 Massachusetts Ave. N.W.,
Washington, D.C. 20008
202-483-2400

Ivory Coast Development Office,
  Economic Counselor
  521 Fifth Ave., New York, N.Y.
  10017
  212-869-1700

Consulate of the Ivory Coast
  9000 Sunset Blvd., Suite 1402, Los
  Angeles, Calif. 90069
  213-272-5158

JAMAICA

Jamaica Industrial Development Corp.
  200 Park Ave., New York, N.Y.
  10017
  212-OX 7-1188

JAPAN

Japan Trade Center
  393 Fifth Ave., New York, N.Y.
  10016
  212-532-7191

Japan Trade Center
  232 North Michigan Ave., Chicago,
  Ill. 60601
  312-726-4390

Japan Trade Center
  1737 Post St., San Francisco,
  Calif. 94115
  415-922-0234

Japan Trade Center
  727 West 7th St., Los Angeles,
  Calif. 90017
  213-625-0731

Japan Trade Center
  Melrose Bldg., 1127 Walker St.,
  Houston, Tex. 70002
  713-227-8318

Japan Trade Center
  2 Canal St,., New Orleans, La. 70130
  504-525-8266

KENYA

Embassy of Kenya
  2249 R St. N.W., Washington, D.C.
  20008
  202-234-4350

KOREA

Korea Trade Promotion Center
  (KOTRA)
  Suite 4601, Empire State Bldg., 350
  Fifth Ave., New York, N.Y. 10001
  212-594-9464

Korea Trade Center, Occidental
  Center
  1149 South Hill St., Los Angeles,
  Calif. 90015
  213-748-5331

Korea Trade Center
  111 East Wacker Dr., Suite 519,
  Chicago, Ill. 60601
  312-644-4324

Korea Trade Center
  Room 250-C, World Trade Center,
  Ferry Bldg., San Francisco, Calif.
  94111
  415-391-2637

Korea Trade Center
  1142 1 Main Pl. Bldg., Dallas, Tex.
  75250
  214-748-9341

LESOTHO

Embassy of the Kingdom of Lesotho
  1601 Connecticut Ave. N.W., Suite
  300, Washington, D.C. 20009
  202-462-4190

LIBERIA

Embassy of Liberia
  5201 16th St. N.W., Washington,
  D.C. 20011
  202-723-0437

B. M. Lawrence & Co.
  351 California St., San Francisco,
  Calif. 94104
  415-981-3650

LUXEMBOURG

Luxembourg Consulate General
  200 East 42nd St., New York, N.Y.
  10017
  212-687-3166

MALAYSIA

Embassy of Malaysia Trade Office,
    Attn: Trade Attache (Counselor)
845 Third Ave., 16th Floor, New
York, N.Y. 10022
212-355-5028

MALI

Embassy of Mali
2130 R St. N.W., Washington, D.C.
20008
202-332-2249

MARTINIQUE, GUADELOUPE, AND FRENCH GUIANA

French Commercial Counselor in
    Washington, Embassy of France
1100 Connecticut Ave. N.W.,
Washington, D.C. 20036
202-223-6710

MOROCCO

Embassy of Morocco, Attn:
    Commercial Counselor, Economic
    Section
1601 21st St. N.W., Washington,
D.C. 20009
202-462-7979

Office of Commercialization and
    Exportation
597 Fifth Ave., New York, N.Y.
10020
212-758-2625

NETHERLANDS

Industrial Commissioner for the
    Netherlands in the U.S.
1 Rockefeller Plaza, 11th Floor,
New York, N.Y. 10020
212-246-1429

NETHERLANDS ANTILLES

Netherland Antilles Economic
    Mission
866 UN Plaza, New York, N.Y.
10017
212-421-3360

NEW ZEALAND

Office of the Minister (Commercial),
    New Zealand Embassy
1145 19th St. N.W., Washington,
D.C. 20036
202-338-8820

New Zealand Government Trade
    Commissioner
630 Fifth Ave., New York, N.Y.
10021
212-586-0060

New Zealand Government Trade
    Commissioner
153 Kearny St., San Francisco,
Calif. 94108
415-982-6780

New Zealand Government Trade
    Commissioner
510 West 6th St., Los Angeles,
Calif. 90014
213-624-1491

NICARAGUA

Embassy of Nicaragua, Commercial
    Section
1627 New Hampshire Ave. N.W.,
Washington, D.C. 20009
202-332-1643

NIGERIA

Consulate General of Nigeria, Attn:
    Nigerian Commercial Officer
575 Lexington Ave., New York,
N.Y. 10022
212-752-1670

Embassy of Nigeria, Office of
    Economic Affairs
1333 16th St. N.W., Washington,
D.C. 20036
202-234-4800

NORWAY

Embassy of Norway, Attn:
    Commercial Attache
3401 Massachusetts Ave. N.W.,
Washington, D.C. 20007
202-333-6000

PAKISTAN

Pakistan Investment Center, Consulate
General of Pakistan
12 East 65th St., New York, N.Y.
10021
212-879-5800

PANAMA

Embassy of Panama, Attn:
Commercial Counselor
2862 McGill Terrace, Washington,
D.C. 20008
202-387-7400

Panama Government Investment
Development Center
405 Park Ave., New York, N.Y.
10022
212-371-4343

PARAGUAY

U.S. Paraguay Trade Assn.
1134 National Press Bldg.,
Washington D.C. 20004
202-NA 8-9439

PHILLIPINES

Embassy of the Phillippines, Attn:
Commercial Attache
1617 Massachusets Ave. N.W.,
Washington, D.C. 20036
202-265-2043 or 202-462-1400

Office of the Commercial Attache
17 Battery Pl., Room 309, New
York, N.Y. 10004
212-269-0840

Office of the Foreign Trade Promotion
Republic, Philippine Consulate
General
6 North Michigan Ave., Suite 907,
Chicago, Ill. 60602
312-332-6458

Office of the Foreign Trade Promotion
Republic, Philippine Consulate
General
2433 Pali Highway, Honolulu,
Hawaii 96817
595-6316 or 595-6318

Office of the Foreign Trade Promotion
Republic, Philippine Consulate
General
3075 Wilshire Blvd., Los Angeles,
Calif. 90005
213-384-8075

Office of the Foreign Trade Promotion
Republic, Philippine Consulate
General
L-275 World Trade Center, Ferry
Bldg., San Francisco, Calif. 94111
415-982-2354

Office of the Foreign Trade Promotion
Republic, Philippine Consulate
General
1440 International Trade Mart, New
Orleans, La. 70130
504-524-2755

Office of the Foreign Trade Promotion
Republic, Philippine Consulate
General
835 Central Bldg., Third Ave. &
Columbia St., Seattle, Wash. 98104
206-MA 4-7703

PORTUGAL

Casa de Portugal
570 Fifth Ave., New York, N.Y.
10036
212-581-2450

ROMANIA

Romanian Trade Office
95 Madison Ave., New York, N.Y.
10016
212-532-4077

SINGAPORE

Singapore Economic Development
Board
500 North Michigan Ave., Suite 42,
Chicago, Ill. 60611
312-644-3730

Singapore Economic Development
Board
745 Fifth Ave., Suite 1509, New
York, N.Y. 10022
212-421-2203

Singapore Economic Development
Board
44 Montgomery St., Suite 4261,
San Francisco, Calif. 94104
415-391-0756

SPAIN

Commercial Office of Spain
2558 Massachusetts Ave. N.W.,
Washington, D.C. 20008
202-265-8600

Commercial Office of Spain
Chrylser Bldg., 32nd Floor, 405
Lexington Ave., New York,
N.Y. 10017
212-661-4959

Commercial Office of Spain
55 East Washington St., Chicago,
Ill. 60602
312-782-7799

Commercial Office of Spain
Flood Bldg., Suite 542, 870
Market St., San Francisco,
Calif. 94102
415-397-1853

Commercial Office of Spain
1840 International Trade Mart,
New Orleans, La. 70130
504-524-1401

SURINAM

Consulate General of The Netherlands
1 Rockefeller Plaza, 11th Floor,
New York, N.Y. 10020
212-246-1436

SWAZILAND

Embassy of the Kingdom of
Swaziland
2233 Wisconsin Ave. N.W.,
Washington, D.C. 20007
202-362-6683

SWEDEN

Swedish Industrial Development
Corp.
63 East 64th St., New York, N.Y.
10021
212-628-0320

TANZANIA

Embassy of Tanzania
2721 Connecticut Ave. N.W.,
Washington, D.C. 20008
202-483-4116

THAILAND

Bangkok Bank Ltd.
44 Wall St., New York, N.Y.
10005
212-944-5925

TRINIDAD AND TOBAGO

Trinidad & Tobago Industrial
Development Corp.
400 Madison Ave., Suite 712-
714, New York, N.Y. 10017
212-PL 5-9360

TUNISIA

Embassy of Tunisia
2408 Massachusetts Ave. N.W.,
Washington, D.C. 20008
202-AD 4-6644

TURKEY

Turkish Embassy, Office of the
Commercial Counselor
2523 Massachusetts Ave. N.W.,
Washington, D.C. 20008
202-483-6366

Turkish Embassy, Office of the
Commercial Counselor
Room 542, Empire State Bldg., 350
Fifth Ave., New York, N.Y. 10001
212-564-4880

UGANDA

Embassy of Uganda
5905 16th St. N.W., Washington,
D.C. 20011
202-726-7100

Commercial Section, Permanent
Mission of Uganda to the UN
801 Second Ave., New York, N.Y.
10017
212-689-3780

The Uganda Coffee Marketing Board
110 Wall St., New York, N.Y. 10005
212-943-2410

UNITED KINGDOM

The Director, British Trade
Development Office, British
Consulate-General
150 East 58th St., New York, N.Y.
10022
212-593-2258

H. M. Consul General, British Consulate-General
Suite 912, 225 Peachtree St. N.E.,
Atlanta, Ga. 30303
404-524-2691

H. M. Consul General, British Consulate-General
Suite 4740, Prudential Tower,
Prudential Center, Boston, Mass.
02199
617-542-2810

H. M. Consul General, British Consulate-General
33 North Dearborn St., Chicago, Ill.
60602
312-346-1810

H. M. Consul General, British Consulate-General
1828 Illuminating Bldg. 44 Public
Square, Cleveland, Ohio 44113
216-621-7676

H. M. Consul General, British Consulate-General
1008 Detroit Bank & Trust Bldg.,
211 Fort St. West, Detroit,
Mich. 48226
313-962-4776

H. M. Consul General, British Consulate-General
1005 World Trade Center, Houston,
Tex. 77002
713-223-2301/2/3/4

H. M. Consul General, British Consulate-General
3324 Wilshire Blvd., Los Angeles,
Calif. 90010
213-385-7381

H. M. Consul General, British Consulate-General
932 Ingraham Bldg., 25 Southeast
Second Ave., Miami, Fla. 33131
305-371-7544/5/6

URUGUAY

Embassy of Uruguay, Commercial
Section
1918 F St. N.W., Washington, D.C.
20006
202-628-1336

YUGOSLAVIA

Embassy of Yugoslavia
2410 California St. N.W., Washington, D.C. 20007
202-462-6566

Yugoslav Consulate General, Attn:
Economic Counselor
488 Madison Ave., New York,
N.Y. 10022
212-838-2300

Yugoslav Consulate General
625 Stanwix St., Pittsburgh, Pa.
15222
412-471-6191

Yugoslav Consulate General
188 West Randolph St., Suite 3000,
Chicago, Ill. 60601
312-332-0169

Yugoslav Consulate General
1919 Sacramento St., San Francisco,
Calif. 94127
415-776-4941

Yugoslav Federal Chamber of Economy
Trade Office
1900 Ave. of the Stars, Suite 758,
Los Angeles, Calif. 90067
213-553-2648

Federal Economic Chamber of Yugoslavia
Mid-West Trade Office, 15 South
5th St., Suite 1252, Minneapolis,
Minn. 55402
612-332-3961

MULTINATIONAL ORGANIZATIONS

ADELA Development Corp. of the
U.S.
1211 Connecticut Ave. N.W., Washington, D.C. 20006
202-296-3412

International Finance Corp.
1818 H St. N.W., Washington,
D.C. 20433
202-EX 3-6360

International Finance Corp.
120 Broadway, New York, N.Y.
10005
212-964-6100

Overseas Private Investment Corp.
1129 20th St. N.W., Washington,
D.C. 20527
202-632-1854

33. Foreign Firms Listed on the New York and American Stock Exchange

Alcan Aluminum Ltd.
1 Place Ville Marie, Montreal,
Canada

Alliance Tire & Rubber Co., Ltd.
Hadera, Israel

Atlas Consolidated Mining and
Development Corp.
A. Soriano Bldg., Makati, Rizal,
Philippines

Benguet Consolidated, Inc.
P.O. Box 817, Manila,
Philippines

British American Tobacco Company,
Ltd.
Westminster House, London S. W. 1,
England

British Petroleum Co., Ltd.
Britannic House, London E. C. 2Y
9 BU, England

Campbell Red Lake Mines, Ltd.
360 Bay St., Toronto, Ontario,
Canada

Canada Southern Railways
6 Penn Center Plaza, Philadelphia,
Pa. 19104

Canadian Breweries, Ltd.
79 St. Clair Ave. East, Toronto
7, Canada

Canadian Pacific, Ltd.
Windsor Sta., Montreal 3, Quebec,
Canada

Courtaulds, Ltd.
18 Hanover Square, London W. 1,
England

Distillers Corp.-Seagrams, Ltd.
1430 Pul St., Montreal 110, Quebec,
Canada

Dome Mines, Ltd.
South Porcupine, Ontario,
Canada

Genstar, Ltd.
1 Place Ville Marie, Montreal 113,
Quebec, Canada

Granby Mining Co., Ltd.
1111 West Georgia St., Vancouver,
B. C. 5, Canada

Hudson Bay Mining & Smelting Co.,
Ltd.
P.O. Box 28, Toronto Dominion
Centre, Toronto 1, Ontario,
Canada

Imperial Tobacco Group, Ltd.
1 Grosvenor Pl., London SWOX
7HB, England

International Nickel Co. of Canada,
Ltd.
Cooper Cliff, Ontario, Canada

McIntyre Porcupine Mines, Ltd.
55 Yonge St., Toronto1, Ontario,
Canada

Marinduque Mining & Industrial Corp.
2283 Pasong Tamo Extension,
Makati, Rizal, Philippines D 708

Massey-Ferguson, Ltd.
200 University Ave., Toronto 1,
Ontario, Canada

Norlin Corp.
Calle Aquilino de la Guardia # 8,
Panama, Republic of Panama

Northern & Central Gas Corp., Ltd.
4600 Toronto-Dominion Centre,
Toronto 1, Ontario, Canada

Northgate Exploration, Ltd.
Toronto-Dominion Centre,
Toronto 1, Ontario, Canada

O'Okiep Cooper Co., Ltd.
Nababeep, Cape Province, South
Africa

Pacific Petroleums, Ltd.
P.O. Box 6666, Calgary, Alberta,
Canada

Philippine Long Distance Telephone
Co.
Legazpi St., Makati, Rizal, Phil-
ippines

Roan Selection Trust, Ltd.
Kafue Honse, Cairo Rd., P.O. Box
851, Lusaka, Zambia

Royal Dutch Petroleum Co.
30 Card van Bylandtlaan, The
Hague, Netherlands

San Carlos Milling Co.
222 Buendia Ave., Makati, Rizal,
Philippines

Shell Transport & Trading Co., Ltd.
Shell Centre, London S.E. 1,
England

Sumitomo Chemical Co., Ltd.
15, 5-Chome, Kitahama,
Higashiku, Osaka, Japan 541

Syntex Corp.
P.O. Box 7386, Panama 5, Republic of Panama

Tubos De Acero De Mexico S. A.
Pans No. 15, Mexico City 4, D. F.,
Mexico

Hiram-Walker-Gooderham & Worts,
Ltd.
2072 Riverside Dr., East Walkerville,
Ontario, Canada

Westcoast Transmission Co., Ltd.
1333 West Georgia St., Vancouver 5,
British Columbia, Canada

PUBLICATIONS AND REFERENCE SERVICES

34. Financial and Investment Advisory Publications

BANK LETTERS

No charge. Apply directly.

Business in Brief
Chase Manhattan Bank, 1 Chase Manhattan Plaza, New York, N.Y. 10015

Business Bulletin
Cleveland Trust Co., Euclid & East 9th St., Cleveland, Ohio 44101

Monthly Letter on Business and Economic Conditions
First National City Bank of New York, 399 Park Ave., New York, N.Y. 10022

FEDERAL RESERVE BANK PUBLICATIONS

No charge. Apply directly.

Business Conditions: A Review
Federal Reserve Bank of Chicago, P.O. Box 834, Chicago, Ill. 60690

Business Review
Public Information Dept., Federal Reserve Bank of Philadelphia, Philadelphia, Pa. 19101

Business Review
Federal Reserve Bank of Dallas, Dallas, Tex. 75222

Economic Review
Research Dept., Federal Reserve Bank of Cleveland, Cleveland, Ohio 44101

Monthly Review
Federal Reserve Bank of Atlanta, Atlanta, Ga. 30303

Monthly Review
Federal Reserve Bank of Kansas City, Federal Reserve Sta., Kansas City, Mo. 64198

Monthly Review
Federal Reserve Bank of New York, 33 Liberty St., New York, N.Y. 10045

Monthly Review
Federal Reserve Bank of Richmond, Richmond, Va. 23212

157

Monthly Review
Federal Reserve Bank of San Francisco, 400 Sansome St., San Francisco, Calif. 94120

Review
Federal Reserve Bank of St. Louis, P.O. Box 442, St. Louis, Mo. 63166

DAILY AND WEEKLY NEWSPAPERS

American Banker
525 West 42nd St., New York, N.Y. 10036

Barron's National Business & Financial Weekly
30 Broad St., New York, N.Y. 10004

Commercial and Financial Chronicle
25 Park Pl., New York, N.Y. 10036

Financial World
17 Battery Pl., New York, N.Y. 10004

Journal of Commerce
99 Wall St., New York, N.Y. 10005

New York Times
229 West 43rd St., New York, N.Y. 10036

Wall Street Journal
30 Broad St., New York, N.Y. 10004

Wall Street Transcript
54 Wall St., New York, N.Y. 10005

Weekly Bond Buyer
77 Water St., New York, N.Y. 10005

BROKERAGE HOUSE LETTERS

Most of the major brokerage firms publish some type of market letter for their clients. Interested investors should contact these firms. A weekly publication, *The Wall Street Transcript*, reprints a number of market letters of interest to the investment community. Information about a subscription can be obtained by writing to: The Wall Street Transcript, 54 Wall St., New York, N.Y. 10005.

MAJOR INVESTMENT NEWSLETTERS

The following section has been provided by Select Information Exchange, a New York City-based subscription agency specializing in handling only investment and business service publications. They provide a special trial subscription plan for most of their publications. This allows an individual or company an opportunity to review a number of publications at a nominal rate. Information and subscription rates for the following publications can be obtained by writing to Select Information Exchange, Box 770, Wall St. Sta., New York, N.Y. 10005. No part of this section may be reproduced in any form by any means without permission in writing from Select Information Exchange.

Active Stocks

Marketlines. F.B.P. Publishing, Inc. A weekly market advisory letter devoted to the most active listed stocks, whose analysis is based on the theory of sponsorship. The service traces the interest of the professionals, chartists, and emotional public who are behind every stock and offers buy—hold—sell recommendations for each stock reviewed. Special trading section and special situations are included with each issue. 1 year, 51 issues, $150.

Art Investment

The Print Collector's Newsletter. The only comprehensive newsletter devoted to original prints, with auction prices, new prints published, books reviewed, catalogs reviewed, feature articles, new multiples published. International. Illustrated. 1 year, 6 issues, $12.

Washington International Arts Letter. Leads to the best tax-deductible arts organizations are provided regularly in this digest of support programs, 20th-century patronage, investments, and developments in the arts. 1 year, 10 issues, $27.

Asian Business and Investments

An Asian Notebook. The Tokyo-based magazine telling Asia like it is for those who really want to know. Will help the businessman understand what makes Asia tick and provide interesting, factual reading at the same time. 2 years, 24 issues, $24.

The Investor. Leading business, investment, and trade magazine published in Thailand. Must reading for the businessman and investor interested in South East Asia. 1 year, 26 issues, $33.75.

Pacific Basin Report Service. Culls the essence of hundreds of significant business and financial developments in the Asia-Pacific region. Current activities of major U. S., Japanese, and European firms in Pacific Basin countries—revealing ownership and financing, tracing supply links, focusing especially on multinational ventures. Fully indexed by company and country. 1 year, 24 issues, $144.

Australian Investments

Extel Australian Company Service. Extel Statistical Services, Ltd. Comprehensive weekly card service covering Australian security market. Company activities, subsidiaries, directors, capital, voting rights, dividend record, profit and loss details (10 yrs.), turnover analysis, interim statements, share quotations, P-E ratios, balance sheets, net asset value, mergers, acquisitions, etc. 1 year, 52 issues, $84.

Comsec Australian Industry Report. Report in industry group sequence of all listed stocks on Sydney Exchange showing price ranges, yields, P.E., marketability, and industry averages. 1 year, 12 issues, $125.

Comsec Market Indicators & Weekly Highlight Sheet. Technical indicators and market summary, including all listed stocks showing technically interesting situations in the Australian stock market. 1 year, 52 issues, $200.

Comsec 200 Speculative Daily Bar Charts. Charts showing high, low, last sale prices on semi-log scale, and turnover on 200 speculative Australian stocks. 1 year, 52 issues, $200.

Comsec 200 Leading Weekly Bar Charts. Charts showing high, low, last sale prices on semi-log scale, and turnover on 200 leading Australian stocks. 1 year, 52 issues, $200.

Kompass Australia. The computerized directory of Australian industry. 8,300 companies, 296,000 product, material, and service entries. Sponsored by the Associated Chambers of Commerce of Australia. Annually published in Spring. 1 issue, $45.

Bahamas Investments

The Darragh Letter. Weekly business and investment newsletter of the Bahamas. Written in the islands and mailed from Florida every Saturday. Covers the growing Bahamian securities market, direct investment opportunities, real estate, business, and political climate. Edited by Charles Darragh, consultant on the Bahamas. 1 year, 52 issues, $50.

Banking and Investments

Promotion Newsletter. Dan Newman Co. A confidential personal monthly publication for advertising and marketing executives in banking and savings and loan institutions. Ideas for increasing business. 1 year, 12 issues, $25. 2 years, 24 issues, $40.

Bank Management Services

Bank Automation Newsletter. Warren, Gorham & Lamont, Inc. The only publication devoted to digesting all news involving bank automation: products, installations, personnel, law, research, marketing, maintenance, book reviews, personalities. 1 year, 12 issues, $36.

Senior Bank Executive's Report. Warren, Gorham & Lamont, Inc. Twice a month, eight-page newsletter with marketing, law, personnel, money matters, management, operations. Tightly edited, well-written. 1 year, 24 issues, $60.

The Bankers Magazine. Established in 1846, this quarterly presents articles in depth on all phases of banking management with particular emphasis on lending, money management, banking history, ethics, marketing, and management strategies. Aimed at the top executive and those who will be top executives. 1 year, 4 issues, $28.

Bank Auditing and Accounting Report. Warren, Gorham & Lamont, Inc. A professional information letter report service that will keep you completely informed regarding new laws, procedures, practices, and developments in bank accounting, auditing, and control systems. 1 year, 12 issues, $36.

Bank Installment Lending Newsletter. Warren, Gorham & Lamont, Inc. A professional information letter report service that will keep you completely informed regarding new laws, procedures, practices, and developments in bank accounting, auditing, and control systems. 1 year, 12 issues, $36.

Bank Loan Officers Report. In six tightly packed pages you will find a distillation of the best information available in the commercial loan field. Written for the creative bank loan officer. 1 year, 12 issues, $36.

Bank Marketing Report. Warren, Gorham & Lamont, Inc. Selling techniques, market research, training bank personnel, advertising, public relations, employee relations, officer call programs. It is for hard-working bank marketing officers who need help, need new ideas, need new techniques, and need them now. 1 year, 12 issues, $36.

Bank Director's Report. Warren, Gorham & Lamont, Inc. Apprises the bank director of his legal responsibilities, his liabilities, and gives him the tools to make his bank more successful and more profitable. Legal pitfalls, management techniques, marketing ploys for both large and small banks. 1 year, 12 issues, $28.

Bank Investment Portfolio Planner. Warren, Gorham & Lamont, Inc. In addition to reporting on current trends and developments, this service digs out case history material unavailable elsewhere. Coverage includes: money market investments; industrial & financial dealer paper; bankers acceptances; tax-exempt securities; securities regulations; adjusting the money position; alternative sources of liquidity; collateral loans vs. repurchase agreements; federal funds market; asset allocation; etc. 1 year, 24 issues, $55.

Bank Operations Report. Warren, Gorham & Lamont, Inc. A monthly reporting service providing authoritative guidance and practical information for the people who manage banking's vital internal support functions; systems and automation; internal controls; organization and personnel; security arrangements; accounting; office management; physical plant and equipment. Special in-depth reports are sent periodically. 1 year, 12 issues, $36.

Bank Personnel Report. Warren, Gorham & Lamont, Inc. Covers all aspects, new techniques, and new procedures, including news in federal and state regulation and legislation affecting bank personnel practices. Also includes pension plans, profit sharing, suggested systems and salary administration, psychological tests, work evaluation tests, training programs, automation, clerical time management programs, etc. 1 year, 12 issues, $29.

The Bank Security Report. Warren, Gorham & Lamont. An expert, practical information service dealing exclusively with bank security methods and training programs, shows how you can stop disasters before they take place. Information about new security equipment, forged checks, identifications, training devices. 1 year, 12 issues, $36.

Bank Teller's Report. Warren, Gorham & Lamont, Inc. Trains tellers in all phases of banking, marketing, operations, techniques, personal grooming, public relations, customer relations. 1 year, 12 issues, $24.

Bankers Handbook of Federal Aids to Financing. Warren, Gorham & Lamont, Inc. An instant information retrieval system to find where the monies are, what agencies to approach, who is eligible to apply, how to process applications for federal financing in: real estate financing assistance; small business programs; natural resource programs; housing; export financing; mobile homes; farm loans; nursing homes; veterans loans; disaster loans. Fully indexed by subject. 1 issue, $34.50.

Branch Banker's Report. Warren, Gorham & Lamont, Inc. Covers bank discipline, operations and marketing, public relations, community relations, business development, loan profitability, employee training and relations. New management ideas and procedures, new trends, developments, legal, etc. 1 year, 12 issues, $28.

Payment Systems Newsletter. The only monthly 8-page newsletter which is devoted to digesting technological changes in the payment system as it affects commercial banks, mutual savings banks, savings and loan associations, credit unions, retailers, brokerage firms, insurance companies, etc. Contents include systems and software, payment systems standards, research and marketing developments, and industry reviews. 1 year, 12 issues, $37.50.

The Tax Report of Banking and Trusts. Warren, Gorham & Lamont, Inc. Covers Federal and State court bank tax decisions, digest and reference to articles in tax and legal periodicals. Congressional committee reports, proposed and new legislation in fields of federal and state taxation of banks and trusts, bank and trust planning laws, specimen filled-in income tax returns for small, medium, and large banks, new ideas for tax planning and savings. 1 year, 24 issues, $44.

Washington Banktrends. A financial newsletter that alerts banks and other financial institutions to critical financial trends and capsulizes relevant news. 1 year, 52 issues, $50.

Banking Statistics Interpretation—Investment Counsel Based on Banking Statistics Analysis

The Bank Credit Analyst. Monetary Research, Ltd. A continuous appraisal of U. S. money and credit, pointing up the trends in business and investments of all types—inventories and capital outlays, as well as stocks and bonds. 1 year, 12 issues, $150.

The International Bank Credit Analyst. Monetary Research, Ltd. A continuous appraisal of the money and credit situation of ten Free World countries pointing up the trends in business and investments of all types—inventories and capital outlays as well as stocks and bonds. 1 year, 12 issues, $250.

Financial Markets Review. Finacor, Inc. A monthly analysis of trends in money, bank credit, and spending with timing recommendations for investments in the stock and bond markets. 1 year, 12 issues, $85.

Money and Credit Reports. Capital Advisors, Inc. News reports on trends and developments in the money and credit areas, on how they affect business, securities, and real estate investments. What the current interest rate charges mean is one of many topics covered in this letter edited by J. I. Weiss. 1 year, 24 issues, $60.

Bond and Money Market Services

Baxter International Economic Research Bureau. A weekly investment and economic service which analyzes business conditions, market trends, and international monetary conditions. Individual stock recommendations are made with emphasis on sound growth situations. Published since 1926 by William J. Baxter & Staff. 1 year, 51 issues, $90.

Fitch Corporate Bond Ratings. Fitch Investors Service. An authoritative comprehensive service on the corporate bond market which presents in alphabetical arrangement the quality rating, bank eligibility, and legal status of the outstanding issues of almost 1,000 corporations. Close to 1,300 different issues, both domestic and foreign, are covered. Monthly supplements on a cumulative basis cover new issues and changes in ratings, eligibility, and legal status. Unlimited inquiry privilege. 1 year, 12 issues, $30.

Goldsmith, Nagan Bond and Money Market Letter. Goldsmith-Nagan, Inc. A bi-weekly analysis, and interpretation of bond price and interest-rate trends, covering corporate bonds. Government securities and all money market instruments. 1 year, 26 issues plus specials, $75.

Investment Guidelines. McConnell Craig Capital Advisor, Ltd. A comprehensive letter for the experienced businessman and investor. Dealing with the trends of bonds, bullion (gold & silver), interest rates, money markets, real estate and stocks as viewed from the international scene. American and Canadian markets regularly featured. Recommendations made for domestic and foreign issues. 1 year, 24–30 issues, $75.

British Investments

Extel British Company Information. Extel Statistical Services, Ltd. Comprehensive daily card service covering British security market. Company activities, subsidiaries, directors, capital, voting rights, dividend record, profit and loss details (10 yrs.), turnover analysis, interim statements, share quotations, P. E. ratios, balance sheets, net asset value, mergers, acquisitions, etc. 1 year, 260 issues, $600.

Extel Unquoted Equities Service. Extel Statistical Services, Ltd. Comprehensive weekly card service covering the unquoted British equities market. Company activities, subsidiaries, directors, capital, voting rights, dividend record, profit and loss details (ten yrs.), turnover analysis, interim statements, major shareholders, balance sheets, net asset value, mergers, acquisitions, etc. 1 year, 52 issues, $420.

Fleet Street Letter. A weekly economic and investment letter written anonymously by a team of Fleet Street's top city journalists. Also contains inside information of world affairs and U.K. politics, essential for right investment decisions. 1 year, 48 issues, $40.

International Securities Locator—United Kingdom Securities. Scheinman Ciaramella International, Inc. Lists by security every U.K. security held by over 2000 investment companies in U.K., U.S., Canada, and 22 other countries. Shows number of shares held by each fund, previous position, net change. Also names, addresses, telephone, telex, and cable address of funds. 1 year, 4 issues, $520.

Investors Chronicle & Stock Exchange Gazette. The leading British financial weekly journal established over a half century giving complete information to the investor and the investment counsellor. Each issue offers a careful and responsible review of the British and European stock market from both the investment and the speculative viewpoints. 1 year, 52 issues, $33.60.

Business Cycles

Business Conditions Digest. U. S. Government. Reports on the latest changes and developments of more than 100 different series of economic indicators grouped according to their usual timing in relation to major changes in the economy; leading, coincident, or lagging. 3 years, 36 issues, $45.

Business and Financial News

Business Week Letter. McGraw-Hill, Inc. A complete financial service for businessmen and investors, from the editors of *Business Week*, which relates current economic trends, and important new developments in the financial sector, to the profitable operation of your business. To backstop your investment decisions, you'll find sophisticated market analysis; news of stocks, bonds, funds; recommendations from leading securities analysis; periodic computer coverage of moving stock groups. Also, new ideas from experts in planning, taxes, insurance pension-planning—plus on-the-spot Washington coverage of political developments affecting businessmen and investors. 1 year, 26 issues, $50.

Business Trends

Survey of Current Business. U. S. Government. Gives information on trends in industry, the business situation, outlook, and other points pertinent to the business world. 3 years, 36 issues, $27.

California Investments

California Business. A leading source of investment information about California corporations both large and small. The exclusive over-the-counter review, in depth corporate analyses, investment news plus earnings projections and reports provide vital data and insight for investment decisions. 1 year, 50 issues, $24.

Business West. A monthly magazine covering western business and finance in depth, particularly those companies and corporate activities in California, Oregon, and Washington. It keeps the investor interested in Western opportunities informed on corporate developments and unveils promising new companies. 1 year, 12 issues, $9.

Canadian Investments

Bauman's Monday Market. A weekly market letter featuring sample performance portfolios specializing in Canadian mining and oil stocks and also featuring industrial and junior industrial situations. 1 year, 52 issues, $75.

Canadian Business. The work book of Canadian management, it is designed to help executives face up to the everyday corporate problems. Editorial coverage includes articles on: executive development, better management techniques, scientific and technological developments now facing modern business and industry plus in-depth business forecasts of the Canadian business scene. 1 year, 12 issues, $9.

Canadian Business Service Weekly Bulletin. Canadian Business Service. A weekly market letter providing a general view of the economic and business trends influencing the canadian stock market. It also includes Canadian Business Service 43 Group Indices of 175 stocks and a supplement on the U. S. stock market. 1 year, 52 issues, $75.

Canadian Business Service Special Surveys and Industries. Four complete special surveys weekly on well-known Canadian companies including financial summary, earnings outlook, dividend prospects, stock charts, and specific comments on the security at the current market. Also published each week is a study of one of the more important industries. 1 year, 260 issues, $135.

The Canadian Investor. Maclean-Hunter, Ltd. A highly respected weekly investment letter, edited by Frank Kaplan, one of the most widely followed journalists on the Canadian investment scene and features, specific stock and industry recommendations, including a rundown of penny shares, extractive industry shares, and news of special interest to corporate investors. 1 year, 48 issues, $100; 2 years, 96 issues, $180.

Canadian Mines Handbook. Northern Miner Press, Ltd. Contains the latest information on more than 4,500 Canadian mining companies, financial position, investments, earnings, production, ore reserves, properties, mine development, capitalization, 8-year range table of stock prices, and much more. $8.

Daily Record. Toronto Stock Exchange. Daily publication of shares traded on the Toronto Stock Exchange, showing opening and closing prices, closing Bid and Asked, plus pertinent and current information on all listed securities. 1 year, 260 issues, $80.

Directory of Directors. Maclean-Hunter, Ltd. This richly bound, 770-page book is an indispensable businessman's guide to the men and companies in Canada that make the big buying decisions. Contains an alphabetical list of over 13,000 key executives with their titles, directorships, business, and home addresses plus a list of over 2,400 leading Canadian companies with head office addresses and the names of officers and directors. Published annually. 1 issue, $25.

Industrial Canada. Canadian Manufacturers Assn. This publication for Canadian industrial management includes articles of general interest and training lectures to educate management in specialized areas. Also contains Canadian news on newly established industries, new plants, expansion of existing ones, international trade developments, transportation, tariff changes, and sales tax rulings. 1 year, 9 issues, $10.

The Dempsey Canadian Newsletter. Canentco Ltd. A fortnightly news digest of Canadian business, labor government, and finance affairs. 1 year, 26 issues, $30.

The Financial Post. Maclean-Hunter, Ltd. Canada's leading journal of business, investment, and public affairs. It gives wide coverage on Canadian mining, oil, gas, and industrial stocks, including stock quotations. On the business front, it keeps readers posted on what's happening today and what the outlook is ahead plus comment and reports on government plans and moves. 1 year, 52 issues, $12.

The Garnet Letter. S. L. Garnet Co. A weekly investment letter specializing in Canadian and U. S. securities. It includes a watching service covering all Canadian public companies with automatic reports and news bulletins. Subscription also includes *S. L. Garnet Pink Sheet.* 1 year, 50 issues, $50.

S. L. Garnet Pink Sheet. S. L. Garnet Co. A weekly investment newsletter specializing in Canadian speculatives, mining, oil, and junior industrials. It includes a watching service which issues automatically any news bulletins pertaining to subscribers holdings. 1 year, 50 issues, $50.

Garnet Letter plus *Garnet Pink Sheet* special combination subscription offer. 1 year, 50 issues of both, $85.

Investment Survey of Canada. A weekly investment letter providing comprehensive coverage of the Canadian securities and business markets. Regular features include specific investment recommendations, quality investments, and trading situations, surveys of growth companies, action of the money managers, profit trends and developments, industrial group analyses, insider reports, resources review, assessments of the current business situation with leading and lagging business indicators. 1 year, 48 issues, $98; 6 mos., 24 issues, $65.

Investor's Digest of Canada. Publishes company and industry studies by research departments of leading Canadian brokerage houses; speeches by corporate executives to analysts; technical analyses. Monthly interview with a top mutual fund manager or investment analyst; plus "On the Inside" by Roger Croft, a column which ferrets out special situations in the Canadian market. 1 year, 24 issues, $50.

The Northern Miner. Over 54 years old, this recognized authority provides the most complete, factual, up-to-date news available on Canada's ever-expanding mining industry. Complete statistics for mining trading on the Toronto, Montreal, and Vancouver stock exchanges, as well as quotations for the most active unlisted mining stocks. 1 year, 52 issues, $15; 3 years 156 issues, $37.50.

The Northern Miner Special Microfilm Service for Libraries. The entire publishing of the *Northern Miner* weekly, dating back to September 4, 1915, on microfilm. Each complete year on a 35-mm positive film. $25.

Ottawa Week. A weekly newsletter dealing with developments in government affairs which may affect business and industry in Canada. 1 year, 50 issues, $50.

Survey of Industrials. Maclean-Hunter, Ltd. Here's a wealth of information to help you pick industrial securities with profit potential. Includes comparative condensed balance sheets and earnings statements, dividend histories, capital structure, and funded debt, plus names of officers and directors and transfer agents. Also included is a stock price range table for the past 7 years. Published annually. 1 issue, $9.

Survey of Investment Funds. Maclean-Hunter, Ltd. Provides detailed coverage of Canada's fast growing investment funds including mutual, closed-end, and other equity funds. Gives pertinent data on history, policies, and operating methods of individual funds together with information on restrictions, capitalizations, and redemption options. Also includes data on performance of funds, fees charged for management services, description or portfolios, and dividend policies. Published annually. 1 issue, $9.

Survey of Markets. Maclean-Hunter, Ltd. Here is a reference book for executives, public officials, speakers, writers—everyone who wants to be well-informed on the growth and development of Canada's markets for consumer and industrial goods and services. Included are area-by-area market characteristics—population, number of households, average weekly earnings, number of taxpayers, labor force, consumer price trends, housing figures, and a big marketing map of Canada. Published annually. 1 issue, $11.

Survey of Mines. Maclean-Hunter, Ltd. Provides complete investment information on mining companies in Canada. On producing companies, full reports of production, ore reserve, earnings, dividends, officers, and directors. On company under development: present status of operations. Includes a large map section for the principal mineral areas and a 7-year price range of stocks. Published annually. 1 issue, $9.

Survey of Oils. Maclean-Hunter, Ltd. Gives significant investment facts to invest knowledgeably in Canada's oil and gas securities. Information includes: officers and directors, 7-year price range of stocks, drilling records, dividend histories, earnings, working capital, property locations. Includes maps of principal Western oil and gas areas. Published annually. 1 issue, $10.

Stock Market Trends. Independent Investors Counselling, Ltd. Canada's oldest and most widely read technical advisory service. Specific buy and sell recommendations are made, including complete followup coverage of their supervised list. Discussion on Indicators and overall technical state of the market. 1 year, 24 issues, $84; 6 mos., 12 issues, $50.

Toronto Stock Exchange Review. Toronto Stock Exchange. Monthly volume, high and low; year to date volume, high and low; dividend record, outstanding shares, earnings of all stocks listed on the TSE, plus many other features. The official TSE publication. 1 year, 12 issues, $8.

Western Canada Business Letter. Century Publishing, Ltd. A fortnightly newsletter concentrating on business developments in the western northern parts of Canada, including oil, gas, mining, and forestry industries. 1 year, 25 issues, $30.

Chart Services

Chartcraft Monthly NYSE-ASE Chartbook. Chartcraft Inc. Point and figure charts on all NYSE and ASE stocks in a large-sized (8½ X 11 in.) 256-page volume. Provides a review of technical trend indicators, charts of the leading indicators, charts on 80 industry groups, and much more. 1 year, 12 issues, $150. (1 issue, $15)

Chartcraft O-T-C Monthly Chartbook. Chartcraft, Inc. Point and figure charts on nearly 1,800 O-T-C stocks, plus a sophisticated review of trends, indicators, and industries. 1 year, 12 issues, $150.

Chartcraft Weekly O-T-C Service by Electronic Computer. Chartcraft, Inc. Price changes for point and figure charting, taken from NASDAQ bid prices and ultimately covering 3,000 O-T-C stocks. Includes buy and sell signals, price objectives, stop-loss points, and relative strengths. Plus trend reversals from bearish to bullish, and from bullish to bearish; four charts on stocks of particular interest; a P & F chart of the NQB 35 O-T-C Industrials; bullish-bearish percentages of the NQB Industrials, and bullish-bearish percentages of all O-T-C stocks in the service. 1 year, 52 issues, $150.

Chartcraft Trend Reversal Service. Chartcraft, Inc. Point and figure charts by electronic computer on all "breakout stocks" on NYSE and ASE sent to subscribers, each week. Shows buy and sell signals on active stocks. Excellent for timing. 1 year, 52 issues, $150.

Graphic Stocks. F. W. Stephens Co. Over 1,600 charts showing monthly high, low, close, and volume statistics. Also shows earnings, dividends, capitalizations, splits, yields and 1929–1935 price ranges. Also contains 60 charts of group average plus the Dow Jones averages on rails, utilities, and industrials from 1929 to date. All 1600 charts are shown for over 11 years. 1 year, 6 issues, $100; single copy, $20.

Graphic Stocks Special Edition 1924-1935. F. W. Stephens Co. The only chart book of its kind showing early prices. 774 charts showing monthly highs and lows over a period of 12 years for stocks listed on the NYSE and the ASE (1924-1935). $25.

Graphic Stocks 100 Blue-Chips Charts. F. W. Stephens Co. 100 blue-chip stocks going back to 1924 through end of 1968. $15.

Mansfield NYSE Stock Chart Service. R. W. Mansfield Co. Provides large comprehensive charts on every stock listed on the NYSE. Each chart depicts a comprehensive technical, statistical, and analytical research picture. In addition, it includes every week sixteen pages of general market information, stock and group averages, technical indicators, statistical barometers, and analytical comments. 1 year, 52 issues, $327.

Mansfield ASE Stock Chart Service. R. W. Mansfield Co. Provides large comprehensive charts on every stock listed on the ASE. Each chart depicts a comprehensive technical, statistical, and analytical research picture. In addition it includes each week sixteen pages of general market information, stock and group averages, technical indicators, statistical barometers, and analytical comments. 1 year, 52 issues, $327.

Mansfield OTC Stock Chart Service. R. W. Mansfield Co. Provides large comprehensive charts for every issue in the NSTA active list, about 1100 issues. Each chart depicts a comprehensive technical, statistical, and analytical research picture, including weekly H-L-C, performance ratio, weighted 30-week moving average, annual ranges, percentage scale, capitalization, STAQ symbol, earnings, and dividends. 1 year, 52 issues, $327.

Mansfield NYSE Daily Basic Stock Chart Service. R. W. Mansfield Co. Provides large comprehensive daily basis charts on every stock listed on the NYSE. Each chart depicts a comprehensive technical, statistical, and analytical research picture and includes 21 points of critical value, 11 of which are exclusive Mansfield features. 1 year, 52 issues, $400.

Point and Figure Change Service. Morgan, Rogers & Roberts, Inc. For investors who keep their own point & figure price charts. Divided into 5 sections: Section 1—Full daily coverage, one-point price changes; for every NYSE common stock; Section 2—Full daily coverage, one-point price changes, for every ASE common stock; Section 5—commodity futures price change service on the outstanding contracts of the leading commodity futures; Section 6— (weekly) All ASE stocks; Section 7—(weekly) All NYSE stocks. Sections 1 or 2—1 year, $110; Section 5—1 year, $85; Sections 6 or 7—1 year, $95; Sections 1, 2, 5, 6, and 7—1 year, $260.

Reliance Chart Paper. A "Grand Slam" assortment of 8½ X 11 in. and 11 X 17 in. graph papers. Point and figure, semi-logarithmic, and arithmetic chart grids and tabular record sheets, totaling 80 in the reliance line at half of the listed price per sheet. Brochure included. $5.

300 Selected Stocks. Chart Service Institute, Inc., Charts of the 300 most active stocks highlighting their key resistance and support areas, breakouts, reversals, and established trends, plus R & S charts on the popular market averages along with commentary on timing, trends, and advice. Also features special selections with complete analyses and recommendations. 1 year, 50 issues, $95.

Securities Research Complete Service. Securities Research Co., Div. of United Business Service. Complete annual subscriptions to 975 security charts (issued monthly), 975 Cycli-graphs (issued quarterly), and the current Wall Chart. 1 year, $59.

975 Cycli-graphs. Securities Research Co., Div. of United Business Service. Long term 12-year charts on 975 issues. Covers earnings, dividends, prices, and volume relative to market action. 1 year, 4 issues, $27 (1 issue, $8).

975 Security Charts. Securities Research Co., Div. of United Business Service. Each month these charts present the up-dated graphic record of weekly price ranges and volume plotted against earnings and dividends for 975 issues. Each chart is for a 21-month period and depicts advances, declines, support, and resistance levels. Trends and patterns, market diagram comparators, etc., including commentary, where appropriate. 1 year, 12 issues, $45.

Large 22" X 42" Wall Chart of Market Averages. Securities Research Co., Div. of United Business Service. Portrays the broad panorama of stock and bond trends over the past 20 years. Covers DJ industrials, rails, utilities, 40-bond averages, price, and volume fluctuations are charted on weekly basis. Special 53-year inset chart depicts the DJ industrials, rail & bond averages from 1914. 1 year, 4 issues, $9. (1 issue, $3).

Resistance & Support Chartbook. Chart Services Institute. Contains two indices charts of the six most useful indicators with comments as to each week's probable action. Trading section, with current suggestions, also follow-up from previous suggestions. Listing of stocks whose 200-day averages changed direction that week, R & S charts of 1800 stocks for "at-a-glance" indication of probable direction and extent of each price move. This information is not available elsewhere. 1 year, 50 issues, $195.

Wall Street's Top 50. Security Market Research, Inc. Daily basis chart service of 50 selected high performance, high potential stocks including timing indices. Also includes short-and long-term market timing indices. Telephone service in New York, Chicago, Denver, Los Angeles for daily updating of market and stock indices. Instruction Manual included. 1 year, 52 issues, $142.

China Investments

The China Letter. The Asia Letter, Ltd. A complete business intelligence service for firms or individuals interested in keeping up with the developing China market. Trade prospects, case studies, regulations, addresses of Peking contacts for your products. Edited by world-reknown China business expert, Arthur C. Miller. 1 year, 12 issues, $175.

Taiwan Trade Monthly. Epoch Publicity Agency. The most widely circulated business publication of the Republic of China. Taiwan business and investment opportunities are intelligently and professionally discussed. Statistics are official and the information accurate. 1 year, 12 issues, $6.

Coins Investment Advisory Service

The Forecaster. Bill Willoughby Coin Exchange. A weekly newsletter reporting investment ideas and information on both the Monetary and Numismatic Markets. 1 year, 48 issues, $40.

National Coin Reporter. Surveys the coin investment market each month. Covers U. S. coins, silver bullion, and gold coin speculation. Also, covers general economic, predictions with emphasis on how not to lose by the coming devaluation, etc. 1 year, 12 issues, $18.

Commodity Investments

Advanced Commodity Trading Systems. 19 different methods for trading commodities. All the methods were written after 1970. Each method sold separately.

Agricultural Economic Research. U. S. Government. Contains papers relating to economic and statistical research in agriculture by Government bureaus and other cooperating agencies. 3 years, 12 issues, $3.

Agricultural Research. U. S. Government. Contains results of U. S. Department of Agriculture research projects in livestock management, crops, soils, fruits and vegetables, poultry, and related agricultural fields. 3 years, 36 issues, $4.50.

Agricultural Situation. U. S. Government. Contains statistics and general information regarding crops and other agricultural products and includes brief summaries of economic conditions. 3 years, 36 issues, $3.

Berkley Commodity Futures Trading Methods. Berkley Associates. 29 different methods for trading commodities. Each method sold separately.

Chartcraft Commodity Service. Chartcraft Inc. Point and figure charts on all active and major commodities, plus comprehensive readings giving buy signals, sell signals, and reversal points. 1 year, 52 issues, $120.

Commodities—The Magazine of Futures Trading. Investor Publications Inc. A monthly magazine designed and edited to provide in-depth information and education for those interested in and actively involved in the commodity futures market. No buy or sell recommendations are made, but authoritative articles by known experts offer a fund of knowledge about commodities and the factors and forces that bear upon the prices of futures. 1 year, 12 issues, $28.

Commodity Advices Point & Figure Technique. Morgan, Rogers & Roberts Inc. A specific technical commodity advisory service issued twice every week which attempts to call to the attention of its readers the few commodities offering the best opportunities for good percentage trades. Includes buy points, sell points, stops, and likely trading objectives. $25 month.

Commodity Charts. Futures Publishing Co. Vertical line chart service published each Friday, covering wheat, corn, soybeans, rye, oats, meal, oil, porkbellies, beefcattle, eggs, potatoes, greaswool, sugar, copper, hides, coffee, KC wheat, Wpg rye, and flax. Special chart paper enables easy pinpointing of price levels. Weekly & monthly range charts and spread charts sent periodically. Each issue also includes general chart comments, and an analysis of price possibilities for coming week. 1 year, 52 issues, $135.

Commodity Chart Service. Commodity Research Bureau Inc. Comprehensive weekly chart service providing over 150 different price charts for virtually every actively traded commodity futures contract in the U. S. and Canada. Charts up-dated each week showing daily high, low, and close as of Friday's trading—mailed to subscribers same day. Additional features include weekly technical comment interpreting significant chart formations and a trend indicator based on mathematical calculations. 1 year, 52 issues, $200.

Commodity Year Book—Statistical Abstract Service. Commodity Research Bureau, Inc. Provides the latest available statistics for updating the statistical tables appearing in *Commodity Year Book.* It is published five times yearly— January, March, July, September, and November. 1 year, 5 issues, $35.

Commodity Computer Report. Scientific Investment Research. Weekly publication which monitors 20 commodities on seven exchanges by means of electronic computer. The four most active commodities are selected and stops are set each week by computer. 1 year, 52 issues, $92.

Commodity Futures Forecast. Weekly advisory letter, recommending a limited portfolio of positions in commodity futures. Each recommendation is coupled with a stop. Positions are closely followed, with specific advice for taking profits, making purchases and sales. Collect wire service covers crises. 1 year, 52 issues, $200.

Commodity Exchange Bulletin. National Commodity Research & Statistical Service, Inc. A weekly commodity service published after the market close each Friday with specific recommendations and an analysis of the current technical and fundamental condition of the market. Covers commodities of current interest on all U. S. Exchanges with several spread recommendations. 1 year, 52 issues, $80.

Commodity Microanalysis. A daily commodity advisory service with specific recommendations for action on 14 active commodity markets. Subscribers also receive a complimentary copy of *Commodities for Potential Gains* plus a free telephone recorder service, a special situations program, and several individually tailored trading programs to meet their individual need. 1 year, 250 issues, $195.

Commodity Futures Statistics Service. Using computer researched statistics, this service points out growth opportunities and special situations in silver, cocoa, bellies and all rapidly developing commodities. It lists margin requirements: buy, sell, and stop loss points: major chart support and resistance points; and much more. Free call collect privileges for all subscribers. 1 year, 50 issues, $120.

Commodity Research Institute Weekly Advisory Letter. A weekly letter which gives specific buy and sell points based on technical action in the market. Updated daily via telephone recorder service. 1 year, 27 issues, $75.

Commodity Timing. This service offers a new approach to trading the commodity market by using their timing index and fundamental index available to subscribers on a daily basis for the commodities they follow. When the timing index crosses above zero a buy signal is given; when it crosses below zero a sell signal is given and buying is only done when the fundamental index is bullish while short selling is done only when the fundamental index is bearish. 1 year, 52 issues, $100.

The Commodity Trader. A revolutionary approach to commodity trading. Gives projected prices on all commodities covered. Techniques are technical and fundamental. Model accounts are updated daily. Special delivery and telegram services are also available. 1 year, 52 issues, $100.

The Commodity Trader. S.T.S. Bulletin. A complete course of instruction on the professional approach to commodity trading, covering every phase from the most basic to the most sophisticated trading techniques. Features include: personal coaching, newsletters, commodity workshops, special reports and sample trading letters.

Commodity Traders Course. Sibbet-Hadady Publications. Fourteen Lesson course: formula plan, contrary opinion, fundamental analysis, seasonal, open interest, price-volume, buying power vs. selling pressure, price momentum, chart patterns, cumulative average, moving averages, spreads, catching histori-cal lows, catching large bear markets, placing orders, stops, point & figure, Dow Theory, converting short-term gains into long term. 1 volume, $50.

Commodity Trend Service. Bi-weekly bulletin giving advice on all U. S. and Canadian commodity futures markets. Forecasting is based primarily on so-phisticated chart interpretations, seasonal tendencies, relative strengths, con-trary opinion, and important technical data—since 1945. 6 mos., 14 issues, $150; 3 mos., 8 issues, $95; 1 mo., 5 issues, $35.

Commodex. Daily technical bulletins based on the Commodex system for antic-ipating trends in commodity futures. Text, explaining system, together with periodic three-color charts are part of the service. 1 year, 250 issues, $250.

Com-Mod-Trend. A commodity advisory service built entirely on a set of com-puter programs eight years in development by a mathematician and veteran commodity trader. Their hot line phone service gives subscribers recorded sig-nals telling exactly when to buy and sell. A weekly newsletter summarizes the week's action and results. 1 year, 52 issues, $200.

Consensus. A national commodity futures weekly newspaper that comprehen-sively covers the commodity futuresmarket. This publication contains com-modity market letters, charts of all active commodities, special commodity reports, daily quotations of all traded commodities, monthly commodity calendar, U.S.D.A. statistics, and news releases from the major commodity ex-changes. 1 year, 52 issues, $121.

Daily Commotrace. Delivered daily, plus hot line telephone privileges after 9:30 a.m. Fully computerized service gives unhedged buy and sell signals, sliding stops adjusted daily, 3-and 20-day moving averages, 3-and 20-day price trends, weekly summary. Explanatory material included. Covers 44 futures contracts, usually about 15 daily. Developed by two physicists— claims to detect major trends automatically. 1 year, 250 issues, $250.

Daily Traders Guide. Commodity Decisions Corp. Daily commodity trading recommendations cover over 150 futures in 30 commodities. Buy limits and stops are specified for each recommendation. Each daily issue carries adjusted stops for the futures on the current recommendation list. 1 month, 22 issues, $30.

Economics of Futures Trading. By Thomas A. Hieronymus. Commodity Research Bureau, Inc. A basic study of the fascinating world of commodity markets by a leading national authority. Assuming no prior knowledge on the readers' part, the author guides him through the full complexity of market operation and evaluation. 350 pages. Hard cover. 1 issue, $12.95.

Dunn & Hargitt Commodity Service. A weekly commodity service giving daily bar charts with moving averages unique to each chart; P & F charts selected for superior profit results; specific buy, sell advice and complete follow-up of each trading position; fundamental comments; probability table showing how far a minor trend swing will be for each commodity; a ledger of commissions, exchange margins, and minimum fluctuations; telephone message during week to up-date weekend letter. 1 year, 52 issues, $200.

Farm Index. Contains articles based largely on research of the Economic Research Service and on material developed in cooperation with State agricultural experiment stations. 3 years, 36 issues, $6.

Foreign Agriculture. U. S. Government. World agricultural trade, especially as it affects U. S. agriculture, reports on current crop and livestock developments abroad. Foreign trends in production, policies, prices, supplies, and consumption of farm products and other factors affecting world demand for U. S. agricultural products. 3 years, 156 issues, $30.

Futures Market Service. Commodity Research Bureau, Inc. The famous "blue sheet," published every Friday, is probably the most widely distributed commodity advisory service in the world. It is issued in the form of an 8-page bulletin tersely discussing developments affecting the future of commodity supply and demand, including opinions as to probable price trends. Two pages of charts are included weekly. 1 year, 52 issues, $75.

Guide to Commodity Price Forecasting. Commodity Research Bureau, Inc. This unusual 275-page book contains 24 exclusive studies that explain forecasting with the aid of (a) chart interpretation and other technical analysis techniques, and (b) analysis of fundamental (supply-demand) and seasonal pressures. 1 issue, $17.50.

Lessons in Commodities. Commodity Futures Statistics Service. Ten-lesson advanced commodities course covers: computer-based trading systems; P & F chart construction; portfolio trading; counter trend trading techniques; seasonal position Trading with actual seasonal bullishness ratings; chart patterns; moving average; spreads; special situations; official stop buy and stop sell bar chart levels. Three months course via mail. $21.

The Lombard Letter. A monthly preview of seasonal factors that will affect commodity futures. Few specific buy or sell recommendations. Intended for experienced traders and brokers. Trades require patience. Some technical comment. 1 year, 12 issues, $100.

Market Vane Commodity Service. Sibbet-Hadady Publications, Inc. Presents in graphical form the bullish consensus of more than 30 other leading commodity advisory services. Buy, sell, and stop recommendations on contrarian and non-contrarian trades followed through to close out. Confidential phone number with daily up-dated recorded market report with recommendations included with regular subscription. 1 year, 52 issues, $200.

Modern Commodity Futures Trading. By Gerald Gold. Commodity Research Bureau, Inc. A practical book, devoted primarily to the techniques and methods for successful trading in the commodity markets. It explains trading methods, what makes prices go up and down, seasonal price patterns, chart trading, and much more. 254 pages. Hard cover, 1 issue, $10.

NCA Advisory Service. National Commodity Advisors weekly letter plus daily phone recorder service. Recommendations are placed into four risk groups according to account size. Service specializes in finding situations they feel are about to produce long and sustained moves which would then be exploited using pyramid techniques. Service claims to have produced enormous profits for all risk groups. 1 year, 52 issues, $180.

Parris & Company Commodity Service. Parris & Co. A weekly letter on commodities specializing in spreads and straddles. All recommendations are supported by practical explanations and by long-term charts. 1 year, 52 issues, $240.

Quintus Associates Weekly Commodity Market Letter. Quintus Associates, Inc. A masterful, comprehensive analysis of some 22 commodities on a weekly basis with specific recommendations to buy and sell. 1 year, 52 issues, $85.

Siegel Weekly Newsletter. Siegel Trading Co., Inc. Analysis and specific recommendations for most actively traded commodities each Thursday night. Reports mailed on Friday. 1 year, 52 issues, $150.

SMR Commodity Chart Service with Timing Indices. Security Market Research, Inc. A daily basis commodity chart-book containing 58 contracts covering 22 commodities, each complete with the famous SMR timing indices. Instruction Manual included. 1 year, 52 issues, $200.

Special Trading Situations Bulletin. This publication uses an econometric approach to commodity trading which includes contrary opinion. Price-trend analysis and fundamental information as well as floor traders' opinions. Each trade is given a risk rating and support and resistance zones are included. A unique trendicator covering all active commodities is also included. 3 mos., 13 issues, $55.

S.T.S. Chartmaster Service. A complete weekly chart service covering 12 of the most active commodities, and featuring: 2-color large bar charts, support and resistance zones, technical comments, price trend information, and specific trading advice. It also provides a daily telephone recorder service, special monthly reviews and a unique price momentum oscillator that closely follows price action. 1 year, 52 issues, $95.

TARA Market Master Weekly Cattle Letter. Texas Agricultural Research Associates, Inc. In-depth economic analyses and specific forecasts with futures trading recommendations. Daily telephone privileges. 1 yr., 52 issues, $225.

TARA Market Master Weekly Hog & Pork Letter. Texas Agricultural Research Associates, Inc. In-depth analyses and forecasts on live hogs and pork including pork bellies, with futures trading recommendations on live hogs and pork bellies. Daily telephone call privileges. 1 year, 52 issues, $200.

TARA Market Master Monthly Cattle Letter. Texas Agricultural Research Associates, Inc. In-depth economic analyses and forecasts prepared following monthly cattle on feed report with tips on futures trading, weekly telephone call privileges. 1 year, 12 issues, $60.

TARA Market Master Monthly Hog & Pork Letter. Texas Agricultural Research Associates, Inc. In-depth economic analyses and forecasts on live hogs and pork including pork bellies, with tips on trading live hogs and bellies, with weekly telephone privileges. 1 year, 12 issues, $60.

TARA Chart Master. Texas Agricultural Research Associates, Inc. Modified weekly Point & Figure charts and related TARA Chart Master on most options of all actively traded commodities. 1 year, 52 issues, $100.

Technical and Mathematical Analysis of Trends in the Commodity and Stock Markets. Commodity Research Institute. A 16-lesson course of instruction. 1 issue, $100.

Weekly Weather and Crop Bulletin, National Summary. U. S. Government. Gives a synopsis of weather conditions and their effect on crops and farming operations in the U. S. and snow and ice conditions during the winter season. 3 years, 156 issues, $15.

Communications and Communications Stock Investments

Cablecast. Paul Kagan Associates, Inc. Twice-monthly analysis of the CATV Industry's fundamentals, featuring updates of statistics of CATV stocks. Published by well-known CATV security analyst Paul Kagan. 1 year, 24 issues, $150.

Communications Investor. Paul Kagan Associates, Inc. Twice-monthly market letter on communications stocks. Covers such diverse communications industries as CATV, microwave, data communications, broadcasting, publishing, telephone, facsimile. 1 year, 24 issues, $96.

Datacast. Paul Kagan Associates, Inc. Twice-monthly analysis of the microwave network and data communications industries. Publication's goal is to relate the various subgroups within telecommunications to one another for investment purposes. 1 year, 24 issues, $150.

Computer Investment Services

The Anticipator Report. Scientific Investment Research. Quality stocks, computer-selected for possible capital gains, using regression analysis equations. Report features Computiming Index to help select favorable buying times. 1 year, 26 issues, $66.

The BLP Forecast. A weekly investment advisory letter generated by a computerized portfolio management system which makes use of technical analysis of general market conditions and produces individual stock recommendations. 1 year, 52 issues, $50.

Bull Bear Indicator. Bull-Bear Indicator, Inc. An advisory letter that features the stocks that Ira U. Cobleigh believes will make the greatest percentage gains over the next six months and in the three, five year period. It includes the only simulator (computer model) of the NYSE going back to 1897. This computer model which provides the indicator for the service defines the safe periods for investment in the stock market, during which the investor should be 100% long. During other periods (bear market), the investor should be 100% in cash. Edited by Dr. Ira U. Cobleigh, the economist, and Royden Brown, it publishes on the 10th and 25th of each month, excepting the months of December, June, July, and August. 1 year, 20 issues, $200.

Chartcraft Compustrength Service. Chartcraft, Inc. A new computer-based statistical service which combines the criterion of relative strength with that of ultra high volume to determine which stocks to buy and sell—and exactly, when to do it. This complete service also spots bullish and bearish trends, detects changes in trends, and advises on shorting and timing of purchases and sales. Covering every common stock on the NYSE and ASE, spotting short-term, intermediate-term, and long-term trends, and pinpointing your selection of stocks, this is the most revolutionary, newest, and most complete service published by Chartcraft and represents the culmination of efforts, experience, and technical research of this fine, progressive 20-year-old investment service. 1 year, 52 issues, $240.

Computab Stockrecommendations. Concerted Investment Services. A highly sophisticated service that utilizes a combination of the top-performing systematic approaches to investing. Continually analyzes new approaches with sound statistical sampling and the laws of probability and adds or replaces approaches as the latest results warrant. Only stocks that meet the criteria of these approaches are recommended. 1 year, 12 issues, $100.

Computab Combination Stock and No-Load Mutual Fund Recommendations. Concerted Investment Services. Same as above but includes no-load fund recommendations. 1 year, 12 issues, $150.

Comput-Alert. A highly technical, simply understood computer stock selection service, using the latest "envelope" selection techniques giving buy-sell-sell short—cover signals, supplemented with a daily hot line giving current market forecasts and signals. Uses a $25,000 model portfolio. 1 year, 44 issues, $98.

Computer-Gram. Sibbet-Hadady Publications, Inc. Represents the last word in the application of sophisticates aerospace and computer technology to analyze and sort stocks. Evaluates more than 2,350 NYSE and ASE stocks in alphabetical order with six different evaluation indexes on each stock. Also 24 sortings to find stocks that meet specific objectives. Trend forecast of DJIA, relative strength of various industries, and price and volume charts on selected stocks included. Specific stocks recommended and followed till closed out. 1 year, 52 issues, $150.

Computer P/V Charts. Scientific Investment Research. Bi-weekly publication which selects the "top 10" stocks on the NYSE and ASE and presents computer drawn P/V charts (price vs. volume). 1 year, 26 issues, $66.

Com-Stat Recommendations. Spear & Staff, Inc. Computer-based stock research service with regular supervision of an operational account. Computer rating analyses attempt to select issues with the greatest possibility of advancing the furthest and the fastest. 1 year, 52 issues, $500.

Com-Trac. Spear & Staff, Inc. The independent computer-based shorter-term stock trading module of Com-Stat, covering more than 200 issues every week.

Technical research analysis attempts to isolate issues capable of maximum stock market gains in 3 to 20 weeks. 1 year, 52 issues, $300.

The Dikewood Stock Report. Edde Securities Corp. A weekly investment report rating all NYSE stocks by price performance as based on a computer program analysis. Included are portfolios and weekly computer-based buy and sell recommendations. 1 year, 52 issues, $1,200.

Communications and Communications Stock Investments

EVM Letter. EVM Analysts, Inc. The reported earnings of every listed company are studied and a forecast for the next quarter is made. Those companies whose earnings support either purchase or short sale are subjected to extensive technical analyses. Recommendations are made depending upon the status of three overall market indicators. Specific price objectives and stop losses are calculated for each recommendation until closed out. Regular subscribers receive an analysis of their personal portfolio each month. 1 year, 52 issues, $150.

ISEC 250. A special purpose electronic analog investment computer for sale to investors including an operating manual that allows any stock to be analyzed for relative fundamental values. No subscriptions are necessary. Purchase price: $275.

The ISEC Report. A weekly service consisting of a general market discussion, charts of both exchanges, and an in-depth study of an individual security combining both technical and fundamental analysis. All recommendations are followed until the position is closed out. 1 year, 52 issues, $250.

The Predictor. Specific buy-hold-sell advice based on a mathematically programmed computer analysis of the technical action of all listed stocks. Fundamental evaluations of the most dynamic situations are introduced yielding specific recommendations with weekly follow-up for those stocks having sound fundamentals, superior technical action, and proper timing. Each recommendation offers reasons for its selection and specific price objectives. 1 year, 50 issues, $165.

The Stock Market Alert. Minimum 100 issues yearly published on "Alert" basis as and when changes in trend occur. Sophisticated technical and fundamental service for both the short-term trader and the longer-term professional investor. All stocks NYSE and AMEX monitored daily by four independent computer programs to show market and stock trends. Strong stocks are alerted by use of a number of independent approaches. Blocks and Groups into which big money flow are highlighted, and major market turns are shown. Stocks recommended are also analyzed fundamentally. Original monetary indicators employed in continuously revaluing current earnings and dividends. 1 year, 100 issues, $175.

Trade Levels Report. A weekly statistical service listing computer-calculated intermediate-term trends of over 1,500 common stocks as well as industry averages. Also listed are measurements of short-term buying and selling forces acting on stocks and industry groups. Each week computer-calculated listings of: strongest uptrends, severest downtrends, stocks under greatest accumulation, and stocks under greatest distribution. Monthly are computer-calculated support and resistance levels for over 750 stocks listing a strength rating for each level. 1 year, 52 issues, $145.

Consensus Investment Services

Consensus of Insiders Advisory Service. Authored by Perry F. Wysong, whose dynamic successes have been widely acclaimed throughout the securities field and discussed in full-length articles in *Fortune Magazine*, the *New York Times*, and many other respected business publications, this complete service offers an effective, practical, yet completely original approach to selecting stocks and accurately predicting market trends by analyzing the total number of transactions by company insiders and stock exchange specialists. Featuring the twenty stocks favored by the most company officials and supported by specialist's risk exposure ratio, this new, power-packed service is a must for the sophisticated investor. 1 year, 52 issues, $72.

Demand/Supply Index. A factual, pocket-sized report which uncovers the 10 listed stocks that have been bought most by individual Corporate Insiders, Mutual and Pension Funds each month. Reports are airmailed bi-weekly. Index Wires, Direct Dial Tele-Tape, the Market Specialists Pressure Index, timing devices and 14 other features are all part of this unique service. All are bound with the Basic Approach Booklet in an attractive, pocket-sized vinyl binder. 1 year, 23 issues, $100.

Investors Intelligence. A twelve-page report giving a consensus of all major advisory services and brokers letters and providing the 10 stocks most mentioned by all services, a technical review of promising low-priced stocks, fundamental and technical recommendations of interest to the investor, and more. 1 year, 24 issues, $60.

Wall Street Reports. A monthly roundup of professional investment news and information. Includes comments on the economy, statistics on NYSE stocks, reports from leading brokers (both company studies and industry surveys), and a selection of speeches before security analyst societies. 1 year, 12 issues, $10.

Convertible Securities

Chartcraft Convertible Bond Chartbook. Chartcraft, Inc. Point and figure charts of over 140 convertible bonds. Issued semi-annually. 1 issue, $12.50.

IMR Convertible Bond Selections. A monthly service presenting convertible bond investments. The selections are arranged by bond quality ratings and on the basis of trading for high yields and at limited premiums over common stock conversion values. 1 year, 12 issues, $15.

KV Convertible Fact Finder. Kalb, Voorhis & Co. Statistical research recommendations and continuous research in the Convertible Bond Market. 1 year, 52 issues, $90.

Value Line Convertible Survey. Arnold Bernhard & Co., Inc. Studies and reports on over 1,000 different convertible bonds, convertible preferred stocks, and warrants and their underlying common stocks, plus special situations involving mergers, acquisitions, recapitalizations, and exchange and tender offers. Provides information, analyses, and recommendations, as well as specific trading instructions for using the sophisticated techniques of professionals. Includes leverage projections and estimates of the actual current value of the convertible bond, warrant, or preferred stock under study. In mergers and acquisition situations, a special section carries in tabular format key data on the surviving company, evaluation of the exchange offer, analysis of potential advantages. 1 year, 38 issues, $192.

Corporation Law

Securities Regulation and Transfer Report. Warren, Gorham & Lamont, Inc. Authoritative, complete, and dependable reports of all important court decisions, regulations, and rulings affecting the issuance, transfer, and registration of securities. Covers new SEC proceedings, disciplinary actions, stock exchange developments, and trend setting developments affecting securities, registrations, mergers, tender offers, and proxy statements. 1 year, 24 issues, $44.

Currencies, Gold and Gold Stock Investments

Green's Commodity Market Comments. Economic News Agency. A highly regarded, sophisticated bi-weekly review specializing in monetary matters, related fields of gold, silver, other precious metals, and foreign exchange. An authority in its field, it is indispensable reading for investors and traders. 1 year, 24 issues, $120.

International Monetary Issues. Israel Business Books, Ltd. A comprehensive roundup of international economic and monetary news plus a penetrating, hard-hitting analysis to help guide investment and policy decisions. For those institutions and individuals involved in international monetary and economic issues, this Israeli-based publication is must reading. 1 year, 24 issues, $35.

International Reports of Finance and Currencies. Weekly reports come in three sections: (1) Evaluation of Basic World Monetary Trends and Events; (2) International Finance Market Letter, including international survey of hedging opportunities in foreign exchange, foreign financing prospects, country by country, trend of free gold market, international interest arbitrage; (3) Statistical Market Letter on International Finance and Currencies, including free market foreign exchange rates, New York rates for all sterling categories, I.R. guidance rates for foreign exchange futures, free market gold prices; silver and platinum prices, etc. 1 year, 52 issues, plus consultation privilege, $320.

The Lynch International Investment Survey. Lynch-Bowes, Inc. A weekly letter authored by Mr. Walter A. Lynch, well-known economist and expert on gold and silver, which covers all aspects of the international and domestic money markets as well as specific recommendations on individual securities. 1 year, 52 issues, $100.

Pick's World Currency Report. Pick Publishing Corp. A monthly publication accepted all over the globe as an outstanding authority on currency rates, analyses, and forecasts. Practical appraisals of monetary situations, the latest discounts, and possibilities for use of leading international trade and investment units; the most comprehensive listing of free market gold, metals, and diamond prices available anywhere; plus much more. Also, inquiry privilege for "fresh" on-the-spot quotations, valuable contracts, and other desired information, included with subscription price. 1 year, 12 issues, $275.

Cylinder Theory

Cylinder Theory Report. Fortnightly investment letter largely based on the teachings of the Cylinder Theory as contained in a book by the same title authored by Dr. C. M. Flumiani. Specific stock recommendations, market timing, price objectives for stocks. D-J index objectives for market timing, commentary on monetary indicators and on international politics. 1 year, 24 issues, $36.

Dow Theory Concept

Dow Theory Letters. Written by Richard Russell, internationally known expert on the Dow Theory and author of many books and articles written for Barron's and leading financial publications. Deals with the trend of the market as interpreted under Dow Theory, plus all other items of general interest to investors. Gold, silver, bonds, interest rates, bank credit, odd-lots, economic fundamentals, and much more are covered. Specific comments on individual stocks in each issue. 1 year, 36 issues, $75.

Dow Theory Comment. Rhea, Greiner & Co. Originated by Robert Rhea in 1932 and written since his death in 1939 by Rhea's former associate and partner, Perry Greiner. These letters, using Dow's time-tested basic principles, have an enviable record of forecasting the major and secondary stock price trends since 1932. 1 year, 35 issues, $40.

Dynamic Synthesis Investment Concept

Dynamic Synthesis Stock Market Forecast. The Institute of Dynamic Synthesis, Inc. A weekly commentary with buy and sell signals based on original stock price forecasting methods described in the books by Walter Heiby, *Stock Market Profits through Dynamic Synthesis* and *The New Dynamic Synthesis*. 1 year, 52 issues, $95.

Euromarket Investment

Euromarket Surveys. A. E. Walsh & Partners, Ltd. Series of quarterly studies, authored by A. E. Walsh & Dr. John Paxton, in which some aspect of the economics of the Common Market and E.F.T.A. countries is analyzed in depth with particular reference to trade and investment. 1 year, 4 issues, $38.

European Business and Investment

Business Europe. Business International. A weekly eight-page report on opportunities and dangers for firms doing business with, within, and from Europe, emphasizing the EEC, EFTA, and European marketing, financing, taxation and management. 1 year, 52 issues, $198.

European Investments

Extel European Company Service. Extel Statistical Services, Ltd. Comprehensive weekly card service covering the European securities market. Company activities, subsidiaries, directors, capital, voting rights, dividend record, profit and loss details (ten years), turnover analysis, interim statements, share quotations, P-E ratios, balance sheets, net asset value, mergers, acquisitions, etc. 1 year, 52 issues, $180.

Stock Exchange Official Yearbook. A new unique fortnightly advisory letter, authored by Charles M. Whitmore, Jr. dealing with Canadian extractive companies, unusual investment situations, and utility-type investments in the U.S.A. A century of family experience investing in American resources is employed in research and recommending. Model portfolio shown. 1 yr., 26 issues, $50.

Franchise Investments

Franchise Journal. A monthly magazine edited for those interested in an investment or for those desiring an owner/manager relationship in a franchise business. Contains listings of new franchises, stock reports, and general news of the franchise world. 1 year, 12 issues, $6.

Franchising Around the World. Edited for individuals, groups, firms seeking investments, income opportunities, and equity-building offerings. The news articles feature new offerings and up-dated material on established firms. 1 year, 6 issues, $5.

Specialty Salesman Magazine. A monthly round-up of news and information on specialty products and franchises available for sale by independent sales people. Each issue contains a gold mine of listings of new appealing products and services to add onto lines of independent sales people. 1 year, 12 issues, $5.

Fundamental—Technical Complete Investment Advisory Services

The Adams Letter. Croesus Capital Corp. Weekly market letter with in-depth commentary on market and the economy. Specific buy and sell signals given for market. Specific and continuously up-dated stock recommendations and industry reports. Buy zones for lists of glamour issues and weekly advice on their performance. Specializes in undervalued stocks. 1 year, 52 issues, $120.

The Equity Forecast. American Equity Counselling Service. Offers fundamental and technical analysis of general market conditions and gives specific recommendations of issues, offering buy zones, stop losses, etc. 1 year, 52 issues, $95.

American Investors Service. Chestnutt Corp. A comprehensive, highly regarded technical weekly market letter giving: 70-industry group trend analyses, ratio lines and percentage-strength for posting industry group charts; and stocks ranked by percentage-strength to show the long-term price trends of 1,000 stocks processed by an elaborate, professional electronic computer program. 1 year, 52 issues, $240.

Barry Market Letter. Barry Management Co. Offers a model portfolio, a news commentary on socio-political-economic events, a technical review of the overall market, and individual security recommendations. 1 year, 51 issues, $60.

The Bartlett Letters. A weekly investment advisory service recommending purchases and sales of securities, based on a supervised list averaging about ten stocks. Detailed reports on three model funds are published about once a month—speculative fund, small investors fund, and investment fund. 1 year, 52 issues, $45.

Borchert's Market and Group Timing Bulletin. A complete professional service for the private investor. Covers the market trends, stock groups, recommended portfolio, when to buy or sell funds, when to get in or out of the market, stressing timing for maximun safety and profits. Special bulletins at important market turns when deemed necessary. 1 year, 12 issues, $12.

Buck Investment Letter. A weekly investment advisory service with recommendations based on both fundamental and technical data, supervised by Frank H. Buck, Jr. Maintains a continuously supervised security list and covers economic and cyclical trends. 1 year, 50 issues, $36.

The Cabot Market Letter. For longer term investors this investment advisory service utilizes the unique Cabot trend lines for market timing of primary trends. Then uses fundamentals and technical considerations for selecting quality stocks which are followed until closed out. Model account employed. 1 year, 26 issues, $60.

Carter Index. A weekly letter designed to help subscribers buy and sell strong momentum stocks in conjunction with the movements of the important market cycles. The adviser claims to invest his own money in the same manner and he publishes the results each week. This service is for the more serious investor only. 1 year, 52 issues, $300.

The Consultant. Utilizing investor psychology and highly sophisticated technical devices to call turns in both the market and individual stocks, this weekly investment advisory service analyzes the stock market on a continuing basis and offers both long-term and short-term recommendations. Individual stock recommendations are followed up until closed out. Speed resistance lines and the unit concept are uniquely employed in timing purchases and sales and evaluating the DHA. Telephone consultation and telegraphic services are also available to active traders. 1 year, 44 issues, $100.

Ford Value Report. Ford Investors Service. A unique monthly advisory service which assigns dollars and cents values to over 1,100 common stocks each month. Values are based on earnings, dividends, growth rate, etc. Subscribers compare value with price to determine whether stocks are underpriced or overpriced. Also frequent special reports on a variety of investment subjects. 1 year, 12 issues, $18.

Guardian Investment Letter. N. M. Corp. A monthly investment letter which will assist the subscriber in selecting securities that will yield above average capital gains without subjecting himself to undue risks. The letter provides adequate information to permit a logical comparison and gives the subscriber a basis for deciding whether to accept or reject its recommendation. 1 year, 12 issues, $48.

The Holt Investment Advisory. T. J. Holt & Co., Inc. A truly professional service for the private investor. Published semi-monthly and averages 18 pages each. Includes sophisticated studies of market, economy, and money and credit as well as technical analysis. Recommends unequivocal investment strategy and specific stocks to buy or avoid. Contains many revealing charts. 1 year, 24 issues, $120.

Extractive Industries Investment Service

Whitemore Investment Letter. A new unique fortnightly advisory letter, authored by Charles M. Whitemore, Jr. dealing with Canadian extractive companies, unusual investment situations, and utility-type investments in the U.S.A. A century of family experience investing in American resources is employed in researching and recommending. Model portfolio shown. 1 year, 26 issues, $50.

Investment Bulletin. American Institute Counselors, Inc. Twelve issues discuss significant economic developments and trends, inflation, statistical indicators, industrial production, and securities markets. Eight issues analyze specific industries' growth prospects, companies' performances, and investment suitability under three investment plans. Four quarterly issues summarize advisable investments. This highly respected service offers adequate advice for long-term sensible investment programs for investors with modest means. 1 year, 24 issues, $15.

Investment Letter & Supervised Growth Leaders. Investment Counsel, Inc.

Published since 1930, this letter discusses economic developments which
have a bearing on security prices, suggestions for the management of investments, industry studies, individual company studies. Once a month the list
of dynamic fast-growth leaders and supplemental approved stocks is published with recommendations for purchase. 1 year, 24 issues, $75.

Investment Strategy. Crosby-Ware Trusts. A weekly review of economic lead
indicators which have historically preceded stock market turns. Fine tuning
by technical price swing analysts. Specific recommendations on each of the
30 Dow Jones industrials. The author is a graduate economist with 26 years
of investment experience. 1 year, 50 issues, $265.

Investment Survey of America. A weekly investment letter providing comprehensive coverage of the American Securities and business markets. Regular
features include: Specific investment recommendations—quality investments
and trading situations, surveys of growth companies; action of the money
managers, profit trends and developments; industrial group analyses; insider
reports; investing for international strength; commentary on bond and money
markets; resources review; assessments of the current business situation with
leading and lagging business indicators. 1 year, 24 issues, $72.

Investor Forecast. Heese & Associates. This monthly bulletin recommends
at least three buy situations in each issue and includes a list of all previous
recommendations which have not yet reached a sell position, the date and
price when recommended, along with the high and percent change since that
date. A personal portfolio review and continuous portfolio surveillance for
the extent of the subscription period is also included with the subscription.
1 year, 12 issues, $45.

Jubb's Managed Portfolio. Jubb Co., Inc. A managed growth portfolio whose
advisor seeks high annual returns. Specific buy and sell recommendations
along with periodic up-dates of past recommendations. Research usually
includes personal visits to companies under study and technical methods for
timing. Subscribers receive a recommendation report and background folder
on each security recommended. 1 year, 12 issues, $100.

The Markstein Letter. Features stocks chosen for hopeful profits according
to the methods listed in David Markstein's bestseller books. Offers weekly
explanation of economic happenings and current outlook. Shows three model
portfolios designed to help readers invest successfully. Complete phone or
mail consultation privilege with each subscription. 1 year, 45 issues, $501.

New Scientific Investor. Scientific Investment Research. Monthly studies-in-
depth of all the fundamental and technical tools used by investment analysts,
using a Scientific Data Systems on-line computer for analysis and an IBM
360-75 computer and SC-4020 plotter for chart selection and plotting, to
determine optimum profit methods and strategy. 1 year, 12 issues, $20.

The Professional Investor. Lynatrace, Inc. "Which investment advisory services
perform best?" which analyzes the performance of over 70 services. This
unique service is designed and written for the sophisticated investor and the
professional. Combines analysis of technical, psychological, and fundamental
indicators. Spotlights one or two stock per issue. Unhedged calls on market
turns. Sophisticated investment techniques and trading advice. 1 year, 24
issues, $125.

The Professional Tape Reader. Radcap, Inc. Utilizing the author's years of
experience on the NYSE floor, this twice-monthly service analyzes what the
specialists are doing in conjunction with many other significant technical and

fundamental indicators to produce unhedged practical advice about what both traders and investors should do in the market. All specific stocks recommended are constantly followed up. This unique service also features instructive material based on how specialists and other members of the Exchange trade for their own accounts to help subscribers improve techniques. 1 year, 24 issues, $85.

Pursell's Argus Watching Service. A personal investment letter for the busy professional man or for investors residing in foreign lands. Written by Admiral Ion Pursell, who has been teaching estate planning, investing, and money management since 1917, this letter offers a personalized watching and reporting service. Personal letters are written regarding all holdings and recommending changes as needed. Special letters and telegrams supplement the bi-monthly mailings. 1 year, 24 issues, $150.

The Rand Market Report. A revolutionary approach to stock market timing and security selection employing unparalleled market studies that utilize a totally new concept. Rand Index Rationale through computer application weighs the combined fundamental and technical positions of individual stocks and market trends. Specific buy, hold, sell-short sale recommendations and portfolio positions. Published every two weeks plus frequent bulletins in advance of important stock moves. 1 year, 48 issues, $78.

Research Institute Investors Service. Investment recommendations, including Special Situations, issued on a flexible schedule. Includes full-length depth studies of professional caliber. In addition, detailed follow-up reports on open recommendations. Market commentary, aggressive growth model portfolio, economic analysis for investors, technical analysis, funds' activity. 1 year, 52 issues, $192.

RMI Investment Letter. AMI Corp. A complete weekly service for aggressive speculators seeking maximum gain as well as for serious, prudent long-term investors. Trend Through chart techniques tell when to buy and sell. RMI Market Signal flashes major market turns. In depth analysis of selected recommendations. Bonus monthly Statistical Monthly Summary. 1 year, 52 issues, plus 12 stock summaries, $88.

Sophisticated Wall Streeter. A monthly investment letter offering total money management to its subscribers and which seeks out growth stocks, special situations, short sales, bonds, convertibles, warrants, options, commodities, etc. that possess strong profit potential. Risk incurred, time needed, price to buy and to sell, are stated for each recommendation. Model portfolios of $1,000, $3,000, $10,000, and $50,000 are followed in each issue. 1 year, 14 issues, $30.

Spear Market Report. Spear & Staff, Inc. A carefully prepared weekly investment letter which discusses the outlook for business and investments; market policy advances, advices on market-wide stock investment opportunities plus advices on stock opportunities in fast-moving areas of scientific development. Specific buy-hold-sell recommendations on individual issues. 1 year, 52 issues, $125.

Systems Approach. H. H. Quigley & Co., Inc. A weekly stock market investment letter that covers three broad areas: (1) economics, (2) technical indicators of the market, and (3) individual stock recommendations. Their unique economic commentary gives insight into government policy, changes in monetary trends and their effect on the market and price of your stocks. 1 year, 50 issues, $90.

Scientific Market Analysis. "The Nighmare German Inflation"—SMA's unique booklet on history's wildest inflation—is sent with each. Also *market analysis,* detailing SMA's carefully researched system for judging major market trends, with SMA's 10-year record. For serious investors, not for the in-and-out trader. 1 year, 24 issues, $44.

The Tillman Survey. A weekly investment advisory report with background business and market discussions, short-term market analyses, industry reviews and ratings of group performance, portfolios for various purposes and specific buy and sell recommendations for stocks and bonds based on both fundamental and technical analysis. 1 year, 52 issues, $85.

Investment Quality Trends. A 12-page bi-monthly report, which includes three special individual stock reports and charts, and which determines and rates the value of each of 350 important blue chip stocks from dividend yield extremes at undervalue and overvalue levels. Service includes four quarterly reviews. 1 year, 24 issues, $95.

Scalisi Investment Advisory Service. Investment recommendations in this weekly letter are based on economic factors, political factors, business cycles, as well as market factors, technical and fundamental. Separate warning letters are mailed to subscribers when danger signals appear. 1 year, 52 issues, $100.

Surf Writer. Royal Hawaiian Advisors, Inc. A weekly investment letter from Hawaii based on the methods outlined in this advisor's copyrighted booklet sent to all subscribers. Detailed investment strategy directed toward maximum capital gains for the performance-oriented trader as well as the conservative investor. 1 year, 52 issues, $85.

Trendway Advisory Service. Long-established, comprehensive service for experienced investors, traders, professionals. Features widely acclaimed breadth indexes for major trend signals, intermediate and short-term timing. Continuous picture of stock group movements; in-depth group analyses. Individual stock recommendations include select few for major commitment during bull markets; short sales in bear periods. 1 year, 52 issues, $95.

United Business Service. A weekly 12-page report that brings to the investor a concise summary of business and investment developments, including Washington news, commodity price trends, industry surveys, the outlook for the stock market, and specific buy-hold-sell advices on stocks and bonds recommended for growth, income, or profit. 1 year, 52 issues, $98.

Value Line Investment Survey. Arnold Bernhard & Co., Inc. A complete investment service offering comprehensive information on 1,400 stocks and 68 industries. Published in three parts: *Ratings & Reports* features full-page reports weekly on each of more than 110 stocks and their industries, including growth ratings, earnings forecasts, charts, etc.; a comprehensive *Weekly Summary of Advices and Index* including up-to-date investment ratings on each of 1,400 stocks; and *Selection and Opinion.* Value Line's 8–12 page editorial section highlighting important trends, forecasts, and opinions, including an Especially Recommended Stock or Special Situation each week. 1 year, 52 issues, $189.

Value Line Selection & Opinion. Arnold Bernhard & Co., Inc. The 8–12 page editorial section of the *Value Line Investment Survey* available as a separate service. Features an especially recommended stock or special situation each week. Includes the value line view of business, the economy and the market, and advice on how to adapt your investment strategy to meet new developments. Plus special industry reports, model portfolios, new issues, and regular reports on insider transactions and investment company transactions. 1 year, 52 issues, $49.

Wall Street Pipeline. Baker & Co. An audio-tapereporting service containing market experts' opinions, in their own voice, on investment opportunities and important trends. Ideas are fresh (each tape made the previous week), sound (respondents are working professionals in the street), and fast-paced (twenty different opinions in each thirty-minute standard cassette). 1 year, 12 issues, $99.50.

The Whitehall Market News Letter. A comprehensive service for predicting important market moves based on a three part analysis: psychometrics, fundamentals, and technical factors, complete with charts. Subscription includes monthly letter plus bulletins when necessary. A portfolio kept current each month with buy and sell recommendations plus in-depth research reports. 1 year, 12 issues, $15.

Zehnder's Letter. A weekly newsletter summarizing news of vital interest to investors, including specific stock recommendations and follow-ups. 1 year, 52 issues, $12.

Fundamental Statistical Investment Services

Fact's History Tapes. Facts, Inc. Monthly history tapes containing same data as daily services for all NYSE and AMEX stocks. $150 per month.

Fact's Stock Prices on Magnetic Tape. Facts, Inc. Daily and weekly prices on all NYSE and AMEX stocks, plus on a large number of OTC issues. Data can include close, high, low, open, volume, earnings, dividends, etc. Per month quotations; daily data, $285; weekly data, $110.

Fund Raisers Tax and Counsel Service

J. K. Lasser's Taxes for Fund Raisers. Business Reports, Inc. A continuing service for nonprofit organizations especially prepared by the J. K. Lasser Tax Institute. Contains authoritative information on new tax developments plus creative editorial comment and suggestions for applying them to the raising of funds for educational, religious, and charitable institutions. 1 year, 12 issues, $42.

Georgia Investments

Georgia Business News. Securities News Publishing Corp. Weekly statewide source of Georgia financial and business information. Corporate listings and new securities registrations are published. In-depth company analyses, investment news, earnings, projections, dividends, and company reports provide the reader with insight into the rapidly expanding Georgia market. 1 year, 52 issues, $6.

Government Securities Investment Service

Reporting on Governments. A weekly analysis and forecast on U.S. Government securities, the economic outlook, monetary and fiscal policies and interest rate trends—edited for 25 years by Sylvia Porter. 1 year, 52 issues, $89.

Growth Stock Investments

America's Fastest Growing Companies. John S. Herold, Inc. Lists approximately 150 companies selected on the basis of past earnings record, 50 to 60 pages per issue. Follows progress on a continuing basis, rating each company on its attractiveness for investment. New companies are added, old ones delisted, as changes develop. Operates growth stock portfolio and reports results. Two special supplements are issued quarterly, "Growth Stock Digests" and "The Panograph." 1 year, 12 issues, $78.

Connors Report. Connors Investor Services, Inc. In-depth research on small but fast-growing companies. Only six recommendations are made each year—each thoroughly documented in a professional research report more than twenty pages in length. Companies are recommended only after personal, on-site discussions with management and interviews with customers, competitors, and suppliers. 1 year, 6 complete reports plus updating materials, $100.

Forecaster, Growth Stock, Inc. Aims to identify small emerging growth companies before they become well known. All recommendations are written in a concise easily read one-page report. The progress of all recommendations are reported periodically to subscribers. 1 year, 12–24 issues, $24.00.

Growth Stock Digest. Stock Information Reporting Service, Inc. A new quarterly magazine featuring over 200 growth companies. Includes earnings per share by quarters, percentage increase over prior years, monthly closing prices, price/earnings ratio, and estimated earnings per share. Growth stocks are selected on proven basis of five continuous years of earnings growth without decline. All stocks rated on 4-year increase in earnings. P/E data grouped by industry and up-dated quarterly. Listings include NYSE, ASE, and OTC. 1 year, 4 issues, $20.

Growth Stock Facts. Value Research, Inc. Up to 50 growing companies listed on the basis of size and earnings rate. Includes an investment philosophy and a mechanism for aiding future analysis. Fact sheets become work sheets. Company fortunes are followed, some delisted, new ones identified. 1 year, 12 issues, $90.

Growth Stock Outlook. For experienced professionals and sophisticated investors, this service lists 90–100 rapidly growing companies (NYSE, ASE, and OTC) and keeps tabs on each unit delisted when growth slackens. It includes all new recommendations for prior 12 months or longer. Issued twice monthly, plus new listing reports, it offers concise, fast reading. 1 year, 24–36 issues, $35.

Wall Street Investors Service. A new statistical service that analyzes the analysts, edited by John H. Logan. Over 100 analysts' current selections are listed in each issue and ranked for profit potential. One or two unusual values are selected from these listings. Each special situation must show a capital gains potential of more than 30% within the next 12 months. Only stocks on the NYSE or ASE are considered. All must have outstanding past, present, and future growth records of sales and earnings and be undervalued in relation to their current P/E Ratio. 1 year, 24 issues, $100.

Hedge Advisory Services

The Hedge Advisory Stock Service. A monthly investment letter specializing in hedging common, warrants, and convertible bonds, and authored by an investor with over twenty years of hedge experience. 1 year, 12 issues, $50.

Hong Kong Business and Investments

Red Book—Hong Kong. Who exports what in Hong Kong. Computer compiled directory of products, producers, and traders. 1 issue, $15.

India Business and Investments

Advertlink. The bi-weekly tabloid on India's advertising and marketing business. 1 year, 26 issues, $10.

Kothari's Economic Guide and Investment Handbook of India. Introduction to the Indian economy and listing of major Indian companies by industry and service categories. 1 issue, $22.

Indicator Consensus Services: Investment Counsel Based on Indicators of Stock Market Direction

Technical Indicator Review. Chartcraft, Inc. Weekly 4-page report on trend of the market, leading and meaningful indicators and group ratings with charts. 1 year, 52 issues, $48.

Technical Trends. Merrill Analysis, Inc. Weekly investment letter, edited by Arthur A. Merrill, which presents leading market barometers in graphic form. Also, includes subscription to *Report on Growing Companies.* 1 year, 50 issues, $32.

Insider Reports

Official Summary of Security Transactions and Holdings. U. S. Government. Made up of security holdings figures showing owners, relationships to issuers, amounts of securities bought and sold by each owner, their individual holdings reported at end of reported month, and types of securities. Popularly known as the "insider reports." 3 years, 36 issues, $19.50.

Weekly Insider Report. Stock Research Corp. A weekly report of all insider trades of 1,000 or more listed shares (not including stock dividends, exercise of options, intra-family gifts). The publisher claims to send the material several weeks ahead of any other source. Reports weekly multiple sales or purchases by company, a sell-to-buy ratio; also monthly reports of companies acquiring their own stock. 1 year, 52 issues, $35.

International Business Management & Investment

Business International. A weekly eight-page report to management on worldwide business problems and opportunities and how firms are meeting them. Highlights case studies of solutions to all forms of international management problems, practical interpretations of new U.S. and foreign laws and regulations, political and business forecasts of key markets. 1 year, 52 issues, $198

Department of State Bulletin. U. S. Government. Provides information on the development of foreign relations, operations of the State Department, statements by the President and Secretary of State, and special articles on international affairs. 1 year, 52 issues, $16.

Financing Foreign Operations. Business International. A 400-page basic volume, updated as major changes occur of international financing techniques, cross-border financing and domestic financing in 24 major countries. 1 year, 1 volume with monthly updates, $198.

Investing, Licensing & Trading Conditions Abroad. Business International. A monthly updating service which provides a complete, continuous reference to the rules, regulations and laws of 56 countries as they apply to organizing, financing, labor, taxes, remittances, licensing, and trade. 1 year, 1 volume with monthly updates, $240.

Institutional Investment Services

International Investment Companies Yearbook. Scheinman, Ciaramella International, Inc. Hard-bound two volumes per year. Describes approximately 2,400 funds from 39 countries. Gives objective investment policy, investment restrictions, officers and directors, management fee, plans, redemption charges, minimum accepted, reporting and dividend dates, addresses and historical record, etc. Each country prefaced by local investment company laws. 1 year, 2 issues, $195.

International Securities Locator—U.S. and Canadian Securities. Scheinman, Ciaramella International, Inc. List by security every U.S. and Canadian Security held by over 2,000 investment companies, in U.S., Canada, and 23 other countries. Shows number of shares held by each fund, previous position, net change. Also names, addresses, telephone, telex, and cable numbers of funds. Bound, updated 8 times annually. 1 year, 8 issues, $350.

Money Market Directory. Considered the bible of the institutional investment community, this unique reference volume offers a comprehensive and authoritative reference service on the total population of institutional investors and portfolio managers, 6,000 tax-exempt funds representing $190 billion in assets and 4,000 investment management services with assets of $840 billion are listed, as well as every other major investment institution. Each entry includes the name, address, and telephone number of the fund, the name of the administrator responsible, the amount of money under management, and the corporate trustees and/or counselors who make the investment decisions. 1 issue, $150.

Portfolios of the World—U. S. and Canadian Securities. Scheinman, Ciaramella International, Inc. Approximately 600 pages in each quarterly issue. Gives holdings of U. S. and Canadian Securities held by approximately 1,400 mutual funds and investment companies located in U.S., Canada, and 18 other countries. Shows name of security and number of shares arranged by country and funds alphabetically within each country. 1 year, 4 issues, $130.

Insurance Stocks

Insurance Advocate. A weekly insurance news magazine reporting overall industry problems and developments, statistics on underwriting experience, announcements of mergers, acquisitions, and new capitalizations. Includes discussions of insurance stock trends, and investments of both life and fire and casualty companies. Meetings of regulatory authorities and legislative hearings are also covered. 1 year, 52 issues, $7.

Insurance Stock Market Service. A 6-page investment report covering more than 200 publicly owned life insurance companies. It contains specific buy recommendations with regular follow-up advice, a life stock master list, traders section, market comments, mergers, dividends, and interim operational reports. Also a special 4-page quotation report. 1 year, 25 issues, $50.

Life Insurance Advisory Service. A personal advisory service covering only Life Stocks. (1) Personal consultation privileges. (2) Annual portfolio review. (3) Quarterly newsletter. (4) Copy of "Annual Comparative Analysis of Life Companies," covering 156 companies and offering 71 columns of vital statistics on each company. 1 year, 5 issues, $25.

Stocks of the Future. Maintains a small list of four to six stocks of strong OTC insurance companies with excellent growth records that it feels offer the greatest potential for capital appreciation. Suitable for long-term investment only—periods of at least 3 years. 1 year, 6 issues, $12.

International Investments

Capital International Perspective. The Capital Group, Inc. Covers over 1,000 leading stocks (including 36 gold stocks) and 200 convertible debentures traded in Europe, Japan, Australia. Quarterly issues have price charts for each security, and recent operating and financial data. Monthly issues contain end-of-month prices, P/E, yield, and performance ranking of 1,000 stocks. Special market indexes for each country. 1 year, 16 issues, $250.

Investment Clubs

Better Investing Magazine, National Association of Investment Clubs. Designed to help the individual better understand various investment principles, it features columnists and articles discussing growth stocks, errors made by investors, stock selection techniques, model portfolios, and the investment principles and procedures suggested by the National Association of Investment Clubs. 1 year, 12 issues, $4.

Israel Investments

Business Diary. Gabriel Alon Publications. A thorough digest and complete analysis and evaluation of all Israel business news and trends. For 23 years this concisely written, authoritative business paper has provided the International business community with a unique intelligence and insight on Israel business. 1 year, 12 issues, $35.

Israel Investors' Report. A financial newsletter offering information and analysis on U. S.—Israel trade relations; Investment in Israel stocks, industry, and real estate; and on Israeli economy and finance. Published since 1961. 1 year, 22 issues, $20.

Japan Business and Investments

Extel Japanese Company Service. Extel Statistical Services, Ltd. Comprehensive daily card service covering Japanese Security market. Company activities, subsidiaries, directors, capital, voting rights, dividend record, profit and loss details, interim statements, share quotations. P/E ratios, balance sheets, net asset value, mergers, acquisitions, etc. 1 year, 260 issues, $600.

1972 Japan Company Directory. Comprehensive reports on 800 major companies and banks with special reference to their past records, present showings, and future possibilities. Names directors, dividends, net worth, equipment, references, cable address, capital changes, business results, business prospects, major stockholders, number of employees, date of establishment, principal business lines, number of stockholders, stocks held by foreigners, average age of personnel, details of specialized lines, total liabilities and net worth, production and sales amounts, head office and overseas branches, share price changes over past several years. Also includes "Who's Who" supplement listing the names and biographies of 1,000 leaders in Japanese business, industry, and finance. 1 issue, $20.

Japan Economic Journal. Weekly economic newspaper published by the *Nihon Keisai Shimbun*, Japan's economic and business newspaper with over 1 million daily circulation. Journal is foremost source of news for businessmen, includes stock tables. 1 year, 52 issues, $36.50.

Japan Economic Yearbook. A comprehensive encyclopedia of major economic, industrial and commercial events and developments in Japan during the year it covers. 1 issue, $10.

Japan Electronic Industry. Electronics are booming in business and innovation in Japan. This monthly magazine keeps thousands of subscribers worldwide up-to-date on what is happening. 1 year, 12 issues, $17.

Japan Electronics Buyers' Guide. Leading annual directory to electrical-electronics manufacturers and products. Published by Dempa Shimbun. 1 issue, $20.

The Japan Stock Journal. Complete weekly price range of listed Japanese stocks on the Tokyo Stock Exchange; Japan's economic, industrial, and financial news and review; development of foreign trade; corporate report; report on joint ventures of Japanese firms and foreign firms. 1 year, 52 issues, $21.

Machine Tools in Japan Today. Comprehensive guide to Japan's machine tool industry and its products. 1 issue, $8.

Meri. The semi-annual analysis of Japan's top companies by the Mitsubishi Economic Research Center. 1 year, 2 issues, $36.

Motor & Parts Trade News. Trade magazine of the Japanese automotive and parts industries. 1 year, 12 issues, $15.

The Oriental Economist. The oldest English language economic monthly in Japan, reporting on the latest trends and developments in Japanese politics, its economy, investment ideas and opportunities, financial and industrial areas. 1 year, 12 issues, $25.

Photo Review. Trade magazine of Japan's camera and photographic industries. 1 year, 12 issues, $15.

Standard Trade Index of Japan. Over 9,000 Japanese manufacturers, business concerns, traders listed in 2,000 pages. 30,000 commodity and service items listed in commodity index. Published by Japan Chamber of Commerce. Annually published in mid-Spring. 1 issue, $30.

Technical Japan. A quarterly magazine covering Japanese industry and its latest technical advances. 1 year, 4 issues, $10.

Zosen Shipping & Shipbuilding. The monthly magazine on Japan's fast expanding shipping and shipbuilding industry. 1 year, 12 issues, $16.20.

Zosen Yearbook. The annual directory to the Japanese shipping and shipbuilding industry. 1 issue, $10.

Korean Business and Investments

Comprehensive Media Guide: Korea. 1969–1970. The first and only directory to South Korea's newspaper, magazine and broadcast media. 1 issue, $5.

Korea Directory. Lists all authorized foreign traders in South Korea. Classified lists of makers, Government, foreign firms, residents. Best basic guide to booming Korea economy. Annually published in spring. 1 issue, $12.

Low-Priced Speculative Stock Situations

Cumulative Stock Profits. The CSP Advisor. By technical chart and fundamental analysis, this service attempts to build up capital by small but quick cumulative stock profits. Selects two–four low-priced stocks every other week and gives specific price range to buy and exact price to sell. 1 year, 24 issues, $95.

Low-Priced Stock Selector. Three low-priced stock recommendations presented monthly, each one based on the following yardsticks of low-priced stock value; sales and earnings growth, financial strength, quality product or service, low price/earnings, ratio, and low dilution of equity. Up-dated information and continuing buy, hold, sell recommendations are contained in subsequent issues. 1 year, 12 issues, $28.

Penny Stock Reporter. The only national publication devoted to stocks in the extremely low price range. Many stocks now listed on the AMEX and NYSE were once penny stocks. Features Stock-of-the-Month, timely articles, news items, latest prices. 1 year, 12 issues, $18.

The Penny Speculator. F.B.P. Publishing, Inc. Low-priced most active stocks followed weekly where the actual price is given to buy, sell, and/or switch. Popular Special Situations are issued periodically. Tape action, market psychology, and the effects of sponsorship are delved into with each stock reviewed. For investors, traders, and speculators. 1 year, 51 issues, $95.

Personal Service in Low-Priced Stocks. Cen-Com, Inc. A unique service specializing in low-priced AMEX listed stocks. Unlimited telephone and mail privileges. A basic loose-leaf book is provided, containing specific recommendations on approximately 90 stocks; weekly change pages and periodical news letters keep the information continuously current. 1 year, 50 issues, $100.

Manufacturing Companies' Financial Statistics

Quarterly Financial Report for Manufacturing Corporations. U. S. Government. Shows the financial characteristics and operating results for all U. S. Manufacturing corporations, arranged by industry grouping. 3 years, 12 issues, $6.

Mergers & Acquisitions. The Journal of Corporate Venture. This hardbound journal deals with the phenomena of merger and acquisition in United States corporate development and growth. It is a "how-to" journal, aimed at making the subscriber an insider in this billion dollar business. 1 year, 6 issues, $48.

Mexican Investments

Actevsia Mexico Reports. Monthly business, financial, stock market, real estate, and economic reports on current events and their effect on the investor. English and Spanish. 1 year, 12 issues, $18.

Mexletter. Semi-monthly Mexican business and investment advisory service. English and Spanish. 1 year, 24 issues, $40.

Mutual Funds Investments

Computab No-Load Mutual Fund Recommendations. Concerted Investment Services. A highly sophisticated service that utilizes a combination of the top-performing systematic approaches to investing. Continually analyzes new approaches with sound statistical sampling and the laws of probability and adds or replaces approaches as the latest results warrant. Only no-loads that meet the criteria of these approaches are recommended. 1 year, 12 issues, $50.

Converse Fund Reports. A monthly advisory report on leading investment companies. Two model mutual fund portfolios, selected closed-end and open-end funds, market analysis and commentary, statistical section. Directory of more than 800 funds and loose-leaf binder for filing reports included in annual subscription. 1 year, 12 issues, $36.

Fundicator Performance/Rankings of Mutual Funds. This new service provides performance and performance/ranking grades (A, B, C, D, E) on over 350 mutual funds, including over 120 maximum growth funds and over 60 no-load funds, every four weeks. It also includes a sample chart system for recording performance information and a list of fund addresses. 1 year, 13 issues, $18.

Current Data on Mutual Funds. Kalb Voorhis & Co. Performance record for 12-month period on more than 240 funds whose total net assets are $1 million or more. 1 year, 12 issues, $8.

Fund Investment Engineering. A monthly service which recommends to stay invested in packages of the best performing no loads. Rates the better performing no loads every month and sets up three "best of funds" portfolios of high gain-risk, aggressive growth, and conservative growth which are kept under constant surveillance. 1 year, 12 issues, $36.

Fund Guide International. A monthly periodical informing an international readership about fund investment opportunities throughout the world. Concentrates on 100 selected funds and focuses on "hard currency" countries such as Holland, Germany, Switzerland, Australia, U.K., Japan, Canada, and USA. 1 year, 12 issues, $30.

Fundline. David H. Menashe & Co., A 40-page handbook of no-load fund charts, including 26-week moving averages of each fund, unique dual ratings, recommended investment strategy, as well as the Master Indicator Chart. Complete handbook published every 4th week; update of ratings and prices sent 2 weeks later. 1 year, 26 issues, $48.

Fundscope Magazine. The only mutual fund magazine in the country distributed generally to both investors and industry representatives. Complete comprehensive, up-to-date coverage of mutual funds. 1 year, 12 issues, $50.

Growth Fund Guide: The Investors Guide to Dynamic Growth Funds. Growth Fund Research, Inc. An unbiased fund service offering up-to-date logarithmic charts, sample portfolios, market comment, fundratings, and latest news and developments. A transparent % ruler and indices charts for easy comparisons are also provided. 1 year, 12 issues, $36.

KV Selletter for the Mutual Fund Salesman. Kalb, Voorhis & Co. A monthly 8-page 5½ X 8½-in. publication with sales ideas and methods. 1 year, 12 issues, $5.

Mutual Funds Scoreboard. Yale Hirsch Organization. Current news, views, and performance ratings on over 530 mutual funds by the publisher of *The Manual of Mutual Funds* and the *Stock Traders Almanac.* 1 year, 4 issues, $6.50.

Mutual Fund Reporter. Investors Research Service. A monthly report giving the comparative performance of 160 of the largest mutual funds, including 34 "performance" funds and 24 "no-load" funds. Funds are classified by investment objective and emphasis is given the 30 top performing funds. 1 year, 12 issues, $12.

No-Load Buyer's Guide. An all no-load mutual fund advisory service. Each issue includes charts to show performance, statistics on funds for the last 3½ years, market comment, supervised list of no-loads, and letters from fund managers. 1 year, 12 issues, $37.

No-Load Fund Digest. A comprehensive monthly analysis of no-load (no sales charge) mutual funds including detailed performance charts, performance summaries, and no-load fund ratings. Forecast analysis and technical indicators. More than 110 no-load funds are covered including many small, unpublicized growth funds. 1 year, 12 issues, $33.

Performance Fund Selector Report. Indicates which, where, how to buy the most promising no-load mutual funds when an up-market is predicted by the service. Follow-up on all recommendations until sell recommendation. Model Portfolio is maintained. Service emphasizes buy-sell recommendations. 1 year, 12 issues, $35.

Performance Guide Publications. Designed for professionals. Over 480 mutual funds are competitively ranked by year to date performance and published weekly. All new funds are added as they become available to the public. Monthly interviews with leading portfolio managers, market and fund analysis. All no-load funds are included. 1 year, 45 issues, $35.

The Pocket Summary of Mutual Funds. Kalb, Voorhis & Co. A four by seven inch book, featuring a full page to each fund, citing all important facts and figures. 10-year history of more than 250 different funds, all those sold through investment dealers. 1 year, 2 issues, $6.

Wiesenberger's Charts & Statistics. An annual, graphic presentation of 15-year investment results for funds with assets of $10 million or more. Also, shows records of accumulation plans, and a statistical compendum of 5′, 10′, 20′, and 25-year investment results. An important aid in planning one's financial future. 1 issue, $45.

Wiesenberger Dealer Service. The most complete source of factual and statistical information available on mutual funds. 19 different publications and newsletters provide complete, up-to-date information on every mutual fund and in-depth analysis of the industry. The dealer service allows you to easily compare the different funds, their objectives, performance, and investment programs. 1 year, complete service, $350.

Wiesenberger's Guide to Mutual Fund Withdrawal Plans. Learn how to use and evaluate plans, the unique feature of mutual funds designed for retirement income or as a supplement to ordinary income. Use the charts to investigate over 195 possibilities before investing. This is the only book published which is devoted to mutual fund withdrawal plans exclusively. 1 issue, $20.

Wiesenberger's Insurance/Fund Selling. The semi-monthly newsletter designed to provide ideas and "how-to" stories on the big-ticket combination sale of insurance and mutual funds—individual financial planning, corporate pension and profit sharing plans, and trusts. The articles are in-depth treatments, written in everyday terms, covering events and current leaders in the combined sales area. 1 year, 26 issues, $96.

Wiesenberger's Investment Companies. The annual "bible" of the mutual fund industry. It gives the facts, figures, and commentary needed to make sound mutual fund investment decisions. Also, included are quarterly management results, an invaluable way to keep on top of short- and long-term performance of the funds. 1 issue, plus quarterly up-dates, $55

Wiesenberger's Facts on the Funds. Covers the major portfolio transactions of the 165 largest mutual funds in America. This report is issued in four quarterly large editions with regularly issued supplements to up-date the information and with special roundup bulletins. 1 year, 4 issues, $75.

Wiesenberger Mutual Fund Performance Monthly. Wiesenberger Services, Inc. Provides Alpha and Beta performance evaluations for each of 350 mutual funds, reflecting portfolio selectivity and market sensitivity. It also shows percent change in net asset value for the latest month, year to date, the last 12 months, and the previous year. It includes performance evaluations for each of the funds covered for the latest five- and ten-year periods. For easy reference, funds covered in the report are categorized and ranked in three separate sections, including an alphabetical section, a section grouping the funds according to a variety of stated objectives and policies, and a third section ranking the funds by size (dollar value of assets). 1 year, 12 issues, $280.

National Stock Exchange

National Stock Exchange Informer. Stocks on the National. A market letter providing coverage of all issues listed on the National Stock Exchange. It makes specific recommendations, highlights most active National issues and all new listings as well as providing a substantial amount of additional information for the individual who likes to make up his own mind. 1 year, 12 issues, $30.

National Stock Exchange Review. Stocks on the National. A reference manual consisting of individual 5½ X 8½-in. fact sheets for each of the more than 140 National listings. Each fact sheet contains the company's financial history, a description of its business, and recent developments. They are pre-punched to fit in a vinyl binder. 1 year, 12 issues, $33.

New Issues

New Issues 1971. Descriptions of over 1,000 companies offering stock for first time to investing public. Published in November. 1 issue, $10.

New Issue Outlook. Provides weekly comprehensive two-page advance reports on companies planning to go public and follow-up computer reports on the price movements of the securities they offer, including latest earnings and P/E figures. 1 year, 52 issues, $250.

New Issue Performance Directory. New Issue Outlook. A master guide to the performance of the new issue market, divided into three large sections, containing all the pertinent statistics one needs to know to judge the performance of particular new issue stocks, new issue underwriters, and the performance of new issues by industry. 1 copy, $25.

New Issue Research. Investment Bankers Research. Contains analyses of companies offering their stock to the public for the first time. Released prior to offering dates. Outlook comments for each issue. For institutions and private investors. 6 months, 6 issues, $16.

Securities and Exchange Commission News Digest. U. S. Government. Presents brief summaries of financial proposals filed with and actions by the SEC. 3 years, approx. 780 daily issues, $45

North Carolina Investments

Carolina Financial Times. Weekly newspaper covering the North Carolina business and financial community. General business and investor news coverage, in-depth articles and regular features: OTC stock quotes, security analysis, estate planning, export sales leads, new incorporations. Monthly special issues. 1 year, 52 issues, $18.

Northwest Investments

Northwest Investment Review. Williamette Management Associates, Inc. A twice monthly publication with commentary on national economic and market trends, but with primary emphasis on Northwest companies and markets. Coverage includes regular analysis of insider transactions, market performance, earnings and corporate news for over 100 Northwest companies. Specific buy and sell recommendations are given. 1 year, 24 issues, $120.

Obsolete Securities

Obsolete Security Reports. R. M. Smythe & Co., Inc. Fully researched customs written reports on securities (stocks or bonds) thought to be worthless. These reports can be used for tax purposes or to locate any underlying value, and are written by authorities in the field. $10 each report.

Inactive Securities Report. L. Richard Cooper, Inc. On securities that are inactive and not quoted, this service will research and provide up-to-date information for valuation and also documentation required to establish tax losses. $10 each report.

Oil and Other Energy Investment News

Advanced Battery Technology. Robert Morey Associates. The only monthly publication that follows all important aspects of the international battery industry—research, engineering, manufacturing, sales, and financial news. 1 year, 12 issues, $30.

Annual Overseas Exploration Report. Petroconsultants, S.A. A complete listing of public and private companies holding overseas concessions for petroleum exploration and exploitation. Published once a year in Spring. Two volumes, $250.

Energy Info. Robert Morey Associates. A monthly executive summary of key events occurring in the fields of power generation and research, including advanced energy conversion, nuclear, utilities, oil industry, fossil fuel utilization, gas turbines, total-energy, mining, and related business and financial news. 1 year, 12 issues, $25.

Foreign Scouting Service. Petroconsultants, S.A. Consists of individual monthly reports, maps, and other data on 125 countries covering current and past oil exploration activity. Information on each country shows sedimentary basins, concession boundaries and owners, open areas, drilling wells and depths, oil fields, production, dry holes, geophysical work, etc. Covers most oil producing countries throughout Europe, Near and Middle East, Latin America, North Africa, Central and South America, Far East, and Australia. 1 year, 12 issues, $120–360.

International Oil News. William F. Bland Co. A weekly news report of significant and timely international oil intelligence. No interpretation or comment; strictly factual information obtained first hand from prime sources. 1 year, 52 issues, $110.

Oil & Gas Discoveries. John S. Herold, Inc. A highly sophisticated and authoritative report designed for oil men and investors that relates important industry developments to specific companies involved. Tables and charts are uniquely designed to guide investors to making the proper decisions in selecting investments in this area. 1 year, 6 issues, $80.

Oil Industry Comparative Appraisals. John S. Herold, Inc. A manual-type service which gives in-depth basic information on asset values of approximately 130 oil companies. Appraised net worth per share for each company is determined by estimating the earning power of all the assets. Revised continually. 1 year, $240.

Oil Statistics Bulletin & Canadian Oil Reports. Oil Statistics Co., published since 1923, an affiliate of Apear & Staff, Inc. Covers developing stock investment opportunities throughout the world in the oil and gas industries. Follow up and sale advice is provided in each recommendation. 1 year, 26 issues, $125.

Petrochemical News. William F. Bland, Co. A weekly news report which gives current news about business developments in the petrochemical business. Coverage is worldwide. No interpretation or comment; strictly factual information obtained first hand from prime sources. 1 year, 52 issues, $120.

Petroleum Outlook. John S. Herold, Inc. A monthly news digest for those executives or investors interested in the economics, trends, and important events concerning the oil industry. Used widely by investors, analysts, and oil men. 1 year, 12 issues, $45.

Over-The-Counter Securities

Space Age Market Research. A special situation service that specializes in over-the-counter securities. Organized in 1958, this service claims over 30% of its recommendations listed on major exchanges after selections. 1 year, 12 issues, $40.

Dynamic OTC Growth Letter. Authored by Alfred C. Rizzo, this service employs innovative fundamental research to uncover OTC stocks that have unusually strong growth potential. Believing that the biggest gains are made by investors who buy undervalued OTC stocks before the Street's security analysts discover them, he uses in his selection process 20 checkpoints, which are sent free. 1 year, 24 issues, $125.

The O-T-C Market Chronicle. William B. Dana Co. A new weekly publication devoted to over-the-counter companies. Each issue covers general market trends, earnings reports, new products, research studies, personnel investment feature articles, SEC registrations, technical market strength, and comprehensive stock quotation coverage. 1 year, 52 issues, $20.

Over-the-Counter Securities Handbook. Factual description of 2,000 OTC companies—dividends, financial condition, current ratio, balance sheet, assets, per share sales, net income, etc. 5 year record. Published in September, 1 issue, $10.

Over-the-Counter Securities Review & Listed Securities Journal. Monthly 9 X 12-in. journal covering OTC securities and providing information on dividends, recent and proposed listings, broker bulletin earnings, initial public offerings, etc. 1 year, 12 issues, $15.

Over-the-Counter Newsletter. A bi-weekly newsletter presenting current, concise, and comprehensive information about the over-the-counter market. 1 year, 25 issues, $40.

Over-the-Counter Special Reports. Specific recommendations on individual issues, backed up by well-ordered analysis from which the publishers develop recommendations in logical fashion. Worthwhile source of investment intelligence. 1 year, 12 issues, $50.

OTC Informer. National Corporate Sciences, Inc. A comprehensive investment advisory service for all investors interested in the rich profit possibilities of the OTC market. Each 10-14-page report contains: a New Issues section giving advanced information on all companies planning initial public stock offerings, including Reg. A's; a special situations section containing in-depth recommendations; and a reports section including stocks not found in standard references. 1 year, 21 issues, $75.

The Informer. National Corporate Sciences, Inc. The advisory staff of this service will extensively research any active or inactive OTC stock to help you find the true value of your investment. For an additional fee a thorough investment analysis will be made. $30 per report. $50 per report with investment analysis.

Pacific Northwest Business

Marple's Business Roundup. A newsletter published on alternate Wednesdays and devoted solely to business in the Pacific Northwest. From time to time it reviews various industries and carries short items on individual companies doing business in the area. Founded 1949. Subscribers include every bank in Washington and Oregon with more than $60 million in deposits. 1 year, 26 issues, $18.

Pension and Profit Sharing Planning

The Prototype Planner. A monthly publication edited by Jack McKinley discussing new developments and trends in the design and marketing of qualified pension and profit sharing plans for small and medium size employer companies with slightly more emphasis on corporate master and prototype plans. 1 year, 12 issues, $36.

Digest of Selected Pension Plans. U. S. Government. Summarizes the principal features of selected pension plans for employees under collective bargaining and selected pension plans for salaried employees. 1 year, $5.

Phillipine Business and Investments

Economic Monitor. Weekly news and analysis of Phillipine business, investment, and economy. 1 year, 52 issues, $35.

Portfolio Appraisal Service

CPA: Computerized Portfolio Accounting. Schield Stock Service, Inc. Based on duplicate confirmation slips from your broker(s), this service provides monthly statement of current position, recent price history, initial cost, and current market value for each security rank ordered by total rate of return to date: Quarterly profit and loss statements; year end tax statement. 1 year, $225.

Psychological Interpretative Based Investment Services

Contrary Investor. Fraser Publishing Co. James L. Fraser applies contrary opinion theory to investment and speculation. Objectives are to watch and report popularity in shares, mention neglected shares, give psychological over-bought early warning signals, comment on crowd approach to market, endeavor to ferret out occasional unusual vehicles for investing speculative portions of your investment funds. 1 year, 26 issues, $30.

Contrary Investor Follow Up. Fraser Publishing Co. Offers buy-hold-sell recommendations on past contrary opinion selections. Purpose is to keep readers informed on current price projections and to prune choices that have acquired too much crowd appeal. All selections are followed up until closed out, usually with long-term gains in mind. 1 year, 26 issues, $20.

Contrary Investor Personal Service. Fraser Publishing Co. Designed for individuals who have neither time nor inclination to manage own investment portfolios. Subscribers receive all their published newsletters, plus monthly investment and speculative portfolios. Personal mail consultation privileges important. 1 year, $200.

Neill Letter of Contrary Opinion. Fraser Publishing Co. Humphrey B. Neill's expositions on economic and sociopolitical problems together with contrary discussions that suggest opposite probabilities. The only financial newsletter based with clearly defined logic and fact. 1 year, 26 issues, $27.50.

Real Estate Investments

Construction Review. U. S. Government. Brings together under one cover virtually all of the Government's current statistics that pertain to construction. 3 years, 36 issues, $19.50.

Current Housing Reports. U. S. Government. Reports on housing vacancies and housing characteristics. Gives percent distributions of rental vacancies and homeowner vacancies, bb facilities, number of rooms, monthly rent asked, and sales price asked, etc., compared with same quarter of previous year. 3 years, 12 issues, $4.50.

Housing & Realty Investor. Audit Investment Research, Inc. Hard-nosed, independent and confidential investment advice on the rewards and risks in construction and housing securities. Once monthly all new stock offerings by companies with a stake in the industry are reviewed and a regular portfolio planner provides continuing guidance to investors. 1 year, 24 issues, $96.

Housing Starts. U. S. Government. Contains number of new nonfarm and total housing units started, by ownership, location, and type of structure. 3 years, 36 issues, $6.

Housing Authorized by Building Permits and Public Contracts. U. S. Government. Contains monthly statistics on the number of new housing units authorized by building permits and public contracts in the U. S. 3 years, 36 issues, $24.

HUD Newsletter. Reports on significant and newsworthy events and developments in housing, urban affairs, mortgage market, credit, and related matters of particular interest to builders, planners, social welfare groups, and State and City officials. 3 years, 156 issues, $4.50.

Mortgage Banker. Covers all areas pertaining to real estate finance and investment, including government policies and regulations affecting same, economic conditions, new financing techniques, loan administration and operations, urban problems in the housing field, etc. 1 year, 12 issues, $8.

Mortgage and Real Estate Executives Report. Warren, Gorham & Lamont, Inc. An in-depth information and idea reporting service for the real estate attorneys and executives. Covers new mortgage lending techniques, new Federal aids to real estate financing, new forms and checklists for real estate loans, legal, and tax decisions affecting real estate. 1 year, 24 issues, $38.

Modern Real Estate and Mortgage Forms. Warren, Gorham & Lamont, Inc. 750 pages of forms supplied by large mortgage and real estate investors, developers, and lenders throughout the U.S. An encyclopedia of forms for every mortgage and real estate transaction. 1 issue, $35.

Our Public Lands. U.S. Government. Features all news about the 460-million acre public domain, such as how to buy public lands, where to hunt and fish, new laws and regulations, scenic and natural areas, new camping sites, conservation highlights, Alaskan opportunities, and ancient ruins. 3 years, 12 issues, $6.

Commercial Expansion Report. Prospector Research Services, Inc. A monthly service which keeps salesmen and businessmen informed of plans for new commercial and institutional expansions. Construction plans are reported for shopping centers, office buildings, stores, hotels, motels, banks, hospitals, nursing homes, apartment houses, and other community developments. Reports are available for regional or national coverage. 1 year, 12 issues, $39.

Sales Prospector. Prospector Research Services, Inc. A monthly prospect research report for salesmen and other businessmen interested in industrial expansions and relocations for manufacturing firms, distribution centers, and transportation terminals, in new or existing buildings. Reports are available for regional and national coverage. 1 year, 12 issues, $39.

Real Estate Advisor's News. A service giving a general investment plan plus individual guidance and advice. Regular subscribers get personal financial master plan, personal consultation privileges, quarterly newsletter, survey of U. S. land developers, and seven investment bulletins. 6 mos., $90.

Real Estate Insider Newsletter. Atlantic Commercial Enterprises, Inc. A weekly newsletter devoted to the latest developments in the world-wide real estate market. Geared to the investor, realtor, attorney, appraiser, and general real estate professional. 1 year, 52 issues, $38.

Real Estate Law Report. Warren, Gorham & Lamont, Inc. Reports of significant legislative changes, cases, decisions, rulings, and regulations— real estate law, taxations, truth-in-lending, banking law, landlord-tenant, labor law, etc. Federal and State coverage. Analysis and opinion of what you should be doing now in response to these changes. Reports on what other professionals in your field are doing. 1 year, 12 issues, $36.

Real Estate Review. Warren, Gorham & Lamont, Inc. Provocative articles written by the dynamic industry leaders of our time. If you want to share their pragmatic thinking about today's opportunities and their vision of the future, this is the magazine to read. 1 year, 4 issues, $28.

Real Estate Syndication Digest. A comprehensive monthly review of national real estate syndication activity. Offers national reporting coverage, analyses of new syndications, acquisitions, reports, updates on regulatory decisions, innovative financial techniques, and presentations by noted authorities. 1 year, 12 issues, $75.

Real Estate Trusts: America's Newest Billionaires. Audit Investment Research, Inc. Packed with facts and analyses, this 467-page book includes a series of computerized internal operating ratios for major trusts that you will find invaluable in making investment decisions. Ample charts, tables, graphs, and specific case studies clarify and document the wealth of data both on the industry and on individual trusts. 1 issue, $24.

Realty Trust Review. Audit Investment Research, Inc. Authoritative, detailed coverage of the emerging Real Estate Investment Trusts—the industry's closest counterpart to mutual funds. Because they pay 90% of earnings to shareholders, trust securities offer unusual opportunities for capital gains potential, with above average dividends. Each issue contains an exclusive summary of nearly one thousand financial facts on all major trusts. 1 year, 24 issues, $84.

Value of New Construction Put in Place. U. S. Government. Reports on value of new construction put in place, bb type. 3 years, 36 issues, $7.50.

Savings and Loan Company Investments

Savings and Loan Investor. A semi-monthly publication devoted exclusively to the savings and loan industry. Comprehensive, detailed, and current information on specific companies and industry performance. Insider data. Investment by mutual funds. Charts on all NYSE, ASE, and OTC-NASDAQ stocks. Buy and sell recommendations. 1 year, 24 issues, $25.

Science and Technology Stock Investments

Computer Industry Newsletter. Securities Publishing Co. An informational service to provide an account of recent developments in the computer industry. Published twice monthly, the newsletter reports about specific companies and specific segments within the industry, and it is designed for the intelligent and performance-minded individual who can evaluate such information. 1 year, 24 issues, $60.

Computerworld. Written and edited for computer community, the management, professional, and technical people who design, analyze, program, and manage the use of automatic data systems. News columns report the technical and business developments in computer hardware, software, communications, services, education, etc. Special features include stock market report and index, conference news, new products, new investment opportunities, etc. 1 year, 52 issues, $9.

New Medical Technology. Published bi-weekly by a former executive of Dow Jones and the *Wall Street Journal* to satisfy a growing need for continuous, accurate, authoritative information on companies, products, equipment, research projects, contracts, financial reports, mergers, acquisitions, and all pertinent news of medical instrumentation and electronics. Written from a non-technical viewpoint, consistent with needs of businessmen and investors who know how to measure growth possibilities before they become full grown. 1 year, 26 issues, $52.

Technology Breakout Letter. DCM Associates. Offers early warnings of significant technological advances having a potential for imminent profit. Follow-up addresses are provided, but investment advice is not offered. Covers growth industries: knowledge, civic, ecology, robotics, ocean, leisure, materials, biomedical, energy, transportation, food, developing economics. 3 mos., 3 issues, $125.

Securities Industry News

Wall Street Letter. A confidential report about the securities industry and the people, firms and publications that make it tick. Edited by Myron Kandel, former financial editor of the N.Y. *Herald Tribune.* 1 year, 50 issues, $60.

Securities Statistics

Bank & Quotation Record. William B. Dana Co. One of the most comprehensive, authoritative, statistical tools for professional investors, this large 8½ X 12½-in., 96-page thick monthly statistical record is packed with quotations and quotation ranges of all listed stocks including those of probably the most comprehensive categorized lists of OTC securities. Other statistical information contained includes call loan rates, DJ averages, foreign exchanges, money market, NYSE indexes, volume of trading, prime bankers acceptances, securities called for redemption, time loan rates, exchange seats, etc. 1 year, 12 issues, $75.

Statistical Bulletin. U.S. Government. Includes statistical summaries of new securities, securities sales, common stock prices, stock transactions, and other phases of securities exchange. 3 years, 36 issues, $4.50.

Singapore Business and Investments

Who's Who in Malaysia and Singapore. Contains approximately 2,000 introductions to men who are the leaders in business, industry, professions, and government. 1 issue, $11.

Market Indicators Digest. The Fred Macaskill Investment Service. An international investment letter, based on the Dow theory, that gives in-depth coverage to the fundamental, technical, monetary, and psychological factors that influence markets. The international monetary situation and gold stocks are discussed in detail. A model international portfolio is maintained. 1 year, 25 issues, $66.

South and Central American Business & Investments

Business Latin America. Business International. First business paper for the whole of Latin America, serving executives responsible for operations throughout the region or in any Latin American nation. Interprets the new opportunities and obstacles being created by LAFTA and CACM, as well as reporting political, economic, and corporate trends and events in every country. 1 year, 52 issues, $198.

Special Situations Investment Services

Forbes Special Situation Survey. Forbes Investors Advisory Inst. A highly professional service for a limited group of sophisticated investors who are willing to accept carefully selected risks for unusually large capital gain potentials. Reports on 12 special situations, continuously followed up with special supplements on new developments and close out reports when a situation has reached its price objective. 12 reports, $150.

Maximum Gains Service. J. L. Spillane Co. Recommends undervalued stocks for unusually large capital gains and with minimal relative risk. Emphasis on extensive fundamental research with attention to technical timing and market psychology. Free test of stock market knowledge included. 1 yr., 24 issues, $100.

Prognosticator's Survey. A biweekly special situations letter designed for speculators. Definitely buy / short sale / stop loss / price objective figures provided for securities selected from N.Y. and American Exchanges. Number of recommendations limited with continuous review provided until transaction is closed. Discussion of general market conditions and basis for recommendations are not usually included. 1 year, 26 issues, $75.

Comp/Vest Alert. Scientific Investment Research. Bi-weekly selection of particular stock on NYSE or ASE which has both favorable fundamentals and technical strength on bar charts and also P/V charts (price vs. volume). 1 year, 52 issues, $125.

The Red Herring. Objective of this service: substantial capital appreciation over the intermediate to long term during generally favorable market conditions; conservation of capital during bear markets. Its medium: special situations, principally OTC stocks of rapidly growing companies judged likely to achieve greater investor recognition; also, selected new issues evaluated prior to their offering. Economic fundamentals and market prospects assessed periodically. 1 year, 24 issues, $50.

Titan Special Situations Service. Tital Investing Corp. An advisory service which selects three to five listed stocks annually for capital appreciation. Follow-up reports are issued until sales are recommended. 1 year, 3 to 5 issues, $30.

Tralick Investors Advisory. An investment letter that offers advice on the price to buy and the price to sell on stocks and features: a "Stock Star of the Month," recommends three stocks in the long-term section. Three stocks in the short-term section, four stocks in the action section, and eight stocks in the bounce section. 1 year, 12 issues, $24.

Value Line OTC Special Situations Service. Arnold Bernhard & Co., Inc. One or more special situation recommendations each month on OTC or ASE stocks, supported by a detailed 4-page report including key statistical data and charts. The service also provides supervisory reviews detailing performance records of every special situation recommended following up each at least once each quarter until close out, and more often if developments require. A summary index, updated twice a month contains current advice (especially recommended—buy-hold-sell) for each special still held. 1 year, 24 issues, $145.

Tax Counsel

Federal Tax Forms Service. Warren, Gorham & Lamont, Inc. A looseleaf-bound compilation of every Internal Revenue Service and U. S. Tax Court Form and accompanying instructions that you are very likely to need. These many hundreds of documents are organized by their official form number and scrupulously cross-referenced by subject. They are all actual size for reproduction and cover all taxpayers. Quarterly supplements up-date the information. 1 issue, plus 4 supplements, $37.50.

Foundations Federal Tax Letter. Callahan Publications. A comprehensive news digest of information and the ideas regarding Federal government actions affecting tax exempt organizations. 1 year, 24 issues, $125.

The Kess Tax Practice Report. Warren, Gorham & Lamont, Inc. An expert helps you to keep your information about day-to-day tax problems encountered in your professional work absolutely current. Alerts you to new tax legislation, the latest tax-saving ideas and strategies, and much more. 1 year, 24 issues, $36.

Tax Services for Investors

J. K. Lasser Tax Report. Business Reports, Inc. A semi-monthly 4-page report on tax saving ideas on investments, business, family and estate planning, plus monthly in-depth studies of tax sanctuaries and subjects of special tax interest. 1 year, 24 issues, $36.

Tax Shelters for Investors

Tax Shelter Advisory Service. In-depth research, evaluation by oil, cattle, real estate industry professionals of SEC-registered public investment offerings as to profit and/or income potential. Sole purpose is to help sophisticated investors and investment advisors maximize investor asset base through meaningful investment of tax dollars. 1 year, 25–30 reports, $500.

Technical: Investment Advisory Services.

Chartcraft Weekly NYSE–ASE Service by Electronic Computer. Chartcraft, Inc. Comprehensive weekly price changes for P. & F. charting covering all NYSE and ASE stocks, plus a complete analysis of the DJIA, a report of leading industry groups, and NYSE and ASE bullish percentage report, a listing of issues turning from bullish to bearish and those turning from bearish to bullish, nine selected trading opportunities with buy and sell signals, price objectives and stop-loss points, as well as relative strength ratings. 1 year, 52 issues, $150.

Comparative Market Indicators. Service of technical market timing including the unique CMI market trading index and trading indices for a selected group of stocks. Chart of 46 daily and weekly indicators, technical market commentary, and illustrated research topics. All updated, printed, and mailed every Friday. 1 year, 50 issues, $80.

Consistent Profits in the Stock Market. By Curtis Dahl. A book which presents a definite procedure to follow price trends and produce excellent profits year after year in the stock market. Proof provided through presenting a detailed application and results on a great many individual stocks between 1935 and May 1968. Latest revised issue, $20.

Market Kinetics. Sibbet-Hadady Publications, Inc. Forecasts changes in the market price trend, provides buy/sell recommendations of specific stocks, followed through to close out, and general investment recommendations on silver, gold, real estate, land, bonds, mortgages, etc. Optional phone service with daily up-dated market report and recommendations available. 1 year, 52 issues, $95.

The Master Indicator. A weekly letter edited by John Goddess. Analyzes advances and declines, upside-downside volume. NYSE member and nonmember trading, and other technical aspects of market activity. Interprets buying and selling pressures to find the industry groups and stocks about to become market leaders. Flash bulletins on buy and sell signals. 1 year, 24 issues, $68.

The Strongest Stocks. A stock market letter written by Gilbert Haller, author of the Haller theory book. The strongest stocks on the AMEX and NYSE are listed according to percentage price changes. Fast moving stocks are selected for specific recommendations. Stock market trends are analyzed and interpreted according to the Haller theory and other market indicators. The top performing mutual funds are also listed. 1 year, 24 issues, $50.

Up-Trend Report. Scientific Investment Research. Bi-weekly publication which monitors 3,600 stocks on the NYSE, ASE, Regional Exchange, and OTC markets in search of stocks "mostly likely to advance in the next six months." 1 year, 26 issues, $66.

Williams Reports. A complete service featuring the Williams theory for predicting important market moves. Subscription includes a monthly letter, plus bulletins whenever a buy or sell signal is given, plus a selection of recommended stocks, whose recommendations are based on a unique combination rating system which includes analysis of velocity, relative strength, time channels, moving averages, etc. Each recommendation is uniquely qualified, fundamentally strong, and technically ready for trading with the Williams trading method. 1 year, 36 issues, $50.

Technical: Short-Term Advisory Services

Todd Market Barometer Short Term. F. B. Todd & Co. Weekly reports based on F. Beaman Todd's original concept using the daily spread and daily price changes. Formula unaltered since its origin in 1938. This study results in anticipating most moves of 10 to 20 points, plus the larger moves. 1 year, 52 issues, $200.

Key-Volume Strategies. Using the tried approach that volume is key to forecasting move durations and reversals, recommendations appear weekly with a fully described original method to select one–four stocks called "MWP" for mid-week pricing technique. Readers are also regularly introduced to tools to convert their daily newspaper to a daily market advisor. 1 year, 48 issues, $58.

Technical: Long-Term Advisory Services

Long-Term Technical Trends. Stone & Mead, Inc. Monthly market service for professional or sophisticated investors. Each issue contains 9-year charts on major technical indicators. Service is unique in that it provides background information to support all conclusions. Its major value is for investors who want to think for themselves. Short interim reports are sent when necessary. 1 year, 12 issues. $100.

Texas Investments

Texas Metro Magazine. Texas Metropolitan Publications. General editorial, class-oriented regional magazine on subjects of management interest—business, stocks, marketing, social, science and technology, travel living—with emphasis on North Central Texas, among three leading growth areas of U. S. 1 year, 12 issues, $5.

Thailand Business

Thailand Year Book. The leading business directory of Thailand. 1 issue, $12.

Timing Investment Advisory Services

Business and Investment Timing. Anthony Gaubis & Co. A unique service based on privately developed studies of economic maladjustments, decennial patterns, and technical factors which tend to anticipate turning points in the stock market cycle. A weekly investment letter, published since January 1934, which includes bimonthly reviews of earnings and price prospects of 240 stocks and special reports on issues recommended for purchase. 1 year, 48 issues, $60.

The Short-Term Market Timing Report. Stock Fundamentals Co. Pertinent comments issued twice monthly. Flash bulletins mailed when important volume index signals short term up or down market moves. Based on daily up volume versus daily down volume combined with daily Dow price action and institutional buying and selling trends. Includes 6-year research summary. 1 year, 24 issues plus flash bulletins, $65.

Studies in the Movements of Stock Prices. Parnell C. McKenna. To anticipate stock market turning points is the basic objective. Cycles are stressed, and objective measurements provide indications of the strength and phase of the dominant stock market cycle. The cyclical status of stocks with superior appreciation potentials are discussed. Supplemented with special bulletins when judged to be warranted. 1 year, 12 issues, $60.

Trendicator. Demand/Supply Index. A unique market signalling service that daily evaluates the ratio of short transactions conducted in private accounts of all NYSE specialists, floor traders, and affiliate members to the general public short position. Based on studies since 1955 and performance records since 1966, this service claims that specialists activity can signal market turns and provides its subscribers with buy or sell signals via direct telephone, confirming them by airmail. 1 year, $100.

Traders' Investment Services

Dunn & Hargitt Letter. A weekly stock market service giving moving average trendline data on 1,500 stocks; specific buy, sell advice on undervalued growth stocks based on earnings analysis of 5,000 stocks; market picture and trend evaluation based on charts of key market indicators, computerized analysis of 99 industry groups; 50 strongest stocks based on relative strength; model investment portfolios; fastest growing companies with low P/E ratios; charts of selected growth stocks, buying and selling pressure analysis based on uptick-downtick volume data; overvaluation-undervaluation index for long-range market timing. 1 year, 52 issues, $129.

The Phillips Report. A concise, technical weekly letter for active traders. Recommends specific trades for each of four medium to high risk supervised portfolios. Short-term trades advised daily by telephone. All recommendations are followed up, and track record is shown weekly. Market trends and technical strength of all portfolio stocks updated daily. 1 year, 44 issues, $85.

Stollman's Techno-Monetary Pulse. This service offers buy and sell signals on volatile high volume stocks via daily telephone recordings. Clear, action-pointed market policy, updated every day, is offered via telephone each business day. As techno-monetary indicators flash buy or sell signals, the message is continually changed. 1 year, $50.

The Technicraft Trader. A weekly market letter especially designed for short term traders, using a unique timing method for today's market and featuring the strongest stocks, plus two or three hi-flyer trades and daily advice by phone. All commitments are protected by stop-loss. 1 year, 50 issues, $100.

The Trading Corner. E. J. Investment Service. A weekly market letter giving specific recommendations to buy, sell, or sell short specific securities based primarily on technical considerations assessing buying and selling pressures. Results of previous recommendations are recapped on a regular basis. Model portfolio for the long term investor is maintained and results tabulated. 1 year, 52 issues, $125.

Warrant Investments

C & P Warrant Analysis. Designed for the investor seeking detailed coverage of the unique investment opportunities provided by warrants. Provides bi-weekly coverage of all actively traded U.S. and Canadian warrants. A unique computer model is used to assign warrant values, assisting in the identification of warrants which are technically attractive. Complete information and calculations for over 300 warrants. Includes "About Warrants" and 3-ring binder. 1 year, 26 issues, $85.

Convertible Preferred and Warrant Chart Book. Kalb, Voorhis & Co. Published irregularly about once a year, this one-of-a-kind book provides charts showing common price in relation to preferred or warrants. A four-week trial subscription to *KV Convertible, Fact Finder Service* is provided with each purchase of this unique book, but because of its infrequent publication, book is likely to be dated by as much as 9–10 months. 1 issue, $10.

FRA Warrant Service. Financial Research Associates. Oriented toward the sophisticated investor desiring hedge/arbitrage warrant situations and to the trader seeking maximum leverage from selected speculative commitments. Each issue contains 30–50 pages of detailed hedge and reverse hedge analyses, two warrant valuations, leverage projections, recommendations, and a summary containing over 50 pieces of easily referenced dates for each warrant. 1 year, 12 issues, $60.

Investment Survey of Warrants. Independent Survey Co. Ltd. A weekly warrant investment letter providing comprehensive coverage of over 100 active American and Canadian warrants. It examines warrant economics, the technical picture, the common stock value and finally the warrant potential and when it reaches a buying area. 1 year, 48 issues, $58.

35. Financial Periodicals

ACB Management
  Associated Credit Bureaus, Inc.,
    6767 Southwest Freeway,
    Houston, Tex. 77036
  Eds.: Joan D. Masterson and Susan
    L. Strong
  Monthly, $5.00/year

Advertising Forum
  National Consumer Finance Assn.
  1000 16th St. N.W., Suite 701,
    Washington, D.C. 20006
  Ed.: Howard Cohagen
  Quarterly, free

American Banker
  525 West 42nd St., New York, N.Y.
    10036
  Ed.: Willard C. Rappleye, Jr.
  5 per week, $150.00/year

American Investor
  American Stock Exchange
  American Stock Exchange Bldg., 86
    Trinity Pl., New York, N.Y. 10006
  Ed.: Robert M. Keane
  10 per year, $5.00/year

Bank Administration
  Bank Admin. Institute
  P.O. Box 500, Park Ridge, Ill. 60068
  Ed.: Frank G. McCabe
  Monthly, $8.00/year

Bank Installment Lending Newsletter
  Management Reports, Inc.
  89 Beach St., Boston, Mass. 02111
  Monthly, $37.50/year

Bank Marketing Management
  Bank Marketing Assn.
  309 West Washington St., Chicago,
    Ill. 60606
  Ed.: Charles E. Bartling
  Monthly, $6.00/year

Bank News
  Financial Publications, Inc.
  912 Baltimore Ave., Kansas City,
    Mo. 64105
  5 per month, $20.00/year

Banker & Tradesman
  Warren Publishing Corp.
  89 Beach St., Boston, Mass. 02111
  Ed.: William A. Mallard
  Weekly, $42.00/year

Bankers Digest
  Robert M. Pinson
  Suite 1302, 1512 Commerce, Dallas,
    Tex. 75201
  Ed.: Bonita Bell
  Weekly, $5.00/year

Banker's Letter of the Law
  Warren, Gorham & Lamont
  89 Beach St., Boston, Mass. 02151
  Monthly, $18.00/year

Bankers Magazine
Warren, Gorham & Lamont, Inc.
89 Beach St., Boston, Mass. 02111
Ed.: Theodore L. Cross
Quarterly, $28.00/year

Bankers Monthly
Bankers Monthly, Inc.
1528 Skokie Blvd., Northbrook,
Ill. 60062
Ed.: A. M. Youngquist, Jr.
Monthly, $9.00/year

Banking
Simmons-Boardman Publishing
Corp.
350 Broadway, New York, N.Y.
10013
Ed.: Harry Waddell
Monthly, $8.00/year

Banking Law Journal
Warren, Gorham & Lamont, Inc.
89 Beach St., Boston, Mass. 02111
Monthly, $34.00/year

Banking News
Maryland Bankers Assn.
P.O. Box 822, Baltimore, Md. 21203
Ed.: William B. Elliott
Monthly, $5.00/year

Banking Systems & Equipment
Gralla Publications
1501 Broadway, New York, N.Y.
10036
Ed.: Alan Richman
Monthly, $5.00/year

Barron's
30 Broad St., New York, N.Y.
10004
Ed.: Robert M. Bleiberg
Weekly, $18.00/year

Bond and Money Market Review
First National Bank of Chicago
1 First National Plaza, Chicago, Ill.
60670
Monthly, free

Burroughs Clearing House
P.O. Box 299, Detroit, Mich. 48232
Ed.: Harry V. Odle
Monthly, contract circulation

Business and Financial Indicators
Federal Reserve Bank of Richmond
Research Dept., 9th & Franklin Sts.
Richmond, Va. 23213
Monthly, free

Business Conditions
Federal Reserve Bank of Chicago
Research Dept., P. O. Box 834
Chicago, Ill. 60690
Ed: Karl A. Scheld
Monthly, free

Business Review
Federal Reserve Bank
Public Information Dept.
Philadelphia, Pa. 19101
Monthly, free

Business Review
Federal Reserve Bank of Dallas
Sta. K, Dallas, Tex. 75222
Monthly, free

California Savings and Loan Journal
California Savings & Loan League
P. O. Box R, Pasadena, Calif. 91109
Ed.: Robert L. Kocher
Monthly, $5.00/year

Canadian Banker
Canadian Bankers' Assn.
P. O. Box 282, Royal Trust Tower
Toronto, Dominion Centre
Toronto, 111, Ontario, Canada
Ed.: Pamela Arnould
6 per year, $2.00/year

Canadian Trends
CUNA International, Inc.
P. O. Box 431, Madison, Wisc.
53701
Ed.: Dr. Walter Polner
Bi-monthly, Canada $1.00 ($1.50)
for 100 nos.

Collector
American Collectors Assn., Inc.
4040 West 70th St., Minneapolis,
Minn. 55435
Ed: Mrs. Eileen M. Johnson
Monthly, $10.00/year

Commercial Financing
National Commercial Finance
Conference, Inc.
29 Broadway, New York, N.Y.
10006
Ed.: Leonard Machlis
Bi-monthly, $20.00/year

Commercial West
Suburban Newspapers, Inc.
6601 West 78th St., Minneapolis,
Minn. 55435
Ed.: Roger J. Lewis
Weekly, $8.00/year

Consumer Finance News
National Consumer Finance Assn.
1000 16th St. N.W., Washington,
D. C. 20036
Ed.: Lawrence E. Baker
Monthly, $6.00/year

Credit and Financial Management
National Assn. of Credit
Management
475 Park Ave. South, New York,
N.Y. 10016
Ed.: Thomas F. Kenny
Monthly, $5.00/year

Credit and Financial Newsletter
National Assn. of Credit
Management
475 Park Ave. South, New York,
N.Y. 10016
Ed.: Thomas F. Kenny
Monthly, $5.00/year

Credit Executive
New York Credit & Financial
Management Assn.
71 West 23rd St., New York, N.Y.
10010
Ed.: Barrett R. Tanner
Monthly, membership

Credit Manager
Institute of Credit Management in
Southern Africa
P. O. Box 687, Johannesburg,
South Africa
Ed.: Donald Begley
Bi-monthly, R.2-$4.00

Credit Trend Service
Institute for Trend Research
South Rd., Hopkinton, N.H.
03301
Ed.: Chapin Hoskins
Monthly, $25.00/year

Credit Union Executive
CUNA International, Inc.
Publications Dept., Madison, Wisc.
53701
Ed.: Paul Zagorski
Quarterly, $6.50/year

Credit Union Magazine
Credit Union National Assn.
Publications Dept., P. O. Box 431
Madison, Wisc. 53701
Ed.: Paul D. Butler
Monthly, $3.00/year

Credit World
International Consumer Credit Assn.
375 Jackson Ave., St. Louis, Mo.
63130
Ed.: Richard K. Klein
Monthly, $6.00/year

Cu-Vues
New York State Credit Union
League
204 Fifth Ave., New York, N.Y.
10010
Ed.: Milton B. Schulman
Bi-monthly

Farm Credit News
Farm Credit Banks of Omaha
P. O. Box 1229, Omaha, Nebr.
68501
Ed.: Terry Bentley
Quarterly, free

*Federal Reserve Bank of Atlanta.
Monthly Review*
Federal Reserve Bank of Atlanta
Atlanta, Ga. 30303
Monthly, free

*Federal Reserve Bank of Kansas City.
Monthly Review*
Federal Reserve Bank of Kansas City
Kansas City, Mo. 64198
Ed.: Clarence W. Tow

Monthly (bi-monthly—June &
September), free

Federal Reserve Bank of New York.
Monthly Review
Federal Reserve Bank of New York
33 Liberty St., New York, N.Y.
10045
Monthly, free

Federal Reserve Bank of Richmond.
Monthly Review
Federal Reserve Bank of Richmond
Richmond, Va. 23213
Monthly, free

Federal Reserve Bank of St. Louis.
Review
Federal Reserve Bank of St. Louis
P. O. Box 442, St. Louis, Mo.
63166
Monthly, free

Federal Reserve Bulletin
Federal Reserve System
Bd. of Governors, Washington, D. C.
20551
Ed.: Board
Monthly, $6.00/year

Finance
P. O. Box G, Lennox Hill Sta.
New York, N.Y. 10021
Ed.: James P. Roscow
Monthly, $25.00/year

Finance and Development
International Monetary Fund &
International Bank for
Reconstruction & Development
(World Bank)
19th & H Sts. N.W., Washington,
D. C. 20431
Ed.: John D. Scott
Quarterly, free

Finance Facts
National Consumer Finance Assn.
Educational Services Div., 701 Solar-
Bldg., 1000 16th St. N.W.,
Washington, D. C. 20036
Monthly

The Financial Daily
P. O. Box 26565, Richmond, Va.
23261
Weekly, $50.00/year

Financial Executive
Financial Executives Institute
50 West 44th St., New York, N.Y.
10036
Ed.: Ben Makela
Monthly, $12.50/year

Financial World
17 Battery Pl., New York, N.Y.
10004
Ed.: R. J. Anderson
Weekly, $28.00/year

First National Bank of Chicago.
Business and Economic Review
First National Bank of Chicago
1 First National Plaza, Chicago, Ill.
60670
Monthly, free

First National Bank of Chicago.
International Economic Review
First National Bank of Chicago
1 First National Plaza, Chicago, Ill.
60670
Monthly, free

I B A Municipal Statistical Bulletin
Investment Bankers Assn. of
America
425 13th St. N.W., Washington
D. C. 20004
Quarterly, membership

Illinois Banker
Illinois Bankers Assn.
188 West Randolph St., Chicago, Ill.
60601
Ed.: Helen M. Kreisch
Monthly, $3.50/year

Independent Banker
Independent Bankers Assn. of
America
P. O. Box 267, Sauk Centre, Minn.
56378
Ed.: Bill McDonald
Monthly, $6.00/year

Industrial Banker
American Industrial Bankers Assn.
1629 K St. N.W., Washington, D. C.
20006
Ed.: Esther W. Lewis
Monthly, $6.00/year

International Financial Statistics
International Monetary Fund
Secretary, 19th & H Sts. N.W.,
Washington, D. C.
Monthly, $10.00/year

*International Monetary Fund. Staff
Papers*
International Monetary Fund
19th & H Sts. N.W., Washington
D. C. 20431
Ed.: Norman K. Humphreys
3 per year, $6.00/year

Journal of Commercial Bank Lending
Robert Morris Associates
1432 Philadelphia National Bank
Bldg., Philadelphia, Pa. 19107
Ed.: Clarence R. Reed
Monthly, membership (nonmembers
$10.00/year)

*Journal of Consumer Credit
Management*
Society of Certified Consumer
Credit Executives
7405 University Dr., St. Louis, Mo.
63130
Ed.: Miss Mary Alice Minney
Individuals, $8.00; educational
institutions, $5.00

Journal of Finance
Grad. School of Bus. Admin.
New York Univ.
100 Trinity Pl., New York, N.Y.
10006
Eds.: D. Luckett, Robert A. Kavesh
5 per year, $15.00/year

*Journal of Financial and Quantitative
Analysis*
Grad. School of Bus. Admin.
Univ. of Washington
209 Mackenzie Hall, Seattle, Wash.
98105
Ed.: Dr. Charles A. D'Ambrosio
5 per year, $12.00/year

Journal of Money, Credit & Banking
Ohio State Univ. Press
Journals Dept., 2070 Neil Ave.
Columbus, Ohio 43210
Quarterly, students $6.00/year;
others, $12.00/year

Kansas Banker
Kansas Bankers' Assn.
707 Merchants National Bank Bldg.
Topeka, Kans. 66612
Ed.: Roger D. Kirkwood
Monthly, $3.00/year

Kentucky Banker
Kentucky Bankers Assn.
425 South Fifth St., Louisville, Ky.
40202
Ed.: Ralph Fontaine
Monthly, $3.00/year

Magazine of Bank Administration
Bank Admin. Institute
303 South Northwest Highway,
P. O. Box 500, Park Ridge, Ill.
60068
Ed.: Frank G. McCabe
Monthly, $8.00/year

Mid-Continent Banker
408 Olive St., St. Louis, Mo. 63102
Ed.: Ralph B. Cox
13 per year, $7.00/year

Mid-Western Banker
161 West Wisconsin Ave., Milwaukee
Wisc. 53203
Ed.: Bernard A. Beggan, Jr.
Monthly, $6.00/year

Mississippi Banker
Mississippi Bankers Assn.
Box 37, Jackson, Miss. 39205
Ed.: John R. Hubbard
Monthly, $5.00/year

Monetary Notes
Economists' National Committee on
Monetary Policy
79 Madison Ave., New York, N.Y.
10016
Ed.: Walter E. Spahr
Monthly, free

Monthly Bank Clearings
Dun & Bradstreet, Inc.
Business Economics Dept., 99
Church St., New York, N.Y.
10007
Ed.: Rowena Wyant
Monthly, $3.00/year

Monthly Economic Letter
First National City Bank
399 Park Ave., New York, N.Y.
10022
Monthly, free

Morgan Guaranty Survey
Morgan Guaranty Trust Co. of
New York
23 Wall St., New York, N.Y. 10015
Ed.: Milton W. Hudson
Monthly, free

Mountain States Banker
Colorado, New Mexico, Wyoming &
Utah Bankers' Assn.
1150 National Bank Bldg., Denver
Colo. 80202
Ed.: Ariel Parker
Monthly, $5.00/year

*National League Journal of Insured
Savings Associations*
1200 17th St. N.W., Washington,
D. C. 20036
Ed.: Andrew R. Mandala
Monthly, $7.00/year

New Jersey Banker
New Jersey Bankers Assn.
P. O. Box 573, Princeton, N.J.
08540
Ed.: W. Walter Asmus
Quarterly, $3.00/year

New York State Banker
New York State Bankers Assn.
405 Lexington Ave., New York,
N.Y. 10017
Ed.: Yvonne Ludlam
Weekly, $7.50

*New York University Graduate School
of Business Administration.
Institute of Finance Bulletin*
New York Univ.

Grad. School of Bus. Admin.
Institute of Finance, 100 Trinity
Pl., New York, N.Y. 10006
4-6 per year, $5.00/year (teachers
$1.00)

Ohio Banker
Ohio Bankers Assn.
33 North High St., Columbus, Ohio
43215
Ed.: Don Buckley
Monthly, $4.00/year

*Quarterly Financial Report for
Manufacturing Corporations*
Superintendent of Documents
Government Printing Office,
Washington, D. C. 20402
Quarterly, $2.00/year

*Royal Bank of Canada. Monthly
Letter*
Royal Bank of Canada
Monthly Letter Dept., Box 6001,
Montreal, Quebec, Canada
Monthly, free

Safe Deposit Bulletin
New York State Safe Deposit Assn.
521 Fifth Ave., New York, N.Y.
10017
Ed.: Raymond J. Walter
Monthly, $10.00/year

Savings and Loan News
United States Savings & Loan
League
111 East Wacker Dr., Chicago, Ill.
60601
Ed.: Hoyt A. Mathews
Monthly, $6.00/year

Savings Association News
Savings Assn. League of New York
State
700 White Plains Rd., Scarsdale,
N.Y. 10583
Ed.: Walter Kaner
Monthly, write for subscription rates

Savings Bank Journal
National Assn. of Mutual Savings
Banks
200 Park Ave., New York, N.Y.
10017

Ed. & Publisher: Richard E.
  Pokriefke
Monthly, $14.00/year

Southern Banker
McFadden Business Publications
2119 Warren Dr., Norcross, Ga.
  30071
Ed.: R. W. Gibbs
Monthly, $5.00/year

Tarheel Banker
North Carolina Bankers Assn.
911 Durham Life Bldg., Raleigh,
  N.C. 27602
Ed.: Harry Gatton
Monthly, $3.00/year

Tempo
Touche Ross & Co.
P. O. Box 919, Radio City Sta.,
  New York, N.Y. 10019
Ed.: Carol Murray
Quarterly, free

Tennessee Banker
Tennessee Bankers Assn.
22nd Floor, Life & Casualty Tower,
  Nashville, Tenn. 37219
Ed.: Robert M. Gilliam
Monthly, $2.00/year

Third Federal Savings & Loan
  Association of Cleveland, Ohio
  News
7007 Broadway, Cleveland, Ohio
Ed.: Gerome Rita Stefanski
Free

U. S. Federal Home Loan Bank
  Board Journal
Federal Home Bank Board
101 Indiana Ave. N.W., Washington,
  D. C. 20552
Ed.: Watson Fenimore
Monthly, $3.50/year

U. S. Treasury Department.
  Treasury Bulletin
Superintendent of Documents
Government Printing Office,
  Washington, D. C. 20402
Monthly, $13.50/year

Wall Street Journal
Dow Jones & Co., Inc.
30 Broad St., New York, N.Y.
  10004
Exec. Ed.: Edward R. Cony
Daily, $32.00/year

Weekly Bank Clearings
Dun & Bradstreet, Inc.
Business Economics Dept., 99
  Church St., New York, N.Y.
  10007
Ed.: Rowena Wyant
Weekly, $10.00/year

World Reporter
CUNA International, Inc.
World Extension Dept., 1617
  Sherman Ave., P. O. Box 431
  Madison, Wisc. 53701
Quarterly, contract free circulation

36. Major Financial Reference Books

GUIDES TO SOURCES OF ADDITIONAL INFORMATION

Angel, J., *Handbook of International Investment Facts and Information Sources.* New York: Regents Publishing Co., 1967

Coman, E. T., *Sources of Business Information.* Berkeley: Univ. of California Press, 1964.

Guide to Business and Investment Books. New York: Select Information Exchange, 1970.

Investment Sources and Ideas. New York: Select Information Exchange, 1972 (free of charge)

Klein, B., *Guide to American Directories.* New York: Klein Publishing Co., 1972

McNierney, M., *Directory of Business and Financial Services.* New York: Special Libraries Assn., 1963

Woy, J. B., *Investment Information: A Detailed Guide to Selected Sources.* Detroit: Gale Research Co., 1970

INDEXES TO FINANCIAL PERIODICALS

Funk and Scott Index of Corporations and Industries. Cleveland: Predicasts, Inc., weekly.

The New York Times Index. New York: The New York Times, Bi-weekly; annual cumulation.

PAIS Bulletin. New York: Public Affairs Information Service, weekly.

Wall Street Journal Index. New York: Wall Street Journal, monthly.

Wall Street Transcript. New York: Wall Street Transcript, weekly.

GLOSSARIES OF FINANCIAL AND BANKING TERMS

Horn, Stefan F., *Glossary of Financial Terms in English, French, Spanish and German.* New York: American Elsevier Publishing Co., 1965

Ricci, Julio. *Elsevier's Banking Dictionary in Six Languages.* New York: American Elsevier Publishing Co., 1966

DIRECTORIES OF U.S. COMPANIES

Angel, J. L., *Directory of American Firms Operating in Foreign Countries.* New York: World Trade Academy Press, 1969

Middle Market Directory. New York: Dun & Bradstreet, annual.

Million Dollar Directory. New York: Dun & Bradstreet, annual.

News Front Directory of 25,000 Leading U.S. Corporations. New York: News Front Magazine, annual.

Standard and Poor's Register of Corporations, Directors and Executives. New York: Standard & Poor's Corp., annual.

Thomas' Register of American Manufacturers. New York: Thomas Publishing Co., annual.

DIRECTORIES OF FOREIGN FIRMS

Angel, Juvenal L., *Directory of Foreign Firms Operating in the U.S.* New York: Simon & Schuster, 1971

Beerman's Financial Yearbook of Europe. New York: International Publications Service, annual.

Dun and Bradstreet Exporter's Encyclopedia. New York: Dun & Bradstreet, 1969

Financial Times of London Yearbook: Business Information. New York: St. Martin's Press, 1972

Jane's Major Companies of Europe. New York: McGraw-Hill Book Co., 1972

HANDBOOKS AND ENCYCLOPEDIAS

Baughn, W. H. and Walker, C. E., *The Banker's Handbook.* Homewood, Ill.: Dow Jones-Irwin Publishing Co., 1966

Bogen, Jules I. and Shipman, Samuel. *Financial Handbook.* New York: Ronald Press, 1970

Commodity Yearbook. New York: Commodity Research Bureau, annual.

Dow Jones Investors Handbook. Princeton, N.J.: Dow Jones Books, 1972

Encyclopedia of Stock Market Techniques. Larchmont, N.Y.: Investors Intelligence, 1972

The McGraw Hill Dictionary of Modern Economics; A Handbook of Terms and Organizations. New York: McGraw-Hill Book Co., 1964

Munn, G. G., *Encyclopedia of Banking and Finance.* Boston: Bankers Publishing Co., 1962

Van Arsdell, Paul, *Corporation Finance.* New York: Ronald Press, 1970

Vancil, Richard F., *Financial Executive's Handbook.* Homewood, Ill.: Dow Jones-Irwin Publishing Co., 1969

Zarb, Frank G. and Kerekes, Gabriel T., eds., *The Stock Market Handbook.* Homewood, Ill.: Dow Jones-Irwin Publishing Co., 1970

LEGAL TOPICS

Bromberg, Alan R., *Securities Law: Fraud: Securities and Exchange Commission Rule 10b-5.* New York: McGraw-Hill Book Co., 1969

Decisions and Reports of the Securities and Exchange Commission. Washington, D.C.: U.S. Government Printing Office, subscription. Apply.

Federal Bank Service. Englewood Cliffs, N.J.: Prentice-Hall Inc., loose-leaf service

Federal Banking Law Reports. Chicago: Commerce Clearing House, weekly. Loose-leaf service

Gadsby, Edward N., *The Federal Securities Exchange Act of 1934.* New York: Matthew Bender & Co., 1970

Securities Regulation Service. Englewood Cliffs, N.J.: Prentice-Hall Inc., weekly. Loose-leaf service

Security Transactions. Chicago: Commerce Clearing House, weekly. Loose-leaf service

Stock Transfer Guide. Chicago: Commerce Clearing House, weekly. Loose-leaf service

Study of the Securities Industry, Part I. Hearings of the Subcommittee on Commerce and Finance of the House Committee on Interstate and Foreign Commerce. Washington, D.C.: U.S. Government Printing Office, 1971

Trust and Estate Law Reports. Chicago: Commerce Clearing House, weekly. Loose-leaf service

BIOGRAPHICAL INFORMATION SOURCES

Directory of Directors (Canada). New York: MacLean-Hunter Ltd.

Standard and Poor's Register of Corporations, Directors and Executives. Part II. New York: Standard & Poor's Corp., annual.

Who is Who in British Finance. New York: Stechert-Hafner, Inc., 1972

Who's Who in Finance and Industry. Chicago: Marquis Publishing Co., biennial.

DIRECTORIES LISTING INDIVIDUALS AND FINANCIAL INSTITUTIONS

Broker-Dealer and Investment Advisor Directory. U.S. Securities and Exchange Commission. Washington, D.C.: U.S. Government Printing Office, annual.

Directory and Guide to the Mutual Savings Banks in the United States. New York: National Assn. of Mutual Savings Banks.

Directory of American Savings and Loan Associations. Baltimore: T. K. Sanderson Organization, annual.

Directory of Municipal Bond Dealers in the U.S. New York: The Bond Buyer, annual.

Investment Banker-Broker Almanac. New York: Finance Magazine, annual.

Membership Directory. New York: Financial Analysts Federation, annual.

Polk's Bank Directory. North Nashville, Tenn.: R. L. Polk & Co., annual.

Rand McNally International Bankers Directory. Chicago: Rand McNally & Co., semiannual.

Security Dealers of North America. New York: Standard & Poor's Corp., semiannual.

MUTUAL FUND DIRECTORIES

Hirsch, Yale, *The 1970 Manual of Mutual Funds.* Lynbrook, N.Y.: Enterprise Press.

Investment Companies. New York: Weisenberger Services, 1972, annual.

Mutual Fund Directory. Los Angeles: FundScope, Inc., annual.

Mutual Fund Directory. New York: Dealer's Digest Publishing Co., semiannual.

Survey of Canadian Investment Funds. New York: McLean-Hunter Publishing Co.

STOCK EXCHANGE DIRECTORIES

American Stock Exchange Membership Directory. Chicago: Commerce Clearing House, semiannual.

New York Stock Exchange Directory. Chicago: Commerce Clearing House, semiannual.

Stock Market Official Yearbook. New York: Iliffe & NTP, Inc., annual.

INVESTMENT INFORMATION SOURCES

Corporate Financial Directory. New York: Investment Dealer's Digest, Inc., annual.

Industry Surveys. New York: Standard & Poor's Corp.

Moody's Bank and Finance Manual. New York: Moody's Investors Service, Inc., annual with updating service.

Moody's Bond Survey. New York: Moody's Investors Service, Inc., weekly.

Moody's Handbook of Common Stocks. New York: Moody's Investors Service, Inc., four per year.

Moody's Industrial Manual. New York: Moody's Investors Service, Inc., annual with updating service.

Moody's Municipal & Government Manual. New York: Moody's Investors Service, Inc., annual with updating service.

Moody's Public Utility Manual. New York: Moody's Investors Service, Inc., annual with updating service.

Moody's Stock Survey. New York: Moody's Investors Service, Inc., weekly.

Moody's Transportation Manual. New York: Moody's Investors Service, Inc., annual with updating service.

National Monthly Bond Summary. New York: National Quotation Bureau.

National Monthly Stock Summary. New York: National Quotation Bureau.

The Outlook. New York: Standard & Poor's Corp., weekly.

Over-the-Counter and Regional Exchange Stock Reports. New York: Standard & Poor's Corp.

Security Owner's Stock Guide. New York: Standard & Poor's Corp., monthly.

Security Price Index Record. New York: Standard & Poor's Corp.

Standard & Poor's Earnings and Ratings Bond Guide. New York: Standard and Poor's Corp., monthly.

Standard Corporation Records. New York: Standard and Poor's Corp., loose-leaf service.

United Business and Investment Report. Boston: United Business Service, weekly.

United Mutual Fund Selector. Boston: United Business Service, semi-monthly.

Value Line Investment Survey. New York: Value Line Investment Survey, weekly.

37. Sources of Financial Information

FINANCIAL RATINGS AND RANKINGS

Annual Report on American Industry. Forbes, Inc. Annual (January issue).
Ranks corporations by industry groups. Includes aerospace and defense, automotive, building materials, chemicals, consumer goods, distribution, electronics, energy, finance, forest products, industrial equipment, information processing, leisure and education, metals, multi-companies, conglomerates, transportation, and utilities. Issue may be purchased. Apply.

Directory of 25,000 Leading U.S. Corporations. News Front Books. Annual.
Lists 25,000 major companies by standard industrial classification, approximate sales, profits, assets, etc. Publication can be purchased. Apply.

Fortune Directory Issues. Fortune Magazine. Annual (July and August issues).
Ranks the top 500 corporations; largest banks, retail chains, transportation, insurance, and utilities companies; top 200 foreign corporations. Data includes rank by sales, assets, net profits, etc. Single issue may be purchased. Apply.

Middle Market Directory. Dun & Bradstreet. Annual.
Lists about 18,000 U.S. companies with a worth of $500,000 to $999,-999. Lists Officers, standard industrial classification, approximate sales, and number of employees. Publication is leased. Apply.

Million Dollar Directory. Dun & Bradstreet. Annual.
Lists about 25,000 U.S. companies with a worth of $1 million or more. Lists officers, standard industrial classification, approximate sales, and number of employees. Publication is leased. Apply.

FINANCIAL DATA ABOUT SPECIFIC CORPORATIONS

The following organizations provide services and information about U.S. and foreign corporations. Apply directly to each for specific information about services, subscription costs, etc.

Bureau of International Commerce
U.S. Department of Commerce,
Washington, D.C. 20230

Leasco Services
200 Park Ave., New York, N.Y.
10017

Xerox International Financial File
c/o University Microfilms, 300 N.
Zeeb Rd., Ann Arbor, Mich. 48106

CREDIT INFORMATION ABOUT SPECIFIC CORPORATIONS

The following organizations provide credit reporting services about U.S. and foreign companies. Apply directly to each for specific information about services, subscription costs, etc.

Bureau of International Commerce
U.S. Department of Commerce,
Washington, D.C. 20230

Dun & Bradstreet, Inc.
99 Church St., New York, N.Y.
10007

Foreign Credit Interchange Bureau
c/o National Assn. of Credit Management, 475 Park Ave. South, New
York, N.Y. 10016

Retail Credit Co.
P.O. Box 4081, Atlanta, Ga. 30302

FINANCIAL RATIOS

Accounting Corp. of America
Research Dept., P.O. Box 1471, San
Diego, Calif. 92112
Barometer of Small Business. Two
issues per year. Apply. Balance
sheet and operating data for 48 lines
of small retail and service businesses.

Reported by sales volume and geographical location groupings. Includes selected ratios. Studies are developed from monthly financial reports submitted by clients of the Accounting Corp.

Dun & Bradstreet
99 Church St., New York, New
York 10007
The following publications are free of charge in single copies. *Key Business Ratios for 125 Lines; Cost of Doing Business—Corporations; Cost of Doing Business—Proprietorships and Partnerships.*

Fairchild Publications
7 East 12th St., New York, N.Y.
10003
Financial Manual of Retail Stores.
Annual.

Robert Morris Associates
The Philadelphia National Bank
Bldg., Philadelphia, Pa. 19107
*Sources of Composite Financial Data—A Bibliography—*3rd ed.
($1.00). Lists sources of nongovernmental data for 300 industries.
Annual Statement Studies. A collection of composite balance sheets and income statements for different lines of business including manufacturing, wholesaling, retailing, and services. Publication may be purchased. Apply.

Prentice-Hall, Inc.
Englewood Cliffs, N.J. 07636
Leo Troy, *Almanac of Business and Industrial Financial Ratios.* Presents data on 266 major and minor industries classified by standard industrial classification. Twenty-two ratios are provided for each industry. Publication may be purchased. Apply.

Standard & Poor's Corp.
345 Hudson St., New York, N.Y.
10007
Standard and Poor's Industry Sur-

vey. Annual. Surveys about 50 industries. Provides some ratios.

U.S. Government Printing Office Washington, D.C. 20402
Quarterly Financial Report for Manufacturing Corporations. A subscription publication of the Securities Exchange Commission and Federal Trade Commission. $1.25 per year. Apply.

FOREIGN EXCHANGE QUOTATIONS

The following organizations and publications provide information concerning up-to-date foreign exchange rates.

Commercial and Financial Chronicle
25 Park Pl., New York, N.Y. 10007
The Monday edition of this publication includes current rates.

First National Bank of Chicago
International Section, 1 First National Plaza, Chicago, Ill. 60670

Manufacturers Hanover Trust Co.
Foreign Exchange Trading Dept., 4 New York Plaza, New York, N.Y. 10015

U.S. Board of Governors of the Federal Reserve System
Washington, D.C. 20551
Foreign Exchange Rates. Monthly. Free
Foreign Exchange Rates for the Week. Free

38. Major Sources of Financial Statistics

Andriot, John D., *Guide to Government Statistics.* McClean, Va.: Documents Index, 1967

Bank and Quotation Record. New York: William B. Dana Co., twelve per year.

Business Statistics. Office of Business Economics. U.S. Dept. of Commerce. Washington, D.C.: U.S. Government Printing Office, monthly by subscription.

Commodity Yearbook. New York: Commodity Research Bureau, annual.

Directory of Non-Federal Statistics for States and Local Areas. Bureau of the Census. Washington, D.C.: U.S. Government Printing Office.

Economic Almanac. New York: The Conference Board, biennial.

Economic Indicators. U.S. Joint Economic Committee. Washington, D.C.: U.S. Government Printing Office, monthly.

Federal Reserve Bulletin. Board of Governors of the Federal Reserve System. Washington, D.C.: U.S. Government Printing Office, monthly by subscription.

Federal Reserve Chart Book. Board of Governors of the Federal Reserve System. Washington, D.C.: U.S. Government Printing Office, monthly by subscription.

Financial Times of London Yearbook. New York: St. Martins Press, 1972

Handbook of Basic Economic Statistics. Washington, D.C. Economic Statistics Bureau of Washington, monthly with an annual compilation.

Historical Chart Book. Board of Governors of the Federal Reserve System. Washington, D.C.: U.S. Government Printing Office, annual.

International Financial Statistics. Washington, D.C.: International Monetary Fund, monthly.

The Investment Outlook. New York: Bankers Trust Co., annual.

Monetary Statistics of the U.S. Estimates, Sources and Methods. New York: National Bureau of Economic Research, 1970

Official Summary of Security Transactions and Holdings. Securities & Exchange Commission. Washington, D.C.: U.S. Government Printing Office, monthly by subscription.

Report of the Special Study of Securities Markets. Securities & Exchange Commission. Washington, D.C.: U.S. Government Printing Office, 1971

Statistical Abstract of the United States. U.S. Bureau of the Census. Washington, D.C.: U.S. Government Printing Office, annual.

Statistical Bulletin. Securities & Exchange Commission. Washington, D.C.: U.S. Government Printing Office, monthly by subscription.

Statistical Yearbook. New York: United Nations, Secretariat's Statistical Office, annual.

Survey of Current Business. U.S. Dept. of Commerce. Washington, D.C.: U.S. Government Printing Office, monthly by subscription.

Trade and Securities Statistics. New York: Standard & Poor's Corp., monthly with cumulations.

Treasury Bulletin. U.S. Treasury Dept. Washington, D.C.: U.S. Government Printing Office, monthly by subscription.

Wasserman, Paul, *Statistics Sources.* Detroit: Gale Publishing Co., 1971

EDUCATIONAL PROGRAMS AND RESOURCES

39. College and University Programs

FINANCE MAJOR

Alabama

Birmingham-Southern Coll.
Birmingham 35204
Oakwood Coll.
Huntsville 35806
Samford Univ. (formerly Howard
Coll.)
800 Lakeshore Dr., Birmingham
35209
Univ. of Alabama
University 35486

Alaska

Univ. of Alaska
College 99701

Arizona

Arizona State Univ.
Tempe 85281
Northern Arizona Univ.
Flagstaff 86001
Univ. of Arizona
Park Ave. at East 3rd St., Tucson
85721

Arkansas

Little Rock Univ.
Little Rock 72204
Ouachita Baptist Univ.
Arkadelphia 71923
Univ. of Arkansas
Fayetteville 72701

California

Armstrong Coll.
222 Harold Way, Berkeley 94704
California State Coll. at Long Beach
6101 East 7th St., Long Beach
90801
California State Coll. at Los Angeles
Los Angeles 90032
Loyola Univ. of Los Angeles
7101 West 80th St., Los Angeles
90045
Sacramento State Coll.
6000 J St., Sacramento 95819
San Diego State Coll.
San Diego 92115
San Francisco State Coll.
San Francisco 94132

Univ. of San Francisco
San Francisco 94117

Univ. of Santa Clara
Santa Clara 95053

Univ. of Southern California
University Park, Los Angeles 90007

Colorado

Univ. of Colorado
Boulder 80302

Univ. of Denver
University Park, Denver 80210

Connecticut

Fairfield Univ.
Fairfield 06431

Univ. of Connecticut
Storrs 06268

Delaware

Univ. of Delaware
Newark 19711

District of Columbia

The American Univ.
Massachusetts & Nebraska Aves.
N.W., Washington 20016

Georgetown Univ.
37th & O Sts. N.W., Washington
20007

Howard Univ.
Washington 20001

Southeastern Univ.
1736 G St. N.W., Washington 20006

Florida

Florida State Univ.
Tallahassee 32306

Florida Technological Univ.
Orlando 32801

Univ. of Florida
Gainesville 32601

Univ. of Miami
Coral Gables 33124

Univ. of Palm Beach
660 Fern St., West Palm Beach
33401

Univ. of South Florida
Tampa 33620

Georgia

Georgia Southern Coll.
Statesboro 30458

Univ. of Georgia
Athens 30601

Valdosta State Coll.
Valdosta 30601

Hawaii

Univ. of Hawaii
Honolulu 96822

Illinois

DePaul Univ.
Chicago 60604

Loyola Univ.
820 North Michigan Ave., Chicago
60611

Northern Illinois Univ.
DeKalb 60115

Roosevelt Univ.
430 South Michigan Ave., Chicago
60605

Southern Illinois Univ.
Carbondale 62903

Southern Illinois Univ.
Edwardsville 62025

Univ. of Illinois, Chicago Circle
Campus
Box 4348, Chicago 60680

Univ. of Illinois, Main Campus
Urbana-Champaign Campus 61803

Indiana

Indiana Univ.
Bloomington 47401

St. Joseph's Coll.
Rensselaer 47978

Univ. of Evansville
Evansville 47704

Univ. of Notre Dame
Notre Dame 46556

Valparaiso Univ.
Valparaiso 46383

Iowa

Drake Univ.
Des Moines 50311

Univ. of Iowa
Iowa City 52240

Kansas

Kansas State Univ.
Manhattan 66502

Kansas State Coll. of Pittsburg
Pittsburg 66762

Wichita State Univ.
Wichita 67208

Kentucky

Eastern Kentucky Univ.
Richmond 40475

Univ. of Kentucky
University Sta., Lexington 40506

Univ. of Louisville
Louisville 40208

Louisiana

Louisiana Polytechnic Institute
Ruston 71270

Louisiana State Univ.
Baton Rouge 70803

Loyola Univ.
6363 St. Charles Ave., New Orleans
70118

Northeast Louisiana State Coll.
Monroe 71201

Univ. of Southwestern Louisiana
Lafayette 70501

Maine

Husson Coll.
157 Park St., Bangor 04401

Maryland

Univ. of Baltimore
1420 North Charles St., Baltimore
21201

Univ. of Maryland
College Park 20740

Massachusetts

American International Coll.
170 Wilbraham Rd., Springfield
01109

Babson Coll.
Babson Park (Wellesley) 02157

Boston Coll.
Chestnut Hill 02167

Merrimack Coll.
North Andover 01845

Nichols Coll. of Bus. Admin.
Dudley 01572

Northeastern Univ.
360 Huntington Ave., Boston 02115

Simmons Coll.
300 The Fenway, Boston 02115

Michigan

Michigan State Univ.
East Lansing 48823

Muskegon Business Coll.
145 Apple Ave., Muskegon 49443

Univ. of Detroit
Detroit 48221

Wayne State Univ.
Detroit 48202

Western Michigan Univ.
Kalamazoo 49001

Minnesota

St. Cloud State Coll.
St. Cloud 56301

Mississippi

Mississippi State Univ.
State College 39762

Univ. of Southern Mississippi
Hattiesburg 39401

Missouri

Univ. of Missouri
Columbia 65201
Kansas City 64110
Rolla 65401
St. Louis 63121

Northwest Missouri State Coll.
Maryville 64468

Southwest Missouri State Coll.
Springfield 65802

St. Louis Univ.
St. Louis 63103

Washington Univ.
St. Louis 63130

Montana

Univ. of Montana
Missoula 59801

Nebraska

Creighton Univ.
2500 California St., Omaha 68131

Univ. of Nebraska
Omaha 68101

Nevada

Univ. of Nevada
Reno 89507

New Jersey

Fairleigh Dickinson Univ.
Florham Park, Madison 07940
Rutherford 07070
Teaneck 07666

Rider Coll.
Trenton 08602

Seton Hall Univ.
South Orange 07079

New Mexico

Eastern New Mexico Univ.
Portales 88130

New Mexico State Univ.
Las Cruces 88001

Univ. of New Mexico
Albuquerque 87106

New York

Adelphi Univ.
Garden City 11530

Fordham Univ.
Bronx 10458

Hofstra Univ.
1000 Fulton Ave., Hempstead
11550

Long Island University, Merriweather
Campus
Greenvale 11548

Pace Coll.
41 Park Row, New York 10038

Siena Coll. (St. Bernardine of Siena
Coll.)
Loudonville 12211

St. Bonaventure Univ.
St. Bonaventure 14778

St. John Fisher Coll.
3600 East Ave., Rochester 14618

St. John's Univ.
Grand Central & Utopia Parkways,
Jamaica 11432

Syracuse Univ.
Syracuse 13210

Utica Coll. of Syracuse Univ.
Syracuse 13210

Ohio

Ashland Coll.
Ashland 44805

John Carroll Univ.
University Heights, Cleveland 44118

Cleveland State Univ.
Euclid-24th St., Cleveland 44115

Dyke Coll.
1375 E. Sixth St., Cleveland 44114

Kent State Univ.
Kent 44240

Miami Univ.
Oxford 45056

Ohio State Univ.
Columbus 43210

Ohio Univ.
Athens 45701

Univ. of Akron
302 East Buchtel Ave., Akron 44304

Univ. of Cincinnati
Cincinnati 45221

Univ. of Toledo
2801 West Bancroft St., Toledo
43606

Walsh Coll.
North Canton 44720

Wright State Univ.
Dayton 45431

Xavier Univ.
Victory Parkway, Cincinnati 45207

Oklahoma

Oklahoma State Univ.
Stillwater 74074

Univ. of Oklahoma
Norman 73069

Univ. of Tulsa
Tulsa 74104

Oregon

Univ. of Oregon
Eugene 97403

Univ. of Portland
5000 North Willamette Blvd.,
Portland 97203

Pennsylvania

Duquesne Univ.
Pittsburgh 15219

Gannon Coll.
Erie 16501

LaSalle Coll.
Olney Ave. at 20th St., Philadelphia
19141

Lehigh Univ.
Bethlehem 18015

Pennsylvania State Univ.
University Park 16802

Susquehanna Univ.
Selinsgrove 17870

Temple Univ.
Broad & Montgomery, Philadelphia
19122

Univ. of Pennsylvania
Philadelphia 19104

Puerto Rico

Univ. of Puerto Rico
Rio Piedras 00931

Rhode Island

Univ. of Rhode Island
Kingston 02881

Tennessee

Carson-Newman Coll.
Jefferson City 37760

East Tennessee State Univ.
Johnson City 37601

Memphis State Univ.
Memphis 38111

Middle Tennessee State Univ.
Murfreesboro 37130

Tennessee Technological Univ.
Cookeville 38501

Univ. of Tennessee
Knoxville 37916

Texas

Baylor Univ.
Waco 76703

East Texas State Univ.
Commerce 75428

Univ. of Houston
3801 Cullen Blvd., Houston 77004

McMurry Coll.
South 14th St. & Sayles Blvd.,
Abilene 79605

North Texas State Univ.
Denton 76203

Southern Methodist Univ.
Dallas 75222

St. Edward's Univ.
Austin 78704

St. Mary's Univ.
San Antonio 78228

Texas A & I Univ.
Kingsville 78763

Texas A & M Univ.
College Station 77843

Texas Christian Univ.
Fort Worth 76129

Texas Technological Coll.
Lubbock 79409

Texas Woman's Univ.
Denton 76214

Univ. of Texas at Austin
Austin 78712

West Texas State Univ.
Canton 79015

Utah

Univ. of Utah
Salt Lake City 84112

Vermont

Univ. of Vermont
Burlington 05401

Virginia

Old Dominion Univ.
Norfolk 23508
Univ. of Richmond
Richmond 23173
Univ. of Virginia
Charlottesville 22903

Washington

Gonzaga Univ.
East 502 Boon Ave., Spokane 99202
Seattle Univ.
Seattle 98122
Univ. of Washington
Seattle 98105

West Virginia

Marshall Univ.
Huntington 25701

Wisconsin

Marquette Univ.
1131 West Wisconsin Ave.
Milwaukee 53233
Univ. of Wisconsin-Milwaukee
3203 North Downer Ave.
Milwaukee 53201
Wisconsin State Univ.
17th & State Sts., LaCrosse 54601
Oshkosh 54901
Whitewater 53190

FINANCIAL MANAGEMENT MAJOR

California

California Baptist Coll.
8432 Magnolia Ave., Riverside 92504
California State Coll. at Hayward
25800 Hillary Rd., Hayward 94542
Sacramento State Coll.
6000 J St., Sacramento 95819

District of Columbia

George Washington Univ.
20006

Florida

Univ. of Palm Beach
660 Fern St., West Palm Beach 33401

Maryland

Univ. of Baltimore
1420 North Charles St., Baltimore 21201

Massachusetts

Babson Coll.
Babson Park (Wellesley) 02157

Minnesota

St. Cloud State Coll.
St. Cloud 56301

Nebraska

Wayne State Coll.
Wayne 68787

New York

New York Univ.
Washington Square, New York 10003
Pace Coll.
41 Park Row, New York 10038

Ohio

Dyke Coll.
1375 E. Sixth St., Cleveland 44114
Kent State Univ.
Kent 44240

Pennsylvania

Temple Univ.
Broad & Montgomery, Philadelphia 19122

Puerto Rico

World Univ.
Ave. Barbosa y Guayama, Hato Rey 00917

Vermont

Royalton Coll.
South Royalton 05068

Wisconsin

Wisconsin State Univ.
Whitewater 53190

GRADUATE STUDY IN BUSINESS

California

Stanford Univ. Office of the Doctoral
Program, Grad. School of Bus.
Stanford 94305

United States International Univ.
Grad. School of Bus. Admin.
8655 East Pomerado Rd., San
Diego 92124

Univ. of California, Berkeley, Grad.
School of Bus. Admin., Berkeley
94720

Univ. of California, Grad. School of
Bus. Admin., Los Angeles 90024

Univ. of Southern California, Grad.
School of Bus. Admin., Los
Angeles 90007

Colorado

Univ. of Denver, Coll. of Bus. Admin.,
Grad. Div., Denver 80210

District of Columbia

American Univ., School of Bus.
Admin., 20016

The George Washington Univ., School
of Government and Bus. Admin.
20006

Georgia

Emory Univ., Grad. School of Bus.
Admin., Atlanta 30322

Illinois

Northwestern Univ., Grad. School of
Management, 339 East Chicago
Ave., Chicago 60611

The Univ. of Chicago, Grad. School of
Bus., Chicago 60637

Indiana

Indiana Univ. Grad. School of Bus.,
Bloomington 47401

Massachusetts

Harvard Univ., M.B.A. Program,
Harvard Bus. School, Soldiers
Field, Boston 02163

Massachusetts Institute of Technology,
Alfred P. Sloan School of
Management, Grad. Committee,
50 Memorial Dr., Cambridge
02139

Michigan

Michigan State Univ., Grad. School of
Bus. Admin., Eppley Center, East
Lansing 48823

Univ. of Michigan, Grad. School of
Bus. Admin., Ann Arbor 48104

Missouri

Washington Univ., Grad. School of
Bus. Admin., St. Louis 63130

New Hampshire

Dartmouth Coll., Amos Tuck School
of Bus. Admin., Hanover 03755

New Jersey

Rutgers—The State Univ., Grad.
School of Bus. Admin., 18
Washington Pl., Newark 07102

Seton Hall Univ., School of Bus.
Admin., South Orange 07079

New York

The Bernard M. Baruch Coll., The City
Univ. of New York, Graduate Div.
17 Lexington Ave., New York
10010

Columbia Univ., Bus. School
Admissions Office, 105 Uris Hall,
Grad. School of Bus., New York
10027

Cornell Univ., Grad. School of Bus.
and Public Admin., Malott Hall,
Ithaca 14850

New York Univ., Chmn., Admission
Committee, Grad. School of Bus.
Admin., 100 Trinity Pl., New
York 10006

Syracuse Univ., Grad. School, Coll. of Bus. Admin., Syracuse 13210

The Univ. of Rochester, Coll. of Bus. Admin., Rochester 14627

North Carolina

Univ. of North Carolina, Grad. School of Bus. Admin., Chapel Hill 27514

Ohio

Case Western Reserve Univ., School of Grad. Studies, Cleveland 44106

Ohio State Univ., Dir. of Grad. Programs, Coll. of Administrative Science, Columbus 43210

Pennsylvania

Carnegie-Mellon Univ., GSIA Dir. of Admissions, Pittsburgh 15213

Duquesne Univ., Grad. School of Bus. Admin., Pittsburgh 15219

Pennsylvania State Univ., Grad. Studies in Bus. Admin., 102 Boucke Bldg., University Park 16802

Temple Univ., School of Bus. Admin., Grad. Div., Philadelphia 19122

Univ. of Pittsburgh, Grad. School of Bus., Pittsburgh 15213

The Wharton School (Univ. of Pennsylvania), Wharton Grad. Admissions, W-103 Dietrich Hall, Philadelphia 19104

South Carolina

Univ. of South Carolina, Dir. of Grad. Studies, Coll. of Bus. Admin., Columbia 29208

Virginia

Univ. of Virginia, Grad. School of Bus. Admin., 3607 University Sta., Charlottesville 22903

Washington

Univ. of Washington, Grad. School of Bus. Admin., Seattle 98105

Washington State Univ., Dean of the Grad. School, Coll. of Economics and Bus., Pullman 99163

40. Educational Materials for Qualifying Examinations in the Securities Industry

ARCO Publishing Co.
219 Park Ave. South, New York, N.Y. 10003
Securities Representative Examinations. $5.00

Assn. of Stock Exchange Firms
120 Broadway, New York, N.Y. 10005
Manual for Registered Representatives. $1.00; *Gifts of Securities or Money to Minors.* $.25

Commerce Clearing House
420 Lexington Ave., New York, N.Y. 10017
New York Stock Exchange Guide, Volume 3, Federal Securities Law and Regulations. Publication may be purchased. Apply.

Dept. of Member Firms
New York Stock Exchange
4 New York Plaza, New York, N.Y. 10004
Study Outlines for Registration Examinations; Member, Allied Member and Coordinate Examinations; Supervisory Analysts Examination; and Branch Office Manager Examination. No charge. Apply.

National Assn. of Securities Dealers
888 17th St. N.W., Washington, D.C. 20006
What You Must Know $.55; *NASD Training Guide* $.40; *NASD Manual,* $1.00; *The NASD and the Registered Representative,* $.25; *Over-the Counter Trading Handbook,* $.25;

Study Outline for Qualification Examination, $.15; *National Commodity Futures Examination for Registered Representatives,* free.

New York Institute of Finance
2 New York Plaza, New York, N.Y. 10004
Background and Operations of the Securities Industry. A programmed learning text. $7.95; *Mutual Funds. A Training Guide.* $3.00; *New York Stock Exchange Training Kit.* $8.95; *Securities Transfer-Principles and Procedures.* $4.95; *Review Tests for Investment Industry Employees* (revised edition), Series I $3.00; Series II $3.00

John Nuveen & Co.
61 Broadway, New York, N.Y. 10006
Investment Company Manual. $40.00

Prentice-Hall, Inc.
Englewood Cliffs, N.J. 07632
Loll, Leo M. Jr. *The Over-the-counter Securities Market.* 2nd ed.; Sauvin, Harry. *Investment Management.* 3rd ed.; Loll, Leo M. Jr. *Questions and Answers on Securities Markets.*

Presidents Publishing House
575 Madison Ave., New York, N.Y. 10022
Tomlinson, Lucille, Ed. *How to Start, Operate and Manage Mutual Funds.*

Pride Publishing Co.
160 Broadway, New York, N.Y. 10038
How to Pass the Registered Representative Examination. $8.95.

41. Film and Filmstrip Sources

PRODUCERS/DISTRIBUTORS

The following associations and organizations have films and/or filmstrips on banking and finance topics for either loan, rental, and/or purchase.

American Bankers Assn.
1120 Connecticut Ave. N.W., Washington, D.C. 20036

American Express Co.
65 Broadway, New York, N.Y. 10004

American Management Assn.
Film Dept., 135 West 50th St., New York, N.Y. 10020

Associated Credit Bureaus, Inc.
6767 Southwest Freeway, Houston, Tex. 77035

Bailey Films
6509 Delongpre Ave., Hollywood, Calif. 90028

Bank Admin. Institute
303 South Northwest Highway, P.O. Box 500, Park Ridge, Ill. 60068

Bank Public Relations & Marketing Assn.
231 South LaSalle St., Chicago, Ill. 60604

Business Education Films
5113 16th St., Brooklyn, N.Y. 11204

Carousel Films, Inc.
1501 Broadway, New York, N.Y. 10036

City Coll. of New York
Audio-Visual Extension Service,
New York, N.Y. 10010

Eye Gate House, Inc.
146-01 Archer Ave., Jamaica, N.Y.
11435

Federal Reserve Bank of Atlanta
Atlanta, Ga. 30303

Federal Reserve Bank of Boston
Boston, Mass. 12106

Federal Reserve Bank of Chicago
Chicago, Ill. 60690

Federal Reserve Board
Washington, D.C. 20551

Indiana Univ.
Audio Visual Center, Bloomington,
Ind. 47401

Insurance Information Institute
110 William St., New York, N.Y.
10038

Joint Council on Economic Education
1212 Ave. of the Americas, New
York, N.Y. 10036

Journal Films, Inc.
909 West Diversey Parkway,
Chicago, Ill. 60614

McGraw-Hill Text Films
330 West 42nd St., New York, N.Y.
10036

National Assn. of Manufacturers
277 Park Ave., New York, N.Y.
10017

National Consumer Finance Assn.
1000 16th St. N.W., Washington,
D.C. 20036

New York Stock Exchange
11 Wall St., New York, N.Y.
10005

The New York Times
229 West 43rd St., New York,
N.Y. 10036

Sterling Educational Films
P.O. Box 8497, Universal City,
Calif. 91608

U.S. National Audio-Visual Center
National Archives & Records Service,
Washington, D.C. 20409

Universal Education & Visual Arts
221 Park Ave. South, New York,
N.Y. 10003

Visual Education Consultants
2066 Helena St., Madison, Wisc.
53701

Westminster Films, Ltd.
Toronto, Canada

FILM LIBRARIES

Alabama

Univ. of Alabama, Audio Visual
Services, P.O. Box 1991, University
35486

Arizona

Univ. of Arizona, Bureau of AV Services,
Tucson 85721

California

Los Angeles Public Library, Audio-Visual
Dir., 630 West 5th St., Los Angeles
90017

Univ. of California, Media Center,
Berkeley 94720

Colorado

Univ. of Colorado, Bureau of AV
Instruction, Extension Div., Boulder
80302

Connecticut

Univ. of Connecticut, Audio-Visual
Dept., Storrs 06268

Delaware

Univ. of Delaware, Div. of University
Extension, Newark 19711

District of Columiba

The Public Library, Periodicals Div.,
499 Pennsylvania Ave. N.W., Washington 20001

Florida

Florida Atlantic Univ., Learning Resources Center, University Site, Boca Raton 33432

University of Florida, Dept. of Visual Instruction, General Extension Div., Gainesville 32601

Georgia

Univ. of Georgia, Georgia Center for Continuing Education, Communication Div., Athens 30601

Hawaii

Library of Hawaii, Film Section, King & Punchbowl Sts., Honolulu

Univ. of Hawaii, Coordinator of AV Activities, Honolulu 96813

Idaho

Idaho State Coll., Film Library, Pocatello 83201

Illinois

Chicago Public Library, Visual Materials Center, 78 East Washington St., Chicago 60602

Southern Illinois Univ., Audio-Visual Service, Carbondale 62901

Univ. of Illinois Visual Aids Service, 704 South 6th, Champaign 61820

Indiana

Indiana Univ., Audio-Visual Center, Bloomington 47401

Iowa

Iowa State Univ., Visual Instruction Service, 121 Pearson Hall, Ames 50010

State Univ. of Iowa, Bureau of AV Instruction, Iowa City 52240

Kansas

Univ. of Kansas, Bureau of Visual Instruction, Lawrence 66044

Kentucky

Univ. of Kentucky, School Film Library Service, Coll. of Education, Lexington 40506

Maine

Univ. of Maine, Audio-Visual Service, Stevens Hall South, Orono 04473

Maryland

Enoch Pratt Free Library, Films Dept., 400 Cathedral St., Baltimore 21201

Massachusetts

Boston Public Library, A-V Dept., Copley Square, Boston 02116

Boston Univ., Film Library, School of Education, Boston 02215

Univ. of Massachusetts, AV Center, Amherst 01002

Michigan

AV Education Center, Frieze Bldg., 720 East Huron, Ann Arbor 48104

Detroit Public Library, Educational Film Dept., 5201 Woodward Ave., Detroit 48202

Minnesota

Univ. of Minnesota, AV Extension Service, 2037 University Ave. S.E., Minneapolis 55414

Mississippi

Univ. of Mississippi, AV Service, P.O. Box 51, University 38677

Missouri

Kansas City Public Library, 311 East 12th St., Kansas City 64152

St. Louis Public Library, Film Library Service, Olive, 13th & 14th Sts., St. Louis 63103

Nebraska

Univ. of Nebraska, Bureau of AV Instruction, Lincoln 68508

Nevada

Univ. of Nevada, AV Communications, Reno 90407

New Hampshire

Univ. of New Hampshire, AV Education, Durham 03824

New Jersey

State Museum, Extension Service, Dept. of Education of New Jersey, Trenton 08608

New York

The New York Public Library, Film Library, Donnell Library Center, 20 West 53rd St., New York 10019

New York Univ., Film Library, 26 Washington Pl., New York 10003

Rochester Public Library, Reynolds AV Dept., 115 South Ave., Rochester 14604

Syracuse Univ., Educational Film Library, Bldg. D-7, Syracuse 13210

North Carolina

Univ. of North Carolina, Bureau of AV Education, Abernethy, Box 1050, Chapel Hill 27514

North Dakota

Univ. of North Dakota, AV Center Center, Grand Forks 58201

Ohio

Cleveland Public Library, Film Bureau, 325 Superior Ave., Cleveland

Toledo Public Library, Film Service, 325 Michigan St., Toledo 43624

Oklahoma

Univ. of Oklahoma, Educational Materials Service, Norman 73069

Oregon

Oregon State System of Higher Education, Office of AV Services, Corvallis 97330

Pennsylvania

Pennsylvania State Univ., AV Aids Library, University Park 16802

Puerto Rico

Univ. of Puerto Rico, AV Education Center, School of Education, Rio Piedras 00928

South Carolina

Univ. of South Carolina, Extension Div., Columbia 29208

South Dakota

South Dakota State Coll., Film Library, Brookings 57006

Tennessee

The Univ. of Tennessee, Film Services, Knoxville 37916

Texas

The Univ. of Texas, Visual Instruction Bureau, Div. of Extension, Main University, Austin 78712

Utah

Brigham Young Univ., Dept. of AV Communications, Provo 84601

Utah State Univ., AV Aids, Logan 84321

Vermont

Univ. of Vermont, AV Services Div., Burlington 05401

Washington

Seattle Public Library, Order Dept. Serials Div., 4th & Madison, Seattle,

Univ. of Washington, AV Services, Lewis Hall, Seattle 98105

West Virginia

West Virginia Univ., AV Library, Dept. of Radio, TV & Motion Pictures, Morgantown 26505

Wisconsin

Univ. of Wisconsin, Bureau of Visual Instruction, 1312 West Johnson St., Madison 53715

Wyoming

Univ. of Wyoming, AV Services, Adult Education & Community Services, Laramie 82070

42. Correspondence Courses

COMMERCIALLY SPONSORED

American Institute of Management
125 East 38th St., New York, N.Y.
10016

Assn. of Commodity Exchanges, Inc.
82 Beaver St., New York, N.Y.
10005
Commodity Futures Correspondence Course—14 lessons.

Commodity Futures Statistics Service
P.O. Box 799, Wall St. Sta., New York, N.Y. 10005
Commodity Lessons—10 lessons.

Dun & Bradstreet, Bus. Education Div.
P.O. Box 860, Radio City Sta., New York, N.Y. 10019
Fundamentals of the Credit Function; Credit and Financial Analysis; Advanced Credit and Financial Analysis.

Forbes, Inc.
60 Fifth Ave., New York, N.Y.
10003
Forbes Stock Market Course.

Hershey Video Systems, Inc.
John Hancock Center, 875 North Michigan Ave., Chicago, Ill. 60611
General Securities Training—Videotape course. New York Stock Exchange Registered Representative.

New York Institute of Finance
37 Wall St., New York, N.Y. 10005
Work of the Stock Exchange; Brokerage Office Procedures; Registered Representative Course.

Training & Audio-Visual Communications
2975 Far Hills Ave., Dayton, Ohio 45419
Fundamentals of Banking and Finance—24-Cassette tape course.

Weisenberger Financial Services
5 Hanover Square, New York, N.Y.
10004
Self-Tutor for NASD Mutual Fund Salesman Examination.

HOME STUDY SCHOOLS

The following schools offering finance courses are approved and accredited by the National Home Study Council, Washington, D.C. A complete listing of all accredited private home study schools can be obtained free of charge from the National Home Study Council, 1601 Eighteenth St. N.W., Washington, D.C. 20009

American School
Drexel Ave. at 58th St., Chicago, Ill. 60637

American Technical Society
850 East 58th St., Chicago, Ill. 60637

Britannica Schools, Inc.
425 North Michigan Ave., Chicago, Ill. 60611

International Accountants Society
209 West Jackson Blvd., Chicago, Ill. 60606

International Correspondence Schools
Scranton, Pa. 18515

LaSalle Extension Univ.
417 South Dearborn St., Chicago, Ill. 60605

North American School of Accounting
4401 Birch St., Newport Beach, Calif. 92660

UNIVERSITY SPONSORED

The following colleges and universities offer finance courses through independent study. These colleges and universities are members of the Division of Correspondence Study of the National University Extension Association.

Univ. of Alabama
Director of Correspondence Study, P.O. Box 2987, University, Ala. 35486
Corporation; Investments & Securities; Public Finance.

Univ. of California
Head, Correspondence Instruction, Berkeley, Calif. 94720
Analysis of Financial Statistics; Corporation; Financial Management; Public Finance.

Univ. of Colorado
Director, Correspondence Study, 1165 Broadway, Boulder, Colo. 80302
Business; Financial Institutions; Financial Management.

Univ. of Georgia
Supervisor, Independent Study, Center for Continuing Education, Athens, Ga. 30601
Business.

Indiana Univ.
Director, Correspondence Study, Owen Hall, Bloomington, Ind. 47401
Analysis of Financial Statistics; Public Finance.

Indiana State Univ.
Asst. Director, Correspondence Study, Div. of Extended Services, Terre Haute, Ind. 47809
Financial Management.

Univ. of Kansas
Director, Independent Study, Lawrence, Kans. 66044
Business.

Univ. of Kentucky
Director, Correspondence Study, Lexington, Ky. 40506
Financial Management; Investments & Securities.

Louisiana State Univ.
Head, Correspondence Study, 169 Pleasant Hall, Baton Rouge, La. 70803
Bank Administration; Corporation; Investments & Securities; Personal.

Univ. of Minnesota
Acting Director, Independent Study, Nicholson Hall, Minneapolis, Minn. 55455
Business; Corporation; Investments & Securities.

Univ. of Southern Mississippi
Dean, Div. of Continuing Education, Southern Sta., P.O. Box 55, Hattiesburg, Miss. 39401
Corporation; Personal.

Mississippi State Univ.
Director, Correspondence Study, P.O. Box 1534, State College, Miss. 39762
Business.

Univ. of Missouri
Coordinator, Correspondence Study Dept., Columbia, Mo. 65201
Investments and Securities.

Ohio Univ.
Director, Independent Study through Correspondence, Athens, Ohio 45701
Public Finance.

Univ. of Oklahoma
Director, Correspondence Study, 1700 Asp Ave., Norman, Okla. 73069
Business; Financial Management; Personal.

Oklahoma State Univ.
Asst. in Charge, Correspondence Study, Stillwater, Okla. 74074
Financial Management.

Pennsylvania State Univ.
Head, Correspondence Study, 3 Shields Bldg., University Park, Pa. 16802
Corporation.

The Univ. of Tennessee
  Director, University Correspondence,
  Knoxville, Tenn. 37916
  Analysis of Financial Statistics.

The Univ. of Texas
  Asst. Director for Correspondence
  Study, Austin, Tex. 78712
  Business; Corporation.

Southern Methodist Univ.
  Director, Correspondence Div.,
  Dallas, Tex. 75222
  Business.

Texas Technological Coll.
  Director, Div. of Extension,
  Lubbock, Tex. 79409
  Analysis of Financial Statistics;
  Corporation; Personal.

Univ. of Utah
  Director, Home Study, P.O. Box
  200, Salt Lake City, Utah 84110
  Financial Management; Personal.

Utah State Univ.
  Assoc. Director, Extension Div.,
  Logan, Utah 84321
  Business; Personal.

Brigham Young Univ.
  Chairman, Home Study, Provo, Utah
  84601
  Financial Management; Personal.

Univ. of Washington
  Director, Correspondence Study,
  Seattle, Wash. 98105
  Business; Investments & Securities.

Univ. of Wyoming
  Coordinator, Correspondence Study,
  P.O. Box 3294, University Sta.,
  Laramie, Wyo. 82070
  Business; Investments & Securities.

43. Short Courses on Financial Topics

Alpha Executive Planning Corp.
  575 Lexington Ave., New York,
  N.Y. 10022
  212-688-5620

American Management Assn.
  135 West 50th St., New York, N.Y.
  10020
  212-586-8100

Credit Research Foundation
  3500 Marcus Ave., Lake Success,
  N.Y. 11040
  212-725-1700

Grad. School of Credit & Financial
  Management
  475 Park Ave. South, New York,
  N.Y. 10016
  212-725-1700

Jack Karger
  160 Broadway, New York, N.Y.
  10038
  212-267-8844

McGrath Securities Training, Inc.
  77 Seventh Ave., New York, N.Y.
  10011
  212-691-1370

Robert Morris Associates
  Philadelphia National Bank Bldg.,
  Philadelphia, Pa. 19107
  215-LO3-0267

New Jersey Bankers Assn.
  499 N. Harrison St., Princeton,
  N.J. 08540
  609-924-5550

New York Institute of Finance
  2 New York Plaza, New York,
  N.Y. 10004
  212-422-9835

New York Stock Exchange, Dept. of
  Member Firms (Liaison)
  11 Wall St., New York, N.Y. 10005
  212-623-5000

Securities Training Corp.
17 Battery Pl., New York, N.Y.
10004
212-944-0310

Select Information Exchange, Seminar
Dept.
2095 Broadway, New York, N.Y.
10023
212-874-6408

Wall Street Training International
55 Liberty St., New York, N.Y.
10005
212-432-4770

Weis, Voisin & Co., Inc.
17 Battery Pl. North, New York,
N.Y. 10004
212-747-8000

World Trade Institute
1 World Trade Center, Room 1369,
New York, N.Y. 10048
212-285-4452

44. Special Financial Libraries

ATLANTA, GA.

Research Library, Federal Reserve
Bank of Atlanta
Atlanta, Ga. 30303
404-522-4061
Books, periodicals, government
documents, publications of the
Federal Reserve Board and Federal
Reserve Banks.
Hours: 8:30 A.M.–5:00 P.M. Monday–
Friday
Restrictions: Must obtain security
pass from guard force before
admittance to the building.
Copying Machines Available: No

BABSON PARK, MASS.

Babson Coll. Library
Babson Park, Mass. 02157
617-235-1200
Books, periodicals, and company
reports.
Hours: 8:00 A.M.–11:00 P.M. Monday–Friday
9:30 A.M.–5:00 P.M. Saturday
2:00 P.M.–11:00 P.M. Sunday
Restrictions: Local Wellesley community or area company patrons
are welcome.
Copying Machines Available: Yes

BOSTON, MASS.

The First National Bank of Boston
Library
100 Federal St., Boston, Mass.
02110
617-434-8440
12,000 volumes: 118 subject and
country (foreign) file drawers;
900–1000 newspapers, magazines,
newsletters, and government publications.
Hours: 8:45 A.M.–5:00 P.M. Monday–
Friday
Restrictions: Bank employees, customers, graduate students.
Copying Machines Available: No

National Shawmut Bank of Boston
40 Water St., Boston, Mass. 02106
617-742-4900
Books and periodicals on banking,
finance, economics.
Hours: 9:00 A.M.–5:00 P.M. Monday–
Friday
Restrictions: For staff members
only.
Copying Machines Available: Yes

Scudder, Stevens & Clark
10 Post Office Square, Boston,
Mass. 02109

617-482-3990
Finance
Hours: 9:00 A.M.–5:00 P.M. Monday–
Friday
Restrictions: For use in the Research
Dept. only.
Copying Machines Available: Yes

BROOKLYN, N.Y.

Brooklyn Public Library, Bus. Library
280 Cadman Plaza West, Brooklyn,
N.Y. 11201
212-522-4200
About 56,000 reference books;
about 29,000 circulating books;
about 1500 periodicals; about
2500 directories; about 1000 telephone books; rich in corporation
histories, investment information,
loose-leaf services, annual reports,
geographic information.
Hours: 10:00 A.M.–9:00 P.M.–3 days
10:00 A.M.–6:00 P.M.–2 days
10:00 A.M.–5:00 P.M.–1 day
Restrictions: No
Copying Machines Available: Yes

CHARLOTTESVILLE, VA.

Bureau of Population & Economic
Research
1910 Thomson Rd., Lambeth House
(Univ. of Virginia), Charlottesville,
Va. 22903
703-924-3368
Books and periodicals dealing primarily with the economy and
population of Virginia. Extensive
holdings of publications of other
university research organizations.
Hours: 8:00 A.M.–5:00 P.M. Monday–
Friday
Restrictions: Restricted in general
to university community and local
residents, although exceptions are
made.
Copying Machines Available: Yes

CHICAGO, ILL.

Continental Illinois National Bank &
Trust Co. of Chicago Library

231 South LaSalle St., Chicago, Ill.
60693
312-828-4186
Periodicals, books, theses, government hearings, microfiche, research
reports.
Hours: 8:00 A.M.–5:00 P.M. Monday–
Friday
Restrictions: Only bank customers,
librarians allowed (other than bank
employees).
Copying Machines Available: No

Household Finance Corp.
Prudential Plaza, Chicago, Ill. 60601
312-944-7174
Books, periodicals, clippings in con-
sumer finance and related fields.
Hours: 9:00 A.M.–5:00 P.M. Monday–
Friday
Copying Machines Available: Yes

Joseph Schaffner Library, Northwestern Univ.
339 East Chicago Ave., Chicago,
Ill. 60611
312-649-8423
Books, periodicals and other serial
publications, financial services,
corporate annual reports.
Hours: 9:00 A.M.–10:00 P.M. Monday–Friday
9:00 A.M.–5:00 P.M. Saturday
Restrictions: Materials may be used
in the library only. Borrowing
privileges are accorded upon the
payment of a deposit.
Copying Machines Available: Yes

Stein Roe & Farnham
150 South Wacker Dr., Chicago, Ill.
60606
312-368-7840
Books, periodicals, newspapers,
microfilm, microfiche, vertical
files.
Hours: 8:45 A.M.–5:00 P.M. Monday–
Friday
Restrictions: This is a special library
which serves only special cases on
request.
Copying Machines available: Yes

CLEVELAND, OHIO

Business Information Dept., Cleveland
Public Library
Cleveland, Ohio 44114
216-241-1020
150,000 bound volumes in business
and economics; 3600 current periodical and serial titles; some 400
loose-leaf services; pamphlets and
clippings under some 12,000 subject headings; comprehensive collection of trade directories (some
3500 titles); corporate manuals;
comprehensive files of annual reports on over 6000 companies.
Strong in investment, financial,
and management literature. Worldwide coverage to serve business
clientele and graduate students.
Hours: 9:00 A.M.–8:30 P.M. Monday–
Thursday
9:00 A.M.–6:00 P.M. Friday–Saturday
Restrictions: None on reference and
research use.
Copying Machines Available: Yes

DETROIT, MICH.

Detroit Public Library, Business &
Finance Dept.
5201 Woodward Ave., Detroit, Mich.
48202
313-321-1000
Books, periodicals, pamphlets, annual reports, and services.
Hours: 9:30 A.M.–5:30 P.M. Tuesday,
Thursday, Friday, & Saturday
9:30 A.M.–9:00 P.M. Monday &
Wednesday
1:00 P.M.–6:00 P.M. Sunday (Usually October–May)
Restrictions: No
Copying Machines Available: Yes

INDIANAPOLIS, IND.

Indiana State Library
140 North Senate Ave., Indianapolis,
Ind. 46204
317-633-5441

Regional depository for federal documents; Indiana state documents
collection. Moody's services,
Standard & Poor directories; 71
periodicals listed in business periodical index.
Hours: 8:15 A.M.–5:00 P.M. Monday–
Friday
8:15 A.M.–12:00 P.M. Saturdays
(September–May)
Restrictions: No restrictions on use
in library. Borrowing privileges
by individuals restricted to state
personnel.
Copying Machines available: Yes

KANSAS CITY, MO.

Federal Reserve Bank of Kansas City
Federal Reserve Sta., 925 Grand
Ave., Kansas City, Mo. 64198
816-881-2676
Books, periodicals, newspapers, an-
nuals.
Hours: 8:00 A.M.–5:00 P.M. Monday–
Friday
Restrictions: Open to the public,
but check out materials through
interlibrary only.
Copying Machines Available: No

LOS ANGELES, CALIF.

Security Pacific Bank Library
411 South Main St., Room 230,
P.O. Box 2097, Terminal Annex,
Los Angeles, Calif. 90054
213-620-8623
800 monographs economic, business,
finance, marketing; 250 reference
books; 350 periodicals; 5000 vertical file folders; census materials,
population, agriculture, business,
manufacturing
Hours: 8:00 A.M.–4:30 P.M. Monday–
Friday
Restrictions: Materials can only be
checked out by bank employees
or through interlibrary loan; otherwise public may use materials
in library.
Copying Machines Available: Yes

Grad. School of Management Library
UCLA Campus, Los Angeles, Calif.
90024
213-825-4021
The Management Library was authorized in 1958 and first opened for service in 1961. 89,000 monographs and 5000 subscriptions to current journals. Finance and Investments.
Hours: 8:00 A.M.–10:00 P.M. Monday–Thursday
8:00 A.M.–5:00 P.M. Friday
9:00 A.M.–5:00 P.M. Saturday
2:00 P.M.–8:00 P.M. Sunday
Restrictions: Must hold UCLA Library User's card, available to students, faculty, academic personnel; to all others at $25.00 per year, $6.00 per quarter.
Copying Machines Available: Yes ($.05 per print)

MILWAUKEE, WISC.

First Wisconsin National Bank Library
743 North Water St., Milwaukee, Wisc. 53202
414-276-6100
All banking materials, current periodicals, popular magazines, some fictional fun reading, law book sets, and historical material about Milwaukee and Wisconsin. Also offer clipping service of all the area newspapers.
Hours: 8:00 A.M.–4:45 P.M. Monday–Friday
Restrictions: This library is primarily for the use of employees of the bank and for tenants of this building, but also welcomes customers to use facilities.
Copying Machines Available: No

NEW YORK, N.Y.

American Management Assn. Library
135 West 50th St., New York, N.Y. 10020
212-JU6-8100

8500 books, over 250 periodicals received and 175 file drawers of information on the functioning of management from the practitioner's viewpoint.
Hours: 9:00 A.M.–5:00 P.M. Monday–Friday (except holidays)
Restrictions: Members of the association only.
Copying Machines Available: No

Arnold Bernhard & Co. Research Library
5 East 44th St., New York, N.Y. 10017
212-687-3965
600 books, 1000 periodicals, 150 vertical file drawers
Hours: 9:00 A.M.–5:00 P.M. Monday–Friday
Restrictions: Special libraries member, clients of Value Line Investment survey.
Copying Machines Available: Yes

Business International Research Library
757 Third Ave., New York, N.Y. 10017
212-PL9-7700
International economic, financial, and political data.
Hours: 9:00 A.M.–5:00 P.M. Monday–Friday
Restrictions: Clients and graduate students by appointment.
Copying Machines Available: Yes

Documents & Publications Library, Chase Manhattan Bank, N.A.
1 Chase Manhattan Plaza, New York, N.Y. 10015
212-552-4113
Business & finance, 35,000 books, 3000 serial titles.
Hours: 9:00 A.M.–5:00 P.M. Monday–Friday
Restrictions: Customers, staff, and other librarians.
Copying Machines Available: Yes

The Conference Board
845 Third Ave., New York, N.Y.
10022
212-PL9-0900
1500 periodicals (trade, business,
government), 50,000 books (loose-
leaf services, corporate finance,
management, marketing,
economics).
Hours: 5:00 A.M.–9:00 P.M. Monday–Friday
Restrictions: Students not allowed
in; only members of associate
companies.
Copying Machines Available: Yes

Dun & Bradstreet Bus. Library
99 Church St., New York, N.Y.
10007
212-349-3300, exts. 621, 2, 3
Books (12,500), periodicals (250),
indexes (10), vertical file (100
drawers), operating ratios, business
histories.
Hours: 9:00 A.M.–4:45 P.M. Monday–Friday
Restrictions: No loans made to public, just reference service.
Copying Machines Available: Yes
($.25 per page)

Faulkner, Dawkins & Sullivan
1 New York Plaza, New York, N.Y.
10004
212-623-8796
Books, periodicals, financial services,
economic services, newspapers,
periodical indexes, directories,
corporate files consisting of annual
reports, prospectuses, interim
reports, proxy statements, and
other financial data.
Hours: 9:00 A.M.–5:00 P.M. Monday–Friday
Restrictions: Library is open to staff,
clients, and to other libraries.
Copying Machines Available: Yes

Irving Trust Co.
1 Wall St., New York, N.Y. 10015
212-487-6432

Books, periodicals, corporation files,
subject files, microfilm.
Hours: 9:00 A.M.–5:00 P.M. Monday–Friday
Restrictions: Library is open to
Special Library Assn. members,
other librarians, company employees, tenants in building.
Copying Machines Available: Yes

Research Library, Kidder, Peabody &
Co., Inc.
10 Hanover Square, New York, N.Y.
10005
212-747-2504, 2505, 2506
250 periodicals, 1500 books, 6000
Corporation Files, Leasco Dis-
closure Service, investment
banking information files.
Hours: 9:00 A.M.–5:00 P.M. Monday–Friday
Restrictions: SLA members, clients
by appointment, interlibrary loan.
Copying Machines Available: Yes

P. T. Library, Manufacturers Hanover
Trust Co.
350 Park Ave., New York, N.Y.
10022
212-350-4733
10,000 volumes (including bound
periodicals), 170 periodical titles,
255 vertical file drawers.
Hours: 9:00 A.M.–5:00 P.M. Monday–Friday
Restrictions: Membership in the
Special Libraries Assn.
Copying Machines Available: Yes

Moody's Investors Service, Inc.–
Library Dept.
99 Church St., New York, N.Y.
10007
212-267-8800
Complete set of Moody's Manuals
1909–Present (Including: Municipal and government, bank and
finance, industrial, public utility,
transportation); vertical files on
over 20,000 publically held
corporations.

Hours: 9:00 A.M.–5:00 P.M. Monday–Friday
Restrictions: Subscribers to Moody's Investors Service publications.
Copying Machines Available: Yes

National Assn. of Mutual Savings Banks
200 Park Ave., New York, N.Y. 10017
212-973-4704
Reference materials for Savings Bankers
Hours: 9:00 A.M.–4:30 P.M. Monday–Friday
Restrictions: Restricted to Association members.
Copying Machines Available: Yes

New York Stock Exchange–SEC Library
20 Broad St., Room 403, New York, N.Y. 10005
212-623-5060
Corporation Records and Listed N.Y.S.E. Companies only including SEC reports (10K, 10Q, 8K Proxy, Prospectus, NIQ, NIR, etc.) as well as stockholders annual and quarterly reports.
Hours: 9:00 A.M.–4:45 P.M. Monday–Friday
Restrictions: No
Copying Machines Available: Yes

Standard & Poor's Corp.
345 Hudson St., New York, N.Y. 10014
212-924-6400, ext. 478
2500 books, 650 periodical titles, 1600 vertical file drawers, Subjects: corporation records (annual reports, prospectuses, proxies), investments.
Hours: 9:00 A.M.–5:00 P.M. Monday–Friday
Restrictions: Clients only.
Copying Machines Available: No

Statistical Library
140 Broadway, New York, N.Y. 10005

212-676-5072
Research material for all stocks listed, public companies, periodicals, Moody's, Standard & Poor's, etc.
Hours: 9:00 A.M.–5:00 P.M. Monday–Friday
Restrictions: Limited to customers of firm and employees.
Copying Machines Available: Not for public use.

Investment Library–United States Trust Co.
45 Wall St., New York, N.Y. 10005
212-425-4500
2500 books, 400 periodicals.
Hours: 9:00 A.M.–4:45 P.M. Monday–Friday
Restrictions: No
Copying Machines Available: Yes

PHILADELPHIA, PA.

Federal Reserve Bank of Philadelphia
925 Chestnut St., Philadelphia, Pa. 19101
215-WA2-5900
Books & Periodicals–10,000 bound volumes.
Hours: 9:00 A.M.–4:30 P.M. Monday–Friday
Restrictions: No, but bring identification.
Copying Machines Available: No

Business, Science, and Industry Dept., Free Library of Philadelphia
Logan Square, Philadelphia, Pa. 19103
212-MU6-5394-5
Business, financial, and tax services; corporation reports (current and backfiles); financial, economic, and business journals (current and backfiles); up-to-date collection of books on finance, economics, business, and allied subjects.
Hours: 9:00 A.M.–9:00 P.M. Monday–Wednesday

9:00 A.M.-6:00 P.M. Thursday–
Friday
9:00 A.M.-5:00 P.M. Saturday
Restrictions: No
Copying Machines Available: Yes

Mercantile Library (Free Library of
Philadelphia)
1021 Chestnut St., Philadelphia, Pa.
19107
215-MA7-1231 or MU6-5449
Strongest subjects are investments,
accounting, finance, and real
estate. Subscribe to about 500
business trade journals and many
investment services. Total collection about 43,000 volumes, including 10,000 business books.
Hours: 9:00 A.M.-6:00 P.M. Monday,
Tuesday, Thursday, Friday
9:00 A.M.-5:00 P.M. Saturday
9:00 A.M.-9:00 P.M. Wednesday
Summer Hours 9:00 A.M.-
6:00 P.M. Monday–Friday
Restrictions: No
Copying Machines Available: Yes

Pennsylvania Economy League, Inc.,
Eastern Div. Library
Liberty Trust Bldg., Broad & Arch
Sts., Philadelphia, Pa. 19107
215-LO4-6250
20,000 books including bound periodicals, 82 vertical file drawers.
Hours: 9:00 A.M.-5:00 P.M. Monday–Friday
Restrictions: Available to the public
for reference use only. No
borrowing.
Copying Machines Available: Yes

PRINCETON, N.J.

Pliny Fisk Library of Economics &
Finance
Princeton Univ. Library, Princeton,
N.J. 08540
609-452-3211
Reference books, periodicals, government documents, reports, and
pamphlets on economics and finance.

Hours: 9:00 A.M.-5:00 P.M. Monday–
Friday
9:00 A.M.-12:00 P.M. Saturday
7:15 P.M.-10:15 P.M. Sunday
Restrictions: Open to the public for
reference use only. High school
students and undergraduates from
other institutions must have special permission for access.

RICHMOND, VA.

Research Library, Federal Reserve
Bank of Richmond
8th & Franklin Sts., Richmond, Va.
23261
703-648-7271, ext. 415, 309
Books, periodicals. Collection con-
centrates on economic and mon-
etary policy and states in the
Fifth Federal Reserve District
(Md., D.C., Va., W. Va., N.C. &
S.C.)
Hours: 9:00 A.M.-4:30 P.M. Monday–
Friday
Restrictions: Open to the public
by appointment.
Copying Machines Available: Yes

SAN FRANCISCO, CALIF.

Crocker National Bank
1 Montgomery St., San Francisco,
Calif. 94138
415-983-2695
Books, periodicals; Subjects: bank-
ing, economics.
Hours: 8:30 A.M.-5:00 P.M. Monday–
Friday
Restrictions: Interlibrary loan.
Copying Machines Available: No

Research Library, Federal Reserve
Bank of San Francisco
400 Sansome St., San Francisco,
Calif. 94120
415-397-1137, ext. 403
Economics, banking, finance with
particular emphasis on western
United States.
Hours: 8:15 A.M.-5:00 P.M. Monday–
Friday

Restrictions: Reference use only, except for interlibrary loan.
Copying Machines Available: No

Wells Fargo Bank Library
475 Sansome St., San Francisco, Calif. 94144
415-396-3745
Collection mainly includes material on banking and finance.
Hours: 8:15 A.M.–5:00 P.M. Monday–Friday
Restrictions: The library is for the use of bank employees and customers by referral.
Copying Machines Available: Yes

STANFORD, CALIF.

J. Hugh Jackson Library, Grad. School of Bus., Stanford Univ., Stanford, Calif. 94305
415-321-2300, ext. 2161
Reference books, monographs (156,104); corporate reports of companies listed on New York, American, and Over-the-Counter Stock Exchanges (450,000); pamphlets, etc. (1,432); microfilm serials (including periodicals) (4833).
Hours: 7:50 A.M.–11:00 P.M. Monday, Tuesday, Wednesday, Thursday
7:50 A.M.–10:00 P.M. Friday
8:00 A.M.–5:00 P.M. Saturday
1:00 P.M.–10:00 P.M. Sunday
Restrictions: Fee membership ($10 a day, $40 for 3 months, $100 a year).
Copying Machines Available: Yes

WASHINGTON, D.C.

Research Library, Board of Governors of the Federal Reserve System
20th St. & Constitution Ave. N.W., Washington, D.C. 20551
202-737-4171
Books, periodicals, statistical releases, and reports in the fields of banking and finance; monetary, credit and fiscal policy; economic conditions both foreign and domestic, and the Federal Reserve System.
Hours: 8:45 A.M.–5:15 P.M. Monday–Friday
Restrictions: The only restriction is that will not lend to the public.
Copying Machines Available: No

Export-Import Bank of the U.S.
811 Vermont Ave. N.W., Washington, D.C. 20571
202-382-2449
Books on economics and business, U.S. and foreign periodicals, selected U.S. government documents, material from and concerning all countries of the world. Emphasis on current material.
Hours: 8:45 A.M.–5:15 P.M. Monday–Friday
Restrictions: Open to EIB personnel, members of other government agencies, and others with permission of the librarian.
Copying Machines Available: No

Federal Deposit Insurance Corp. Library
550 17th St. N.W., Washington, D.C. 20429
202-389-4314
Banking and finance, law, economics, congressional materials, and pamphlets related to banking.
Hours: 8:30 A.M.–5:15 P.M. Monday–Friday
Restrictions: Employees of other agencies with permission of librarian.
Copying Machines Available: Yes

Joint Bank-Fund Library, International Monetary Fund and World Bank
19th & H Sts. N.W., Washington, D.C. 20431
202-477-3167
100,000 volumes, 2900 periodical and newspaper titles received.

Hours: 9:00 A.M.–5:30 P.M. Monday–
Friday (except holidays)
Restrictions: Not open to the public
but arrangements can be made for
reference use of material not available elsewhere.
Copying Machines Available: Yes
(for staff use)

Securities & Exchange Commission
Library
500 North Capitol St. N.W., Wash-
ington, D.C. 20549
202-755-1464
Economics, engineering, finance,
government, securities law.
Hours: 9:00 A.M.–5:30 P.M. Monday–
Friday
Restrictions: For staff use only.
Library may be used upon spe-
cial request for research by mem-
bers of the public.
Copying Machines Available: No

MONTREAL, QUEBEC, CANADA

Bank of Montreal, Library
129 St. James St. West, Montreal
126, Quebec, Canada
514-877-6890
Books, periodicals, microfilm.
Hours: 9:00 A.M.–5:00 P.M. Monday–
Friday
Restrictions: No
Copying Machines Available: Yes

The Royal Bank of Canada
1 Place Ville Marie, P.O. Box 6001,
Montreal 101, Quebec, Canada
514-874-2452
Books and pamphlets (50,000);
periodicals (800 titles).
Hours: 9:00 A.M.–5:00 P.M. Monday–
Friday
Restrictions: No
Copying Machines Available: Yes

OTTAWA, ONTARIO, CANADA

Library, Dept. of Finance/Treasury
Board Secretariat

K1A OG5 (City Postal Code),
Ottawa, Ontario, Canada
613-992-3006
50,000 books, pamphlets, etc.
Subjects: Public finance, public
administration, management,
personnel management, economics. 400 periodicals, economics,
finance, social sciences.
Hours: 8:30 A.M.–5:00 P.M. Monday–
Friday
Restrictions: Public may use library,
but no library service is provided,
and no borrowing is permitted,
except through other libraries.
Copying Machines Available: No

TORONTO, ONTARIO, CANADA

Information Centre, Canadian Imperial
Bank of Commerce
25 King St. West, Toronto 1,
Ontario, Canada
416-862-3352
15,000 books, 800 periodicals,
1000 subject files, complete
Statistics Canada collection
Hours: 9:00 A.M.–5:00 P.M. Monday–
Friday
Restrictions: Reference only—re-
quest telephone call first.
Copying Machines Available: Yes

Toronto Dominion Bank, Dept. of
Economic Research
55 King St. West & Bay St., Toronto
111, Ontario, Canada
416-866-8068
Books, newspapers, pamphlets,
periodicals.
Hours: 8:45 A.M.–4:30 P.M. Monday–
Friday
Restrictions: By special arrangement
with librarian only—but open to
staff of other libraries.
Copying Machines Available: No

ASSOCIATIONS
AND ORGANIZATIONS

45. Associations in the U.S.

BANKING ASSOCIATIONS

American Bankers Assn.
815 Connecticut Ave. N.W., Washington, D. C. 20006
202-298-9090
Exec. V.P.: Willis W. Alexander
Membership: 18,000–19,000
Publications: *Banking*
Annual meetings: 1971—San Francisco

American Finance Assn.
Grad. School of Bus. Admin., New York Univ., 100 Trinity Pl., New York, N.Y. 10006
212-732-5820
Secy.-Treas.: Robert A. Kavesh
Membership: 5000–6000
Publications: *Journal of Finance*
Annual meetings: 1971—New Orleans

American Industrial Bankers Assn.
1629 K St. N.W., Washington, D. C. 20006
202-296-8766
Exec. V.P.: Max A. Denney
Membership: 450–500
Publications: *Industrial Banker*
Annual meetings: 1972—Houston, 1973—Hawaii

American Safe Deposit Assn.
Box Q, Clarence, N.Y. 14031
Exec. Mgr.: Russell F. Graham
Membership: 2400–2500 Banks
Publications: *Educational Bulletin* and *National News*

American Savings & Loan Institute
111 East Wacker Dr., Chicago, Ill. 60601
312-644-3100
Exec. V.P.: Dale C. Bottom
Membership: 30,000–35,000

Assn. of Bank Travel Bureaus
8265 Washington Blvd., Indianapolis, Ind. 46240
317-253-9338
Secy.: James J. Glover
Membership: 125–150

Assn. of Registered Bank Holding Cos.
730 15th St. N.W., Washington, D. C. 20005
202-393-1158
Exec. Dir.: Donald L. Rogers
Membership: 50–60
Publications: *Bank Holding Company Facts*
Annual meetings: 1971—Minneapolis

Assn. of Reserve City Bankers
105 West Adams St., Chicago, Ill.
60603
312-782-7545
Exec. Secy.: Corwith Hamill
Membership: 400–450
Annual meetings: 1972–Boca
Raton; 1973–Boca Raton

Bank Administration Institute
303 South Northwest Highway, Park
Ridge, Ill. 60068
312-775-5344
Exec. Dir.: Dr. F. Byers Miller
Membership: 7500–8000
Publication: *Bank Administration*
Annual meetings: 1972–Kansas
City; 1973–San Francisco; 1974–
Chicago

Bank Public Relations & Marketing
Assn.
309 West Washington St., Chicago,
Ill. 60606
312-782-7442
Exec. V.P.: R. M. Cheseldine
Membership: 3000–4000
Publication: *Journal*
Annual meetings: 1972–Boston

Bank-Share Owners Advisory League
33 North Dearborn St., Chicago, Ill.
60602
312-346-1866
Secy.: Rolf W. F. Wilhelm
Publication: *Loss Prevention
Bulletin*

Bank Stationers Assn., Inc.
230 West 41st St., New York, N.Y.
10036
212-279-2612
National Secy.: William J. Stevens

Bankers' Assn. for Foreign Trade
First National Bank, Fort Worth,
Tex. 76102
817-336-9161
Secy.: Theodore F. Lange
Membership: 175–200
Annual meetings: 1972–Colorado
Springs; 1973–Boca Raton

Charge Account Bankers Assn.
1401 South Brentwood Blvd., St.
Louis, Mo. 63144
314-962-2063
Managing Dir.: Arthur H. Hert
Membership: 450–500
Annual meetings: 1971–Freeport,
Grand Bahama

Conference of State Bank Supervisors
1101 17th St. N.W., Washington,
D. C. 20036
202-296-2840
Exec. V.P.: Dr. Harry P. Guenther
Membership: 5000–6000
Publications: *A Profile of State
Chartered Banking, Capitol Com-
ments, Supervisor and Banker
Review, The Supervisor*
Annual meetings: 1972–Boca Ra-
ton; 1973–Los Angeles

The Consumer Bankers Assn.
1725 K St. N.W., Washington, D. C.
20006
202-446-2590
Exec. V.P.: Robert A. Fischer
Membership: 225–250
Publications: *CBA News Letter,
Consumer Credit Banker*
Annual meetings: 1972–Boca Raton

Council of Mutual Savings Institutions
50 East 42nd St., New York, N.Y.
10017
212-867-2776
Pres. & Managing Dir.: George L.
Bliss
Membership: 150–175

Council of Savings & Loan Stock Cos.
Suite 710, 900 Wilshire Blvd., Los
Angeles, Calif. 90017
213-628-1279
Pres.: Tom Bane
Membership: 90–100
Publication: *Council Bulletin*

Foundation for Full Service Banks
Philadelphia National Bank Bldg.,
Philadelphia, Pa. 19107
215-561-2345
Exec. V.P.: Richard B. Beal
Membership: 6000–6500

Independent Bankers Assn. of America
P. O. Box 267, Sauk Centre, Minn.
  56378
612-352-2279
Exec. Dir.: Howard F. Bell
Membership: 6500–7000
Publication: *The Independent
  Banker*
Annual meetings: 1972—Miami
  Beach; 1973—San Francisco;
  1974—Freeport, Bahamas; 1975—
  Las Vegas

International Union of Building Soci-
  eties & Savings Assns.
Room 812, 425 13th St. N.W., Wash-
  ington, D. C. 20004
202-638-6334
Secy. General: Josephine Ewalt
Membership: 600–700
Publication: *International Congress*
Annual meetings: 1971—Berlin,
  Germany

Investment Bankers Assn. of America
425 13th St.,N.W., Washington,
  D. C. 20004
202-393-3366
Exec. Dir.: Gordon L. Calvert
Membership: 650–700
Publication: *IBA Washington
  Bulletin*

Mortgage Bankers Assn. of America
1707 H St. N.W., Washington, D. C.
  20006
202-298-9220
Exec. V.P.: Dr. Oliver H. Jones
Membership: 2000–2100
Publications: *Quarterly Economic
  Report, National Delinquency
  Survey, The Mortgage Banker*

National Assn. of Bank-Women, Inc.
111 East Wacker Dr., Chicago, Ill.
  60601
312-644-6610
Exec. Dir.: Phyllis Haeger
Membership: 7500–8000
Publication: *NABW Journal*
Annual meetings: 1972—Chicago

National Assn. of Investors Brokers
Room 125, 1625 Eye St. N.W.,
  Washington, D. C. 20006
202-347-5700
Secy.: Mrs. Martha Norton
Membership: 3500–4000

National Assn. of Mutual Savings
  Banks
200 Park Ave., New York, N.Y.
  10017
212-973-5432
Exec. V.P.: Dr. Grover W. Ensley
Membership: 500–525
Publication: *Savings Bank Journal*
Annual meetings: 1972—Atlanta;
  1973—New York City; 1974—Portland; 1975—Boston

National Bankers Assn.
4310 Georgia Ave. N.W., Washington, D. C. 20011
202-291-6310
Exec. Dir.: Dr. Edward D. Irons
Membership: 20–25 Banks

National Commercial Finance Conference, Inc.
29 Broadway, New York, N.Y.
  10006
212-944-6815
Exec. Dir.: Leonard Machlis
Membership: 125–150
Publication: *Commercial Financing*
Annual meetings: New York City

National Federation of Federal Land
  Bank Assns.
Amboy, Ill. 61310
Secy.-Treas.: Morris Kessinger
Publication: *Country News and
  Views*

National League of Insured Savings
  Assns.
Suite 700, 1200 17th St. N.W.,
  Washington, D. C. 20036
202-659-1955
Exec. Dir.: Kenneth G. Heisler
Membership: 400–450
Publication: *National League
  Journal*
Annual meetings: 1972—Los An-
  geles; 1973—Miami Beach; 1974—
  Honolulu

National Society of Controllers &
Financial Officers of Savings
Institutions
111 East Wacker Dr., Chicago, Ill.
60601
312-644-3100
Exec. V.P.: Charles Borsom
Membership: 2500–3000
Publication: *Bulletin*
Annual meetings: 1972–Dallas &
Chicago; 1973–Chicago; 1974–
Atlanta; 1975–Denver

New York State Safe Deposit Assn.
521 Fifth Ave., New York, N.Y.
10017
212-687-9071
Exec. Secy.: Raymond J. Walter
Membership: 1400–1500

Robert Morris Associates, The National Assn. of Bank Loan &
Credit Officers
1432 Philadelphia National Bank
Bldg., Philadelphia, Pa. 19107
215-563-0267
Exec. Mgr.: Clarence R. Reed
Membership: 1200 banks, 4700
individuals
Publications: *Annual Statement
Studies, The Journal of Commercial Bank Lending*
Annual meetings: 1972–Miami;
1973–Phoenix; 1974–Atlanta;
1975–San Francisco

Savings Institutions Marketing Society
of America
111 East Wacker Dr., Chicago, Ill.
60601
312-644-3100
Exec. V.P.: Harold Jenkins
Membership: 1000–1100
Publications: *Dividends, Idea File,
Newsletter*
Annual meetings: 1971–Hollywood

United Mortgage Bankers of America
840 East 87th St., Chicago, Ill.
60619
312-994-7200
Pres.: Dempsey J. Travis
Membership: 175–200
Publication: *UMBA News Bulletin*

United States Savings & Loan League
221 North LaSalle St., Chicago, Ill.
60601
312-236-2234
Exec. V.P.: Norman Strunk
Membership: 5000–5500
Publication: *Savings and Loan
News*
Annual meetings: 1972–Miami
Beach

CONSUMER ASSOCIATIONS

American Council on Consumer
Interests
238 Stanley Hall, Univ. of Missouri,
Columbia, Mo. 65201
314-449-9331, ext. 224
Exec. Secy.: Edward J. Metzen
Membership: 2200–2300
Publications: *Consumer Education
Forum, Journal of Consumer
Affairs, Newsletter*

Consumer Credit Insurance Assn.
307 North Michigan Ave., Chicago,
Ill. 60601
312-726-9896
General Counsel: Walter D. Runkle
Membership: 100–125

Consumer Federation of America
1012 14th St. N.W., Washington,
D. C. 20005
202-737-3732
Exec. Dir.: Mrs. Erma Angevine
Membership: 150–175
Annual meetings: August–Central
United States

Consumers Union of U.S., Inc.
256 Washington St., Mt. Vernon,
N.Y. 10550
914-664-6400
Exec. Dir.: Walter Sandbach
Memberships: 1,800,000–1,900,000
Publication: *Consumer Reports*

National Consumer Finance Assn.
1000 16th St. N.W., Washington,
D. C. 20036
202-638-1340
Exec. V.P.: Carl F. Hawver
Membership: 14,000–15,000

Publications: *Advertising Forum,
Consumer Finance Law Bulletin,
Consumer Finance News, Finance
Facts Newsletter, Financial Forum*
Annual meetings: 1972—San Juan;
1973—San Francisco; 1974—Montreal; 1975—Las Vegas

National Consumers League
1029 Vermont Ave. N.W., Washington, D. C. 20005
202-347-3853
General Secy.: Sarah H. Newman
Membership: 15,000—16,000
Publication: *Bulletin*

CREDIT ASSOCIATIONS

Advertising Media Credit Executives
Assn. International, Inc.
3101 Strathmoor, Toledo, Ohio
43614
Exec. Secy.-Treas.: Robert Guinsler
Membership: 175—200
Annual meetings: 1972—Phoenix;
1973—Atlanta

Allied Finance Adjusters Conference,
Inc.
Box 489, Stockton, Calif. 95201
Exec. Secy.: E. R. Engdahl
Membership: 175—200
Publications: *Bulletin, Directory*

Aluminum Building Products Credit
Assn.
2217 Tribune Tower, Chicago, Ill.
60611
312-644-0828

American Assn. of Credit Counselors
1803 Washington St., Waukegan, Ill.
60085
312-623-6650
Exec. Secy.: H. Don Morris
Membership: 80—90
Publication: *American Counselor*

American Collectors Assn., Inc.
4040 West 70th St., Minneapolis,
Minn. 55435
612-926-6547
Exec. V.P.: John W. Johnson
Membership: 2500—2600

Publication: *Collector*
Annual meetings: 1972—Las Vegas;
1973—Minneapolis; 1974—White
Sulphur Springs; 1975—Sun Valley; 1976—The Bahamas

American Commercial Collectors
Assn., Inc.
4040 West 70th St., Minneapolis,
Minn. 55435
612-926-6547
Exec. Dir.: John W. Johnson
Membership: 175—200
Publications: *Directory, Newsletter*

American Finance Assn.
Grad. School of Bus. Admin. New
York Univ., 100 Trinity Pl., New
York, N.Y. 10006
212-732-5820
Secy.-Treas.: Robert A. Kavesh
Membership: 5000—6000
Publication: *Journal of Finance*

American Industrial Bankers Assn.
1629 K St. N.W., Washington,
D. C. 20006
202-296-8766
Exec. V.P.: Max A. Denney
Membership: 450—500
Publication: *Industrial Banker*
Annual meetings: 1972—Houston;
1973—Hawaii

American Petroleum Credit Assn.
330 Plymouth Bldg., Minneapolis,
Minn. 55402
612-336-8356
Exec. Secy.: S. J. Haider
Membership: 350—400
Annual meetings: 1972—San Francisco; 1973—Tulsa

American Repossessors Assn., Inc.
4040 West 70th St., Minneapolis,
Minn. 55435
612-926-6547
Exec. Dir.: Lawrence E. Johnson
Membership: 350—400
Publications: *Directory, Recovery,
The Repossessor*
Annual meetings: 1972—Houston;
1973—Orlando, Fla.

Art Material Board of Trade, Inc.
276 Fifth Ave., New York, N.Y.
10001
212-686-2223
Exec. Secy.: Ralph Reichman
Membership: 55–60

Associated Credit Bureaus of America
6767 Southwest Freeway, Houston,
Tex. 77036
713-774-8701
Pres.: John L. Spafford
Membership: 3500–4000
Publication: ACB Management
Annual meetings: 1972—Hawaii

Building Material Dealers Credit Assn.
2351 West 3rd St., Los Angeles,
Calif. 90057
213-382-7151
Exec. V.P.: John M. Addington
Membership: 900–1000
Publication: Bulletin

Charge Account Bankers Assn.
1401 South Brentwood Blvd., St.
Louis, Mo. 63144
314-962-2063
Managing Dir.: Arthur H. Hert
Membership: 450–500

The Consumer Bankers Assn.
1725 K St. N.W., Washington, D. C.
20006
202-466-2590
Exec. V.P.: Robert A. Fischer
Membership: 225–250
Publications: CBA News Letter,
Consumer Credit Banker
Annual meetings: 1972—Boca Raton

Consumer Credit Insurance Assn.
307 North Michigan Ave., Chicago,
Ill. 60601
312-726-9896
General Counsel: Walter D. Runkle
Membership: 100–125

Credit Union National Assn., Inc.
1617 Sherman Ave., Madison, Wisc.
53701
608-244-4721
Managing Dir.: J. Orrin Shipe
Membership: 23–24,000 credit
unions

Publications: CUNA Briefs, Every-
body's Money, The Credit Union
Magazine

Credit Women-International
2051 Railway Exchange Bldg., St.
Louis, Mo. 63101
Exec. Manager: Miss Alexandra
Anagnos
Membership: 13,000–14,000
Annual meetings: 1973—Atlanta

Cues Managers Society
1617 Sherman Ave., Madison, Wisc.
53704
608-244-5675
Exec. Dir.: Robert DeThorne

Foreign Credit Insurance Assn.
250 Broadway, New York, N.Y.
10007
212-349-2160
Pres.: Francis X. Boylan
Membership: 50–55
Publication: FCIA News

Foreign Credit Interchange Bureau
475 Park Ave. South, New York,
N.Y. 10016
212-674-5100
Dir.: J. Stewart Gillies
Membership: 900–1000
Publications: FCIB Bulletin, FCIB
Minutes of Round Table Confer-
ence

Furniture Manufacturers Credit Assn.,
Inc.
P. O. Drawer 591, 107 West Green
St., High Point, N.C. 27761
919-882-8169
Exec. V.P.: Wallace Taylor
Membership: 50–60 Companies

International Consumer Credit Assn.
375 Jackson Ave., St. Louis, Mo.
63130
314-727-4045
Exec. V.P.: William H. Blake
Membership: 55,000–60,000
Publications: Consumer Trends,
ICCA Newsletter, The Credit
World
Annual meetings: 1973—Atlanta

Millinery Credit Assn.
39 West 39th St., New York, N.Y.
10018
212-565-5010
Exec. Secy.: Nathan H. Press
Membership: 125-150

Motion Picture & Television Credit
Managers Assn.
1725 Beverly Blvd., Los Angeles,
Calif. 90026
213-483-4694
Secy.: Murray Wagner
Membership: 40-50

National Assn. of Commercial Collection Agencies, Inc.
5204 Chelsea St., La Jolla, Calif.
92037
714-488-3900
Exec. Secy.: Stanley K. Oldden
Membership: 65-75

National Assn. of Consumer Credit
Administrators
Dept. of Banking, Lew Wallace
Bldg., Santa Fe, N.M. 87501
Secy.-Treas.: T. L. Thomas
Membership: 50-60

National Assn. of Credit Management
475 Park Ave. South, New York,
N.Y. 10016
212-725-1700
Exec. V.P.: Robert D. Goodwin
Membership: 35,000-40,000
Publication: *Credit and Financial
Management*
Annual meetings: 1972—Houston;
1973—Montreal; 1974—Hono-
lulu; 1975—Seattle; 1976—Atlantic
City; 1977—San Antonio

National Assn. of Installment Companies, Inc.
38 West 32nd St., New York, N.Y.
10001
212-239-6520
Exec. Dir.: Edward L. Sard
Membership: 600-700
Publication: *Installment Retailing*

National Chemical Credit Assn.
142 Lexington Ave., New York,
N.Y. 10016

212-683-4370
Secy.: Robert L. Otto
Membership: 90-100

National Commercial Finance Conference, Inc.
29 Broadway, New York, N.Y.
10006
212-944-6815
Exec. Dir.: Leonard Machlis
Membership: 125-150
Publication: *Commercial Financing*
Annual meetings: New York City

National Construction Machinery
Credit Group
165 North Canal St., Chicago, Ill.
60606
312-263-5080
Secy.: W. L. Haney

National Consumer Finance Assn.
1000 16th St. N.W., Washington,
D. C. 20036
202-638-1340
Exec. V.P.: Carl F. Hawver
Membership: 14,000-15,000
Publications: *Advertising Forum,
Consumer Finance Law Bulletin,
Consumer Finance News, Finance
Facts Newsletter, Financial Forum*
Annual meetings: 1972—San Juan;
1973—San Francisco; 1974—Mon-
treal; 1975—Las Vegas

National Fuel Credit Assn.
230 South State St., Chicago, Ill.
60604
312-922-4514
Exec. Secy.: Mrs. L. V. McDonough
Membership: 35-40 companies

National Grain Merchandisers Credit
Assn.
330 Plymouth Bldg., Minneapolis,
Minn. 55402
612-336-8356
Secy.-Treas.: S. J. Haider
Membership: 6-10

National Institute of Credit
44 East 23rd St., New York, N.Y.
10010
212-674-5100

Dir.: George N. Christie
Membership: 2500–2600

National Radiator Manufacturers
Credit Assn.
330 Plymouth Bldg., Minneapolis,
Minn. 55402
612-336-8356
Secy.-Treas.: S. J. Haider
Membership: 11–16

National Suppliers to Food Processors
Credit Assn.
330 Plymouth Bldg., Minneapolis,
Minn. 55402
612-336-8356
Secy.-Treas.: S. J. Haider

Photographic Credit Institute
366 Fifth Ave., New York, N.Y.
10001
212-736-1279
Secy.: Edward A. Donovan
Membership: 60–70

Robert Morris Associates, The National
Assn. of Bank Loan & Credit
Officers
1432 Philadelphia National Bank
Bldg., Philadelphia, Pa. 19107
215-563-0267
Exec. Mgr.: Clarence R. Reed
Membership: 1200 banks, 4700
individuals
Publications: *Annual Statement
Studies, The Journal of Commer-
cial Bank Lending*
Annual meetings: 1972—Miami;
1973—Phoenix; 1974—Atlanta;
1975—San Francisco

Rubber Industry Credit Exchange, Inc.
992 Kenmore Blvd., Box 3756,
Akron, Ohio 44314
216-753-7709
Exec. Secy.: Frank P. Pamer

The Stationery & Office Equipment
Board of Trade, Inc.
200 Fifth Ave., New York, N.Y.
10010
212-675-3430
Exec. V.P.: Edward O. Kallmann
Membership: 225–250

Wool Yarn Jobbers Credit Assn., Inc.
342 Madison Ave., New York, N.Y.
10017
212-682-2930
Exec. V.P.: B. S. Zorwitz

FINANCE ASSOCIATIONS

American Finance Assn.
Grad. School of Bus. Admin. New
York Univ., 100 Trinity Pl., New
York, N.Y. 10006
212-732-5820
Secy.-Treas.: Robert A. Kavesh
Membership: 5000–6000
Publication: *Journal of Finance*

Army Finance Assn.
Box 793, Alexandria, Va. 22313
202-693-1454
Pres.: Brig. Gen. R. J. Richards
Membership: 1700–1800
Publication: *Army Finance Journal*
Semi-Annual meetings: Washington—
Spring/Fall

Assn. of Commercial Finance
Attorneys
22 East 40th St., New York, N.Y.
10017
212-683-5191
Secy.: Paul Coburn
Membership: 175–200

Cues Managers Society
1617 Sherman Ave., Madison, Wisc.
53704
608-244-5675
Exec. Dir.: Robert DeThorne

Financial Executives Institute
50 West 44th St., New York, N.Y.
10036
212-661-3150
Exec. Dir.: James J. Rutherford
Membership: 6000–7000
Publication: *Financial Executive*
Annual meetings: 1972—Detroit;
1973—Minneapolis; 1974—Honolulu; 1975—Boston; 1976—Mexico
City; 1977—Toronto

Institute of Broadcasting Financial
Management
18 South Michigan Ave., Chicago,
Ill. 60603
Exec. Secy.: Catharine E. Serwe
Membership: 375–400
Publication: *IBFM Newsletter*

Institute of Chartered Financial
Analysis
Monroe Hall, Univ. of Virginia,
Charlottesville, Va. 22903
703-924-7111
Exec. Dir.: Dr. C. Stewart Sheppard
Membership: 2400–2500
Publication: *C.F.A. Study Guides*

Municipal Finance Officers Assn. of
U.S. & Canada
1313 East 60th St., Chicago, Ill.
60637
312-324-3400
Exec. Dir.: Donald W. Beatty
Membership: 4000–4500
Publications: *Municipal Finance,
MFOA Newsletter*
Annual meetings: 1972–Denver;
1973–Kansas City; 1974–Las
Vegas

Municipal Treasurers Assn. of the
U.S.
681 Market St., Suite 1085, San
Francisco, Calif. 94105
415-321-7607
Exec. Dir.: Henry Burget

National Assn. of County Treasurers
& Finance Agents
1001 Connecticut Ave. N.W., Wash-
ington, D. C. 20036
202-628-4701
Exec. Secy.: Bernard F. Hillenbrand
Membership: 1100–1200
Annual meetings: With National
Assn. of Counties

National Assn. of Reimbursement
Officers
Div. of Reimbursements, 2100 Guil-
ford Ave., Baltimore, Md. 21218
301-383-3010

Lib.: Russell S. Maranto
Membership: 75–100

National Assn. of Small Business Investment Companies
537 Washington Bldg. N.W., Washington, D. C. 20005
202-638-3411
Exec. V.P.: Walter B. Stults
Membership: 225–250
Publications: *Membership Directory, NASBIC News*
Annual meetings: 1972–Monterey

National Assn. of State Budget
Officers
Council of State Governments, Iron
Works Pike, Lexington, Ky. 40505
Secy.: George A. Bell
Membership: 75–100

National Commercial Finance Confer-
ence, Inc.
29 Broadway, New York, N.Y.
10006
212-944-6815
Exec. Dir.: Leonard Machlis
Membership: 125–150
Publication: *Commercial Financing*
Annual Convention in New York
City

National Consumer Finance Assn.
1000 16th St. N.W., Washington,
D. C. 20036
202-638-1340
Exec. V.P.: Carl F. Hawver
Membership: 14,000–15,000
Publications: *Advertising Forum,
Consumer Finance Law Bulletin,
Consumer Finance News, Finance
Facts Newsletter, Financial Forum*
Annual meetings: 1972–San Juan;
1973–San Francisco; 1974–Mon-
treal; 1975–Las Vegas

National Mutual Fund Managers Assn.
Thomson & McKinnon Auchincloss,
Inc., 2 Broadway, New York,
N.Y. 10004
212-422-5100
Secy.-Treas.: Sal Calafati
Membership: 40–50

Robert Morris Associates, The National Assn. of Bank Loan & Credit Officers
1432 Philadelphia National Bank Bldg., Philadelphia, Pa. 19107
215-563-0267
Exec. Mgr.: Clarence R. Reed
Membership: 1200 banks, 4700 individuals
Publications: *Annual Statement Studies, The Journal of Commercial Bank Lending*
Annual meetings: 1972—Miami; 1973—Phoenix; 1974—Atlanta; 1975—San Francisco

INVESTMENT ASSOCIATIONS

American Assn. of Commodity Traders
286 Fifth Ave., New York, N.Y. 10001
212-736-4610
Pres.: Arthur N. Economou
Membership: 1800–2000
Publication: *Journal of Commodity Trading*

American Conference of Real Estate Investment Trusts
608 13th St. N.W., Washington, D. C. 20005
202-347-9464
Secy.: Milton I. Baldinger

American Institute of Financial Brokers
221 North LaSalle St., Chicago, Ill. 60601
312-346-6080
Secy.: H. J. Van Buskirk
Membership: 200–225

Assn. of Closed-End Investment Cos.
90 Broad St., New York, N.Y. 10004
202-944-3820
Secy.: Howard J. Creelor

Assn. of Mutual Fund Plan Sponsors, Inc.
50 East 42nd St., New York, N.Y. 10017

212-697-9431
V.P.-Treas.: Albro C. Fowler
Membership: 25–30

Assn. of Stock Exchange Firms
120 Broadway, New York, N.Y. 10005
212-227-6722
Pres.: Leon T. Kendall
Membership: 575–600

The Financial Analysts Federation
219 East 42nd St., New York, N.Y. 10017
212-687-3882
Exec. Secy.: Fred Ohles
Membership: 13,000
Publications: *Analysts Directory, Corporate Reporting Critiques, Financial Analysts Journal*
Annual meetings: 1972—New York City; 1973—New York City

Institute of Chartered Financial Analysts
Monroe Hall, Univ. of Virginia, Charlottesville, Va. 22903
703-924-7111
Exec. Dir.: Dr. C. Stewart Sheppard
Membership: 2400–2500
Publication: *C.F.A. Study Guides*

Investment Bankers Assn. of America
425 13th St. N.W., Washington, D. C. 20004
202-393-3366
Exec. Dir.: Gordon L. Calvert
Membership: 650–700
Publication: *IBA Washington Bulletin*

Investment Co. Institute
1775 K St. N.W., Washington, D. C. 20006
202-293-7700
Exec. V.P.: Bruce B. Robe
Membership: 225–250

Investment Counsel Assn. of America, Inc.
49 Park Ave., New York, N.Y. 10016
212-689-3380
Secy.: John M. Wood, Jr.

Membership: 50–60
Publication: *Directory of Member Firms*
Annual meetings: May

Investors League, Inc.
1 The Crescent, Montclair, N.J. 07042
201-675-3633
Pres.: William Jackman
Membership: 85,000–90,000
Publication: *Bulletin*

National Assn. of Investment Clubs
1515 East Eleven Mile Rd., Royal Oak, Mich. 48068
313-543-0612
Exec. Dir.: Thomas E. O'Hara
Membership: 13,000–14,000 clubs; 200,000–225,000 individuals
Publications: *Investment Club Manual, Better Investing*
Annual meetings: 1972—Detroit

National Assn. of Investors Brokers
Room 125, 1625 Eye St. N.W., Washington, D. C. 20006
202-347-5700
Secy.: Mrs. Martha Norton
Membership: 3500–4000

National Assn. of Real Estate Investment Funds
900 Chapel St., New Haven, Conn. 06510
Exec. Dir.: Robert M. Burr
Membership: 100–125
Publication: *NAREIF Handbook of Member Trusts*

National Assn. of Securities Dealers, Inc.
888 17th St. N.W., Washington, D. C. 20006
202-298-7610
Pres.: Gordon S. Macklin
Membership: 4000–4500
Publications: *Annual Report, NASD News*

National Assn. of Small Business Investment Cos.
537 Washington Bldg. N.W., Washington, D. C. 20005

202-638-3411
Exec. V.P.: Walter B. Stults
Membership: 225–250
Publications: *Membership Directory, NASBIC News*
Annual meetings: 1972—Monterey

National Mutual Fund Managers Assn.
Thomson & McKinnon Auchincloss, Inc., 2 Broadway, New York, N.Y. 10004
212-442-5100
Secy.-Treas.: Sal Calafati
Membership: 40–50

Put & Call Brokers & Dealers Assn., Inc.
19 Rector St., New York, N.Y. 10006
212-344-5880
Pres.: Murray E. Gottesman
Membership: 110–125

United Shareowners of America, Inc.
468 Park Ave. South, New York, N.Y. 10016
212-686-4150
Pres.: Benjamin A. Javits

SECURITIES ASSOCIATIONS

American Stock Exchanges
86 Trinity Pl., New York, N.Y. 10006
212-938-2401
Pres.: Ralph S. Saul
Membership: 850–900
Publications: *American Investor, Management & Operations, Weekly Bulletin*

Assn. of Mutual Fund Plan Sponsors, Inc.
50 East 42nd St., New York, N.Y. 10017
212-697-9431
V.P.-Treas.: Albro C. Fowler
Membership: 25–30

The Financial Analysts Federation
219 East 42nd St., New York, N.Y. 10017
212-687-3882

Exec. Secy.: Fred Ohles
Membership: 13,000
Publications: *Analysts Directory,
Corporate Reporting Critiques,
Financial Analysts Journal*
Annual meetings: 1972—New York
City; 1973—New York

Foreign Bondholders Protective
Council, Inc.
1775 Broadway, New York, N.Y.
10019
212-586-6720
Pres.: Donald R. Heath

National Assn. of Securities Dealers,
Inc.
888 17th St. N.W., Washington,
D. C. 20006
202-298-7610
Pres.: Gordon S. Macklin
Membership: 4000-4500
Publications: *Annual Report, NASD
News*

National Detectives & Special Police
Assn.
1029 Vermont Ave. N.W., Washington, D. C. 20005
Secy.: L. D. Ellis
Membership: 19,000-21,000
Publication: *Police Training Bulletin*

National Security Traders Assn., Inc.
208 South LaSalle St., Chicago, Ill.
60604
312-782-2400
Registered Agent: Edward H. Welch
Membership: 5000-6000
Annual meetings: 1972—Sea Island;
1974—Sea Island

New York Stock Exchange
11 Wall St., New York, N.Y. 10005
212-623-3000
Pres.: Robert W. Haack
Membership: 1300-1400

North American Securities Adminis-
trators Assn., Inc.
Room 1202, Lucas State Office
Bldg., Des Moines, Iowa 50319
515-281-5707
Secy.: Larry J. Bryant
Membership: 55-60
Publications: *Court Magazine, Blue
Sky News, NASA Bulletin, Pro-
ceedings*

United Shareowners of America, Inc.
468 Park Ave. South, New York,
N.Y. 10016
212-686-4150
Pres.: Benjamin A. Javits

46. Federal Regulatory Agencies

Commodity Exchange Commission
Dept. of Agriculture Bldg., Washington, D.C. 20250
202-388-6933
The Commission initiates complaints, conducts hearings, and issues cease and desist or suspension orders for violation of the Commodity Exchange Act by any board of trade (commodity exchange) designated as a contract market.

Federal Deposit Insurance Corp.
550 17th St. N.W., Washington, D.C.
20429

202-393-8400
The Corporation was established to promote and preserve public confidence in banks and to protect the money supply through provision of insurance coverage for bank deposits.

Federal Home Loan Bank Board
101 Indiana Ave. N.W., Washington,
D.C. 20552
202-783-5200
The purpose of the Federal Home Loan Bank Board is to encourage thrift and economical home ownership through supervision of the Fed-

eral Home Loan Bank System, the Federal Savings and Loan System, and the Federal Savings and Loan Insurance Corporation.

Federal Reserve System
20th St. & Constitution Ave. N.W., Washington, D.C. 20551
202-737-1100
As stated in the preamble, the purposes of the act are "to provide for the establishment of Federal Reserve Banks, to furnish an elastic currency, to afford means of rediscounting commercial paper, to establish a more effective supervision of banking in the United States, and for other purposes."

Federal Trade Commission
Pennsylvania Ave. at Sixth St. N.W., Washington, D.C. 20580
202-EX3-6800
The basic objective of the Commission is the maintenance of free competitive enterprise as the keystone of the American economic system. Although the duties of the Commission are many and varied under the statutes, the foundation of public policy underlying all these duties is essentially the same: to prevent the free enterprise system from being stifled or fettered by monopoly or corrupted by unfair or deceptive trade practices.

In brief, the Commission is charged with keeping competition both free and fair.

National Credit Union Admin.
1325 K St. N.W., Washington, D.C. 20456
202-382-8727
The mission of the Administration, to provide nationwide administration of the Federal Credit Union program, is achieved through three major activities: Chartering, supervising, and examining Federal credit unions.

Securities and Exchange Commission
500 North Capitol St. N.W., Washington, D.C. 20549
202-755-1200
The general objective of the statutes administered by the Commission is to protect the interests of the public and investors against malpractices in the securities and financial markets.

United States Tariff Commission
E St. between 7th & 8th Sts. N.W., Washington, D.C. 20436
202-628-3947
The Commission serves the Congress and the President as an advisory, factfinding agency on tariff, commercial policy, and foreign trade matters.

47. Internal Revenue Service

REGIONAL OFFICES

National Headquarters, Internal Revenue Service
1111 Constitution Ave. N.W., Washington, D.C. 20224

Central (Ind., Ky., Mich., Ohio, & W. Va.)
550 Main St., Cincinnati, Ohio 45202

Mid-Atlantic (Del., Md., N.J., Pa., Va., & the District of Columbia)
2 Penn Center Plaza, Philadelphia, Pa. 19102

Midwest (Ill., Iowa, Minn., Mo., Neb., N.D., S.D., & Wisc.)
35 East Wacker Dr., Chicago, Ill. 60601

North Atlantic (Conn., Maine, Mass.,
N.H., N.Y., R.I., & Vt.)
90 Church St., New York, N.Y.
10017

Southeast (Ala., Fla., Ga., Miss., N.C.,
S.C., & Tenn.)
275 Peachtree St. N.E., Atlanta, Ga.
30303

Southwest (Ark., Colo., Kan., La.,
N.M., Okla., Tex., & Wyo.)
1114 Commerce St., Dallas, Tex.
75202

Western (Alaska, Ariz., Calif., Hawaii,
Idaho, Mont., Nev., Oreg., Utah, &
Wash.)
870 Market St., San Francisco, Calif.
94102

DISTRICT OFFICES

Alabama
2121 Eighth Ave., N. Birmingham
35203

Alaska
540 Fifth Ave., Anchorage 99501

Arizona
230 North 1st Ave., Phoenix 85025

Arkansas
700 West Capitol, Little Rock 72203

California
300 North Los Angeles St., Los
Angeles 90012
450 Golden Gate Ave., San Francisco
94102

Colorado
1961 Stout St., Denver 80202

Connecticut
450 Main St., Hartford 06103

Delaware
800 Delaware Ave., Wilmington
19801

District of Columbia
(Part of Baltimore District)

Florida
400 West Bay St., Jacksonville
32202

Georgia
275 Peachtree St. N.E., Atlanta, Ga.
30303

Hawaii
Federal Bldg., Honolulu 96813

Idaho
550 West Fort St., Boise 83707

Illinois
17 North Dearborn St., Chicago
60602
325 West Adams St., Springfield
62704

Indiana
Post Office & Courthouse Bldg.,
Indianapolis 46204

Iowa
210 Walnut St., Des Moines 50309

Kansas
412 South Main St., Wichita 67202

Kentucky
Post Office Bldg., Louisville 40202

Louisiana
600 South St., New Orleans 70130

Maine
68 Sewall St., Augusta 04330

Maryland
Federal Bldg., Baltimore 21201

Massachusetts
J.F.K. Federal Bldg., Boston 02203

Michigan
Post Office and Courthouse, Detroit
48226

Minnesota
316 North Robert St., St. Paul
55101

Mississippi
301 North Lamar St., Jackson
39202

Missouri
1114 Market St., St. Louis 63101

Montana
Federal Office Bldg., Helena 59601

Nebraska
106 South 15th St., Omaha 68102

Nevada
300 Booth St., Reno 89502

New Hampshire
80 Daniel St., Portsmouth 03801

New Jersey
970 Broad St., Newark 07102

New Mexico
517 Gold Ave. S.W., Albuquerque 87101

New York
161 Washington Ave., Albany 12210
35 Tillary St., Brooklyn 11201
34 West Mohawk St., Buffalo 14202
120 Church St., New York 10007

North Carolina
320 South Ashe St., Greensboro 27401

North Dakota
653 Second Ave., North Fargo 58102

Ohio
550 Main St., Cincinnati 45202
1240 East 9th St., Cleveland 44199

Oklahoma
200 N.W. 4th St., Oklahoma City 73102

Oregon
319 Southwest Pine St., Portland 97204

Pennsylvania
401 North Broad St., Philadelphia 19108
1000 Liberty Ave., Pittsburgh 15222

Puerto Rico
Office of International Operations, National Office, Ponce de Leon Ave. & Bolivia St., Hato Rey 00917

Rhode Island
130 Broadway, Providence 02903

South Carolina
901 Sumter St., Columbia 29201

South Dakota
640 9th Ave. S.W., Aberdeen 57401

Tennessee
801 Broadway, Nashville 37203

Texas
300 East 8th St., Austin 78701
1600 Patterson St., Dallas 75201

Utah
Post Office and Courthouse, Salt Lake City 84110

Vermont
11 Elmwood Ave., Burlington 05401

Virginia
400 North 8th St., Richmond 23240

Virgin Islands
Office of International Operations, National Office

Washington
2033 Sixth Ave., Seattle 98121

West Virginia
425 Juliana St., Parkersburg 26101

Wisconsin
517 East Wisconsin Ave., Milwaukee 53202

Wyoming
21st & Carey Ave., Cheyenne 82001

48. Securities and Exchange Commission Regional Offices

National Office, Securities & Exchange Commission
500 North Capital St., Washington, D.C. 20549

Arlington
4015 Wilson Blvd., Arlington, Va. 22201

Atlanta
1371 Peachtree St. N.E., Atlanta, Ga. 30309

Boston
John F. Kennedy Federal Bldg., Boston, Mass. 02203

Chicago
U. S. Courthouse and Federal Office Bldg., Chicago, Ill. 60604

Denver
Federal Bldg., Denver, Colo. 80202

Fort Worth
503 U. S. Courthouse, 10th & Lamar Sts., Fort Worth, Tex. 76102

New York
26 Federal Plaza, New York, N.Y. 10007

San Francisco
450 Golden Gate Ave., San Francisco, Calif. 94102

Seattle
Hoge Bldg., 705 Second Ave., Seattle, Wash. 98104

49. Small Business Administration Field Offices

NORTHEASTERN AREA

John Fitzgerald Kennedy Federal Bldg., Boston, Mass. 02203
617-223-3201

Federal Bldg., U. S. Post Office, 40 Western Ave., Augusta, Me. 04330
207-622-6225
55 Pleasant St., Concord, N.H. 03301
603-224-4041

Federal Office Bldg., 450 Main St., Hartford, Conn. 06103
203-244-3600

Federal Bldg., 2nd Floor, 87 State St., Montpelier, Vt. 05601
802-233-8422

702 Smith Bldg., 57 Eddy St., Providence, R.I. 02903
401-528-4580

NEW YORK AREA

26 Federal Plaza, Room 3108, New York, N.Y. 10007
212-264-1481

91 State St., Albany, N.Y. 12207
518-462-6300

255 Ponce De Leon Ave., P.O. Box 1915, Hato Rey, Puerto Rico 00910
765-0404 (Call through Operator)

970 Broad St., Room 1636, Newark, N.J. 07102
201-645-3580

Hunter Plaza, Fayette & Salina Sts., Syracuse, N.Y. 12302
716-473-3460

Federal Bldg., Room 9, 121 Ellicott St., Buffalo, N.Y. 14203
716-842-3240

MIDDLE ATLANTIC AREA

1317 Filbert St., Philadelphia, Pa.
19107
215-597-4705

U. S. Customs House, 6th & King Sts.,
Wilmington, Del. 19801
302-658-6518

1113 Federal Bldg., 31 Hopkins Plaza,
Baltimore, Md. 21201
302-962-3311

Lowndes Bank Bldg., 119 North 3rd
St., Clarksburg, W. Va. 26301
304-624-1365

3410 Courthouse & Federal Bldg., 500
Quarrier St., Charleston, W. Va.
25301
304-343-1227

Room 317, Federal Bldg., 1240 East
9th St., Cleveland, Ohio 44199
216-522-4182

Federal Office Bldg., 134 Summitt St.,
Toledo, Ohio 43602
419-259-6414

Beacon Bldg., 50 West Gay St., Columbus, Ohio 43215
614-469-7310

5026 Federal Bldg., Cincinnati, Ohio
45202
513-684-3175

1900 Commonwealth Bldg., 4th &
Broadway, Louisville, Ky. 40202
502-582-5274

Federal Bldg., 1000 Liberty Ave.,
Pittsburgh, Pa. 15222
412-644-2784

Federal Bldg., 400 North 8th St., Richmond, Va. 23240
703-649-2741

1405 I St. N.W., Washington, D.C.
20417
202-382-3541

SOUTHEASTERN AREA

Hartford Bldg., 100 Edgewood Ave.
N.E., Atlanta, Ga. 30303
404-526-6311

South 20th Bldg., 908 South 20th St.,
Birmingham, Ala. 35205
205-325-3981

Addison Bldg., 222 South Church St.,
Charlotte, N.C. 28202
704-372-7448

1801 Assembly St., Columbia, S.C.
29201
803-253-3373

P.O. Box 2351, 245 East Capitol St.,
Jackson, Miss. 39205
601-948-2333

Federal Office Bldg., 400 West Bay St.,
P.O. Box 35067, Jacksonville, Fla.
32202
904-791-2181

912 Federal Office Bldg., 51 S.W. 1st
Ave., Miami, Fla. 33130
305-350-5533

Security Federal Savings & Loan Bldg.,
500 Union St., Nashville, Tenn.
37219
615-242-5880

Fidelity Bldg., Room 307, 502 Gay
St., Knoxville, Tenn. 37902
615-524-4534

MIDWESTERN AREA

Federal Office Bldg., 219 South Dearborn St., Chicago, Ill. 60604
312-353-4485

New Federal Bldg., Room 749, 210
Walnut St., Iowa 50309
515-284-4610

1200 Book Bldg., 1249 Washington
Blvd., Detroit, Mich. 48226
313-226-7240

502 West Kaye Ave., Marquette, Mich.
49855
906-225-1108

Century Bldg., 36 South Pennsylvania
St., Indianapolis, Ind. 46204
317-633-7124

911 Walnut St., Kansas City, Mo.
64106
816-374-3316

25 West Main, Madison, Wisc. 53703
608-256-4761

Straus Bldg., 238 West Wisconsin Ave.,
Milwaukee, Wisc. 53203
414-272-8600

Reimann Bldg., 816 2nd Ave. South,
Minneapolis, Minn. 55402
612-334-2341

Federal Bldg., 208 North Broadway,
St. Louis, Mo. 64102
314-622-4191

SOUTHWESTERN AREA

Mayflower Bldg., 411 North Akard
St., Dallas, Tex. 75201
214-749-2046

Federal Bldg., 500 Gold Ave. S.W.,
Albuquerque, N.M. 87101
505-843-2871

Niels Esperson Bldg., 808 Travis St.,
Houston, Tex. 77002
713-226-4341

377 P.O. & Courthouse Bldg., 600
West Capitol Ave., Little Rock,
Ark. 72201
501-372-5373

204 Federal Office Bldg., 1616 19th
St., Lubbock, Tex. 79401
806-765-8262

201 Travis Terrace Bldg., P.O. Box
1349, 505 East Travis St., Marshall, Tex. 75670
214-935-5257

Gateway Bldg., 124 Camp St., New
Orleans, La. 70130
504-527-2744

501 Mercantile Bldg., 30 North Hudson, Oklahoma City, Okla. 73102
405-236-2601

301 Broadway, 300 Manion Bldg., San
Antonio, Tex. 78205
512-225-4745

219 East Jackson St., Harlingen, Tex.
78550
512-425-1395

ROCKY MOUNTAIN AREA

Federal Office Bldg., 1961 Stout St.,
Denver, Colo. 80202
303-297-3763

Western Bldg., 300 North Center St.,
Casper, Wyo. 82601
307-265-4310

300 American Life Bldg., 207 North
5th St., Fargo, N.D. 58102
702-237-5131

P.O. Box 1690, 205 Power Block,
Main & 6th Ave., Helena, Mont.
59601
406-442-3245

7425 Federal Bldg., 215 North 17th
St., Omaha, Neb. 68102
402-221-4691

2237 Federal Bldg., 125 State St., Salt
Lake City, Utah 84111
801-524-5804

402 National Bank Bldg., 8th & Main
Ave., Sioux Falls, S.D. 57102
605-336-2980

302-120 Bldg., 120 South Market St.,
Wichita, Kans. 67202
316-267-5655

PACIFIC COASTAL AREA

Federal Bldg., 450 Golden Gate Ave.,
Box 36044, San Francisco, Calif.
94102
415-556-5033

Federal Bldg., Room 4015, 1130 O St.,
Fresno, Calif. 93721
209-487-5189

632 Sixth Ave., Suite 450, Anchorage,
Alaska 99501
277-8622 (Call through operator)

510 Second Ave., Fairbanks, Alaska
99701
452-5101 (Call through operator)

Room 408, Idaho Bldg., 216 North
8th St., Boise, Idaho 83702
208-242-2516

1149 Bethel St., Room 402, Honolulu, Hawaii 96813
546-5020 (Call through operator)

Ada Plaza Center Bldg., P.O. Box 927, Agana, Guam 96910
777-8402 (Call through operator)

849 South Broadway, Los Angeles, Calif. 90014
213-688-2977

300 Las Vegas Blvd., South, Room 4-104, Las Vegas, Nev. 89101
702-385-6271

Central Towers Bldg., 2727 North Central Ave., Phoenix, Ariz. 85004
602-261-3611

700 Pittock Block, 921 Southwest Washington St., Portland, Oregon 97205
503-226-3001

100 West C St., San Diego, Calif. 92101
714-293-5430

1206 Smith Tower, 506 2nd St., Seattle, Wash. 98104
206-583-5676

651 U. S. Courthouse, P.O. Box 2167, Spokane, Wash. 99210
509-838-4129

50. U.S. Department of Commerce Field Offices

Albuquerque
U. S. Courthouse, Albuquerque, N.M. 87101
505-843-2386

Anchorage
412 Hill Bldg., 632 Sixth Ave., Anchorage, Alaska 99501
907-272-6531

Atlanta
Suite 5231, 1401 Peachtree St. N.E., Atlanta, Ga. 30309
404-526-6000

Baltimore
Room 415, U. S. Customhouse, Gay & Lombard Sts., Baltimore, Md. 21202
301-962-3560

Birmingham
Suite 200-201, 908 South 20th St., Birmingham, Ala. 35205
205-325-3327

Boston
Room 510, John F. Kennedy Federal Bldg., Boston, Mass. 02203
617-223-2312

Buffalo
504 Federal Bldg., 117 Ellicott St., Buffalo, N.Y. 14203
716-842-3208

Charleston
Federal Bldg., Suite 631, 334 Meeting St., Charleston, S.C. 29403
803-577-4171

Charleston
3000 New Federal Office Bldg., 500 Quarrier St., Charleston, W.V. 25301
304-343-6181

Cheyenne
6022 O'Mahoney Federal Center, 2120 Capitol Ave., Cheyenne, Wyo. 82001
307-778-2220

Chicago
1486 New Federal Bldg., 219 South Dearborn St., Chicago, Ill. 60604
312-353-4400

Cincinnati
2028 Federal Office Bldg., 500 Main St., Cincinnati, Ohio 45202
513-684-2944

Cleveland
    Room 600, 666 Euclid Ave., Cleveland, Ohio 44114
    216-522-4750

Dallas
    Room 3E7, 1100 Commerce St., Dallas, Tex. 75202
    214-749-3287

Denver
    New Custom House, 19th & Stout Sts., Denver, Colo. 80202
    303-837-3246

Des Moines
    609 Federal Bldg., 210 Walnut St., Des Moines, Iowa 50309
    515-284-4222

Detroit
    445 Federal Bldg., Detroit, Mich. 48226
    313-226-6088

Greensboro
    258 Federal Bldg., West Market St., P.O. Box 1950, Greensboro, N.C. 27402
    919-275-9111

Hartford
    Room 610B, Federal Office Bldg., 450 Main St., Hartford, Conn. 06103
    203-244-3530

Honolulu
    286 Alexander Young Bldg., 1015 Bishop St., Honolulu, Hawaii 96813
    808-546-8694

Houston
    1017 Old Federal Bldg., 201 Fannin St., Houston, Tex. 77002
    713-226-4231

Jacksonville
    P.O. Box 35087, West Bay St., Jacksonville, Fla. 32202
    904-791-2796

Kansas City
    Room 1840, 601 East 12th St., Kansas City, Mo. 64106
    816-374-3141

Los Angeles
    11201 Federal Bldg., 11000 Wilshire Blvd., Los Angeles, Calif. 90024
    213-824-7591

Memphis
    Room 710, 147 Jefferson Ave., Memphis, Tenn. 38103
    901-534-3214

Miami
    Room 821, City National Bank Bldg., 25 West Flagler St., Miami, Fla. 33130
    305-350-5267

Milwaukee
    Straus Bldg., 238 West Wisconsin Ave., Milwaukee, Wisc. 53203
    414-244-3473

Minneapolis
    306 Federal Bldg., 110 South Fourth St., Minneapolis, Minn. 55401
    612-725-2133

New Orleans
    909 Federal Office Bldg. (South), 610 South St., New Orleans, La. 70130
    504-527-6546

New York
    41st Floor, Federal Office Bldg., 26 Federal Plaza, Foley Square, New York, N.Y. 10007
    212-264-0634

Philadelphia
    Jefferson Bldg., 1015 Chestnut St., Philadelphia, Pa. 19107
    215-597-2850

Phoenix
    New Federal Bldg., 230 North 1st Ave., Phoenix, Ariz. 85025
    602-261-3285

Pittsburgh
432 Federal Bldg., 1000 Liberty
Ave., Pittsburgh, Pa. 15222
412-644-2850

Portland
217 Old U. S. Courthouse, 520
Southwest Morrison St., Portland,
Oreg. 97204
503-226-3361

Reno
Room 2028, 300 Booth St., Reno,
Nev. 89502
702-784-5203

Richmond
2105 Federal Bldg., 400 North 8th
St., Richmond, Va. 23240
703-782-2246

St. Louis
2511 Federal Bldg., 1520 Market St.,
St. Louis, Mo. 63103
314-622-4243

Salt Lake City
1201 Federal Bldg., 125 South State
St., Salt Lake City, Utah 84111
801-524-5116

San Francisco
Federal Bldg., Box 36013, 450
Golden Gate Ave., San Francisco,
Calif. 94102
415-556-5864

San Juan
Room 100, P.O. Bldg., San Juan,
Puerto Rico 00902
106-723-4640

Savannah
235 U. S. Courthouse & P.O. Bldg.,
125-29 Bull St., Savannah, Ga.
31402
912-232-4321

Seattle
8021 Federal Office Bldg., 909 1st
Ave., Seattle, Wash. 98104
206-442-5615

PROFESSIONAL SERVICES

51. Major Certified Public Accounting Firms

Arthur Anderson & Co.
1345 Ave. of the Americas, New
York, N.Y. 10019
212-952-7700

Ernst & Ernst
1300 Union Commerce Bldg., Cleveland, Ohio 44115
216-861-5000
140 Broadway, New York, N.Y.
10005
212-943-7800

Elmer Fox & Co.
900 Wichita Plaza Bldg., Wichita,
Kans. 67202
316-265-3231

Alexander Grant & Co.
1 North LaSalle St., Chicago, Ill.
60602
312-732-5100

Harris, Kerr, Forster & Co.
420 Lexington Ave., New York, N.Y.
10017
212-679-2220

Haskins & Sells
2 Broadway, New York, N.Y. 10005
212-422-9600

Hurdman & Cranstoun, Penney & Co.
140 Broadway, New York, N.Y.
10005
212-269-5800

J. K. Lasser & Co.
666 Fifth Ave., New York, N.Y.
10019
212-245-2700

Laventhol Krekstein Horwath &
Horwath
866 Third Ave., New York, N.Y.
10022
212-980-3100

S. D. Leidesdorf & Co.
125 Park Ave., New York, N.Y.
10017
212-697-0200

Lybrand, Ross Bros. & Montgomery
2 Broadway, New York, N.Y. 10005
212-489-1100

Main Lafrentz & Co.
280 Park Ave., New York, N.Y.
10016
212-TN7-9100

McGladrey, Hansen, Dunn & Co.
Davenport Bank Bldg., Davenport,
Iowa 52801
319-323-9911

Peat, Marwick, Mitchell & Co.
345 Park Ave., New York, N.Y.
10022
212-758-9700

Price Waterhouse & Co.
60 Broad St., New York, N.Y.
10004
212-422-6000

A. M. Pullen & Co.
140 Broadway, New York, N.Y.
10005
212-269-7663

Seidman & Seidman
80 Broad St., New York, N.Y.
10004
212-765-7500

Touche Ross & Co.
1633 Broadway, New York, N.Y.
10019
212-489-1600

Arthur Young & Co.
277 Park Ave., New York, N.Y.
10017
212-922-2000

52. Transmitters
of Financial and Securities Data

TICKER INFORMATION

The following companies offer electronic or electromechanical devices
which connect to and reproduce information transmitted on the New York
and American Stock Exchange ticker
networks.

Bunker-Ramo Corp.
277 Park Ave., New York, N.Y.
10017
212-826-7177

Dow Jones & Co., Inc.
30 Broad St., New York, N.Y.
10005
212-422-3115

Scantlin Electronics, Inc.
75 Maiden Lane, New York, N.Y.
10038
212-344-0400

Trans-Lux Corp.
625 Madison Ave., New York, N.Y.
10022
212-751-3110

Ultronic Systems Corp.
100 Wall St., New York, N.Y. 10005
212-425-1470

BID-ASKED INFORMATION

The following companies offer desk
unit devices to transmit sales data and
bid-asked information from the New
York and American Stock Exchanges.

Bunker-Ramo Corp.
277 Park Ave., New York, N.Y.
10017
212-826-7177

Scantlin Electronics, Inc.
75 Maiden Lane, New York, N.Y.
10038
212-244-0400

Ultronic Systems Corp.
100 Wall St., New York, N.Y. 10005
212-425-1470

53. Financial
and Business Mailing Lists

Addresses Unlimited
14760 Oxnard St., Van Nuys, Calif.
91401
213-873-4114
Pres.: Robert K. Spero

Buckley-Dement
555 West Jackson Blvd., Chicago,
Ill. 60606
312-427-3862
Pres.: Harry F. DeLarme

Ed. Burnett, Inc.
176 Madison Ave., New York, N.Y.
10016
212-679-0630
Pres.: Ed Burnett

Business Press, Inc.
32 Broadway, New York, N.Y.
10004
212-269-2122
Pres.: Frederick Nordenson-Stein

Computer List Marketing
176 Madison Ave., New York, N.Y.
10016
212-679-0630
Pres.: Ed Burnett

Consumer Finance Business Service
1316 Lake St., Evanston, Ill. 60201
312-869-4445
Genl. Mgr.: Thomas O'Connor

Creative Mailing Services, Inc.
1100 Stewart Ave., Garden City,
N.Y. 11530
516-333-8100
Pres.: Bernard Fixler

Dependable Mailing Lists, Inc.
425 Park Ave. South, New York,
N.Y. 10016
212-679-7160
Pres.: Jack Oldstein

Doyle Stationery, Inc.
Doyle Bldg., Marshall, Mo. 65340

816-426-2228
Pres.: Dean H. Doyle

Dun & Bradstreet, Inc.
Marketing Services Div., 99 Church
St., New York, N.Y. 10007
212-349-3300
Pres.: Hamilton B. Mitchell

E-Z Addressing Service Corp.
80 Washington St., New York, N.Y.
10006
212-422-9448
Pres.: A. A. Gentile

Ever Ready Mailers, Inc.
4021 Austin Blvd., Island Park, New
York 11558
516-432-0745
Pres.: Arthur Yourish

Gralla Publications
1501 Broadway, New York, N.Y.
10036
212-868-0700
Production Mgr.: Patricia R. Bernato

HSI Computer Mailing Techniques
148 East Lancaster Ave., Wayne, Pa.
19087
215-687-2455
Genl. Mgr.: Kurt J. Schneider

H. H. Harrington/Manhattan Exclusive
482 Court St., Brooklyn, N.Y.
11231
212-UL8-0355
Owner: Helen H. Harrington

The Walter S. Kraus Co.
48-01 42nd St., Long Island City,
N.Y. 11104
212-784-5922
Pres.: Walter S. Kraus

List Management & Marketing
1130 17th St. N.W., Washington,
D.C. 20036
202-293-5750
Pres.: John H. Swain

List Management, Inc.
150 Purchase St., Rye, N.Y. 10580
914-967-5520
Pres.: Fred E. Allen

R. L. Polk & Co.
431 Howard St., Detroit, Mich.
48231
313-961-9470
Pres.: Walter J. Gardner

Research Projects Corp.
1706 Rockaway Ave., Lynbrook,
N.Y. 11563

516-887-2611
Pres.: Bernard Lande

H. K. Simon, Inc.
98 Old Broadway, Hastings-On-Hudson, N.Y. 10706
914-478-2446
List Mgr.: Virginia C. Mozian

Zeller & Letica, Inc.
15 East 26th St., New York, N.Y.
10010
212-685-7512
Pres.: Alvin B. Zeller

54. Financial News Services

AP International Dow Jones & Co.,
Inc.
30 Broad St., New York, N.Y.
10004
212-HA2-3115, ext. 501

Associated Press
50 Rockefeller Plaza, New York,
N.Y. 10020
212-PL7-1111, ext. 291

Dow Jones & Co., Inc.
30 Broad St., New York, N.Y.
10004
212-HA2-3115, ext. 521-529

Moody's Investors Service, Inc.
99 Church St., New York, N.Y.
10007
212-267-8800

The New York Times
229 West 43rd St., New York, N.Y.
10036
212-556-1234

Reuters Economic Services
1212 Ave. of Americas, New York,
N.Y. 10036
212-581-4250

Standard & Poor's Corp.
345 Hudson St., New York, N.Y.
10014
212-924-6400

United Press International
200 East 42nd St., New York, N.Y.
10017
212-MU2-0400 (Ask for Financial
Desk)

The Wall Street Journal
30 Broad St., New York, N.Y.
10004
212-422-3115

Firms that distribute press releases
over private teletype networks:

PR Newswire
247 East 60th St., New York, N.Y.
10022
212-TE2-9400

PR Wire Service
660 First Ave., New York, N.Y.
10016
212-OR9-8998

55. Major Financial Printers

A & R Printing Corp.
228 West Broadway, New York,
N.Y. 10013
212-WA5-1724

Ad Press, Ltd.
21 Hudson St., New York, N.Y.
10013
212-266-4972

Appeal Printing Co.
130 Cedar St., New York, N.Y.
10006
212-WO4-3033

Aquarius Capital Corp.
9 Barrow St., New York, N.Y.
10014
212-989-5980

Bar Press
415 West 55th St., New York, N.Y.
10019
212-CI6-8853

Bowne & Co.
345 Hudson St., New York, N.Y.
10014
212-924-5500

Computer Productions, Inc.
17 Park Pl., New York, N.Y. 10007
212-962-4554

Pandick Press, Inc.
345 Hudson St., New York, N.Y.
10014
212-964-2900

Security Columbian Div. of U. S.
Banknote Corp.
345 Hudson St., New York, N.Y.
10014
212-675-8310

Sorg Printing
80 South St., New York, N.Y.
10038
212-WH3-3040

Charles P. Young
75 Varick St., New York, N.Y.
10013
212-431-5300

56. Financial Writers and Publicists

The following are selected members of
the New York Financial Writers Association:

George Auerbach, Pres.
Public Relations, Inc. 211 East 43rd
St., New York, N.Y. 10017
212-867-1050

Edward Bejan
Financial Public Relations, 5 Hanover Square, New York, N.Y.
10004
212-943-1331

Elliot V. Bell
200 East 66th St., New York, N.Y.
10021
212-TE8-5858

William L. Bennett
World Bank, 1818 H St. N.W., Washington, D.C. 20433
202-DU1-2408

Lawrence J. Bleiberg
Boxwood Associates, 41 West Putnam Ave., Greenwich, Conn.
06830
203-349-2655

Richard E. Blodgett, Ed.
The Corporate Communications Report, 29 Charlton St., New York, N.Y. 10014
212-WA4-6245

Gene M. Brown, Pres.
PR Associates, Inc., 575 Madison Ave., New York, N.Y. 10022
212-688-6900

James H. Cassell, Jr.
Edward Gottleib & Associates, Ltd., 485 Madison Ave., New York, N.Y. 10022
212-421-9220

Jim Catalano
Hill & Knowlton, Inc., 150 East 42nd St., New York, N.Y. 10017
212-697-5600

Carl V. Cefola
7 Hanover St., New York, N.Y. 10005
212-422-1158

Marvin A. Chatinover, Pres.
Forum Financial, 475 Fifth Ave., New York, N.Y. 10017
212-725-5373

Frank J. Cogan, Consultant
Food Trade and Public Relations, 289 West St., Closter, N.J. 07624
201-PO8-0479

Robert J. Duffy
321 Ave. C, New York, N.Y. 10009
212-GR5-0041

David B. Dworsky
The Rowland Co., 415 Madison Ave., New York, N.Y. 10017
212-MU8-1200

Raoul D. Edwards
P.O. Box 50, Park Ridge, Ill. 60068
312-825-3682

John F. Falvey
Financial Public Relations, 7 Hanover St., New York, N.Y. 10005
212-HA2-1158

Richard E. Fiske
Box 324, Pepperell, Mass. 01463

Lee Geist
17 Franklin Rd., Great Neck, N.Y. 11024
516-466-4376

Paul D. Gesner
292 Lantana Ave., Englewood, N.J. 07631
201-LO9-0223

Rolling W. Haxall
Dodgewood Rd., Riverdale, N.Y. 10471
212-KI3-6933

Leonard F. Howard
J. Milbank, 1133 Ave. of the Americas, New York, N.Y. 10036
212-247-0150

Paul A. Johnston, V.P.
Wiesenberger Financial Service, 5 Hanover Square, New York, N.Y. 10004
212-344-8300

Joseph Kaselow, V.P.
Cunningham & Walsh, Inc., 260 Madison Ave., New York, N.Y. 10016
212-683-4900

Stanley Kligfield, Attorney
55 Liberty St., New York, N.Y. 10005
212-227-0187

S. A. Krasney, Pres.
Samuel A. Krasney Associates, 103 Park Ave., New York, N.Y. 10017
212-684-7250

Robert Laffan, Pres.
Public Relations Systems, 200 Park Ave., Suite 4408, New York, N.Y. 10017
212-661-2690

Fred H. Lindemann
Salter-Mathieson & Co. Inc., 133 East 54th St., New York, N.Y. 10022
212-355-5619

Neal M. McMenamin, Senior V.P.
Edwin Bird Wilson, Inc., 30 East
42nd St., New York, N.Y. 10017
212-TN7-7722

J. Leonard Matt, V.P.
Ted Deglin & Associates, Inc., 63
East 80th St., New York, N.Y.
10021
212-628-3550

Trevvett Matthews
Route 2, Box 5, Glen Allen, Va.
23060
703-CO6-1315

Joseph C. Meehan, Pres.
J. C. Meehan Co., 246 Baxter Blvd.,
Portland, Me. 04101
207-773-3070

Emil P. Meier
127-04 22nd Ave., College Point,
N.Y. 11359
212-FL9-5198

Victor F. Morris, V.P.
National Securities & Research Corp.,
120 Broadway, New York, N.Y.
10005
212-BA7-1690

Edward A. Morse
Carl Byoir & Associates, 800 Second
Ave., New York, N.Y. 10017
212-YU6-6100

Frederick Nordenson-Stein
The Haight Hill Co., Inc., 32 Broadway, New York, N.Y. 10004
212-269-2122

Jack O'Dwyer, Ed.
The Jack O'Dwyer Newsletter, 271
Madison Ave., New York, N.Y.
10016
212-679-2471

Dale J. Olmstead
865 First Ave., New York, N.Y.
10017
212-421-0514

Arch Patton
McKinsey & Co., 245 Park Ave.,
New York, N.Y. 10017
212-MU7-3600

Niles N. Peebles
235 East 25th St., New York, N.Y.
10010
212-684-2150

Robert W. Price
The Bugil Co., 500 Fifth Ave., New
York, N.Y. 10036
212-947-2680

M. J. Rossant, Dir.
The Twentieth Century Fund, 41
East 70th St., New York, N.Y.
10021
212-535-4441

Stanley E. Rubenstein
Rubenstein, Wolfson & Co., 230
Park Ave., New York, N.Y. 10017
212-OR9-4334

Merryle S. Rukeyser
21 Glenbrook Dr., New Rochelle,
N.Y. 10804
914-NE6-0200

Alfred Russell, Pres.
Alfred Russell Associates, 1020 15th
St., Denver, Colo. 80202
303-534-0817

Edward Ryan, Senior Ed.
Securities, 80 William St., New York,
N.Y. 10038
212-943-4020

Michael J. Saada, Pres.
Opinion Builders, Inc., 1220 Huron
Bldg., Cleveland, Ohio 44115
216-621-3680

Anthony R. Scalza
Hill & Knowlton, Inc., 150 East
42nd St., New York, N.Y. 10017
212-697-5600

Nelson M. Schneider
Schumacher-Schneider, Inc., 1015
18th St. N.W., Washington, D.C.
20036
202-554-4959

Jerry Sherman
Jerry Sherman Associates, 200 West
57th St., New York, N.Y. 10019
212-245-3700

Charles M. Sievert
McCann-Erickson, Inc., 485 Lexington Ave., New York, N.Y. 10017
212-OX7-6000

Lee Silberman, V.P.
Shearson, Hammell & Co., 14 Wall St., New York, N.Y. 10005
212-588-2158

Carl Spielvogel, Chmn.
McCann-Erickson, Inc., 485 Lexington Ave., New York, N.Y. 10017
212-697-6000

David Steinberg, Exec. V.P.
PR Newswire, Inc., 247 East 60th St., New York, N.Y. 10022
212-TE2-9400

Mack Talbot
Times Publishing Co., Lock Haven, Pa. 17745
717-748-5225

Edward P. Tastrom, Public Relations Dir.
New York Shipping Assn. Inc., 80 Broad St., New York, N.Y. 10004
212-WH3-2740

Peter C. Thompson
Carl Byoir Associates, 800 Second Ave., New York, N.Y. 10017
212-YU6-6100

Edward K. Titus, Writer-Ed.
720 East Broad St., Falls Church, Va. 22046
703-JE4-2839

Lewis A. Webel
Channing Co., Inc., 280 Park Ave., New York, N.Y. 10017
212-661-7700

Phillip Weiner
22 Aldridge Rd., Chappaqua, N.Y. 10514
914-238-3739

Robert G. Woodman
The Shaw-Walker Co., 301 West Washington St., Chicago, Ill. 60606
312-726-8760

57. Major Law Firms

Baker, Botts, Shepherd & Coats
1 Shell Plaza, Houston, Tex. 77002
713-229-1234

Baker & McKenzie
Prudential Plaza, Chicago, Ill. 60601
312-828-0400

Breed, Abbott & Morgan
1 Chase Manhattan Plaza, New York, N.Y. 10005
212-944-4800

Cadwalader, Wickersham & Taft
1 Wall St., New York, N.Y. 10005
212-425-3000

Cahill, Gottlieb, Steen & Hamilton
1250 Connecticut Ave. N.W., Washington, D.C. 20036
202-223-2151

Covington & Burling
888 16th St. N.W., Washington, D.C. 20006
202-293-3300

Cravath, Swaine & Moore
1 Chase Manhattan Plaza, New York, N.Y. 10005
212-422-3000

Davis, Polk & Wardwell
1 Chase Manhattan Plaza, New York,
N.Y. 10005
212-HA2-3400

Debevoise, Plimpton, Lyons & Gates
320 Park Ave., New York, N.Y.
10022
212-PL2-6400

Dewey, Ballantine, Bushby, Palmer &
Wood
140 Broadway, New York, N.Y.
10005
212-344-8000

Donovan, Leisure, Newton & Irvine
2 Wall St., New York, N.Y. 10005
212-732-4100

Fulbright, Crooker, Freeman, Bates &
Jaworski
1140 Connecticut Ave. N.W., Washington, D.C. 20036
202-223-1166

Gibson, Dunn & Crutcher
515 South Flower St., Los Angeles,
Calif. 90012
213-620-9330

Jones, Day, Cockley & Reavis
1100 Connecticut Ave. N.W., Washington, D.C. 20036
202-293-2030

Kaye, Scholer, Fierman, Hays &
Handler
425 Park Ave., New York, N.Y.
10022
212-PL9-8400

Kelley, Drye, Warren, Clark, Carr &
Ellis
350 Park Ave., New York, N.Y.
10022
212-PL2-5800

Kirkland, Ellis, Hodson, Chaffetz,
Masters & Rowe
1776 K St. N.W., Washington, D.C.
20006
202-833-8400

LeBoeuf, Lamb, Leiby & MacRae
1 Chase Manhattan Plaza, New York,
N.Y. 10005
212-HA2-6262

Milbank, Tweed, Hadley & McCloy
1 Chase Manhattan Plaza, New York,
N.Y. 10005
212-422-2660

Morgan, Lewis & Bockius
1140 Connecticut Ave. N.W., Washington, D.C. 20036
202-466-2300

Mudge, Rose, Guthrie & Alexander
20 Broadway, New York, N.Y.
10004
212-422-6767

Mudge, Stein, Baldwin & Todd
20 Broadway, New York, N.Y.
10004
212-422-6767

O'Melveny & Myers
611 West 6th St., Los Angeles, Calif.
90017
213-620-1120

Paul, Weiss, Goldberg, Rifkind, Wharton & Garrison
345 Park Ave., New York, N.Y.
10022
212-935-8000

Pepper, Hamilton & Scheetz
1629 K St. N.W., Washington, D.C.
20006
202-296-1631

Pillsbury, Madison & Sutro
225 Bush St., San Francisco, Calif.
94104
415-421-6133

Reed, Smith, Shaw & McCloy
1155 15th St. N.W., Washington,
D.C. 20005
202-833-3090

Royall, Koegel & Rogers
200 Park Ave., New York, N.Y.
10017
212-972-7000

Shearman & Sterling
53 Wall St., New York, N.Y. 10005
212-483-1000

Simpson, Thacher & Bartlett
1735 I St. N.W., Washington, D.C.
20006
202-296-3424

Squire, Sanders & Dempsey
Union Commerce Bldg., Cleveland,
Ohio 44115
216-696-9200

Sullivan & Cromwell
48 Wall St., New York, N.Y. 10005
212-HA2-8100

Vinson, Elkins, Searls & Smith
First City National Bank Bldg.,
Houston, Tex. 77002
713-225-2411

Webster, Sheffield, Fleischman, Hitch-
cock & Brookfield
1 Rockefeller Plaza, New York, N.Y.
10020
212-582-3370

White & Case
14 Wall St., New York, N.Y. 10005
212-732-1040

Winston, Strawn, Smith & Patterson
1735 I St. N.W., Washington, D.C.
20006
202-833-2626

APPENDIXES

Glossary of Investing Terms

Information provided by the New York Stock Exchange.

Accrued interest. Interest accrued on a bond since the last interest payment was made. The buyer of the bond pays the market price plus accrued interest. Exceptions include bonds that are in default and income bonds. *See also* Flat; Income bond.

All or none order. A market or limited price order which is to be executed in its entirety or not at all, but, unlike a fill or kill order, is not to be treated as cancelled if not executed as soon as it is represented in the Trading Crowd. Bids or offers on behalf of all or none orders may not be made in stocks, but may be made in bonds when the number of bonds is fifty or more. *See also* Fill or kill.

Alternative order—either/or order. An order to do either of two alternatives—such as, either sell (buy) a particular stock at a limit price or sell (buy) on stop. If the order is for one unit of trading when one part of the order is executed on the happening of one alternative, the order on the other alternative is treated as cancelled. If the order is for an amount larger than one unit of trading, the number of units executed determines the amount of the alternative order to be treated as cancelled.

Amortization. A generic term. Includes various specific practices such as depreciation, depletion, write-off of intangibles, prepaid expenses, and deferred charges.

Annual report. The formal financial statement issued yearly by a corporation to its shareowners. The annual report shows assets, liabilities, earnings—how the company stood at the close of the business year and how it fared profitwise during the year.

Arbitrage. A technique employed to take advantage of differences in price. If, for example, XYZ stock can be bought in New York for $10 a share and

279

sold in London at $10.50, an arbitrageur may simultaneously purchase XYZ stock here and sell the same amount in London, making a profit of $.50 a share, less expenses. Arbitrage may also involve the purchase of rights to subscribe to a security, or the purchase of a convertible security—and the sale at or about the same time of the security obtainable through exercise of the rights or of the security obtainable through conversion. *See also* Convertible; Rights.

Assets. Everything a corporation owns or due to it: cash, investments, money due it, materials, and inventories, which are called current assets; buildings and machinery, which are known as fixed assets; and patents and good will, called intangible assets. *See also* Liabilities.

At the close order. A market order which is to be executed at or as near to the close as practicable.

At the opening or **At the opening only order.** A market or limited price order which is to be executed at the opening of the stock or not at all, and any such order or portion thereof not so executed treated as cancelled.

Averages. Various ways of measuring the trend of securities prices, the most popular of which is the Dow-Jones average of 30 industrial stocks listed on the New York Stock Exchange. Use of the term "average" has led to considerable confusion. A simple average for, say, 50 leading stocks would be obtained by totaling the prices of all and dividing by 50. But suppose one of the stocks in the average is split. The price of each share of that stock is then automatically reduced because more shares are outstanding. Thus the average would decline even if all other issues in the average were unchanged. That average thus becomes inaccurate as an indicator of the market's trend.

   Various formulas—some very elaborate—have been devised to compensate for stock splits and stock dividends and thus give continuity to the average. Averages and individual stock prices belong in separate compartments.

   In the case of the Dow-Jones industrial average, the prices of the 30 stocks are totaled and then divided by a divisor which is intended to compensate for past stock splits and dividends and which is changed from time to time. As a result, point changes in the average have only the vaguest relationship to dollar price changes in stocks included in the average. In November 1968, the divisor was 2.011, so that a one-point change in the industrial average at that time was actually the equivalent of 6.7 cents. *See also* NYSE Common Stock index; Point; Split.

Averaging. *See* Dollar cost averaging.

Balance sheet. A condensed statement showing the nature and amount of a company's assets, liabilities, and capital on a given date. In dollar amounts the balance sheet shows what the company owned, what it owed, and the ownership interest in the company of its stockholders. *See also* Assets; Earnings report.

Bear. Someone who believes the market will decline. *See also* Bull.

Bear market. A declining market. *See also* Bull market.

Bearer bond. A bond which does not have the owner's name registered on the books of the issuing company and which is payable to the holder. *See also* Coupon bond; Registered bond.

Bid and asked. Often referred to as a quotation or quote. The bid is the highest price anyone has declared that he wants to pay for a security at a given time; the asked is the lowest price anyone will take at the same time. *See also* Quotation.

Big Board. A popular term for the New York Stock Exchange.

Blue chip. Common stock in a company known nationally for the quality and wide acceptance of its products or services, and for its ability to make money and pay dividends. Usually such stocks are relatively high-priced and offer relatively low yields.

Blue sky laws. A popular name for laws various states have enacted to protect the public against securities frauds. The term is believed to have originated when a judge ruled that a particular stock had about the same value as a patch of blue sky.

Board room. A room for customers in a broker's office where opening, high, low, and last prices of leading stocks are posted on a board throughout the market day.

Boiler room. High-pressure peddling over the telephone of stocks of dubious value. A typical boiler room is simply a room lined with desks or cubicles, each with a salesman and telephone. The salesmen call what are known in the trade as sucker lists.

Bond. Basically an IOU or promissory note of a corporation, usually issued in multiples of $1,000, although $100 and $500 denominations are not uncommon. A bond is evidence of a debt on which the issuing company usually promises to pay the bondholders a specified amount of interest for a specified length of time, and to repay the loan on the expiration date. In every case a bond represents debt—its holder is a creditor of the corporation and not a part owner, as is the shareholder. *See also* Collateral trust bond; Convertible; General mortgage bond; Income bond.

Book. A notebook the specialist in a stock uses to keep a record of the buy and sell orders at specified prices, in sequence of receipt, which are left with him by other brokers. *See also* Specialist.

Book value. An accounting term. Book value of a stock is determined from a company's records, by adding all assets (generally excluding such intangibles as good will), then deducting all debts and other liabilities, plus the liquidation price of any preferred issues. The sum, arrived at is divided by the number of common shares outstanding and the result is book value per common share. Book value of the assets of a company or a security may have little or no significant relationship to market value.

Broker. An agent, often a member of a stock exchange firm or an exchange member himself, who handles the public's orders to buy and sell securities or commodities. For this service a commission is charged. *See also* Commission broker; Dealer.

Brokers' loans. Money borrowed by brokers from banks for a variety of uses. It may be used by specialists and odd-lot dealers to help finance inventories of stocks they deal in; by brokerage firms to finance the underwriting of new issues of corporate and municipal securities; to help finance a firm's own investments; and to help finance the purchase of securities for customers who prefer to use the broker's credit when they buy securities. *See also* Call loan; Customers' net debit balances; Margin.

Bucket shop. An illegal operation now almost extinct. The bucket shop operator accepted a client's money without ever actually buying or selling securities as the client ordered. Instead he held the money and gambled that the customer was wrong. When too many customers were right, the bucket shop closed its doors and opened a new office.

Bull. One who believes the market will rise. *See also* Bear.

Bull market. An advancing market. *See also* Bear market.

Call. *See* Puts and calls.

Call loan. A loan which may be terminated or "called" at any time by the lender or borrower. Used to finance purchases of securities. *See also* Brokers' loans.

Callable. A bond issue, all or part of which may be redeemed by the issuing corporation under definite conditions before maturity. The term also applies to preferred shares which may be redeemed by the issuing corporation.

Capital gain or capital loss. Profit or loss from the sale of a capital asset. A capital gain, under current Federal income tax laws, may be either short-term (6 months or less) or long-term (more than 6 months). A short-term capital gain is taxed at the reporting individual's full income tax rate. A long-term capital gain up to $50,000 ($25,000 in the case of a married individual filing a separate return) is normally taxed at a maximum of 25 percent, depending on the reporting individual's tax bracket. Up to $1,000 ($500 in the case of a married individual filing a separate return) of net capital loss (that is, when you sell securities at a lower price than you paid for them) is deductible from the individual's taxable income during the year reported. If the net capital loss is a long-term capital loss, a deduction is allowed for only one-half of the net capital loss up to the maximum amount of $1,000. If the net capital loss is more than $1,000 in any one year (or $2,000 if the net capital loss is a long-term capital loss), as much as $1,000 annually may be deducted in future years until the amount deductible as a loss has been utilized. The amount of the net capital loss which may be deducted in future years is reduced by the amount of capital gain in such years.

Capital stock. All shares representing ownership of a business, including preferred and common. *See also* Common stock; Preferred stock.

Capitalization. Total amount of the various securities issued by a corporation. Capitalization may include bonds, debentures, preferred and common stock, and surplus. Bonds and debentures are usually carried on the books of the issuing company in terms of their par or face value. Preferred and common shares may be carried in terms of par or stated value. Stated value may be an arbitrary figure decided upon by the directors or may represent the amount received by the company from the sale of the securities at the time of issuance. *See also* Par.

Cash flow. Reported net income of a corporation plus amounts charged off for depreciation, depletion, amortization, extraordinary charges to reserves, which are bookkeeping deductions and not paid out in actual dollars and cents. *See also* Amortization; Depletion; Depreciation.

Cash sale. A transaction on the floor of the Stock Exchange which calls for delivery of the securities the same day. In "regular way" trades, the seller is to deliver on the fifth business day. *See also* Regular way delivery.

Central Certificate Service (CCS). A department of Stock Clearing Corp. which conducts a central securities certificate operation through which clearing firms effect security deliveries between each other via computerized bookkeeping entries thereby reducing the physical movement of stock certificates. *See also* Stock Clearing Corp.

Certificate. The actual piece of paper which is evidence of ownership of stock in a corporation. Watermarked paper is finely engraved with delicate etchings to discourage forgery. Loss of a certificate may at the least cause a great deal of inconvenience—at the worst, financial loss.

Closed-end investment trust. *See* Investment trust.

Collateral. Securities or other property pledged by a borrower to secure repayment of a loan.

Collateral trust bond. A bond secured by collateral deposited with a trustee. The collateral is often the stocks or bonds of companies controlled by the issuing company but may be other securities.

Commission. The broker's basic fee for purchasing or selling securities or property as an agent. The New York Stock Exchange fixes minimum commission rates applicable to orders to purchase or sell NYSE listed stocks involving $500,000 or less. Commissions on portions of orders in excess of $500,000 are subject to negotiation.

Commission broker. An agent who executes the public's orders for the purchase or sale of securities or commodities. *See also* Broker; Dealer.

Common stock. Securities which represent an ownership interest in a corporation. If the company has also issued preferred stock, both common and preferred have ownership rights, but the preferred normally has prior claim on dividends and, in the event of liquidation, assets. Claims of both common and preferred stockholders are junior to claims of bondholders or other creditors of the company. Common stockholders assume the greater risk, but generally exercise the greater control and may gain the greater reward in the form of dividends and capital appreciation. The terms common stock and capital stock are often used interchangeably when the company has no preferred stock. *See also* Capital stock; Preferred stock.

Conglomerate. A corporation seeking to diversify its operations by acquiring enterprises in widely varied industries.

Consolidated balance sheet. A balance sheet showing the financial condition of a corporation and its subsidiaries. *See also* Balance sheet.

Convertible. A bond, debenture, or preferred share which may be exchanged by the owner for common stock or another security, usually of the same company, in accordance with the terms of the issue.

Corner. Buying of a stock or commodity on a scale large enough to give the buyer, or buying group, control over the price. A person who must buy that stock or commodity, for example one who is short, is forced to do business at an arbitrarily high price with those who obtained the corner. *See also* Short position; Short sale.

Correspondent. A securities firm, bank, or other financial organization which regularly performs services for another in a place or market to which the other does not have direct access. Securities firms may have correspondents in foreign countries or on exchanges of which they are not members. Correspondents are frequently linked by private wires. Member organizations of the NYSE with offices in New York City also act as correspondents for out-of-town member organizations which do not maintain New York City offices.

Coupon bond. Bond with interest coupons attached. The coupons are clipped as they come due and are presented by the holder for payment of interest. *See also* Bearer bond; Registered bond.

Covering. Buying a security previously sold short. *See also* Short sale; Short covering.

Cumulative preferred. A stock having a provision that if one or more dividends are omitted, the omitted dividends must be paid before dividends may be paid on the company's common stock.

Cumulative voting. A method of voting for corporate directors which enables the shareholder to multiply the number of his shares by the number of directorships being voted on and cast the total for one director or a selected group of directors. A ten-share holder normally casts ten votes for each of, say 12 nominees to the board of directors. He thus has 120 votes. Under the cumulative voting principle he may do that or he may cast 120 (10 x 12) votes for only one nominee, 60 for two, 40 for three, or any other distribution he chooses. Cumulative voting is required under the corporate laws of some states and permitted in most others.

Curb Exchange. Former name of the American Stock Exchange, second Largest exchange in the country. The term comes from the market's origin on a street in downtown New York.

Current assets. Those assets of a company which are reasonably expected to be realized in cash, sold, or consumed during the normal operating cycle of the business. These include cash, U.S. Government bonds, receivables and money due usually within one year, and inventories.

Current liabilities. Money owed and payable by a company, usually within one year.

Current return. *See* Yield.

Customers' man. *See* Registered Representative.

Customers' net debit balances. Credit of New York Stock Exchange member firms made available to help finance customers' purchases of stocks, bonds, and commodities.

Day order. An order to buy or sell, which if not executed expires at the end of the trading day on which it was entered.

Dealer. An individual or firm in the securities business acting as a principal rather than as an agent. Typically, a dealer buys for his own account and sells to a customer from his own inventory. The dealer's profit or loss is the difference between the price he pays and the price he receives for the same security. The dealer's confirmation must disclose to his customer that he has acted as principal. The same individual or firm may function, at different times, either as broker or dealer. *See also* NASD; Specialist.

Debenture. A promissory note backed by the general credit of a company and usually not secured by a mortgage or lien on any specific property. *See also* Bond.

Depletion. Natural resources, such as metals, oils and gas, and timber, which conceivably can be reduced to zero over the years, present a special problem in capital management. Depletion is an accounting practice consisting of charges against earnings based upon the amount of the asset taken out of the total reserves in the period for which accounting is made. A bookkeeping entry, it does not represent any cash outlay, nor are any funds earmarked for the purpose.

Depreciation. Normally, charges against earnings to write off the cost, less salvage value, of an asset over its estimated useful life. It is a bookkeeping entry and does not represent any cash outlay, nor are any funds earmarked for the purpose.

Director. Person elected by shareholders to establish company policies. The directors appoint the president, vice presidents, and all other operating officers. Directors decide, among other matters, if and when dividends shall be paid. *See also* Management; Proxy.

Discretionary account. An account in which the customer gives the broker or someone else discretion, which may be complete or within specific limits, as to the purchase and sales of securities or commodities, including selection, timing, amount, and price to be paid or received.

Discretionary order. The customer empowers the broker to act on his behalf with respect to the choice of security to be bought or sold, a total amount of any securities to be bought or sold, and/or whether any such transaction shall be one of purchase or sale.

Diversification. Spreading investments among different companies in different fields. Another type of diversification is also offered by the securities of many individual companies because of the wide range of their activities. *See also* Investment trust.

Dividend. The payment designated by the Board of Directors to be distributed pro rata among the shares outstanding. On preferred shares, it is generally a fixed amount. On common shares, the dividend varies with the fortunes of the company and the amount of cash on hand, and may be omitted if business is poor or the directors determine to withhold earnings to invest in plant and equipment. Sometimes a company will pay a dividend out of past earnings even if it is not currently operating at a profit.

Dollar cost averaging. A system of buying securities at regular intervals with a fixed dollar amount. Under this system the investor buys by the dollar's worth rather than by the number of shares. If each investment is of the same number of dollars, payments buy more when the price is low and fewer when it rises. Thus temporary downswings in price benefit the investor if he continues periodic purchases in both good times and bad and the price at which the shares are sold is more than their average cost. *See also* Formula investing.

Do not reduce (DNR) order. A limited order to buy, a stop order to sell, or a stop limit order to sell which is not to be reduced by the amount of an ordinary cash dividend on the ex-dividend date. A do not reduce order applies only to ordinary cash dividends; it is reduced for other distribution such as a stock dividend or rights.

Double taxation. Short for "double taxation of dividends." The federal government taxes corporate profits once as corporate income; any part of the remaining profits distributed as dividends to stockholders is taxed again as income to the recipient stockholder.

Dow Theory. A theory of market analysis based upon the performance of the Dow-Jones industrial and rail stock price averages. The Theory says that the market is in a basic upward trend if one of these averages advances above a previous important high, accompanied or followed by a similar advance in the other. When the averages both dip below previous important lows, this is regarded as confirmation of a basic downward trend. The Theory does not attempt to predict how long either trend will continue, although it is widely misinterpreted as a method of forecasting future action. Whatever the merits of the Theory, it is sometimes a strong factor in the market because many people believe in the Theory—or believe that a great many others do. *See also* Technical position.

Down tick. *See* Up tick.

Earnings report. A statement—also called an income statement—issued by a company showing its earnings or losses over a given period. The earnings report lists the income earned, expenses and the net result. *See also* Balance sheet.

Equipment trust certicicate. A type of security, generally issued by a railroad, to pay for new equipment. Title to the equipment, such as a locomotive, is held by a trustee until the notes are paid off. An equipment trust certificate is usually secured by a first claim on the equipment.

Equity. The ownership interest of common and preferred stockholders in a company. Also refers to excess of value of securities over the debit balance in a margin account.

Exchange acquisition. A method of filing an order to buy a large block of stock on the floor of the exchange. Under certain circumstances, a member-broker can facilitate the purchase of a block by soliciting orders to sell. All orders to sell the security are lumped together and crossed with the buy order in the regular auction market. The price to the buyer may be on a net basis or on a commission basis.

Exchange distribution. A method of disposing of large blocks of stock on the floor of the exchange. Under certain circumstances, a member-broker can facilitate the sale of a block of stock by soliciting and getting other member-brokers to solicit orders to buy. Individual buy orders are lumped together and crossed with the sell order in the regular auction market. A special commission is usually paid by the seller; ordinarily the buyer pays no commission.

Ex-dividend. A synonym for "without dividend." The buyer of a stock selling ex-dividend does not receive the recently declared dividend. Open buy and sell stop orders, and sell stop limit orders in a stock on the ex-dividend date, are ordinarily reduced by the value of that dividend. In the case of open stop limit orders to sell, both the stop price and the limit price are reduced. Every dividend is payable on a fixed date to all shareholders recorded on the books of the company as of a previous date or record. For example, a dividend may be declared as payable to holders of record on the books of the company on a given Friday. Since five business days are allowed for delivery of stock in a "regular way" transaction on the New York Stock Exchange, the Exchange would declare the stock "ex-dividend" as of the opening of the market on the preceding Monday. That means anyone who bought it on and after Monday would not be entitled to that dividend. *See also* Cash sale; Delivery; Net change; Transfer.

Ex-rights. Without the rights. Corporations raising additional money may do so by offering their stockholders the right to subscribe to new or additional stock, usually at a discount from the prevailing market price. The buyer of a stock selling ex-rights is not entitled to the rights. *See also* Ex-dividend; Rights.

Extra. The short form of "extra dividend." A dividend in the form of stock or cash in addition to the regular or usual dividend the company has been paying.

Face value. The value of a bond that appears on the face of the bond, unless the value is otherwise specified by the issuing company. Face value is ordinarily the amount the issuing company promises to pay at maturity. Face value is not an indication of market value. Sometimes referred to as par value. *See also* Par.

Fill or kill. A market or limited price order to be executed in its entirety as soon as it is represented in the Trading Crowd. If not so executed, the order is treated as cancelled. For purposes of this definition a "stop" (*See* Stopped stock) is considered an execution.

Fiscal year. A corporation's accounting year. Due to the nature of their particular business, some companies do not use the calendar year for their bookkeeping. A typical example is the department store which finds December 31 too early a date to close its books after the Christmas rush. For that reason many stores wind up their accounting year January 31. Their fiscal year, therefore, runs from February 1 of one year through January 31 of the next. The fiscal year of other companies may run from July 1 through the following June 30. Most companies, though, operate on a calendar year basis.

Fixed charges. A company's fixed expenses, such as bond interest, which it has agreed to pay whether or not earned, and which are deducted from income before earnings on equity capital are computed.

Flat. This term means that the price at which a bond is traded includes consideration for all unpaid accruals of interest. Bonds which are in default of interest or principal are traded flat. Income bonds, which pay interest only to the extent earned are usually traded flat. All other bonds are usually dealt in "and interest," which means that the buyer pays to the seller the market price plus interest accrued since the last payment date. When applied to a stock loan, flat means without premium or interest. *See also* Short sale.

Floor. The huge trading area—about two-thirds the size of a football field— where stocks and bonds are brought and sold on the New York Stock Exchange.

Floor broker. A member of the Stock Exchange who executes orders on the floor of the Exchange to buy or sell any listed securities. *See also* Commission broker; Two-dollar broker.

Floor trader. *See* Registered trader.

Fluctuation. *See* Point.

Formula investing. An investment technique. One formula calls for the shifting of funds from common shares to preferred shares or bonds as the market, on average, rises above a certain predetermined point—and the return of funds to common share investments as the market average declines. *See also* Dollar cost averaging.

Free and open market. A market in which supply and demand are expressed in terms of price. Contrasts with a controlled market in which supply, demand, and price may all be regulated.

Funded debt. Usually interest-bearing bonds or debentures of a company. Could include long-term bank loans. Does not include short-term loans, preferred or common stock.

General mortgage bond. A bond which is secured by a blanket mortgage on the company's property, but which is often outranked by one or more other mortgages.

Gilt-edged. High-grade bond issued by a company which has demonstrated its ability to earn a comfortable profit over a period of years and pay its bondholders their interest without interruption.

Give up. A term with many different meanings. For one, a member of the Exchange on the floor may act for a second member by executing an order for him with a third member. The first member tells the third member that he is acting on behalf of the second member and "gives up" the second member's name rather than his own. For another, if you have an account with Doe & Co. but you're in a town where Doe has no office, you go to another member firm, tell them you have an account with Doe & Co. and would like to buy some stock. After verifying your account with Doe & Co., the firm may execute your order and tell the broker who sells the stock that the firm is acting on behalf on Doe & Co. They give up the name of Doe & Co. to the selling broker. Or the firm may simply wire your order to Doe & Co. who will execute it for you. The term "give up" has also been applied to a variety of other arrangements, most of which are no longer permitted.

Good delivery. Certain basic qualifications must be met before a security sold on the Exchange may be delivered. The security must be in proper form to comply with the contract of sale and to transfer title to the purchaser.

Good 'Til Cancelled order (GTC) or open order. An order to buy or sell which remains in effect until it is either executed or cancelled.

Government bonds. Obligations of the U.S. Government, regarded as the highest grade issues in existence.

Growth stock. Stock of a company with prospects for future growth—a company whose earnings are expected to increase at a relatively rapid rate.

Guaranteed bond. A bond which has interest or principal, or both, guaranteed by a company other than the issuer. Usually found in the railroad industry when large roads, leasing sections of trackage owned by small railroads, may guarantee the bonds of the smaller road.

Guaranteed stock. Usually preferred stock on which dividends are guaranteed by another company; under much the same circumstances as a bond is guaranteed.

Hedge. *See* Arbitrage; Puts & calls; Selling against the box; Short sale.

Holding company. A corporation which owns the securities of another, in most cases with voting control.

Hypothecation. The pledging of securities as collateral for a loan.

Immediate or cancel order. A market or limited price order which is to be executed in whole or in part as soon as it is represented in the Trading Crowd, and the portion not so executed is to be treated as cancelled. For the purposes of this definition, a "stop" is considered an execution. *See also* Stopped stock.

Inactive post. A trading post on the floor of the New York Stock Exchange where inactive securities are traded in units of ten shares instead of the usual 100-share lots. Better known in the business as Post 30. *See also* Round lot.

Inactive stock. An issue traded on an exchange or in the over-the-counter market in which there is a relatively low volume of transactions. Volume may be no more than a few hundred shares a week or even less. On the New York Stock Exchange many inactive stocks are traded in ten-share units rather than the customary 100. *See also* Round lot.

In-and-out. Purchase and sale of the same security within a short period—a day, week, even a month. An in-and-out trader is generally more interested in day-to-day price fluctuations than dividends or long-term growth.

Income bond. Generally income bonds promise to repay principal but to pay interest only when earned. In some cases unpaid interest on an income bond may accumulate as a claim against the corporation when the bond becomes due. An income bond may also be issued in lieu of preferred stock.

Indenture. A written agreement under which debentures are issued, setting forth maturity date, interest rate, and other terms.

Index. A statistical yardstick expressed in terms of percentages of a base year or years. For instance, the Federal Reserve Board's index of industrial production is based on 1957–59 as 100. In January 1971 the index stood at 165.1, which meant that industrial production that month was about 65 percent higher than in the base period. An index is not an average. *See also* Averages; NYSE common stock index.

Interest. Payments a borrower pays a lender for the use of his money. A corporation pays interest on its bonds to its bondholders. *See also* Bond dividend.

Investment. The use of money for the purpose of making more money, to gain income or increase capital, or both. Safety of principal is an important consideration. *See also* Speculation.

Investment banker. Also known as an underwriter. He is the middleman between the corporation issuing new securities and the public. The usual practice is for one or more investment bankers to buy outright from a corporation a new issue of stocks or bonds. The group forms a syndicate to sell the securities to individuals and institutions. Investment bankers also distribute very large blocks of stocks or bonds—perhaps held by an estate. Thereafter the market in the security may be over-the-counter, on a regional stock exchange, the American Exchange, or the New York Stock Exchange. *See also* Over-the-counter; Primary distribution; Syndicate.

Investment counsel. One whose principal business consists of acting as investment adviser and a substantial part of his business consists of rendering investment supervisory services.

Investment trust. A company or trust which uses its capital to invest in other companies. There are two principal types: the closed-end and the open-end, or mutual funds. Shares in closed-end investment trusts, some of which are listed on the New York Stock Exchange, are readily transferable in the open market and are bought and sold like other shares. Capitalization of these companies remains the same unless action is taken to change, which is seldom. Open-end funds sell their own new shares to investors, stand ready to buy back their old shares, and are not listed. Open-end funds are so called because their capitalization is not fixed; they issue more shares as people want them.

Investor. An individual whose principal concerns in the purchase of a security are regular dividend income, safety of the original investment, and, if possible, capital appreciation. *See also* Speculator.

Issue. Any of a company's securities, or the act of distributing such securities.

Legal list. A list of investments selected by various states in which certain institutions and fiduciaries, such as insurance companies and banks, may invest. Legal lists are often restricted to high quality securities meeting certain specifications. *See also* Prudent man rule.

Leverage. The effect on the per-share earnings of the common stock of a company when large sums must be paid for bond interest or preferred stock dividends, or both, before the common stock is entitled to share in earnings. Leverage may be advantageous for the common when earnings are good but may work against the common stock when earnings decline. Example: Company A has 1,000,000 shares of common stock outstanding, no other securities. Earnings drop from $1,000,000 to $800,000 or from $1 to $.80 a share, a decline of 20 percent. Company B also has 1,000,000 shares of common but must pay $500,000 annually in bond interest. If earnings amount to $1,000,000, there is $500,000 available for the common or $.50 a share. But earnings drop to $800,000 so there is only $300,000 available for the common, or $.30 a share—a drop of 40 percent. Or suppose earnings of the company with only common stock increased from $1,000,000 to $1,5000,000—earnings per share would go from $1 to $1.50, or an increase of 50 percent. But if earnings of the company which had to pay $500,000 in bond interest increased that much—earnings per common share would jump from $.50 to $1 a share, or 100 percent. When a company has common stock only, no leverage exists because all earnings are available for the common, although relatively large fixed charges payable for lease of substantial plant assets may have an effect similar to that of a bond issue.

Liabilities. All the claims against a corporation. Liabilities include accounts and wages and salaries payable, dividends declared payable, accrued taxes payable, fixed or long-term liabilities such as mortgage bonds, debentures, and bank loans. *See also* Assets; Balance sheet.

Lien. A claim against property which has been pledged or mortgaged to secure the performance of an obligation. A bond is usually secured by a lien against specified property of a company. *See also* Bond.

Limit, limited order, or **limited price order.** An order to buy or sell a stated amount of a security at a specified price, or at a better price, if obtainable after the order is represented in the Trading Crowd.

Liquidation. The process of converting securities or other property into cash. The dissolution of a company, with cash remaining after sale of its assets and payment of all indebtedness being distributed to the shareholders.

Liquidity. The ability of the market in a particular security to absorb a reasonable amount of buying or selling at reasonable price changes. Liquidity is one of the most important characteristics of a good market.

Listed stock. The stock of a company which is traded on a securities exchange, and for which a listing application and a registration statement, giving detailed information about the company and its operations, have been filed with the Securities & Exchange Commission, unless otherwise exempted, and the exchange itself. The various stock exchanges have different standards for listing. Some of the guides used by the New York Stock Exchange for an original listing are national interest in the company, a minimum of 1-million shares outstanding with at least 800-thousand shares publicly held among not less than 2,000 shareholders including at least 1,800 round-lot stockholders. The publicly held common shares should have a minimum aggregate market value of $14-million. The company should have net income in the latest year of over $2.5-million before federal income tax and $2-million in each of the preceding two years.

Load. The portion of the offering price of shares of open-end investment companies which covers sales commissions and all other costs of distribution. The load is incurred only on purchase, there being, in most cases, no charge when the shares are sold (redeemed).

Locked in. An investor is said to be locked in when he has a profit on a security he owns but does not sell because his profit would immediately become subject to the capital gains tax. *See also* Capital gain.

Long. Signifies ownership of securities: "I am long 100 U. S. Steel" means the speaker owns 100 shares. *See also* Short position; Short sale.

Management. The Board of Directors, elected by the stockholders, and the officers of the corporation, appointed by the Board of Directors.

Manipulation. An illegal operation. Buying or selling a security for the purpose of creating false or misleading appearance of active trading or for the purpose of raising or depressing the price to induce purchase or sale by others.

Margin. The amount paid by the customer when he uses his broker's credit to buy a security. Under Federal Reserve regulations, the initial margin required in the past 20 years has ranged from 40 percent of the purchase price all the way to 100 percent. *See also* Brokers' loans; Equity; Margin call.

Margin call. A demand upon a customer to put up money or securities with the broker. The call is made when a purchase is made; also if a customer's equity in a margin account declines below a minimum standard set by the Exchange or by the firm. *See also* Margin.

Market order. An order to buy or sell a stated amount of a security at the most advantageous price obtainable after the order is represented in the Trading Crowd. *See also* Good 'til cancelled order; Limit order; Stop order.

Market price. In the case of a security, market price is usually considered the last reported price at which the stock or bond sold.

Matched and lost. When two bids to buy the same stock are made on the trading floor simultaneously, and each bid is equal to or larger than the amount of stock offered, both bids are considered to be on an equal basis. So the two bidders flip a coin to decide who buys the stock. Also applies to offers to sell.

Maturity. The date on which a loan or a bond or debenture comes due and is to be paid off.

Member corporation. A securities brokerage firm, organized as a corporation, with at least one member of the New York Stock Exchange, Inc. who is a director and a holder of voting stock in the corporation. *See also* Member firm.

Member firm. A securities brokerage firm organized as a partnership and having at least one general partner who is a member of the New York Stock Exchange. *See also* Member corporation.

Member organization. This term includes New York Stock Exchange Member Firm and Member Corporation. The term "participant" when used with reference to a Member Organization includes general and limited partners of a Member Firm and holders of voting and nonvoting stock in a Member corporation. *See also* Member corporation; Member firm.

MIP—Monthly Investment Plan. A pay-as-you-go method of buying New York Stock Exchange listed shares on a regular payment plan for as little as $40 a month, or $40 every three months. Under MIP the investor buys stock by the dollars' worth—if the price advances, he gets fewer shares and if it declines, he gets more shares. He may discontinue purchases at any time without penalty. The commission ranges from 6 percent on small transactions to slightly below 1½ percent on larger transactions. *See also* Dollar cost averaging; Odd-lot dealer.

Mortgage bond. A bond secured by a mortgage on a property. The value of the property may or may not equal the value of the so-called mortgage bonds issued against it. *See also* Bond; Debenture.

Municipal bond. A bond issued by a state or a political subdivision, such as county, city, town, or village. The term also designates bonds issued by state agencies and authorities. In general, interest paid on municipal bonds is exempt from federal income taxes.

Mutual fund. *See also* Investment trust.

NASD—The National Association of Securities Dealers, inc. An association of brokers and dealers in the over-the-counter securities business. The association has the power to expel members who have been declared guilty of unethical practices. NASD is dedicated to—among other objectives—"adopt, administer and enforce rules of fair practice and rules to prevent fraudulent and manipulative acts and practices, and in general to promote just and equitable principles of trade for the protection of investors."

Negotiable. Refers to a security, title to which is transferable by delivery. *See also* Delivery; Good delivery.

Net asset value. A term usually used in connection with investment trusts, meaning net asset value per share. It is common practice for an investment trust to compute its assets daily, or even twice daily, by totaling the market value of all securities owned. All liabilities are deducted, and the balance divided by the number of shares outstanding. The resulting figure is the net asset value per share. *See also* Assets; Investment trust.

Net change. The change in the price of a security from the closing price on one day and the closing price on the following day on which the stock is traded. In the case of a stock which is entitled to a dividend one day, but is traded "ex-dividend" the next, the dividend is considered in computing the change. For example, if the closing market price of a stock on Monday—the last day it was entitled to receive a $.50 dividend—was $45 a share, and $44.50 at the close of the next day, when it was "ex-dividend," the price would be considered unchanged. The same applies to a split-up of shares. A stock selling at $100 the day before a two-for-one split and trading the next day at $50 would be considered unchanged. If it sold at $51, it would be considered up $1. The net change is ordinarily the last figure in the stock price list. The mark +1⅛ means up $1.125 a share from the last sale on the previous day the stock traded. *See also* Ex-dividend; Point; Split.

New issue. A stock or bond sold by a corporation for the first time. Proceeds may be issued to retire outstanding securities of the company, for new plant or equipment, or for additional working capital.

Noncumulative. A preferred stock on which unpaid dividends do not accrue. Omitted dividends are, as a rule, gone forever. *See also* Cumulative preferred.

"Not held" order. A market or limited price order marked "not held," "disregard tape," "take time," or which bears any such qualifying notation. An order marked "or better" is not a "not held" order.

NYSE Common stock index. A composite index covering price movements of all common stocks listed on the "Big Board." It is based on the close of the market December 31, 1965 as 50.00 and is weighted according to the number of shares listed for each issue. The index is computed continuously by the Exchange's Market Data System and printed on the ticker tape each half hour. Point changes in the index are converted to dollars and cents so as to provide a meaningful measure of changes in the average price of listed stocks. The composite index is supplemented by separate indexes for four industry groups: industrials, transportation, utilities, and finances. *See also* Averages.

Odd-lot. An amount of stock less than the established 100-share unit or ten-share unit of trading: from one to 99 shares for the great majority of issues, one to nine for so-called inactive stocks. *See also* Round lot; Inactive stock.

Odd-lot dealer. A member firm of the Exchange which buys and sells odd lots of stocks—one to nine shares in the case of stocks traded in ten-share units and one to 99 shares for 100-share units. The odd-lot dealer's customers are commission brokers acting on behalf of their customers. There are one or more odd-lot dealers who, under current practices, are ready to buy or sell, for their own accounts, odd lots in any stock at any time. Odd-lot prices are geared to the auction market. On an odd-lot market order, the odd-lot dealer's price is based on the first round-lot transaction which occurs on the floor following receipt at the trading post of the odd-lot order. The usual differential between the odd-lot price and the "effective" round-lot price is 12½ cents a share for stock selling below $55, $.25 a share for stock at $55 or more. For example: You decide to buy 20 shares of ABC common at the market. Your order is transmitted by your commission broker to the representative of an odd-lot dealer at the post where ABC is traded. A few minutes later there is a 100-share transaction in ABC at $10 a share. The odd-lot price at which your order is immediately filled by the odd-lot dealer is $10.125 a share. If you had sold 20 shares of ABC, you would have received $9.875 a share. *See also* Commission broker; Dealer; Inactive stock; Round lot; Transfer tax.

Off-board. This term may refer to transactions over-the-counter in unlisted securities, or to a transaction involving listed shares which was not executed on a national securities exchange. *See also* Over-the-counter; Secondary distribution.

Offer. The price at which a person is ready to sell. Opposed to bid, the price at which one is ready to buy. *See also* Bid and asked.

Open-end investment trust. *See* Investment trust.

Open order. *See* Good 'til cancelled order.

Option. A right to buy or sell specific securities or properties at a specified price within a specified time. *See also* Puts and calls.

Orders good until a specified time. A market or limited price order which is to be represented in the Trading Crowd until a specified time, after which such order or the portion thereof not executed is to be treated as cancelled.

Overbought. An opinion as to price levels. May refer to a security which has had a sharp rise or to the market as a whole after a period of vigorous buying, which it may be argued, has left prices "too high." *See also* Technical position.

Oversold. An opinion—the reverse of overbought. A single security or a market which, it is believed, has declined to an unreasonable level. *See also* Technical position.

Over-the-counter. A market for securities made up of securities exchange. Over-the-counter is mainly a market made over the telephone. Thousands of companies have insufficient shares outstanding, stockholders, or earnings to warrant application for listing on the N.Y. Stock Exchange, Inc. Securities of these companies are traded in the over-the-counter market between dealers who act either as principals or as brokers for customers. The over-the-counter market is the principal market for U. S. Government bonds and municipals and stocks of banks and insurance companies. *See also* NASD; Off-board.

Paper profit. An unrealized profit on a security still held. Paper profits become realized profits only when the security is sold.

Par. In the case of a common share, par means a dollar amount assigned to the share by the company's charter. Par value may also be used to compute the dollar amount of the common shares on the balance sheet. Par value has little significance so far as market value of common stock is concerned. Many companies today issue no-par stock but give a stated per share value on the balance sheet. Par at one time was supposed to represent the value of the original investment behind each share in cash, goods, or services. In the case of preferred shares and bonds, however, par is important. It often signifies the dollar value upon which dividends on preferred stocks, and interest on bonds, are figured. The issuer of a 3 percent bond promises to pay that percentage of the bond's par value annually. *See also* Capitalization; Transfer tax.

Participating preferred. A preferred stock which is entitled to its stated dividend and, also, to additional dividends on a specified basis upon payment of dividends on the common stock.

Passed dividend. Omission of a regular or scheduled dividend.

Penny stocks. Low-priced issues often highly speculative, selling at less than $1 a share. Frequently used as a term of disparagement, although a few penny stocks have developed into investment-caliber issues.

Percentage order. A market or limited price order to buy (or sell) a stated amount of a specified stock after a fixed number of shares of such stock have traded.

Point. In the case of shares of stock, a point means $1. If General Motors shares rise three points, each share has risen $3. In the case of bonds a point means $10, since a bond is quoted as a percentage of $1,000. A bond which rises three points gains 3 percent of $1,000, or $30 in value. An advance from 87 to 90 would mean an advance in dollar value from $870 to $900 for each

$1,000 bond. In the case of market averages, the word point means merely that and no more. If, for example, the Dow-Jones industrial average rises from 470.25 to 471.25, it has risen a point. A point in this average, however, is not equivalent to $1. *See also* Averages.

Portfolio. Holdings of securities by an individual or institution. A portfolio may contain bonds, preferred stocks, and common stocks of various types of enterprises.

Preferred stock. A class of stock with a claim on the company's earnings before payment may be made on the common stock and usually entitled to priority over common stock if company liquidates. Usually entitled to dividends at a specified rate—when declared by the Board of Directors and before payment of a dividend on the common stock—depending upon the terms of the issue. *See also* Cumulative preferred; participating preferred.

Premium. The amount by which a preferred stock or bond may sell above its par value. In the case of a new issue of bonds or stocks, premium is the amount the market price rises over the original selling price. Also refers to a charge sometimes made when a stock is borrowed to make delivery on a short sale. May refer, also, to redemption price of a bond or preferred stock if it is higher than face value. *See also* Corner; Short sale.

Price-earnings ratio. The current market price of a share of stock divided by earnings per share for a twelve-month period. For example, a stock selling for $100 a share and earnings $5 a share is said to be selling at a price-earnings ratio of 20 to 1.

Primary distribution. Also called primary offering. The original sale of a company's securities. *See also* Investment banker; Secondary distribution.

Principal. The person for whom a broker executes an order, or a dealer buying or selling for his own account. The term "principal" may also refer to a person's capital or to the face amount of a bond.

Proxy. Written authorization given by a shareholder to someone else to represent him and vote his shares at a shareholder' meeting.

Proxy statement. Information required by SEC to be given stockholders as a prerequisite to solicitation of proxies for a security subject to the requirements of Securities Exchange Act.

Prudent man rule. An investment standard. In some states, the law requires that a fiduciary, such as a trustee, may invest the fund's money only in a list of securities designated by the state—the so-called legal list. In other states, the trustee may invest in a security if it is one which a prudent man of discretion and intelligence, who is seeking a reasonable income and preservation of capital, would buy.

Puts and calls. Options which give the right to buy or sell a fixed amount of a certain stock at a specified price within a specified time. A put gives the holder the right to sell the stock; a call the right to buy the stock. Puts are purchased by those who think a stock may go down. A put obligates the seller of the contract to take delivery of the stock and pay the specified price to the owner of the option within the time limit of the contract. The price specified in a put or call is usually close to the market price of the stock at the time the contract is made. Calls are purchased by those who think a stock may rise. A call gives the holder the right to buy the stock from the seller of the contract at the specified price within a fixed period of time. Put and call contracts are written for 30, 60, or 90 days, or longer. If the purchaser of a put or call does not wish to exercise the option, the price he paid for the option becomes a loss.

Quotation. Often shortened to "quote." The highest bid to buy and the lowest offer to sell a security in a given market at a given time. If you ask your broker for a "quote" on a stock, he may come back with something like "45¼ to 45½." This means that $45.25 is the highest price any buyer wanted to pay at the time the quote was given on the floor of the Exchange and that $45.50 was the lowest price which any seller would take at the same time. *See also* Bid and asked.

Rally. A brisk rise following a decline in the general price level of the market, or in an individual stock.

Ratio of collateral to debt. The number of times total stock margin debt is covered by total collateral value: $\dfrac{\text{Collateral Value}}{\text{Stock Margin Debt}} = \text{Ratio}$

Realizing. *See* Profit taking.

Record date. The date on which you must be registered as a shareholder on the stock book of a company in order to receive a declared dividend or, among other things, to vote on company affairs. *See also* Delivery; Ex-dividend; Transfer.

Redemption price. The price at which a bond may be redeemed before maturity, at the option of the issuing company. Redemption value also applies to the price the company must pay to call in certain types of preferred stock. *See also* Callable.

Refinancing. Same as refunding. New securities are sold by a company and the money issued to retire existing securities. Object may be to save interest costs, extend the maturity of the loan, or both.

Registered bond. A bond which is registered on the books of the issuing company in the name of the owner. It can be transferred only when endorsed by the registered owner. *See also* Bearer bond; Coupon bond.

Registered representative. Present name for the older term "customers' man." In a New York Stock Exchange Member Firm, a Registered Representative is a full time employee who has met the requirements of the Exchange as to background and knowledge of the securities business. Also known as an Account Executive or Customer's Broker.

Registered trader. A member of the Exchange who trades in stocks on the Floor for an account in which he has an interest.

Registrar. Usually a trust company or bank charged with the responsibility of preventing the issuance of more stock than authorized by a company. *See also* Transfer.

Registration. Before a public offering may be made of new securities by a company, or of outstanding securities by controlling stockholders—through the mails or in interstate commerce—the securities must be registered under the

Securities Act of 1933. Registration statement is filed with the SEC by the issuer. It must disclose pertinent information relating to the company's operations, securities, management, and purpose of the public offering. Securities of railroads under jurisdiction of the Interstate Commerce Commission, and certain other types of securities, are exempted. On security offerings involving less than $300,000, less information is required.

Before a security may be admitted to dealings on a national securities exchange, it must be registered under the Securities Exchange Act of 1934. The application for registration must be filed with the exchange and the SEC by the company issuing the securities. It must disclose pertinent information relating to the company's operations, securities, and management. Registration may become effective 30 days after receipt by the SEC of the certification by the exchange of approval of listing and registration, or sooner by special order of the Commission.

Regulation t. The federal regulation governing the amount of credit which may be advanced by brokers and dealers to customers for the purchase of securities. *See also* Margin.

Regulation u. The federal regulation governing the amount of credit which may be advanced by a bank to its customers for the purchase of listed stocks.

Return. *See* Yield.

Rights. When a company wants to raise more funds by issuing additional securities, it may give its stockholders the opportunity, ahead of others, to buy the new securities in proportion to the number of shares each owns. The piece of paper evidencing this privilege is called a right. Because the additional stock is usually offered to stockholders below the current market price, rights ordinarily have a market value of their own and are actively traded. In most cases they must be exercised within a relatively short period. Failure to exercise or sell rights may result in actual loss to the holder. *See also* Warrant.

Round lot. A unit of trading or a multiple thereof. On the NYSE the unit of trading is generally 100 shares in stocks and $1,000 par value in the case of bonds. In some inactive stocks, the unit of trading is ten shares.

Scale order. An order to buy (or sell) a security which specifies the total amount to be bought (or sold) and the amount to be bought (or sold) at specified price variations.

Seat. A traditional figure-of-speech for a membership on an exchange. Price and admission requirements vary.

SEC. The Securities and Exchange Commission, established by Congress to help protect investors. The SEC administers the Securities Act of 1933, the Securities Exchange Act of 1934, the Trust Indenture Act, the Investment Company Act, the Investment Advisers Act, and the Public Utility Holding Company Act.

Secondary distribution. Also known as a secondary offering. The redistribution of a block of stock some time after it has been sold by the issuing company. The sale is handled off the NYSE by a securities firm or group of firms and the shares are usually offered at a fixed price which is related to the current market price of the stock. Usually the block is a large one, such as might be involved in the settlement of an estate. The security may be listed or unlisted.

See also Exchange distribution; Investment banker; Primary distribution; Special offering; Syndicate.

Seller's option. A special transaction on NYSE which gives the seller the right to deliver the stock or bond at any time within a specified period, ranging from not less than six business days to not more than 60 days. *See also* Delivery.

Serial bond. An issue which matures in relatively small amounts at periodic stated intervals.

Service charge. In April 1970 an interim service charge was imposed on orders of 1,000 shares or less, pending establishment of a new commission rate schedule. The charge—not less than $15.00 or 50% of the minimum commission applicable to the order, whichever is less—was initially to remain in effect for 90 days. In July 1970, the service charge was extended for an indefinite period. It has been generally assumed that it will terminate with the adoption of a new commission schedule.

Short covering. Buying stock to return stock previously borrowed to make delivery on a short sale.

Short position. Stocks sold short and not covered as of a particular date. On the NYSE, a tabulation is issued once a month listing all issues on the Exchange in which there was a short position of 5,000 or more shares and issues in which the short position had changed by 2,000 or more shares in the preceding month. Short position also means the total amount of stock an individual has sold short and has not covered, as of a particular date. *See also* Margin; Up tick; Short sale.

Short sale. A person who believes a stock will decline and sells it though he does not own any has made a short sale. For instance: You instruct your broker to sell short 100 shares of ABC. Your broker borrows the stock so he can deliver the 100 shares to the buyer. The money value of the shares borrowed is deposited by your broker with the lender. Sooner or later you must cover your short sale by buying the same amount of stock you borrowed for return to the lender. If you are able to buy ABC at a lower price than you sold it for, your profit is the difference between the two prices—not counting commissions and taxes. But if you have paid more for the stock than the price you received, that is the amount of your loss. Stock exchange and federal regulations govern and limit the conditions under which a short sale may be made on a national securities exchange. Sometimes a person will sell short a stock he already owns in order to protect a paper profit. This is known as selling against the box. *See also* Margin; Premium; Up tick.

Sinking fund. Money regularly set aside by a company to redeem its bonds, debentures, or preferred stock from time to time as specified in the indenture or charter.

Special bid. A method of filling an order to buy a large block of stock on the floor of the New York Stock Exchange. In a special bid, the bidder for the block of stock—a pension fund, for instance, will pay a special commission to the broker who represents him in making the purchase. The seller does not pay a commission. The special bid is made on the floor of the Exchange at a fixed price which may not be below the last sale of the security or the current bid in the regular market, whichever is higher. Member firms may sell this stock for customers directly to the buyer's broker during trading hours.

Special offering. Occasionally a large block of stock becomes available for sale which, due to its size and the market in that particular issue, calls for special handling. A notice is printed on the ticker tape announcing that the stock will be offered for sale on the NYSE floor at a fixed price. Member firms may buy this stock for customers directly from the seller's broker during trading hours. The price is usually based on the last transaction in the regular auction market. If there are more buyers than stock, allotments are made. Only the seller pays a commission on a special offering. *See also* Secondary distribution.

Specialist. A member of the New York Stock Exchange who has two functions: First, to maintain an orderly market, insofar as reasonably practicable, in the stocks in which he is registered as a specialist. In order to maintain an orderly market, the Exchange expects the specialist to buy or sell for his own account, to a reasonable degree, when there is a temporary disparity between supply and demand. Second, the specialist acts as a broker's broker. When a commission broker on the Exchange floor receives a limit order, say, to buy a $50 stock then selling at $60—he cannot wait at the post where the stock is traded until the price reaches the specified level. So he leaves the order with the specialist, who will try to execute it in the market if and when the stock declines to the specified price. At all times the specialist must put his customers' interests above his own. There are about 350 specialists on the NYSE. *See also* Book; Limited order.

Specialist block purchase. Purchase by a specialist for his own account of a large block of stock outside the regular Exchange market. Such purchases may be made only when the sale of the block could not be made in the regular market within a reasonable time and at reasonable prices, and when the purchase by the specialist would aid him in maintaining a fair and orderly market. The specialist need not fill the orders on his book down to the purchase price.

Specialist block sale. Opposite of the specialist block purchase. Under exceptional circumstances, the specialist may sell a block of stock outside the regular market on the Exchange for his own account at a price above the prevailing market. The price is negotiated between the specialist and the broker for the buyer. The specialist need not fill the orders on his book down to the purchase price.

Speculation. The employment of funds by a speculator. Safety of principal is a secondary factor. *See also* Investment.

Speculator. One who is willing to assume a relatively large risk in the hope of gain. His principal concern is to increase his capital rather than his dividend income. The speculator may buy and sell the same day or speculate in an enterprise which he does not expect to be profitable for years. *See also* Investor.

Split. The division of the outstanding shares of a corporation into a larger number of shares. A three-for-one split by a company with one million shares outstanding results in three million shares outstanding. Each holder of 100 shares before the three-for-one split would have 300 shares, although his proportionate equity in the company would remain the same; 100 parts of one million are the equivalent of 300 parts of three million. Ordinarily splits must be voted by directors and approved by shareholders. *See also* Stock dividends.

Stock ahead. Sometimes an investor who has entered on order to buy or sell a stock at a certain price will see transactions at that price reported on the ticker tape while his own order has not been executed. The reason is that other buy and sell orders at the same price came in to the specialist ahead of his and had priority. *See also* Book; Specialist.

Stock clearing corporation. A subsidiary of the New York Stock Exchange, Inc. which acts as a central agency for clearing firms in providing a "clearance operation" through which transactions made on the floor are confirmed and balanced and, also, a "settlement operation" which handles the physical delivery of securities and money payments. *See also* Central Certificate Service.

Stock dividend. A dividend paid in securities rather than cash. The dividend may be additional shares of the issuing company, or in shares of another company (usually a subsidiary) held by the company. *See also* Ex-Dividend; Split.

Stockholder of record. A stockholder whose name is registered on the books of the issuing corporation. *See also* Record date; Ex-dividend; Ex-rights.

Stop limit order. A stop limit order to buy becomes a limit order executable at the limit price, or at a better price, if obtainable, when a transaction in the security occurs at or above the stop price after the order is represented in the Trading Crowd. A stop limit order to sell becomes a limit order executable at the limit price or at a better price, if obtainable, when a transaction in the security occurs at or below the stop price after the order is represented in the Trading Crowd.

Stop order. A stop order to buy becomes a market order when a transaction in the security occurs at or above the stop price after the order is represented in the Trading Crowd. A stop order may be used in an effort to protect a paper profit, or to try to limit a possible loss to a certain amount. A stop order to sell becomes a market order when a transaction in the security occurs at or below the stop price after the order is represented in the Trading Crowd. Since it becomes a market order when the stop price is reached, there is no certainty that it will be executed at that price. *See also* Limited order; Market order.

Stopped stock. A service performed—in most cases by the specialist—for an order given him by a commission broker. Let's say XYZ just sold at $50 a share. Broker A comes along with an order to buy 100 shares at the market. The lowest offer is $50.50. Broker A believes he can do better for his client than $50.50, perhaps might get the stock at $50.25. But he does not want to take a chance that he will miss the market—that is, the next sale might be $50.50 and the following one even higher. So he asks the specialist if he will stop 100 at ½ ($50.50). The specialist agrees. The specialist guarantees Broker A he will get 100 shares at 50½ if the stock sells at that price. In the meantime, if the specialist or Broker A succeeds in executing the order at $50.25, the stop is called off. *See also* Specialist.

Street. The New York financial community in the Wall Street area.

Street name. Securities held in the name of a broker instead of his customer's name are said to be carried in a "street name." This occurs when the securities have been bought on margin or when the customer wishes the security to be held by the broker.

Switch order—contingent order. An order for the purchase (sale) of one stock and the sale (purchase) of another stock at a stipulated price difference.

Switching. Selling one security and buying another.

Syndicate. A group of investment bankers who together underwrite and distribute a new issue of securities or a large block of an outstanding issue. *See also* Investment banker.

Tax-exempt bonds. The securities of states, cities, and other public authorities specified under federal law, the interest on which is either wholly or partly exempt from federal income taxes.

Technical position. A term applied to the various internal factors affecting the market; opposed to external forces such as earnings, dividends, political considerations, and general economic conditions. Some internal factors considered in appraising the market's technical position include the size of the short interest, whether the market has had a sustained advance or decline without interruption, a sharp advance or decline on small volume and the amount of credit in use in the market. *See also* Overbought; Oversold.

Thin market. A market in which there are comparatively few bids to buy or offers to sell or both. The phrase may apply to a single security or to the entire stock market. In a thin market, price fluctuations between transactions are usually larger than when the market is liquid. A thin market in a particular stock may reflect lack of interest in that issue or a limited supply of or demand for stock in the market. *See also* Bid and asked; Liquidity; Offer.

Ticker. The instrument which prints prices and volume of security transactions in cities and towns throughout the U.S. and Canada within minutes after each trade on the floor.

Time order. An order which becomes a market or limited price order at a specified time.

Tips. Supposedly "inside" information on corporation affairs.

Trader. One who buys and sells for his own account for short-term profit. *See also* Investor; Speculator.

Trading floor. *See* Floor.

Trading post. One of 18 horsehoe-shaped trading locations on the floor of the New York Stock Exchange at which stocks assigned to that location are bought and sold. About 75 stocks are traded at each post. *See also* Inactive post.

Transfer. This term may refer to two different operations. For one, the delivery of a stock certificate from the seller's broker to the buyer's broker and legal change of ownership, normally accomplished within a few days. For another, to record the change of ownership on the books of the company, dividends, notices of meetings, proxies, financial reports, and all pertinent literature sent by the issuer to its securities holders are mailed direçt to the new owner. *See also* Delivery; Registrar; Street name.

Transfer agent. A transfer agent keeps a record of the name of each registered shareowner, his or her address, the number of shares owned, and sees that certificates presented to his office for transfer are properly cancelled and new certificates issued in the name of the transferee. *See also* Delivery; Registrar; Transfer.

Transfer tax. A tax imposed by New York State when a security is sold or transferred from one person to another. The tax is paid by the seller. On sales by New York State residents, it ranges from $.125 a share to 5 cents a share sold for $20 or more. Sales by out-of-state residents not employed in New York are taxed at reduced rates. There is no tax on transfers of bonds.

Treasury stock. Stock issued by a company but later reacquired. It may be held in the company's treasury indefinitely, reissued to the public, or retired. Treasury stock receives no dividends and has no vote while held by the company.

Turnover. The volume of business in a security or the entire market. If turnover on the NYSE is reported at ten million shares on a particular day, 10,000,000 shares changed hands. Odd-lot turnover is tabulated separately and ordinarily is not included in reported volume.

Two-dollar broker. Members on the floor of the NYSE who execute orders for other brokers having more business at that time than they can handle themselves, or for firms who do not have their Exchange member-partner on the floor. The term derives from the time when these independent brokers received $2 per hundred shares for executing such orders. The fee is paid by the broker and today it varies with the price of the stock. *See also* Commission broker.

Underwriter. *See* Investment banker.

Unlisted. A security not listed on a stock exchange. *See also* Over-the-counter.

Unlisted trading privileges. On some exchanges a stock may be traded at the request of a member without any prior application by the company itself. The company has no agreement to conform with standards of the exchange. Today admission of a stock to unlisted trading privileges requires SEC approval of an application filed by the Exchange. The information in the application must be made available by the exchange to the public. No unlisted stocks are traded on the New York Stock Exchange. *See also* Listed stock.

Up tick. A term used to designate a transaction made at a price higher than the preceding transaction. Also called a "plus-tick." A stock may be sold short only on an up tick, or on a "zero-plus" tick. A "zero-plus" tick is a term used for a transaction at the same price as the preceding trade but higher than the preceding different price. Conversely, a down tick, or "minus" tick, is a term used to designate a transaction made at a price lower than the preceding trade. A "zero-minus" tick is a transaction made at the same price as the preceding sale but lower than the preceding different price. A plus sign, or a minus sign, is displayed throughout the day next to the last price of each company's stock traded at each trading post on the floor of the New York Stock Exchange. *See also* Short sale.

Voting right. The stockholder's right to vote his stock in the affairs of his company. Most common shares have one vote each. Preferred stock usually has the right to vote when preferred dividends are in default for a specified period. *See also* Cumulative voting, Proxy.

Warrant. A certificate giving the holder the right to purchase securities at a stipulated price within a specified time limit or perpetually. Sometimes a warrant is offered with securities as an inducement to buy. *See also* Rights.

When issued. A short form of "when, as and if issued." The term indicates a conditional transaction in a security authorized for issuance but not as yet actually issued. All "when issued" transactions are on an "if" basis, to be settled if and when the actual security is issued and the Exchange or National Association of Securities Dealers rules the transactions are to be settled.

Wire house. A member firm of an exchange maintaining a communications network linking either its own branch offices, offices of correspondent firms, or a combination of such offices.

Working control. Theoretically ownership of 51 percent of a company's voting stock is necessary to exercise control. In practice—and this is particularly true in the case of a large corporation—effective control sometimes can be exerted through ownership, individually or by a group acting in concert, of less than 50 percent.

Yield. Also known as return. The dividends or interest paid by a company expressed as a percentage of the current price—or, if you own the security, of the price you originally paid. The return on a stock is figured by dividing the total of dividends paid in the preceding 12 months by the current market price—or, if you are the owner, the price you originally paid. A stock with a current market value of $40 a share which has paid $2 in dividends in the preceding 12 months is said to return 5 percent ($2.00 ÷ $40.00). If you paid $20 for the stock five years earlier, the stock would be returning you 10 percent on your original investment. The current return on a bond is figured the same way. A 3 percent $1,000 bond selling at $600 offers a return of 5 percent ($30 ÷ $600). Figuring the yield of a bond to maturity calls for a bond yield table. *See also* Dividend; Interest.

Selected Financial Statistics

NOTES TO CHARTS

On the charts an asterisk (*) has been used universally and exclusively to denote a "change in series." (No explanation of the asterisk appears on the face of the chart, but a description of the change in series is included in the notes to that chart.)

310-311 Excess Reserves and Borrowings of All Member Banks Borrowings do not include foreign loans on gold.

312 Loans and Investments of Member Banks, by Class of Bank Comparability of figures by class of bank have been affected somewhat over the years by the following:

1. Changes, in reserve classification of cities or individual banks, such as (a) the redesignation of reserve cities from time to time and (b) reclassification of nine central reserve city banks in New York City as reserve city banks on Oct. 6, 1949, of ten reserve city banks as country banks on Mar. 1, 1954, and 33 reserve city banks as country banks on Feb. 11, 1960.

2. Effective July 28, 1962, central reserve city banks in New York City and in the city of Chicago became reserve city banks, at which time three reserve city banks in each of these cities were added to the "city series," and other reserve city banks were reduced accordingly; in June 1963, three reserve city banks in New York City were reclassified as country banks; in May 1964, one large country bank in New York was reclassified as a reserve city bank.

313 Long- and Short-Term Interest Rates High-grade railroad bonds, annual averages compiled by Standard and Poor's Corporation through 1932; high-grade corporate, annual averages for selected bonds of all types of corporations rated AAA by Standard and Poor's. Basic yields, estimates for the highest grade corporate bonds of 30-year maturity in the first quarter of the year (Feb. since 1959) as compiled by the National Bureau of Economic Research, Inc., 1900–1958, and since 1959 by Scudder, Stevens, and Clark. See notes for pages 316–317 for commercial paper.

314–315 Yields on U.S. Government Securities Securities are classified according to maturity or first call date. Long-term bonds include bonds due or callable after eight years, Jan. 1919–Oct. 1925; after 12 years, Nov. 1925–Dec. 1934; after 15 years, Jan. 1935–Mar. 1952; after 12 years, Apr. 1952–Mar. 1953; and in ten years or more beginning with Apr. 1953. Yields on bills are those for new issues through 1940; thereafter yields are computed on a bank discount basis shown as market yield. Bills included are three-month issues except Mar. 1934–Dec. 1937, when issues were somewhat longer term.

316–317 Short-Term Interest Rates From Oct. 30, 1942, to Apr. 24, 1946, the discount rate shown is the preferential rate on advances secured by Government securities maturing or callable within one year. Rates for commercial paper and bankers' acceptances for the years 1919–1934 are averages of weekly prevailing rates; beginning with 1935, of daily prevailing rates. See notes for pages 314–315 for Treasury bills.

318–319 Bank Rates on Short-Term Business Loans Rates represent: 1919–1927, averages of prevailing rates on commercial loans and time and demand security loans reported monthly by banks in a varying number of cities; Jan. 1928–Feb. 1939, averages of prevailing rates on commercial loans only, as reported monthly by banks in 19 cities; 1939–1966, averages of rates charged on commercial loans maturing within one year made by banks in 19 cities during the first half of Mar., June, Sept., and Dec. beginning with 1967, averages on rates charged by banks in 35 centers on commercial loans made in the first half of Feb., May, Aug., and Nov.

320–321 Bond Yields Monthly averages are based on daily figures except for high-grade municipal and for state and local government Aaa bonds, which are based on Wednesday and Thursday figures, respectively. See notes for pages 314–315 for U.S. Government bonds.

322-323 Stock Market Stock prices since 1957 are monthly averages of daily figures for 425 industrials, 25 railroads, and 50 public utilities; data for earlier years are monthly averages of daily indexes for 90 stocks that have been converted by Standard and Poor's Corporation to a 1941-1943 base. Daily average volume of trading (N.Y. Stock Exchange) is on the basis of a 5½-hour trading day; data before Sept. 29, 1952, when trading was on a 5-hour trading-day basis, have been adjusted to this basis. Stock market credit (discontinued after June 1970) is the sum of (1) customers' debit balances with member firms of the N.Y. Stock Exchange (excluding debt collateralized by U.S. Government securities) and (2) bank loans to others than brokers and dealers for purchasing securities. The latter are as reported by weekly reporting member banks (series revised July 1946, July 1959, and June 1966) and are as of the last Wednesday of the month. All loans secured by U.S. Government securities are excluded through Feb. 1953; for Mar. 1953-July 1959, only loans thus secured at New York and Chicago banks are excluded; thereafter, such loans are excluded at all banks. The level of the series is also affected by changes in the banks included and by loan reclassification in Sept. 1961. Customer credit consists of customers' debit balances (discontinued after June 1970) and bank loans to others as defined above. See also note for page 325.

Brokers' loans quarterly through 1932; call dates 1933-1938; monthly thereafter.

324 Brokers' Loans by Group of Lender Series represents principal groups of lenders. The loans cover primarily loans to brokers and dealers in securities in New York City, most of whom are members of the N.Y. Stock Exchange, but loans to certain investment banking houses that do not have Stock Exchange seats, as well as loans to brokers and dealers belonging to other stock exchanges, are also classified as brokers' loans in the figures reported by banks.

325 Stock Market Credit Figures for Nov. 1931-Aug. 1935 are estimates based on data collected by the N.Y. Stock Exchange; for Sept. 1935-July 1942 and for June and Dec. through 1944, data are those collected by the Federal Reserve. Figures for months other than June and Dec. and for Aug. 1942-Feb. 1945 are Federal Reserve estimates based on reports from a small number of large firms. Beginning with Mar. 1945, data are as reported to the N.Y. Stock Exchange, and money borrowed and customers' debit balances (discontinued after June 1970) exclude amounts secured by U.S. Government securities (included in earlier figures). Beginning with June 1955, figures for money borrowed are for the last Wednesday of the month; data for this series are not available after Feb. 1966.

326 Stock Yields Common stocks: Through 1936, earnings/price and dividend/price ratios are Cowles Commission series. For series beginning with 1936, dividend/price ratio is an annual average of monthly yields for the Standard and Poor's Corporation's 500 stock index (90 stocks before 1957); and earnings/price ratio is an annual average of quarterly data for the same stocks, based on seasonally adjusted quarterly earnings at annual rates and end-of-quarter prices.

Preferred stocks: Yields are annual averages of Standard and Poor's monthly figures.

327 Sales and Redemptions of U.S. Savings Bonds at Issue Price Matured bonds that have been redeemed are included in redemptions. Series E and H are the only savings bonds currently being sold. Sales of series F, G, J, and K bonds (discontinued May 1, 1957) include sale of special offerings in 1948 and 1950. Redemptions of F and G bonds include exchanges for Treasury marketable securities as follows (millions of dollars): 1953, $409; 1959, $692; 1960, $145; 1961, $320; and 1962, $75.

Source: Treasury Dept.

328 Cash Income and Outgo of the U.S. Treasury Data represent two concepts used in measuring Federal receipts and expenditures. The consolidated cash budget, shown here for fiscal years 1940 through 1961, was discontinued in Jan. 1968. At that time, the new unfiled budget, presented in *The Budget of the U.S. Government, Fiscal Year 1969,* replaced the earlier administrative and cash budgets as measures of Federal fiscal operations. Data for cash budget series are from Historical Tables in *The Budget of the U.S. Government, Fiscal Year 1968;* and for new budget series, from Historical Tables in *The Budget of the U.S. Government, Fiscal Year 1971,* and from monthly Treasury statement. Data are plotted at mid-point of fiscal year—for example, fiscal 1960 is plotted at Dec. 31, 1959.

329 State and Local Government Security Issues Data represent principal amounts from sales of long-term securities offered by states, territories, and insular possessions of the United States and their subdivisions, including special districts and local housing authorities. Sales to other state and local government units or to U.S. Government agencies are included. Data for 1956 and earlier years are not strictly comparable with current data. Data beginning with July 1956 from Investment Bankers Association; earlier data from *Bond Buyer.*

330-332 Corporate Security Issues (Securities and Exchange Commission Series) Total includes issues for retirement of securities as well as new capital. Issues for new money are those for plant and equipment and working capital; issues for other purposes are those for repayment of other than security debt and for miscellaneous other purposes. Detailed data for corporate security issues not available after 1967. Types of issues based on gross proceeds, which include flotation costs. All other series based on net proceeds to issuer. For 1934–1947, electric, gas, and water utilities include communication (shown separately thereafter) and "other" transportation (included in transportation thereafter). For 1934–1947, manufacturing includes commercial and miscellaneous, not shown separately thereafter but included in totals.

333 Corporate Profits, Taxes, and Dividends Profits are before allowance for the inventory valuation adjustment. Profits and dividends exclude intercorporate dividends.

Source: Dept. of Commerce.

334 Corporate Profits after Taxes, by Major Industry "All other" includes agriculture, forestry, and fisheries; mining; contract construction; finance, insurance, and real estate; services; and an adjustment to cover receipts in this country of profits earned abroad.

Source: Dept. of Commerce.

335 Total Real Estate Mortgage Debt Outstanding Figures based on data from a variety of sources; estimated when reported data are not available. Financial institutions include commercial banks (including nondeposit trust companies but not trust departments), mutual savings banks, life insurance companies, and savings and loan associations.

336-337   Nonfarm Mortgage Debt Outstanding and/or Holdings Debt estimated by FHLBB (for one- to four-family properties) and by FRB on basis of data from a variety of sources. Government-underwritten debt based on reports of the FHA and VA. Conventional data are a residual.

FNMA, GNMA holdings, shown separately prior to 1968 are those of former FNMA. Holdings of new FNMA from 1954 through 1956 were below $1 billion.

338   Total Consumer Debt Outstanding Mortgage debt on one- to four-family dwellings and nonprofit commercial properties. Security loans based on stock market credit data. "All other" debt consists of nonprofit organizations, policy loans, loans secured by hypothecated deposits (before 1966), trade debt of nonprofit organizations, and deferred and unpaid life insurance premiums. Instalment and noninstalment consumer credit are described in notes to pages 339–340.

339 Short- and Intermediate-Term Consumer Credit Outstanding Estimates are based for the most part on sample reports submitted monthly to the FRS and are adjusted periodically to more comprehensive data. Figures for the period before 1940 based largely on estimates of the Bureau of Foreign and Domestic Commerce (now Office of Business Economics), Dept. of Commerce. For details see "Consumer Credit," Section 16 (new) of *Supplement to Banking and Monetary Statistics.*

340   Types of Consumer Instalment Credit Outstanding Components of instalment credit shown on page 339. Automobile paper and other consumer goods paper represent amounts owed on credit extended for the purpose of purchasing automobiles and other consumer goods. This credit may be extended to the consumer by a retail dealer, arranged by a retail dealer with a financial institution, or extended directly to the consumer by a financial institution. Repair and modernization loans include both FHA-insured and noninsured loans made to finance maintenance and improvement (including purchases and installation of equipment) of owner-occupied dwelling units. Personal loans include all instalment loans outstanding not covered in the above categories made by financial institutions to individuals for consumer purposes.

341   Major Holders of Consumer Instalment Credit For description of data and estimating procedures see "Consumer Credit," Section 16 (new) of *Supplement to Banking and Monetary Statistics.* Consumer finance companies and credit unions (federal and state) account for more than four-fifths of the holdings of "other financial institutions." Nearly three-fourths of the holdings of retail outlets are nonautomotive consumer goods receivables held by department stores (including mail-order outlets) and furniture stores.

342   Consumer Instalment Credit Extended and Repaid Estimates, adjusted for seasonal variation and differences in trading days, are based on information from accounting records of retail outlets and financial institutions and generally include any finance, insurance, and other charges incurred under the installment contract.

The net change in instalment credit outstanding is derived by subtracting instalment credit repaid from instalment credit extended (except for Jan. and Aug. 1959, when the introduction of estimates for outstanding credit for Alaska and Hawaii, respectively, is also reflected). For description see "Consumer Credit," Section 16 (new) of *Supplement to Banking and Monetary Statistics.*

343   Ratio of Consumer Instalment Credit to Income   Ratios of consumer instalment credit extended or repaid to disposable personal income, seasonally adjusted annual rates. Estimates of disposable personal income are from the Department of Commerce. Source for consumer instalment credit extended and repaid is the same as for page 342.

344   Types of Consumer Noninstalment Credit Outstanding   Components of noninstalment credit shown on page 339. Charge-account credit is held mainly by retail outlets; single-payment loans, by commercial banks. Service credit consists principally of amounts owed to doctors, hospitals, and to utility companies.

345   Liquid Liabilities to Foreigners   The term "foreigner" is used to designate foreign official institutions; international and regional organizations; individuals, including U.S. citizens, domiciled in foreign countries; banking and nonbanking corporations created under the laws of a foreign country; and the foreign subsidiaries and branches of U.S. banks and other corporations. Official institutions include foreign central banks and foreign central governments and their agencies, the Bank for International Settlements, and the European Fund, and liabilities to International Monetary Fund arising from gold deposit and gold investment. Nonmonetary international and regional organizations are principally the International Bank for Reconstruction and Development and the Inter-American Development Bank.

346–347   Foreign Exchange Rates   Rates are noon buying rates in New York for cable transfers, in cents per unit of foreign currency.

Rates through May 1921 compiled from various sources; rates shown thereafter are those certified to the Treasury for customs purposes by the Federal Reserve Bank of New York. No rates shown for 1941-1945. For details see "International Finance," Section 15 of *Supplement to Banking and Monetary Statistics,* and Federal Reserve *Bulletins.*

348   U.S. Reserve Assets   Beginning Jan. 1970 total U.S. reserve assets include special drawing rights; initial allocation of SDR's to the United States by the International Monetary Fund (IMF) on Jan. 1, 1970, was $867 million. Total gold stock represents Treasury gold stock plus gold in Exchange Stabilization Fund. Total gold and Treasury gold include gold sold to the United States by the International Monetary Fund with the right of repurchase and gold deposited by the IMF to mitigate the impact on the U.S. gold stock of foreign purchases for the purpose of making gold subscriptions to the IMF under quota increases. Convertible foreign currencies represents holdings of the Federal Reserve System and the U.S. Treasury. U.S. reserve position in IMF represents the U.S. gold tranche position in the IMF (the U.S. quota minus the IMF's holdings of dollars), which is the amount that the United States could purchase in foreign currencies automatically if needed.

Current and back figures: Division of International Finance.

EXCESS RESERVES AND BORROWINGS OF MEMBER BANKS

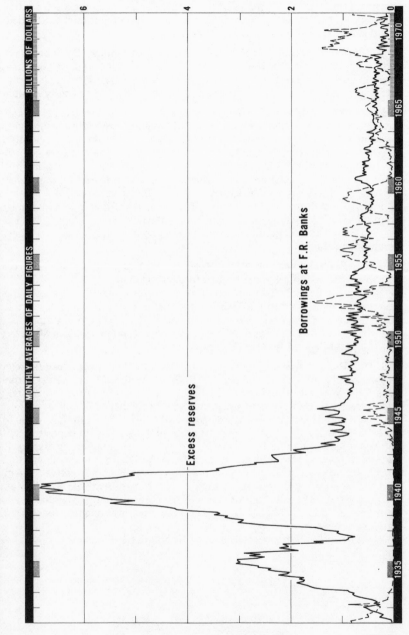

MONTHLY AVERAGES OF DAILY FIGURES

BILLIONS OF DOLLARS

Excess reserves

Borrowings at F.R. Banks

BORROWINGS OF MEMBER BANKS AT FEDERAL RESERVE BANKS

BY CLASS OF BANK

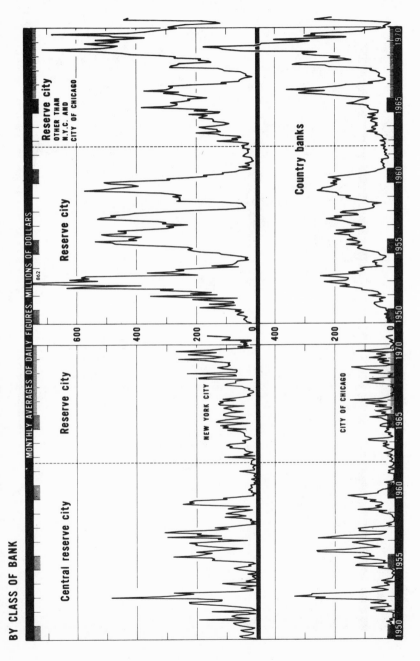

MONTHLY AVERAGES OF DAILY FIGURES, MILLIONS OF DOLLARS

Reserve city
OTHER THAN
N.Y.C. AND
CITY OF CHICAGO

Reserve city

Central reserve city

Reserve city

NEW YORK CITY

Country banks

CITY OF CHICAGO

LOANS AND INVESTMENTS OF MEMBER BANKS
BY CLASS OF BANK

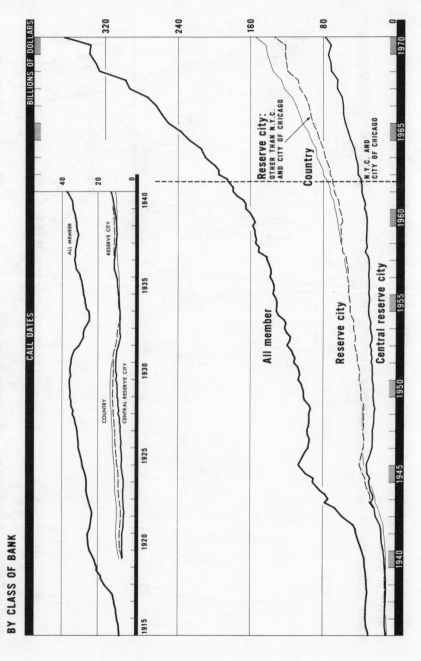

LONG- AND SHORT-TERM INTEREST RATES

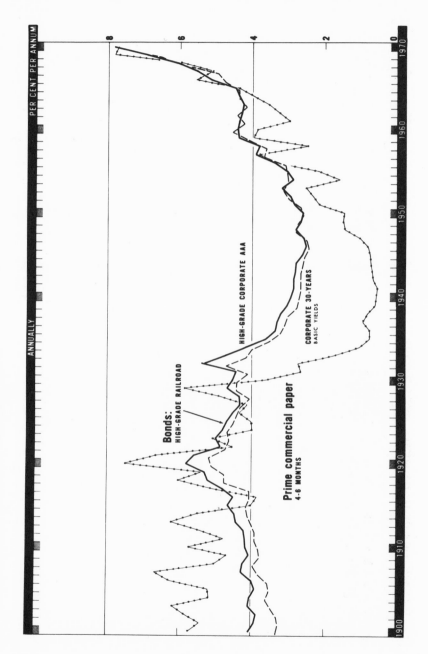

PER CENT PER ANNUM

ANNUALLY

Bonds:
HIGH-GRADE RAILROAD

HIGH-GRADE CORPORATE AAA

CORPORATE 30-YEARS
BASIC YIELDS

Prime commercial paper
4-6 MONTHS

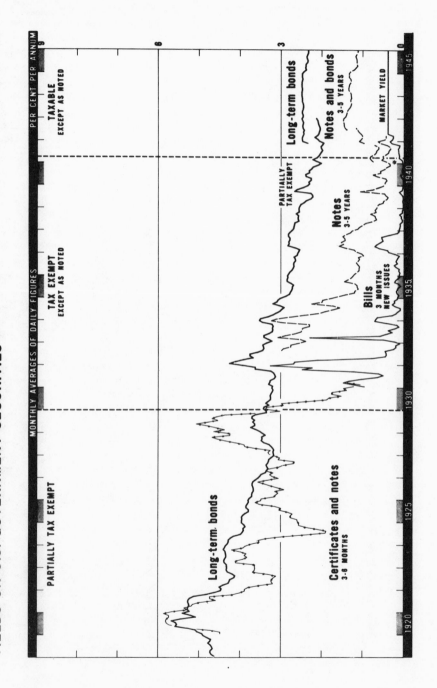

YIELDS ON U.S. GOVERNMENT SECURITIES

YIELDS ON U.S. GOVERNMENT SECURITIES – Cont.

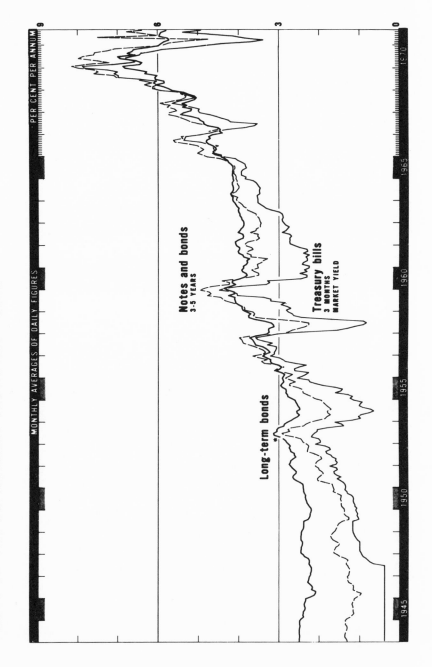

PER CENT PER ANNUM

MONTHLY AVERAGES OF DAILY FIGURES

Notes and bonds
3-5 YEARS

Treasury bills
3 MONTHS
MARKET YIELD

Long-term bonds

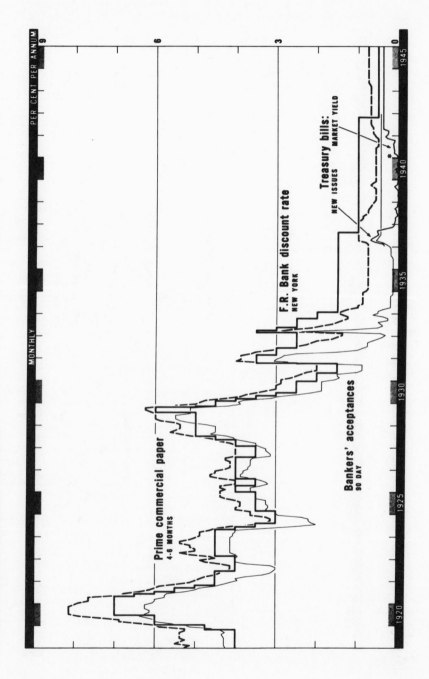

SHORT-TERM INTEREST RATES

MONTHLY

PER CENT PER ANNUM

Prime commercial paper
4-6 MONTHS

F.R. Bank discount rate
NEW YORK

Treasury bills:
NEW ISSUES   MARKET YIELD

Bankers' acceptances
90 DAY

1920   1925   1930   1935   1940   1945

SHORT-TERM INTEREST RATES - Cont.

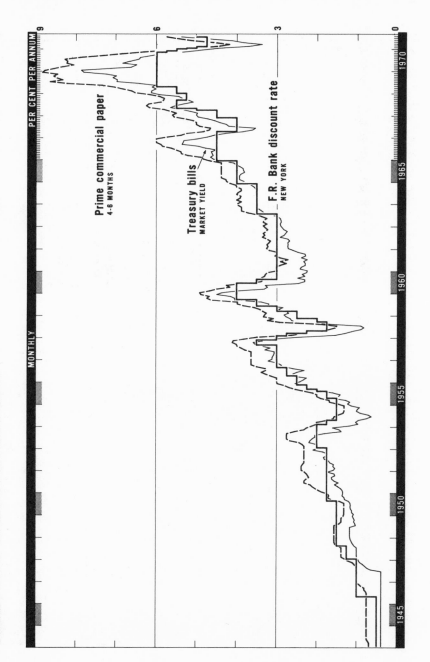

PER CENT PER ANNUM

MONTHLY

Prime commercial paper
4-6 MONTHS

Treasury bills
MARKET YIELD

F.R. Bank discount rate
NEW YORK

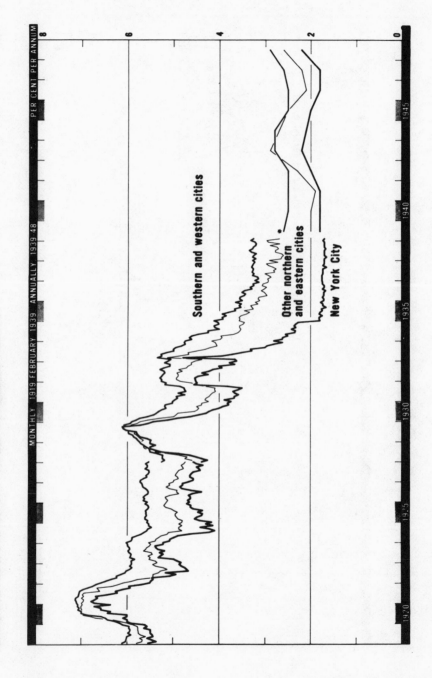

BANK RATES ON SHORT-TERM BUSINESS LOANS

PER CENT PER ANNUM

MONTHLY 1919 FEBRUARY 1939 ANNUALLY 1939-48

Southern and western cities

Other northern
and eastern cities

New York City

BANK RATES ON SHORT-TERM BUSINESS LOANS – Cont.

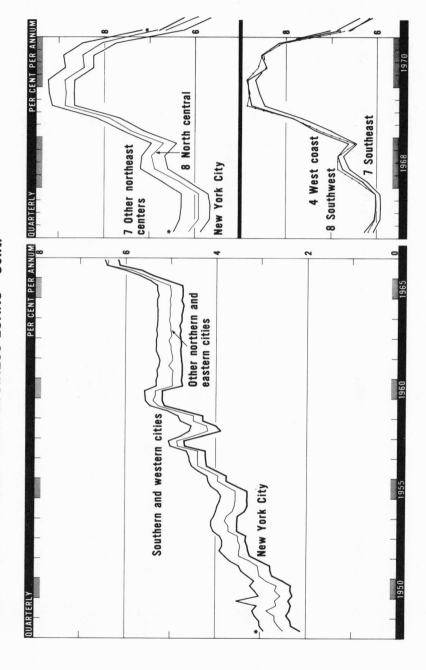

BOND YIELDS

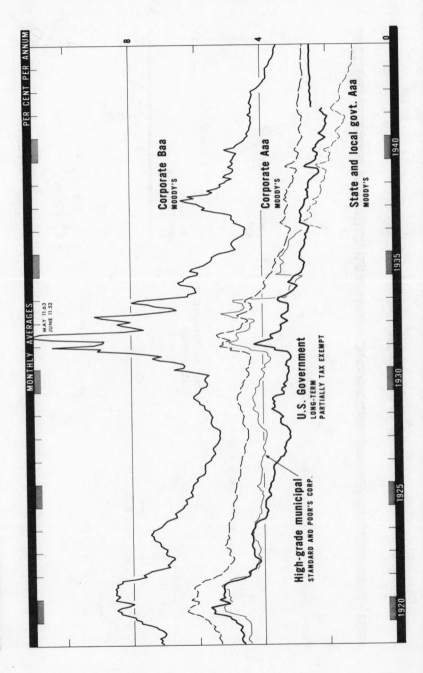

BOND YIELDS – Cont.

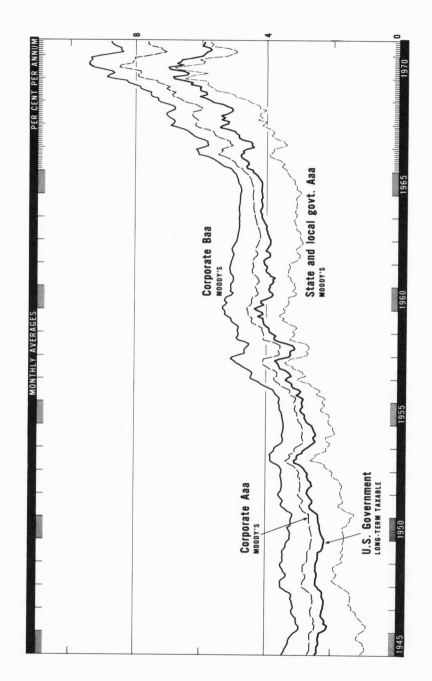

PER CENT PER ANNUM

MONTHLY AVERAGES

Corporate Baa
MOODY'S

State and local govt. Aaa
MOODY'S

Corporate Aaa
MOODY'S

U.S. Government
LONG-TERM TAXABLE

8

4

0

1945

1950

1955

1960

1965

1970

STOCK MARKET

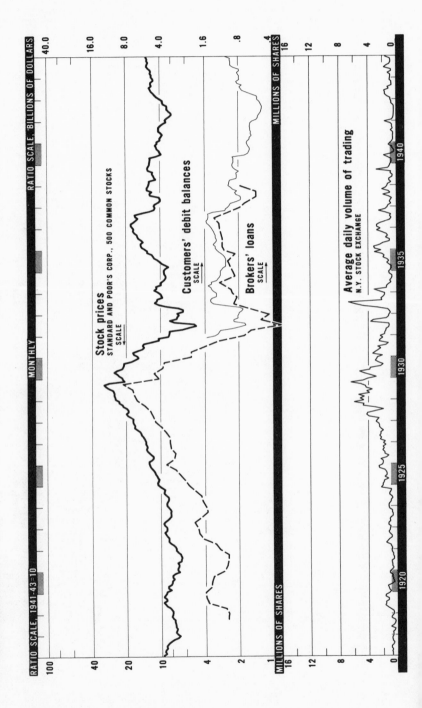

STOCK MARKET – Cont.

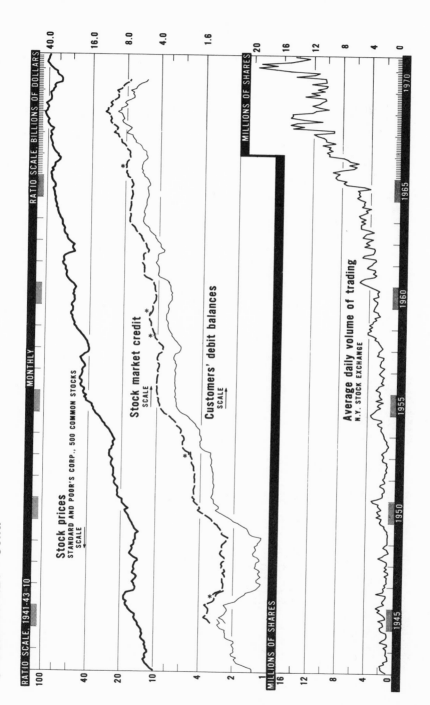

STOCK MARKET – Cont.

RATIO SCALE, 1941-43=10

MONTHLY

RATIO SCALE, BILLIONS OF DOLLARS

Stock prices
STANDARD AND POOR'S CORP., 500 COMMON STOCKS
SCALE

Stock market credit
SCALE

Customers' debit balances
SCALE

MILLIONS OF SHARES

Average daily volume of trading
N.Y. STOCK EXCHANGE

MILLIONS OF SHARES

BROKERS' LOANS BY GROUP OF LENDER

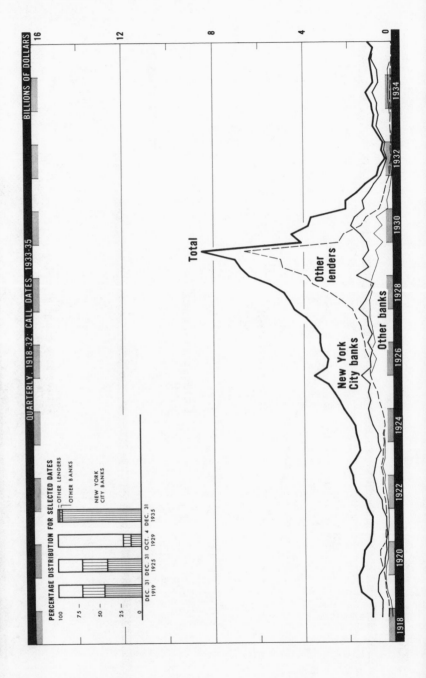

BILLIONS OF DOLLARS

QUARTERLY, 1918-32; CALL DATES, 1933-35

PERCENTAGE DISTRIBUTION FOR SELECTED DATES

OTHER LENDERS

OTHER BANKS

NEW YORK
CITY BANKS

DEC. 31   DEC. 31   OCT. 4   DEC. 31
1919   1925   1929   1935

Total

Other
lenders

New York
City banks

Other banks

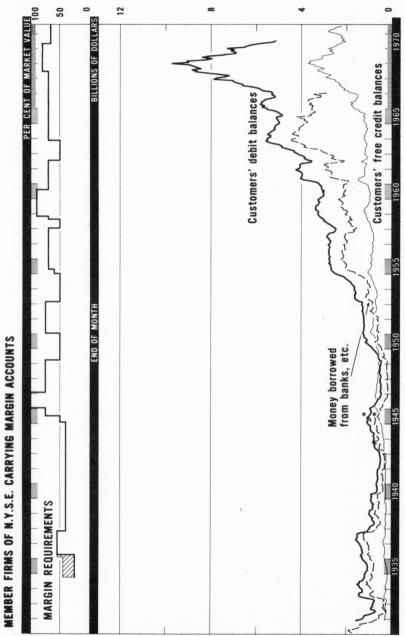

STOCK MARKET CREDIT

MEMBER FIRMS OF N.Y.S.E. CARRYING MARGIN ACCOUNTS

PER CENT OF MARKET VALUE

MARGIN REQUIREMENTS

BILLIONS OF DOLLARS

END OF MONTH

Customers' debit balances

Money borrowed from banks, etc.

Customers' free credit balances

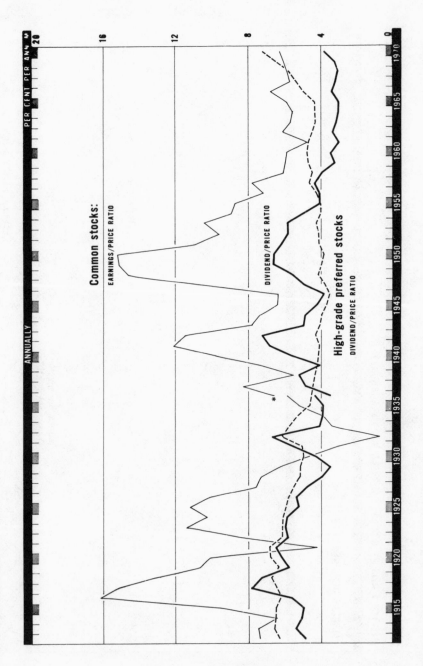

STOCK YIELDS

PER CENT PER ANN M

ANNUALLY

Common stocks:

EARNINGS/PRICE RATIO

DIVIDEND/PRICE RATIO

High-grade preferred stocks
DIVIDEND/PRICE RATIO

20

16

12

8

4

0

1915 1920 1925 1930 1935 1940 1945 1950 1955 1960 1965 19'70

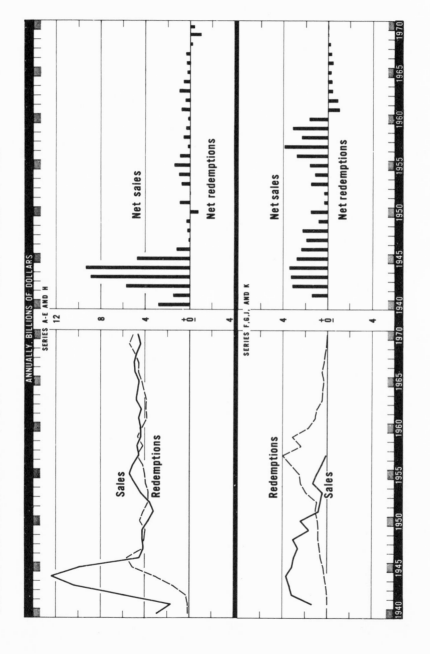

SALES AND REDEMPTIONS OF U.S. SAVINGS BONDS AT ISSUE PRICE

CASH INCOME AND OUTGO OF THE U.S. TREASURY

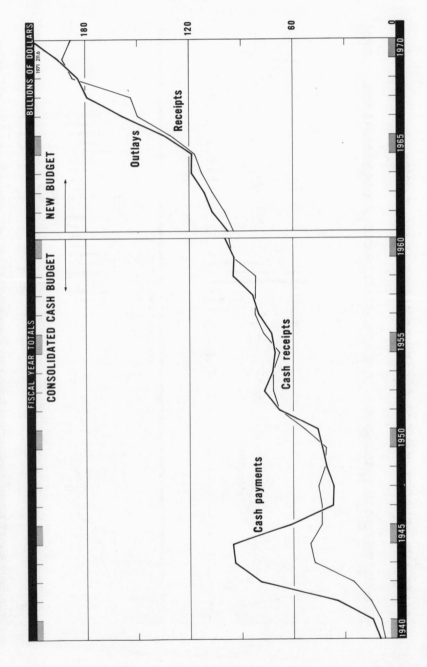

STATE AND LOCAL GOVERNMENT SECURITY ISSUES

ANNUALLY

BILLIONS OF DOLLARS

Refunding

New capital

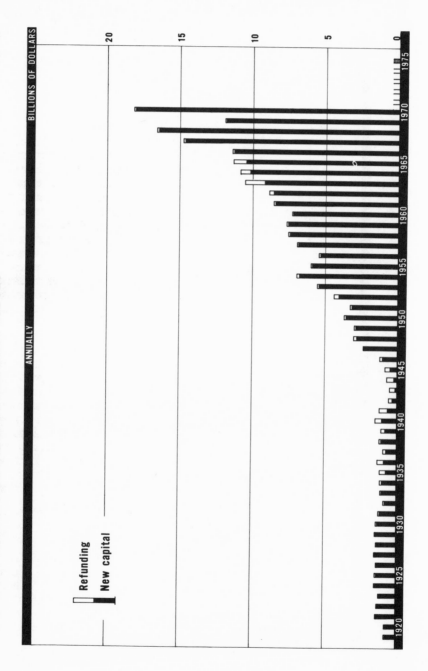

CORPORATE SECURITY ISSUES

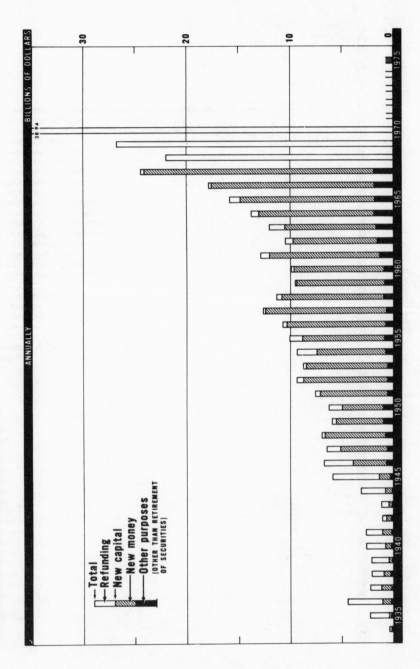

BILLIONS OF DOLLARS

ANNUALLY

Total
Refunding
New capital
New money
Other purposes
(OTHER THAN RETIREMENT
OF SECURITIES)

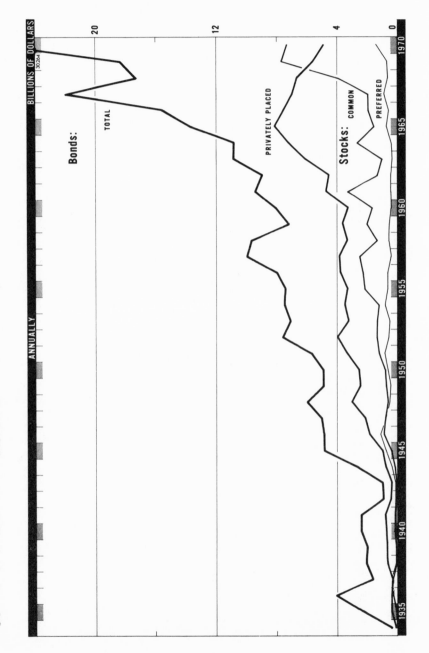

CORPORATE SECURITY ISSUES BY TYPE OF ISSUE

CORPORATE SECURITY ISSUES BY MAJOR ISSUERS (Gross Proceeds)

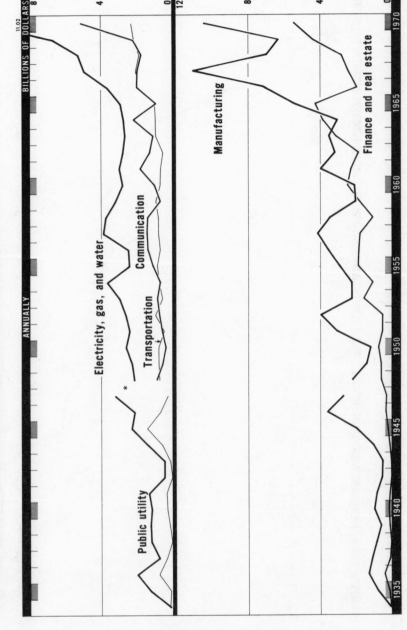

CORPORATE PROFITS, TAXES, AND DIVIDENDS

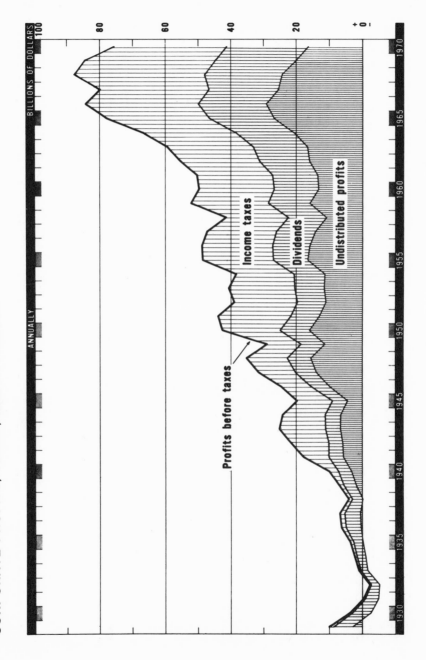

CORPORATE PROFITS AFTER TAXES BY MAJOR INDUSTRY

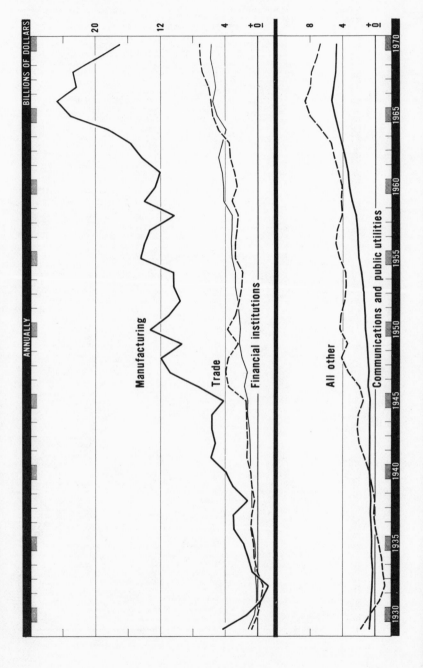

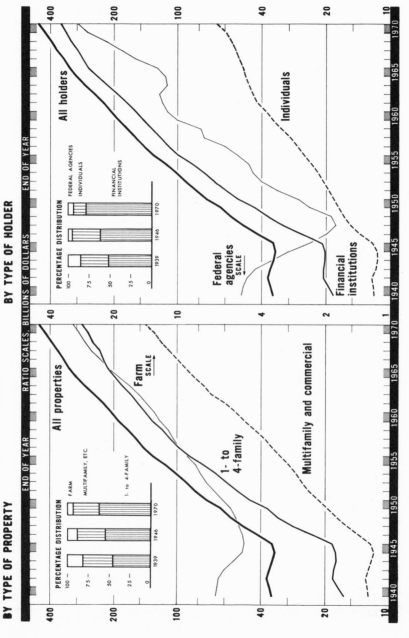

TOTAL REAL ESTATE MORTGAGE DEBT OUTSTANDING
BY TYPE OF PROPERTY
BY TYPE OF HOLDER

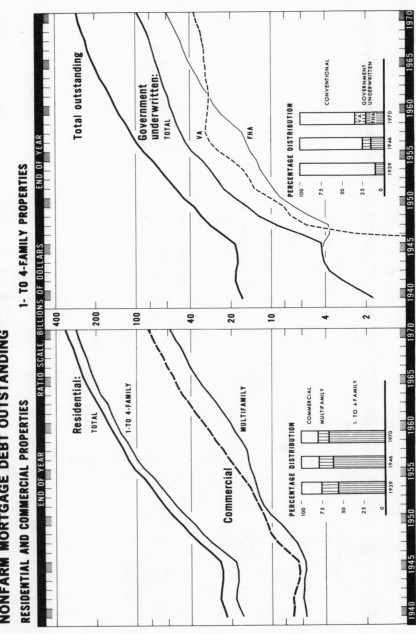

NONFARM MORTGAGE DEBT OUTSTANDING
RESIDENTIAL AND COMMERCIAL PROPERTIES   1- TO 4-FAMILY PROPERTIES

NONFARM MORTGAGE HOLDINGS

BY TYPE OF PROPERTY AND LENDER

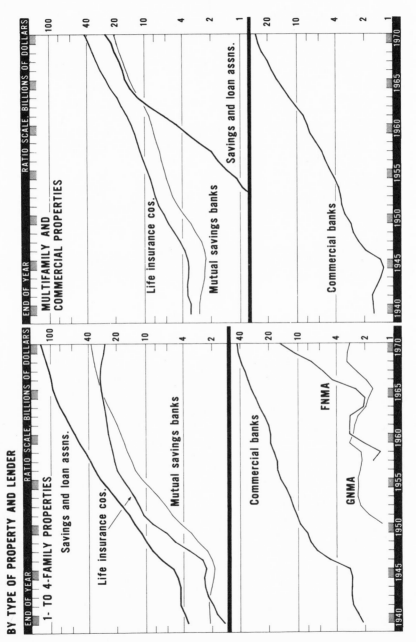

TOTAL CONSUMER DEBT OUTSTANDING

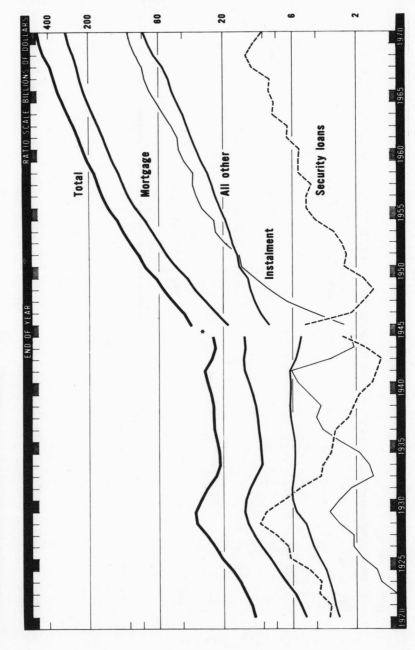

SHORT- AND INTERMEDIATE-TERM CONSUMER CREDIT OUTSTANDING

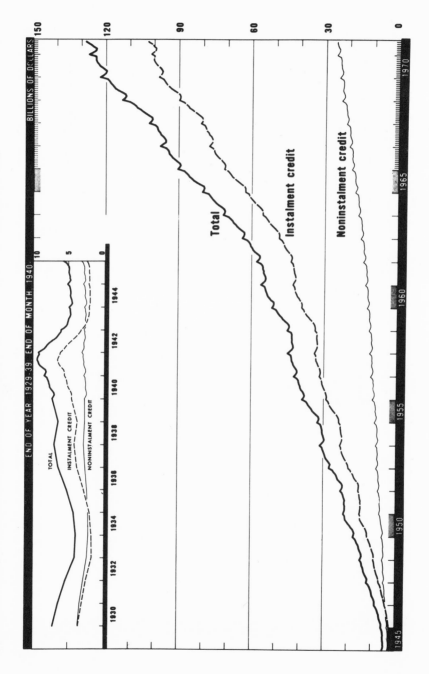

TYPES OF CONSUMER INSTALMENT CREDIT OUTSTANDING

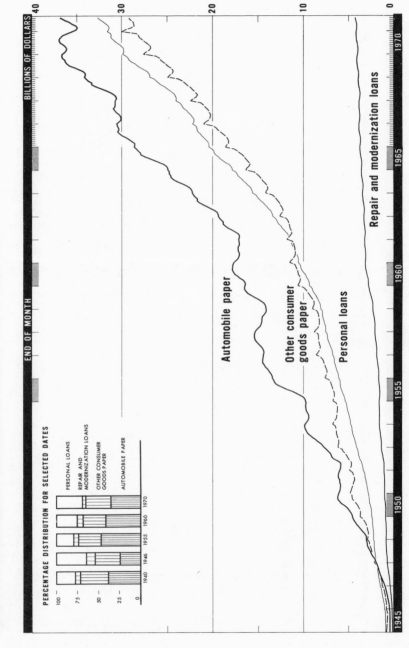

MAJOR HOLDERS OF CONSUMER INSTALMENT CREDIT

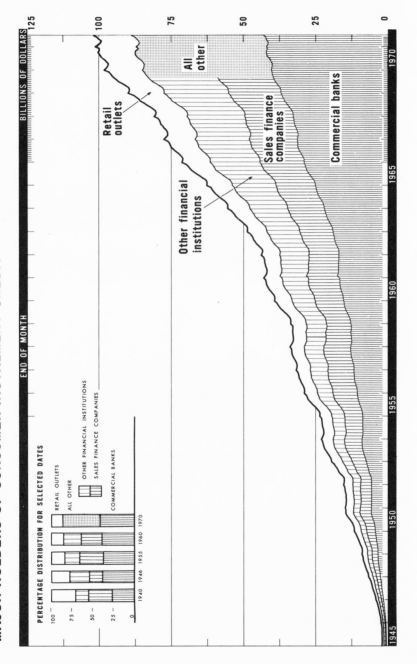

BILLIONS OF DOLLARS

END OF MONTH

PERCENTAGE DISTRIBUTION FOR SELECTED DATES

RETAIL OUTLETS

ALL OTHER

OTHER FINANCIAL INSTITUTIONS

SALES FINANCE COMPANIES

COMMERCIAL BANKS

1940 1946 1955 1960 1970

Retail outlets

Other financial institutions

All other

Sales finance companies

Commercial banks

CONSUMER INSTALMENT CREDIT EXTENDED AND REPAID

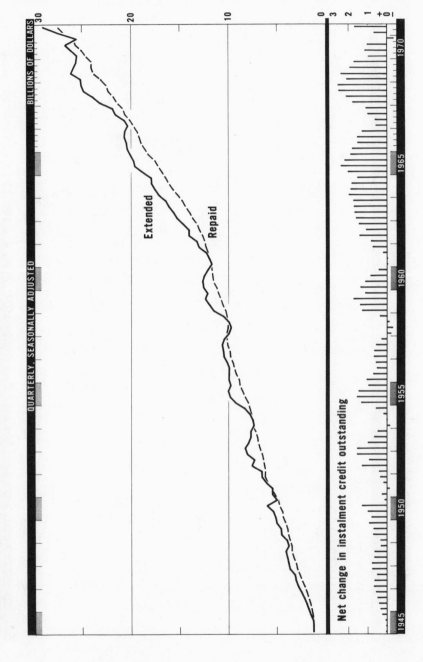

QUARTERLY, SEASONALLY ADJUSTED

BILLIONS OF DOLLARS

Extended

Repaid

Net change in instalment credit outstanding

RATIO OF CONSUMER INSTALMENT CREDIT TO INCOME

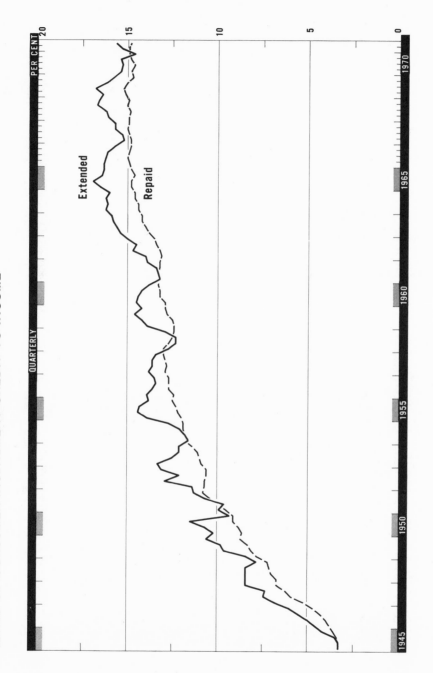

TYPES OF CONSUMER NONINSTALMENT CREDIT OUTSTANDING

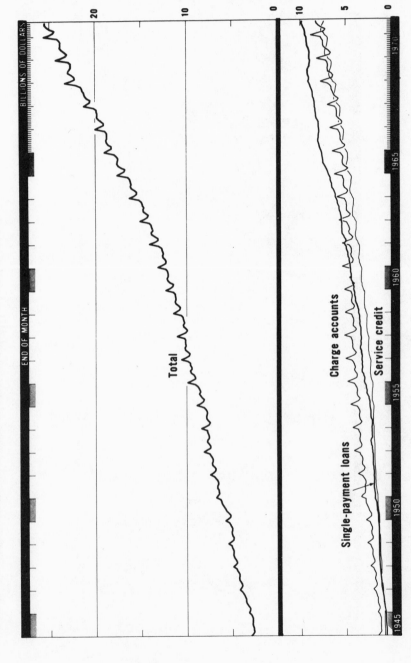

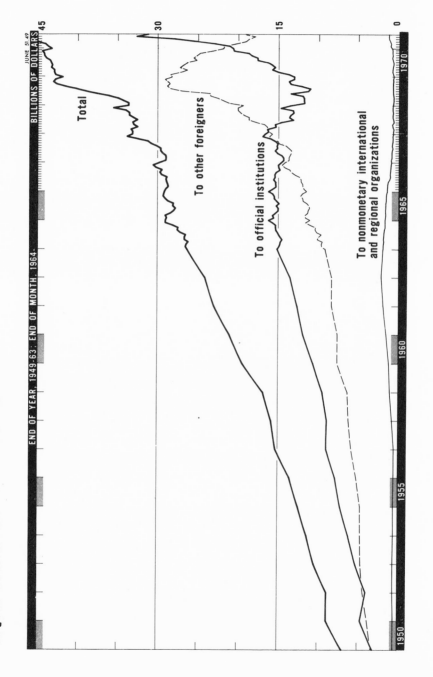

LIQUID LIABILITIES TO FOREIGNERS

BILLIONS OF DOLLARS

END OF YEAR, 1949-63; END OF MONTH, 1964-

JUNE 51.49

Total

To other foreigners

To official institutions

To nonmonetary international
and regional organizations

1950   1955   1960   1965   1970

45   30   15   0

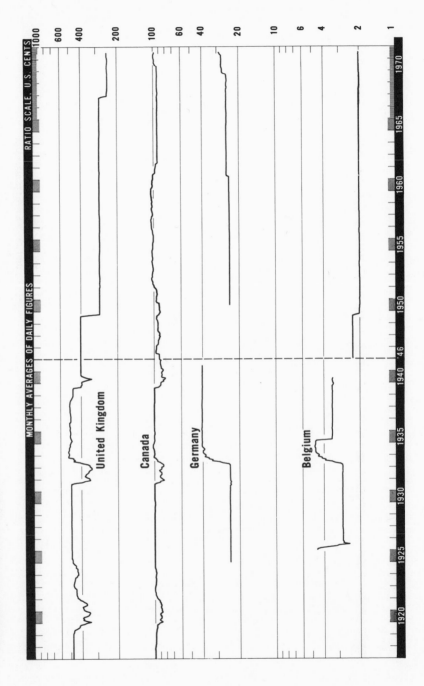

FOREIGN EXCHANGE RATES

FOREIGN EXCHANGE RATES – Cont.

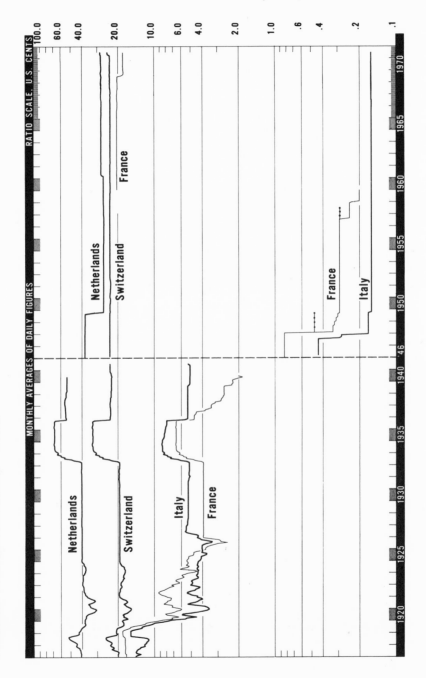

U.S. RESERVE ASSETS

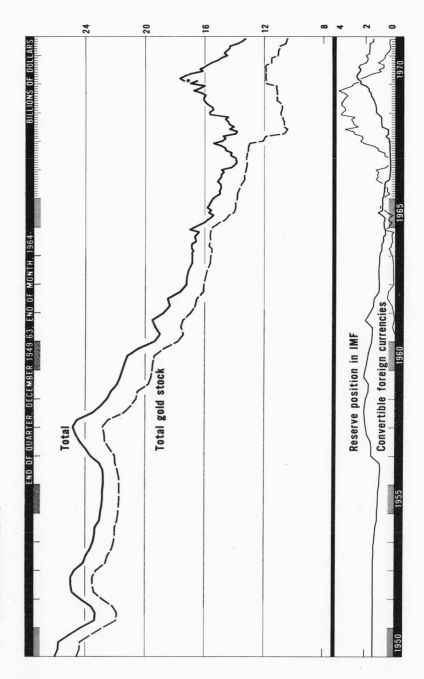

BILLIONS OF DOLLARS

END OF QUARTER: DECEMBER 1949-63; END OF MONTH, 1964-

Total

Total gold stock

Reserve position in IMF

Convertible foreign currencies

24   20   16   12   8   4   2   0

1950   1955   1960   1965   1970

INDEX

In compiling this index, the editor has attempted to list individually those firms and organizations that readers would be most inclined to look for by name. Thus, each of the entries in sections 2, 3, 4, 6–14, 16, 20, 22, 23, 27–32 are listed separately in the index. The remaining sections are listed by subject, with inclusive page numbers.

350 INDEX